Tides of Revolution

Diálogos Series
KRIS LANE, SERIES EDITOR

Understanding Latin America demands dialogue, deep exploration, and frank discussion of key topics. Founded by Lyman L. Johnson in 1992 and edited since 2013 by Kris Lane, the Diálogos Series focuses on innovative scholarship in Latin American history and related fields. The series, the most successful of its type, includes specialist works accessible to a wide readership and a variety of thematic titles, all ideally suited for classroom adoption by university and college teachers.

Also available in the Diálogos Series:

Mexico City, 1808: Popular Politics, Military Power, and the Fall of Silver Capitalism by John M. Tutino

Murder in Mérida, 1792: Violence, Factions, and the Law by Mark W. Lentz

Nuns Navigating the Spanish Empire by Sarah E. Owens

Sons of the Mexican Revolution: Miguel Alemán and His Generation by Ryan M. Alexander

The Pursuit of Ruins: Archaeology, History, and the Making of Modern Mexico by Christina Bueno

Creating Charismatic Bonds in Argentina: Letters to Juan and Eva Perón by Donna J. Guy

Gendered Crossings: Women and Migration in the Spanish Empire by Allyson M. Poska

From Shipmates to Soldiers: Emerging Black Identities in the Río de la Plata by Alex Borucki

Women Drug Traffickers: Mules, Bosses, and Organized Crime by Elaine Carey

Searching for Madre Matiana: Prophecy and Popular Culture in Modern Mexico by Edward Wright-Rios

For additional titles in the Diálogos Series, please visit unmpress.com.

Tides of Revolution

Information, Insurgencies, and the Crisis of Colonial Rule in Venezuela

CRISTINA SORIANO

University of New Mexico Press ✦ Albuquerque

© 2018 by the University of New Mexico Press
All rights reserved. Published 2018
Printed in the United States of America

Library of Congress Cataloging-in-Publication Data
Names: Soriano, Cristina, 1975– author.
Title: Tides of revolution: information, insurgencies, and the crisis of colonial rule in Venezuela / Cristina Soriano.
Description: First edition. | Albuquerque: University of New Mexico Press, 2018. | Series: Diálogos series | Includes bibliographical references and index. |
Identifiers: LCCN 2018001017 (print) | LCCN 2018032059 (e-book) |
ISBN 9780826359872 (e-book) | ISBN 9780826359858 (hardback) |
ISBN 9780826359865 (paper)
Subjects: LCSH: Underground literature—Venezuela—History and criticism. | Foreign news—Venezuela—History—18th century. | Foreign news—Venezuela—History—19th century. | Venezuela—History—War of Independence, 1810–1823—Underground literature. | BISAC: HISTORY / Latin America / Central America.
Classification: LCC PN5102.S67 2018 (e-book) | LCC PN5102.S67 2018 (print) | DDC 079.87—dc23
LC record available at https://lccn.loc.gov/2018001017

Cover illustration: *De la Guayra, on the Spanish Main*, by G. T. Richards (1808), etching, aquatint, work on paper, 14.5 × 24.9 centimeters. Colección Mercantil. Courtesy of Mercantil Arte y Cultura, Caracas. Image by Walter Otto.
Composed in Minion Pro 10.25/13.5

For Julio
and
In memory of my father, Amílcar Soriano M.

Contents

List of Illustrations
ix

Acknowledgments
xi

INTRODUCTION
Prelude to a Storm
Caribbean Winds and Tides of Revolution in Venezuela
1

PART 1
Media

CHAPTER 1
Literacy and Power in Venezuela's Late Colonial Society
15

CHAPTER 2
The Spread of the "Revolutionary Disease"
News, Pamphlets, and Subversive Literacies
47

CHAPTER 3
The Power of the Voice
Imperial Anxieties and Rumors of Revolution
77

PART 2
Movements

CHAPTER 4
The Shadow of Saint-Domingue in the Rebellion of Coro, 1795
117

CHAPTER 5
A Revolutionary Barbershop
Rumors, Texts, and Reading Networks in the La Guaira Conspiracy of 1797
149

CHAPTER 6
The Fear of Foreign Invasion
Black Corsairs in Maracaibo and Other Stories of Black Occupation
183

CONCLUSION
Venezuela and the Revolutionary Atlantic
207

APPENDIX
List and Description of the Prohibited Books Seized in the Libraries of La Guaira's Conspirators during the Investigation and Sent by the Audiencia of Venezuela to Spain in 1802
215

Notes
221

Bibliography
285

Index
311

Illustrations

MAPS

1. Venezuela and the Caribbean	xv
2. Captaincy General of Venezuela (1777–1810)	xvi
3. Province of Caracas (1777–1810)	xvi

FIGURES

1. Pasquinade found in Caracas, May 8, 1790	48
2. First page of the *Gazeta de Madrid*, November 25, 1791	58
3. "An Accurate Map of the West Indies with the Adjacent Coast of America," 1794	83
4. "The Coast of Caracas, Cumaná, Paria, and the Mouths of Río Orinoco," 1775	97
5. "North Western Trinidad and the Coast of Venezuela," 1802	100
6. *De la Guayra, on the Spanish Main*, 1808.	155

TABLES

1. Population of the Province of Caracas (1800)	26
2. Thematic Distribution of Books in Caracas's Private Libraries (1770–1779, 1800–1809)	33
3. Arrival of Dominicans in Maracaibo, January–March 1801	201

Acknowledgments

Tides of Revolution marks the culmination of more than thirteen years of research and reflection about Venezuela and the Atlantic world during the Age of Revolutions. It began as my dissertation project in the Department of History at New York University. There I discovered the powerful dialectical relation that exists between historical mentions and silences, and, inspired by Michel-Rolph Trouillot's *Silencing the Past*, I learned the importance of reformulating questions in order to expand the windows into the past and make silences speak. Throughout the research process for this book, I confronted challenging "moments of silence" in the sources, in the archives, in the historiographic narratives, and while writing; but even when I was sitting in the most obscure and solitary corner of the archive, I never faced these silences alone. During these thirteen years I have been extremely fortunate to have the support of academic institutions and the company and guidance of extraordinary people who made the research experience rich, incredibly constructive, and fascinating.

The initial research of this project was possible thanks to the support of the Centro de Estudios Hispánicos e Iberoamericanos of the Ministerio de Cultura of Spain, the Warren Dean Fellowship from the Department of History of New York University, and the Frank Guggenheim Foundation Dissertation Award. At Villanova University, I was the recipient of the Albert R. Lepage Endowed Professorship in History, which offered me significant support to perform archival research in Venezuela and Spain during the summers of 2012, 2013, and 2014. The Albert R. Lepage Endowed Professorship also provided me with the opportunity to spend an entire academic year on sabbatical finishing the manuscript. In addition, the Wissenschaftskolleg of Berlin and the National Humanities Center in Durham, North Carolina, offered me support to participate in the two-year postdoctoral summer seminar Cultural Encounters: Global Perspectives,

Local Exchanges, 1750–1940 organized by the Summer Institutes for Advanced Studies (SIAS), a space that allowed me to revise and discuss important sections of this manuscript. I am also grateful for receiving the Richard E. Greenleaf Visiting Scholar Award by the Latin American and Iberian Institute at the University of New Mexico, which allowed me to visit and work at the university's Center for Southwest Research.

I very much appreciate the professionalism I found at the different archives I visited in Venezuela, Spain, and the United States. I always encountered friendly and supportive staff who were willing to uncover the silences of the archives with me. In Venezuela, the staff of the Archivo General de la Nación, Archivo Histórico Nacional, and Archivo Arquidiocesano de Caracas guided me with efficiency and cheer. In Spain, the staff of the Biblioteca Nacional in Madrid and the Archivo General de Indias in Seville made my work enjoyable and productive. I am especially grateful to the staff at the photocopy and digitalization center at the AGI for the care and diligence they took while processing my petitions and granting me permissions. I spent several months doing research at the John Carter Brown Library at Brown University, where I had the pleasure to meet Ken Ward, historian of the book and curator of the Latin American Collection. I am grateful for his generosity and friendship.

This book would have not been possible without the incredible inspiration, support, and encouragement I received from my mentors, professors, and classmates at the Universidad Central de Venezuela and at New York University who accompanied me in the process of unveiling historiographic silences. Ramón Aizpurua was the first professor I took history classes with. Ramón not only animated me to explore the past of the slaves and people of color in Venezuela, but he has also supported and guided me throughout my career. I am deeply thankful to my advisor, Sinclair Thomson, for his wise guidance, encouragement, and thoughtful support through graduate school and while I developed this project. I am grateful to Ada Ferrer for inspiring me to begin digging into the representations of Haiti in Venezuela; her splendid work and thoughtful guidance invited me to question historical narratives and build stronger arguments. I will always be thankful to Emanuele Amodio, Antonio Feros, Greg Grandin, Sibylle Fischer, Timothy Reiss, Roger Chartier, Nydia Ruiz, Jürgen Osterhammel, and Harry Liebersohn for how they inspired me in classrooms and seminar rooms. These same rooms were filled with wonderful friends and classmates with whom I share a passion for history; these friends have accompanied me throughout the journey of writing this book. I am particularly grateful to "mis hermanas:" Krisna Ruette, Marcia López, and Yoly Velandria for our never-ending conversations and enduring friendship. I am also in debt to Marcela Echeverri, Michelle Chase, Aisha Finch, Valeria Coronel, Ramón Suárez, Michele Thompson, Natasha Lightfoot, Tanya Huelett, and Edwina Aishe-Nikoi for making the New York phase of this project enriching and enjoyable, both personally and intellectually.

While working as an assistant professor at the Universidad Central de Venezuela, I enjoyed the understanding and generosity of colleagues in the Department of Archeology and Historical Anthropology, particularly Professors Kay Tarble, Emanuele Amodio, Luis Molina, and Rodrigo Navarrete. In my classrooms, I was fortunate to have a wonderful group of students who enthusiastically accompanied me through my research journey, offered challenging questions, and encouraged me to open new paths for historical exploration. I especially thank Rommy Durán, Germán Díaz, Inés Achabal, Nina Soto, Dejaneth Ruza, and Steven Schwartz. Nina, Dejaneth, and Steven worked as research assistants in different phases of this project, offering me immeasurable support.

I am thankful for the support and intellectual stimulation I received from a wonderful group of friends and scholars at Villanova University, including Rebecca Winer, Marc Gallicchio, Paul Rosier, Judy Giesberg, Ed Fierros, Adele Lindenmeyr, Marc Sullivan, Tim McCall, Jeff Johnson, Larry Little, Craig Bailey, Catherine Kerrison, Lynne Hartnett, Joseph Ryan, Chris Haas (†), Andrew Liu, Maghan Keita, and Silvia Nagy-Zekmi. I am especially grateful to Paul Steege, Elizabeth Kolsky, Whitney Martinko, and Hibba Abugideiri for taking the time to review drafts of this project and for offering invaluable suggestions that have helped me strengthen my arguments and structure the book in such a way as to make the most of them.

I have greatly benefited from participating in both formal and informal exchanges with numerous scholars whose works, insightful comments, and critical questioning have challenged me in relevant and productive ways. Many of them read one or several chapters of the book and offered invaluable feedback. I thank Ramón Aizpurua, Pedro Rueda, Roger Chartier, Sinclair Thomson, Ada Ferrer, Marcela Echeverri, Alejandro Cañeque, Michelle Chase, Yuko Miki, Sibylle Fischer, Reuben Zahler, Edward Pompeian, Jesse Cromwell, Clive Griffin, Pedro Guibovich, Natalia Maillard, Ken Ward, Patrick Tardieu, Ann Twinam, Mark Towsey, John French, Pablo Picatto, Caterina Pizzigoni, Clément Thibaud, Alex Borucki, Susan Socolow, Matt

Childs, Charlton Yingling, Rob Taber, Vera Candiani, Alex Bevilacqua, Nurfadzilah Yahaya, Teresa Segura-García, Steffen Rimner, Alejandra Dubcovsky, Carole Leal, Nydia Ruiz, Evelyne Laurent-Perrault, Kathryn Burns, Linda Rupert, Marcel Granier, and Amílcar Soriano.

I would like to thank Thomas Dolinger for his incredible work and patience as he helped me to edit the final manuscript, Aitor Muñoz for designing the maps, and Nina Soto and Jessica Chrisman for their assistance in editing endnotes and preparing the final manuscript. I am deeply thankful to Kris Lane, editor of the Diálogos Series at the University of New Mexico Press, for taking an interest in this project and for providing crucial editorial advice and support throughout the project's various stages. I am very grateful to Clark Whitehorn and the supportive staff of the University of New Mexico Press for their enthusiasm for this project and the care and support they offered me while I prepared the manuscript and as we bring the book into production.

My family and friends have been an incredible source of inspiration and energy throughout my career. I thank my wonderful friends Marcia, Yoly, Krisna, Clau, Gail, Gaby, Lilí, Tina, Martha, and the Peñoneros (Class of '92) for their support, great humor, and endearing company. I am deeply grateful to Nina Panzer for her companionship and guidance while I learned to listen to my own silences. I thank my sister Carolina and my brothers, Luis and Coco, for their profound love and constant companionship; I am so lucky to have you. I would also like to express my appreciation to my aunt Graciela Soriano de García-Pelayo. She awakened my curiosity for the past when I was twelve years old, and her passion and enthusiasm for the study of history remains an inspiration. I owe profound gratitude to my parents, Amílcar and Myriam Soriano, for their support and encouragement throughout my life.

My kids, Vicente and Lucía, grew up holding hands with this project and have always been its most vigorous supporters. I cherish their contagious joy and avid curiosity. My husband and *compañero de vida*, Julio, has been an inexhaustible source of love, strength, and kindness. It is to him that I dedicate this book.

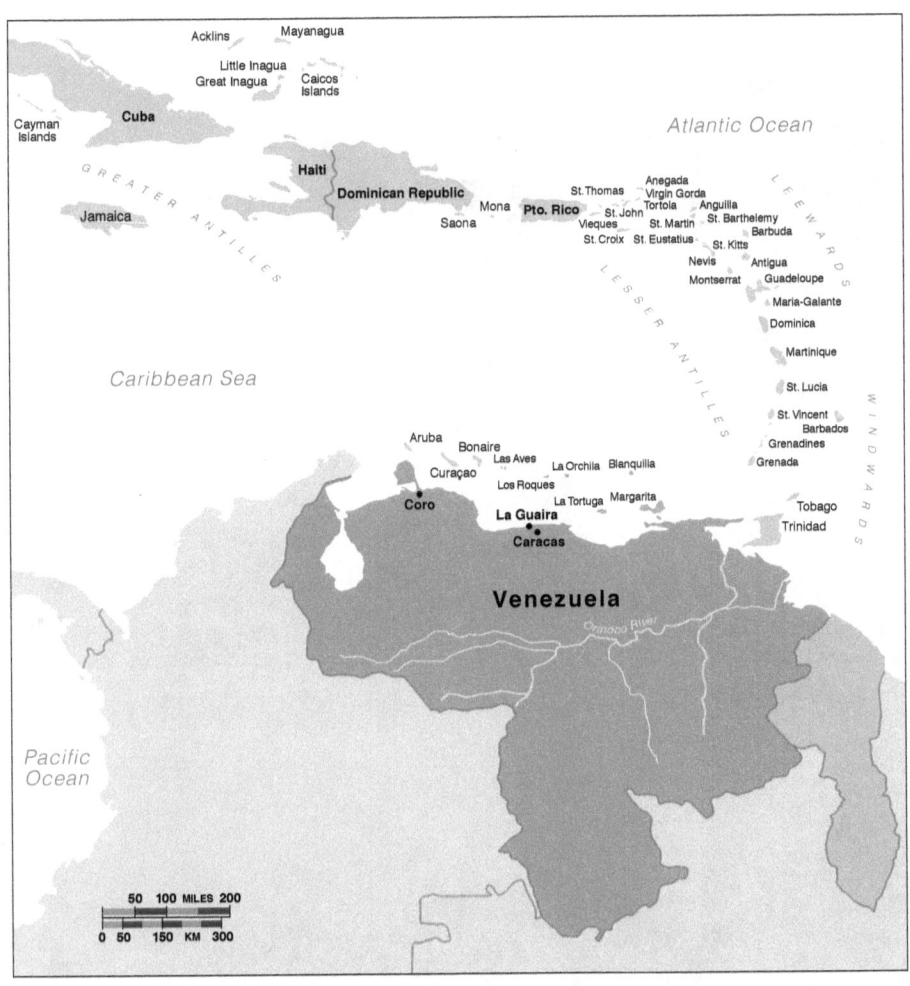

Map 1. Venezuela and the Caribbean. Map created by Aitor Muñoz.

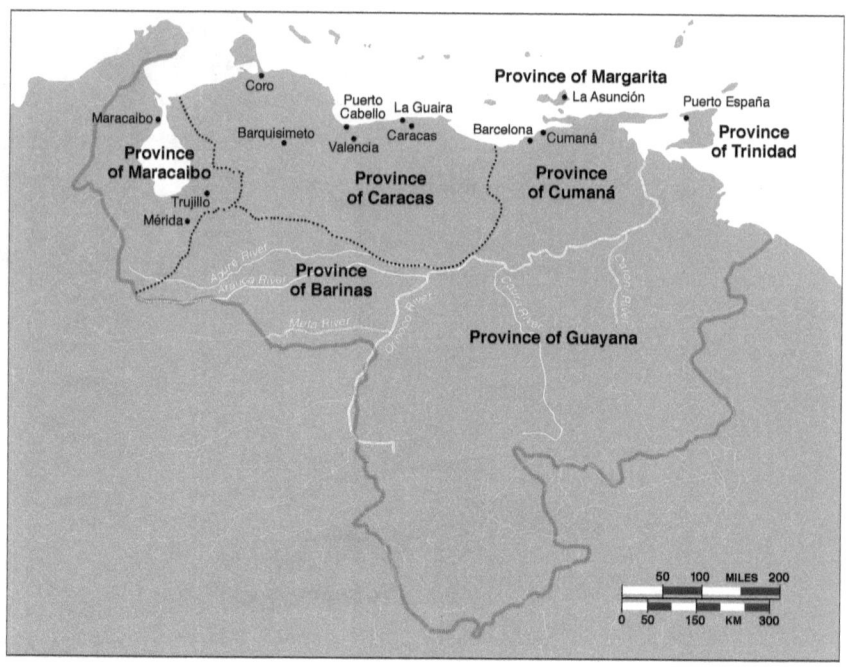

Map 2. Captaincy General of Venezuela (1777–1810). Map created by Aitor Muñoz.

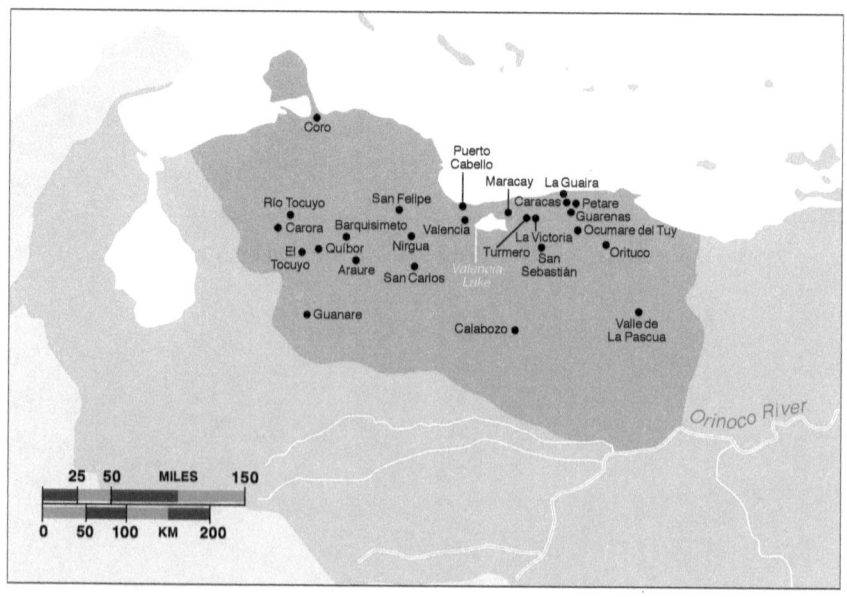

Map 3. Province of Caracas (1777–1810). Map created by Aitor Muñoz.

INTRODUCTION

Prelude to a Storm

Caribbean Winds and Tides of Revolution in Venezuela

⤗ IT WAS A COLD NIGHT, LATE NOVEMBER 1799, WHILE EATING DINNER at an inn along the mountainous road that connected the port of La Guaira to the city of Caracas, when Alexander von Humboldt first heard about revolutionary politics in Venezuela. A heated conversation had erupted among some Caracas-born travelers, whose political convictions and ardent spirits impressed the German explorer; "only the cold wind that seemed to descend from the top of the mountain, covering us in a thick fog, put an end to the agitated conversation."[1] The following morning, an old man who had listened to the conversation the night before reprimanded the group for having such imprudent and dangerous debates: "These conversations," he exclaimed, "should not be taking place anywhere." But in Venezuela, Humboldt reflected, "men carried their political complaints and passions to the highest peaks."[2]

Once in Caracas, Humboldt was welcomed by Venezuela's captain general, don Manuel de Guevara y Vasconcelos, and several distinguished families. At gatherings and dinners, Humboldt noted that white families in Caracas were well educated: they knew the masterpieces of Italian and French literature and were musically cultivated. He found, however, that politics was their favorite subject of discussion:

It seems to me that there is a strong tendency towards a profound study of the Sciences in Mexico and Santa Fé [New Granada], more taste for literature and what the imagination could entertain in Quito and Lima, more light focused on political relations among the nations, and a more extensive perspective about the state of the colonies and the Metropolis, in La Habana and Caracas.[3]

Venezuelans' interest in political affairs, however, was not restricted to elite conversations around the dinner table or during pleasurable excursions to the mountains. Between 1789 and 1808, several political movements and popular rebellions echoing the calls for liberty and equality of the French and Caribbean revolutions erupted across coastal Venezuela, disturbing the tranquility of the entire province and exhibiting the vibrant and challenging political environment of the region. Venezuelans from different socioracial groups were well informed of recent revolutionary events in the Caribbean and Europe, and engaged readily in heated debates on political topics and even planned movements against the colonial government. José Ignacio Moreno, a white creole priest who had been the dean of the University of Caracas, knew all too well that the literate elite was not the only social group partaking in disturbing conversations. According to Moreno, the slave rebellion that rocked Coro in 1795 and the mixed-race republican conspiracy of La Guaira uncovered in 1797 were clear evidence that "the poison of liberty had invaded the hearts of the innocent and less intelligent people."[4] "No one," he wrote in 1797, "can hide from the turbulent and seductive language that the French had spread through the mainland with their voices and papers."[5] For Moreno, it was clear that during the last decade of the eighteenth century, "an evil revolutionary contagion" had poisoned Venezuela.

Largely marginal to the economic and geopolitical interests of the Spanish Empire, the Captaincy General of Venezuela lacked a printing press and relevant intellectual societies, common in other cities and towns of Spanish America.[6] In fact, by the mid-eighteenth century, Venezuela had only two universities (one in Caracas and the other in the Andean town of Mérida), a couple of mechanical arts schools, and a dozen public high schools. Until 1808, Venezuela remained one of only a handful of major provinces in Spanish America without a printing press; as a result, Venezuelans lacked local newspapers and printed materials.[7] The lack of a printing press, and of literary societies, however, did not prevent the Venezuelan public from exchanging ideas during what historians call the Age of Atlantic Revolutions. In fact, as Humboldt and other travelers noted, Venezuelans of all social backgrounds actively participated in networks of information sharing that connected the Spanish South American mainland, or Tierra Firme, with both the Antilles and Europe, creating a vigorous and defiant political environment.

Tides of Revolution explores the circulation of information and the development of political communities in Venezuela during the Age of Revolutions. It covers the period from 1789 to 1808, which saw the development of numerous popular rebellions and conspiracies against the colonial government. Hand-copied materials flooded the cities and port towns of Venezuela; foreigners shared news and rumors of the French and Caribbean revolutions with locals; and Venezuelans of diverse social backgrounds met to read hard-to-come-by texts and to discuss the ideas they expounded. The central argument of this book is that late colonial Venezuela witnessed the emergence of an incipient public sphere that, grounded in semiliterate forms of knowledge transmission and oral information, allowed the participation of a socially diverse population in a wide range of political debates, questioning the monarchical regime and colonial rule, the socioracial hierarchies of colonial society, and the system of slavery.[8]

During this period, colonial authorities became obsessed with silencing local echoes of Franco-Caribbean republican values, which they viewed as seditious and destabilizing. Paradoxically, the absence of printing houses, bookshops, literate societies, and any formal center of debate in Venezuela made these official efforts at control even more futile. Shortly after the Spanish monarchical crisis of 1808, when Napoleon's forces occupied Madrid and exiled the king to Bayonne, Venezuelans became one of the first groups of self-styled "Spanish Americans," or *Españoles Americanos*, to declare independence from Spain and to lead, just a few years later, one of the bloodiest wars of Spanish American independence. The political transformation that gripped early-nineteenth-century Venezuela had less to do with print culture than with the dynamic political atmosphere that had reigned in the region for the previous two decades, since 1789.[9] This book offers an explanation for this political transformation, one that allowed Venezuela, a relative backwater of the late colonial period, to become one of the first regions in Spanish America to declare independence from Iberia and to turn into an influential force for Spanish American independence more broadly.

Caribbean Connections

Although marginal within the Spanish Empire, the Captaincy General of Venezuela was, by virtue of its geography, at the center of the Atlantic revolutions. Between 1789 and 1808, hundreds of political pamphlets and broadsides from the Caribbean were smuggled into the mainland, and waves of French-speaking refugees (Europeans and creoles from the French Caribbean) shared news and subversive ideas with locals. Everyday conversations and discussions transformed the "turbulent" French Caribbean into a common metonymy for a complex set of political ideas and aspirations. This book pays attention to the flow of bodies, goods, and information that connected Venezuelan port cities and the extensive coastal region with the Atlantic world, and argues that Venezuela's unique geographic location and its open and frequent connections with the Caribbean during the Age of Revolutions allowed for the effective entrance and circulation of people and written materials that spread revolutionary information, ideas, and impressions, giving rise to a vibrant political environment.[10]

As Ernesto Bassi argues, the Caribbean region was a space that comprised both islands and continental coasts—a space that was not the exclusive dominion of a single European state but rather simultaneously the Spanish, British, French, and Dutch.[11] Port cities brought together foreigners, migrants from the hinterland, and local inhabitants, who exchanged not only goods but also information. The information that circulated throughout the Caribbean region crossed linguistic and political barriers, but in every port and coastal town, locals adopted specific forms and meanings to their realities.[12]

Thanks to Venezuela's vast and exposed coast, its port cities and coastal towns, such as a La Guaira, Puerto Cabello, Cumaná, La Vela de Coro, and Maracaibo became multicultural and multilingual hubs for encounter and exchange. Socially, port cities were more open, varied, unstable, and dynamic than inland cities because of the fluctuating character of their populations. The configuration of port societies thus facilitated the flow of information about the Atlantic revolutions, but especially about the Haitian Revolution. Of the three Atlantic revolutions—the American, the French, and the Haitian—it was the last that proved most tangible for the inhabitants of Venezuela. In Venezuela, the Haitian Revolution became a locus of shared knowledge, an everyday reference point that was exploited by rebels during negotiations with the colonial elite and, at the same time, by those very elites to justify harsh repression or, alternatively, to make concessions to "calm the spirits" of rebellion in the region. Here it is shown that written and oral information about the French colonies, and especially about Saint-Domingue, circulated freely throughout Venezuela. Waves of gossip and rumor, as well as streams of loose papers or *papeles sueltos* and pamphlets, quickly destabilized the local political climate.[13] Interpretive communities united people of different social backgrounds and promulgated stirring narratives of revolution. On their minds and lips were slave insurrections, anticolonial protests, and the struggle for equality. A central argument of this book is that the Haitian Revolution was not necessarily an antimodel—the product of elites' fearful imagination—but a common language used by both rulers and plebeian groups to make demands and negotiate change.

More important than the classical Enlightenment texts of Rousseau, Voltaire, and Raynal were Caribbean revolutionary pamphlets, anonymous broadsides, and rumors that circulated among Venezuelans. Although distant European political thinkers may have inspired the political debates of the era, in Venezuela these debates were spread, contextualized, discussed, and interpreted by Caribbean and local actors. By paying attention to these Caribbean connections, this book adds to the large body of scholarship on the impact of the Haitian Revolution in the Atlantic world that has emerged in the wake of that event's bicentennial in 2004. This scholarship has analyzed how the Haitian Revolution reshaped politics in different regions of the Atlantic world, especially the French, British, Spanish, and Dutch Caribbean zones but also within European nations and in the United States.[14]

For the Spanish mainland and in particular for Venezuela, scholars have provided rich analysis on how the Haitian republic not only represented an influential political model but also offered logistical support for proponents of creole- or Spanish American–led independence in Venezuela, most importantly Francisco de Miranda and Simón Bolívar.[15] Focused mostly on the early nineteenth century and on the actions of these particular creole leaders, these studies offer only part of the story of Venezuela's Haitian connections: the stories of those exceptional Venezuelans who had direct interactions with Haiti's leaders, who witnessed the political challenges of the nascent republic, and who used Haiti to configure their own political projects. By contrast, *Tides of Revolution* shows that Venezuelans were familiar with Haiti's history long before Francisco de Miranda's expedition to Coro in 1806 and Bolívar's arrival in Haiti in December 1815. This study moves back in time to the moment the first rebellions erupted in Saint-Domingue in 1791, offering an analysis of the complex set of representations and impressions that this theater of revolution left on different communities living in the ports and cities of Venezuela and how these impressions opened new spaces for negotiation between whites and people of color, and between masters and slaves. Following recent portrayals of Haiti as a blueprint for the establishment of American republics, my study offers strong evidence of how familiar Haitian political developments were for most Venezuelans, who would later confront questions of color, racial difference, and abolitionism during their own struggle for independence between 1810 and 1819. Only by reconstructing these early images of the Caribbean revolution in Venezuela, the complex information networks that put them in circulation, and Haiti's influence in the configuration of early political movements can we understand the character and weight of popular support during the war of independence led by the likes of Simón Bolívar and other political leaders, as well as the presence of popular royalism in different regions of Venezuela.[16]

Media and Politics

Tides of Revolution focuses on the circulation of information and the formation of social networks in Venezuelan communities, which, in the absence of printing, developed myriad strategies for spreading and adapting revolutionary ideas. An analysis of local practices of reading and of information sharing—not merely of printed texts—brings into relief the many ways in which ideas and cultural practices crossed the seas and transformed the political landscape of Venezuela during the Age of Revolutions.[17] This book shows that the emergence of semiliterate forms of knowledge transmission in late colonial Venezuela mobilized a socially diverse public that openly debated the monarchical regime, the system of slavery, and the hierarchical socio-racial order. These debates were far from unitary: they took place in different regions, were led by different social groups, and adopted different political narratives. Indeed, the nascent public sphere of late colonial Venezuela would be a place of contestation and struggle, animated by multiple and overlapping discourses of contention.[18]

At the heart of this study is an emergent semiliterate population that kept abreast of developments in the French Caribbean and developed novel strategies for disseminating information broadly. Such strategies ranged from spreading rumors to lending books to producing handwritten pamphlets and pasquinades to holding public readings to performing songs and dialogues. These practices created a platform for the circulation of political knowledge as more social groups became interested in accessing, responding to, and contextualizing news about the political debates that fueled Atlantic revolutions. During this period, more sectors of Venezuelan society, especially plebeian artisans and mixed-race and black laborers, took part in this emergent sphere of public opinion. These groups not only developed strategies for disseminating information among like minds but also planned insurgent movements and stirred political unrest.

The book intervenes in current debates about the impact of printing and reading practices in Latin America, transforming historians' explanations of the process whereby political communities formed during the Age of Revolutions.[19] Traditionally, intellectual and political historians have assumed a straightforward and linear relation between the printed circulation of ideas and the emergence of antimonarchical or anticolonialist movements in Europe and the Americas. This linear relation has been questioned, in turn, by cultural historians, who argue that political and social change results not merely from the intellectual operations of particular groups but from complex transformations of everyday practices, including the dynamics of socialization and literacy. What matters, in other words, is not merely *what* people read but *how* they read and shared ideas.[20] *Tides of Revolution* grafts this discussion onto late colonial Venezuela and expands our notions of literacy in order to encompass the role of revolutionary texts and oral enunciations in the formation of political identities. This book is unique in connecting literate and oral practices of knowledge transmission with political movements in an attempt to understand the place of reading and writing, as well as other forms of semiliterate communication, in the emergence of social networks and movements. To this end, it pays particular attention to the dissemination of information in insurgent movements developing in different regions of Venezuela, such as the slave rebellion that took place outside the town of Coro in 1795, a famous conspiracy centered on Venezuela's main port of La Guaira in 1797, and the less-studied conspiracy that rocked the western port of Maracaibo in 1799.

This study reframes discussions about the character, nature, and relevance of the public sphere in Latin America.[21] It thus offers a new interpretation of the role of information in the emergence of a public sphere in Venezuela, a peripheral province with no printing press that nonetheless became one of the first Spanish American colonies to declare independence. Through this lens, it explores largely neglected topics in the field, including practices of reading among elites and popular groups, the circulation of manuscripts and ephemeral written materials, the role of oral enunciations and rumors, and the centrality of urban centers and port towns in the circulation of revolutionary information.

One of the challenges that historians of late colonial Venezuela often confront is trying to draw a clear picture and offer unequivocal explanations of a period that is characterized by confusion, uncertainty, and ambiguity in regard to possible political scenarios. During the roughly two decades between 1789 and 1808, several sectors of the population struggled with the idea of "revolution" as they were trying to understand what it would mean for their communities and how it would affect their everyday lives and their relationship with the state. Distinct groups understood revolutionary ideas quite differently: rebels in Coro, conspirators of La Guaira, and those in Maracaibo were unsure about how their movements, which certainly produced revolutionary narratives, would ultimately address their discontent and problems.[22] Although it seems clear that most people in Venezuela were not particularly receptive to radical French ideas, here I argue that this emerging public sphere provided fertile ground for the larger population to engage in political debates that questioned colonial rule and its social order, and moreover these debates unfolded new spaces to negotiate with groups of power.

Organization of the Book

This book is divided in two parts: Media and Movements. The first part of the book focuses on the strategies used by Venezuelans of varying social status for obtaining and spreading political knowledge about revolutionary movements taking place throughout the Atlantic basin, most significantly in France and Haiti but also in the fledgling United States. To construct this history of modes of communication and information sharing, I draw on neglected sources spread among different archives in Venezuela, Spain, and the United States. These sources shed light on the everyday forms of communication by which individuals shared their impressions of the revolutionary Atlantic, planned ways to make information available to others, and formed social networks. Part 1 unfolds in three chapters that correspond to three major media for the transmission of ideas: (1) books; (2) newspapers, pamphlets, and pasquinades; and (3) oral information and rumors. These first three chapters are not presented chronologically; rather, each of them covers the period 1789–1808 through the study of a different set of media, communication strategies, and social groups.

The first chapter analyzes the social complexity of colonial Venezuela and the interplay of literacy and power in the social hierarchy. In this stratified society, not all social groups had equal access to the written word, in particular to printed materials. Literate people generally belonged to upper social groups who possessed large libraries, while the majority of the supposedly "nonliterate" people belonged to subordinate social groups that relied largely on oral media for the transmission of information. By the end of the eighteenth century, however, this picture had begun to change. This chapter argues that, although white elites continued to possess the majority of important libraries in urban centers, an expansion of the book market, plus the emergence of networks for the lending and transcription of books, facilitated access to printed materials among less-privileged groups. This chapter also analyzes the composition, numeric expansion, and increasing thematic diversification of private libraries (1770–1810), showing that intellectual life in colonial Venezuela underwent a gradual process of secularization as readers shifted their focus from devotional to Enlightenment texts. In addition, an eruption of new strategies for obtaining and disseminating texts brought a larger proportion of Venezuelan society into contact with potentially subversive written ideas.

The second chapter explores the circulation of printed news, revolutionary broadsides, and pamphlets in the cities and port towns of Venezuela. From 1791 to 1810, revolutionary texts from Europe and the Americas, but especially from France and Saint-Domingue, appeared in the coastal towns of Venezuela. While these pamphlets and broadsheets horrified local officials and elites because of their revolutionary content, they aroused the curiosity of the common people, who had easy access to them. I argue that in this semiliterate colonial social setting, the boundaries between the written and the oral were often slippery: people from different social and educational backgrounds devised (often creative) methods to access the written word and to make it circulate. This chapter pays particular attention to the processes of acquisition, reproduction, and dissemination of these texts among the general population and how these processes required the operation of social networks. Likewise, it also analyzes the content of various texts from the Caribbean, which often raised important questions about slavery and racial inequality in colonial societies. The third chapter traces the migration of people from the revolutionary Atlantic to Venezuela and the forms of oral information they brought with them. Despite the colonial government's attempts to control the entry of foreigners, between 1791 and 1798 more than one thousand French-speaking refugees and prisoners entered Venezuela. Once there, many spread news and rumors of uprisings in the French Caribbean. Here, I chart the emergence of a web of images of the French and Caribbean revolutions, and how these images materialized in the form of real threats to the colonial authorities in the region.

The second part of the book, "Movements," focuses on the role of revolutionary information in the development of three important movements: the slave rebellion of Coro (1795), the conspiracy of La Guaira (1797), and the conspiracy in Maracaibo (1799). These three movements, organized by different socioracial groups, reflected general discontent with Spanish rule as well as with Venezuela's local authorities. The social composition of these movements was diverse and their insurrectional strategies varied, but they all record the effects of the revolutionary tides that inundated the Venezuelan coast. More importantly, these movements reflected the myriad possibilities for political action available to disgruntled subjects who were not just passive recipients of foreign ideas but who actively spread their own political opinions and shaped them into action in their regions.

Chapter 4 analyzes the black-led rebellion of Coro and the different ways that people connected this rebellion to the popular image of Saint-Domingue. The rebellion started in the Coro highlands or *serranía*, a mountainous district in northwestern Venezuela that was largely devoted to the production of sugarcane during the colonial period. According to most historians of colonial Venezuela, Coro's rebels called for the end of sales taxes, the abolition of slavery, and the elimination of Indian tribute, but a more radical interpretation of the rebellion suggests that rebels sought to control the city and, following the example of the revolutionaries in Saint-Domingue, to create a free republic. This chapter offers a new interpretation of the archival sources and reveals a more complex reality. In Coro, the rebels' demands, such as the elimination of taxes and indigenous tributes, were in the main a direct response to local economic and administrative circumstances. Even so, these demands were accompanied by revolutionary calls for the abolition of slavery and, in some cases, the reversal of colonial socioracial hierarchies. In this chapter, I disentangle this intricate set of discourses in order to analyze the threads—imagined or real—that connected the Coro insurrection to Saint-Domingue.

In July 1797, colonial authorities in the port of La Guaira uncovered a subversive republican movement. The movement advocated toppling the colonial state and establishing a republican government in its place. This new republic would embrace free trade, abolish slavery and Indian tributes, and eliminate taxes; additionally, it would be committed to promoting racial harmony, equality, and freedom. The leaders of the movement produced a considerable number of texts intended to instruct their followers and to recruit participants from popular groups. In chapter 5, I analyze the rebels' strategies for disseminating information and their attempt to produce a common language for political opposition. In particular, I show how the leaders, who frequently met in a barbershop, sought to recruit followers from different races and social strata, and how they repurposed political ideas from the French Caribbean to support their cause.

The last chapter explores the so-called Pirela conspiracy, planned in the far western port of Maracaibo in 1799. This movement was supposedly planned by some local *pardos* (free men of color) in conjunction with the captains and crew members of two visiting ships from Port-au-Prince in Saint-Domingue. Only recently has the Pirela conspiracy received scholarly attention, as historians have begun to connect this event to movements in other Caribbean regions—Cartagena de Indias, Cuba, and Curaçao—that were likewise battling "revolutionary contamination from Saint-Domingue." This final chapter analyzes the role of foreigners in the planning of a local republican movement and explores elite fears of a possible invasion and subsequent insurrection. The conspirators' ultimate failure to win broad support from the local population reveals that local pardos, free blacks, and slaves were not interested in following foreign leaders who seemed unaware of their complex local realities.

In an age of Atlantic revolutions, local rebellions, rumored conspiracies, racial hatred, and the presence of foreign agitators made Venezuelan elites and colonial authorities suspicious of people of African descent, undermining a long-standing sense of trust among socioracial groups. This racial fear and lack of confidence did not translate exclusively into blunt repression but surprisingly led officials and elites to also create new strategies of control and to negotiate with popular groups in order to avoid racial violence and social upheaval. These strategies of negotiation and concessions persisted during the early stages of the Venezuelan struggle for independence, when, as Sibylle Fischer reports, Haiti played an important role: it served as a safe haven for patriotic refugees from the mainland, provided military and financial support for the insurgents, and forced the issue of slave emancipation.[23] Saint-Domingue in late colonial Venezuela, therefore, was not merely a specter or object of fear and abhorrence but a central political reference that opened public awareness to complex debates on freedom, equality, and republicanism.

PART 1
Media

CHAPTER 1

Literacy and Power in Venezuela's Late Colonial Society

IN 1792, A YEAR AFTER ACCEPTING A POSITION AS A PRIMARY school instructor, Simón Rodríguez struggled to find the books he needed in Caracas, the capital of the Captaincy General of Venezuela. In a city without a single printing press or bookshop, Caracas's readers, teachers, students, and university professors had to find other ways to access printed material. Bodegas and *pulperías* offered a variety of inexpensive printed materials, such as catechisms, *cartillas*, and devotional books, alongside bottles of olive oil, sacks of grain, soap, and stockings.[1] Hundreds of such texts were sold every year to a public that had learned to read with a Catholic syllabary or with a religious catechism.

Rodríguez, however, did not belong to this massive group of novice readers. He had been educated in one of Caracas's three schools and was well on his way to becoming an advocate for improving primary education in the city. After doing some research, he compiled a list of more than fifteen books, all recently published in Spain, on a range of pedagogical fields, including "the Arts of reading and writing, general instructions on the teaching of Algebra and Arithmetic, and innovative teaching methods for Primary Schools."[2] Desperate, Rodríguez contacted a respected member of the Caracas elite, don Feliciano Palacios, and asked for help in finding these precious printed materials in Spain. Rodríguez had met Palacios in the city council building, where the teacher worked as a scribe.

Palacios sent the book list to his son, Esteban, who was spending some months in Madrid. "I'm sending a list of books for you to buy," Palacios wrote. "Ask Iriarte to give you the money you need. These books are for don Simón, the brother of Cayetanito Carreño." Following his father's directions, Esteban diligently searched for the titles in the bookshops of Madrid. Three months later, he sent the volumes along with a note to his father: "I am sending the books you requested, but not all of them because they are quite expensive."[3] Esteban had spent 270 pesos on Rodríguez's books. Don Feliciano was not pleased to learn of this expenditure (equivalent to the cost of a luxurious piece of furniture or an entire library of sixty used volumes), as he knew he could not ask the humble schoolteacher to pay this sum. He ultimately decided to present the books to Rodríguez as a gift. A year later, Rodríguez would accept the young and rebellious grandchild of Palacios, Simón Bolívar, as a student in his school and would later become his mentor.

The story of Rodríguez's books serves to illustrate the complex networks that connected social and economic status, literacy, and education in colonial Venezuela. Rodríguez himself was an abandoned child, or *hijo expósito*, who was raised, along with his brother, José Cayetano Carreño, in the household of a parish priest, Alejandro Carreño. Although he was an orphan and grew up in a humble home with limited resources, Rodríguez was considered a white creole and was thus able to receive a formal education. This allowed him to work as both a scribe in the city council and a teacher in a primary school.[4] Neither of these positions, however, was particularly lucrative, at least not sufficiently so as to allow Rodríguez to buy the new books he needed. As they had to be imported from Spain, books were expensive luxury items that remained inaccessible to the majority of the population. Venezuela was not, however, a class society in a strict sense, and Rodríguez's lack of money did not prevent him from acquiring these printed materials. His connections to Caracas's elite ultimately provided the economic and logistical means to pursue his goal.

Eighteenth-century Venezuela was notable for its highly stratified but permeable society, offering significant social mobility. Race, family ties, education, occupation, honor, and economic resources all played important roles in defining individual identities. Overlapping social and economic networks, and the absence of a single class hierarchy, facilitated social mobility. Still, not all social groups had equal access to education or to printed matter; literacy and the possession of books represented markers of high social status and power. Literate and formally educated people generally belonged to the white elite. Most members of this group possessed large libraries and the economic means to continue enlarging their book collections, while the majority of the supposedly nonliterate population fit into the lower social groups, who barely had the means to buy a couple of religious broadsides and relied largely on oral media for the transmission of knowledge.[5]

By the end of the eighteenth century, however, this picture had begun to change: the number of people who owned books had increased, and the size and diversity of private libraries had grown significantly. At the same time, an incipient and informal book market had begun to operate, feeding new networks for the circulation of books and printed materials. Many Venezuelans adopted the Spanish reformist model that promoted literacy and formal education for the "common people" while calling for the secularization of knowledge and the promotion of useful sciences (*ciencias útiles*). This movement implicitly entailed the social expansion of literacy, which was coincidently later reinforced by the torrent of printed materials that arrived from the Caribbean during the last years of the eighteenth century.

Although elites continued to possess the majority of important libraries in the urban centers of the province, a more stable book market brought members of lower social groups, such as artisans and laborers, into more regular contact with the printed or at least hand-copied word. In a colonial society with no printing press, books and printed texts were expensive, but it is clear that lack of money did not prevent Venezuelans of modest means from acquiring printed and hand-copied materials: social networks, public auctions (*remates*), an expanding circuit of book lending, and a widespread practice of transcription of texts represented some of the strategies that made written texts accessible to a larger group of people. A number of teachers, including seminary and university professors, sought to open the world of reading to uneducated individuals, and new networks for disseminating texts connected the farthest reaches of the province. During the French and Haitian Revolutions, these incipient networks for the circulation of written materials also served to spread antimonarchical propaganda, abolitionist and egalitarian ideas, and anticolonial sentiments.

From 1789 to 1808, revolutionary texts from Europe and America, as well as Saint-Domingue, Trinidad, and Spanish Santo Domingo, filtered into Venezuela, mortifying local officials and elites and arousing the curiosity of the population. These revolutionary texts arrived at a moment when reading, as a cultural practice, was undergoing important transformations locally.

This chapter explores this complex process of transformation and provides the basis from which to argue that the political and social changes occurring in Venezuela toward the end of the eighteenth century and on the eve of independence resulted not merely from the intellectual endeavors of exceptional individuals but, among other things, from a complex set of modifications of everyday practices of reading and writing, and of changes in readers' relationships with the written word. What matters, in other words, is not so much *what* people read and how these readings influenced their thinking, but rather *how* they read and shared texts, and how these practices of reading led to the emergence of public spaces for the discussion of ideas, political projects, and social prerogatives. What is important to analyze here is the nature of the cultural and social practices that allowed readers (and listeners) to share spaces, connect their texts and readings with their realities, and vice versa.[6]

Although it is certainly important to identify the kinds of books that filled Venezuelan private libraries and to analyze how literary tastes changed over the course of the second half of the eighteenth century, one must analyze also the transformation of reading as a cultural practice that opened new spaces for discussion and debate. A broad question of this book is: How did reading become a tool for socialization and for the integration of political communities in Venezuela at the end of the eighteenth century? This chapter is the first step toward reconstructing late colonial Venezuelans' approach to literacy and to understanding as well the diverse strategies designed to access books and printed materials in the absence of printing presses or bookstores. Practices of lending books, reading excerpts aloud, and transcribing texts crossed social and racial boundaries. These practices, in turn, reveal the sociopolitical dimensions of print culture in late colonial Venezuela.

Curtailing the educational proposals of Spanish reformists who encouraged the education of the masses (peasants, artisans, and laborers), Venezuela's colonial authorities and local elites actively tried to restrain the social expansion of literacy. It was clear for them that this expansion not only compromised socioracial hierarchies but also opened dangerous paths for political awareness. Members of the social and political elite warned that the intellectual simplicity of popular groups would lead novice readers to misunderstand written ideas and thus endanger the tranquility and harmony of the provinces. Colonial officials and church representatives feared that the ongoing tensions between different socioracial groups, the revolutionary events in France and the Caribbean, and the increasing circulation of revolutionary texts would make Venezuelans of lower social status, especially people of color, vulnerable to ideological contagion.[7]

Indexes of prohibited books and papers were read aloud at Sunday mass and posted on the doors of the church and walls around squares; agents of the Inquisition visited private houses to collect or censor prohibited books, or to rip out particularly offensive pages.[8] During Sunday sermons, priests reprimanded readers of seditious tracts and described the hellish punishments they would suffer for reading such evil texts, which promised to spread "revolutionary disease."[9] The lack of printing shops, the absence of formal booksellers, and the prevalence of smuggling activities along Venezuela's long Atlantic coast made efforts at controlling and censoring reading material much more difficult.[10] Samizdat materials—copied by hand—flooded the cities and port towns; networks for borrowing and copying books flourished; and people of diverse social backgrounds soon learned that reading, listening, transcribing, and writing were effective ways to put information in circulation, transmit knowledge, and participate in an emergent sphere of public opinion.

Venezuelan Society on the Eve of the Atlantic Revolutions

By 1750, Venezuela was a stable but not necessarily peaceful province, which just recently had won relevance within the Spanish Empire. The colony remained a province within the Viceroyalty of New Granada (modern-day Colombia, Panama, and Ecuador), yet Venezuelan officials and white elites enjoyed virtual autonomy, as New Granadan officials rarely interfered in local affairs. The creation in 1777 of the Captaincy General of Venezuela, which added six provinces (Maracaibo, Cumaná, Margarita, Trinidad, Guayana, and, later, Barinas) to the jurisdiction of the original Province of Venezuela, confirmed the need for administrative and political centralization, reaffirming the economic importance of the greater Caracas region.[11]

During the eighteenth century, the Venezuelan economy was divided between two main productive activities: the raising of cattle, horses, and mules, and the production of leather in the western plains and on the coast; and the cultivation of export crops—tobacco, cacao, indigo, sugar, and coffee—on the northern coast of the region, also known as the Atlantic littoral or the Costa de Caracas. The cattle economy developed mostly in the western and southern plains, known as the Llanos de Caracas. The geographic conditions of the region allowed for the sustainable and increasing reproduction of cattle with minimal labor investment. However, due to a poor road system that impeded transportation, the presence of plagues and diseases that affected the cattle, and the relatively small internal market for meat and leather products, this economic sector did not expand as quickly and effectively as the cacao-producing sector.[12]

At the beginning of the eighteenth century, small haciendas located along the northern coast of the region and also in the fertile central valleys of the province produced crops such as tobacco, indigo, sugar, coffee, and cacao, which supplied both the small internal market of Venezuela and other nearby Spanish American markets such as Santo Domingo, Cuba, and New Spain. During the mid-eighteenth century, however, the popularity of cacao in European markets grew considerably and sparked the Crown's interest in Venezuela, a region known from the seventeenth century as ideal for cultivating cacao. In fact, Venezuela first drew the careful attention of the monarchy when it received reports of active smuggling of cacao among Venezuelan and Dutch merchants. In order to take advantage of Venezuela's chocolate bounty, in 1728 the Crown authorized the founding of the Compañía Guipuzcoana de Caracas, a Basque company that was not only granted the monopoly over the Venezuelan cacao trade with Spain and, later, with New Spain, but was also charged with the responsibilities of commercializing local products, managing European imports such as textiles, iron, agricultural tools, liquor, and foodstuffs. The so-called Caracas Company was also expected to provide coast guard patrols to curb the contraband trade.[13] The operations of the company in Venezuela increased royal revenues greatly, but local elites and merchants resented the presence of the Basque merchants for many reasons: first, they believed that the company's dominant share of legal commerce endangered their economic interests (due to a drastic and evident drop in prices paid to local cacao producers); second, they complained that the company was not effectively provisioning the region with European goods; and third, they perceived the company as a foreign intruder, representing a threat to local politics. Local discontent with the Caracas Company became most evident in 1749–1751, when Juan Francisco de León led an uprising that mobilized more than four thousand men, making it one of Venezuela's most impressive colonial revolts.[14] Despite tensions with local elites and traders, and several interventions on the part of the Crown to renegotiate the monopoly contract, the Caracas Company's operations (1728–1780) stabilized Venezuela's infrastructure while also encouraging economic and commercial development. All this put the province and its cacao production at the center of the Crown's interests.

By the mid-1700s, the Bourbon dynasty, which had held the Spanish throne since the beginning of the century, enacted a string of new reforms designed to make the empire's administration more effective and to improve economic productivity in the colonies. As part of the reforms, in 1765 the Crown started a process of trade liberalization through the implementation of free trade decrees that allowed different ports of Spanish America to trade legally with one another. On the heels of these decrees, the Crown retracted the Caracas Company's monopoly on Venezuelan cacao in 1781.[15] As a result of unrestricted commercial relations, the Venezuelan economy expanded significantly in the last decades of the eighteenth century, increasing the fortunes of white Spaniards and local hacendados (landed estate owners), merchants, and traders. In the 1780s, cacao from the coastal hills and valleys and the southern slopes of the cordillera represented 70 percent of all legal exports and probably more in terms of illegal trade.[16] Although the cultivation of cacao continued to be the most profitable economic activity, many large landholders switched to other cash crops such as indigo, coffee, tobacco, sugar, and cotton.

The intensification of cacao cultivation in the region and the diversification of agricultural production spurred the demand for labor. As a consequence, the second half of the eighteenth century witnessed a significant increase in the importation of African slaves, the integration of indigenous mission families in the hacienda system, and the growing immigration of poor white laborers from the Basque country and the Canary Islands into the province.[17] By the end of the century, indigenous communities, mixed-race people commonly known as pardos, and free blacks from the western and southern plains dominated the laboring population in Venezuela. In the coastal areas, poor whites, pardos, black domestic laborers, hired workers, and slaves were predominant. Historian José María Aizpurua convincingly argues that a fundamental characteristic of late colonial Venezuela's labor system was its heterogeneity: enslaved laborers, free workers, peasant tenants, small independent producers, and indigenous cultivators were all involved in complex relations of production.[18]

It is important to clarify that Venezuela was a society with slaves, but not a slave-based society. In other words, the system of slavery in this region did not follow the "plantation model" frequently described in nineteenth-century accounts of Caribbean societies.[19] Venezuela's overall economy simply did not rely heavily on slaves; their presence was particularly noticeable only in the coastal region and in the central valleys of the Province of Caracas, where cacao plantations played an important role. In the Andes, the Province of Maracaibo, and the eastern region of Cumaná, by contrast, there were hardly any slaves at all.

Eighteenth-century travelers noticed the striking difference between Venezuela's enslaved population and that of the rest of the Caribbean, and they frequently commented that Venezuelan slaves received better treatment than those in the Caribbean islands. Apparently, Venezuelan landowners were more willing than others to manumit their slaves as a reward for their services, and slaves could also buy their own freedom through *coartación*, or purchase by installments.[20] According to the French traveler Jean-François Dauxion-Lavaysse, local slaves "enjoy a privilege unknown in the French and English colonies: it is that of obliging their masters to liberate them, on their paying the sum of 300 pesos."[21] Masters allowed their slaves to rent or use small plots of land on their haciendas, where they grew their own crops. This was done not necessarily to benefit slaves but rather to exempt Venezuelan masters from the obligation and expense of providing their slaves with housing, food, and clothing. Garden vegetables sold at markets as well as self-hire on off days enabled some slaves to save money for self-purchase.[22]

Hybrid labor arrangements and the relatively small role of slavery within the Venezuelan economy did not mean that Spanish and creole elites in Venezuela supported general manumission. On the contrary, the white elites of Caracas emphatically rejected the abolition of slavery because they were convinced that freeing their slaves would represent an economic loss for their haciendas and a threat to their social power. Elites worried that ex-slaves would join the demographically growing group of pardos and free blacks, whom they regarded as haughty and threatening to the social system. The prospect of abolition thus implied a threat to traditional notions of colonial order and social harmony.

The seemingly ambivalent nature of social divisions during the colonial period has sparked numerous debates about the relative importance and overlapping of socioracial, juridical, and class categories. While historians have traditionally sustained that colonial social stratification in the Spanish Indies depended on the notion of "caste," which reflected racial or physical distinctions, recent scholarship has demonstrated that social divisions were more often based instead on estate distinctions, defined by ancien régime criteria such as occupation, honor, and juridical status. Some authors have argued that, by the end of eighteenth century, expanded access to the means of production led to new forms of exploitation and accumulation, akin to those that operated in class societies, as well as an increasing sense of class differentiation within social groups.[23]

More recent studies have argued that in order to understand the complexity of the colonial Venezuelan social system, scholars must combine traditional feudal notions of social conditions and juridical status with New World realities, namely a socioracial system of classification and emerging class divisions. These historians suggest that the structure of Venezuelan colonial society, like others in Spanish America, reflected the overlapping of socioracial, estate, and class criteria.[24] In fact, these social classifications allowed the colonial state to strategically mold the identities and self-representations of subjects, and they were regularly used to legitimize occupational and social segregation.[25]

In the case of colonial Venezuela, markers of social status were often confusing and unstable, and they changed according to the context in which they were used or contested. Nonetheless, it is possible to identify two broader categories: *calidad* and social estate, which were commonly used to differentiate (and control) groups and to set rules and restrictions in a society that, in theory, was profoundly attached to ideas of order, harmony, and subordination. People in Venezuela understood socioracial or "caste" categories in terms of calidad (literally, "quality"), a comprehensive category that primordially reflected skin color but that also spoke to one's reputation as a whole, representing education, occupation, integrity, and honor, as well as so-called purity of blood.[26] In regions inhabited by peninsular and creole Spaniards, Indians, and blacks, calidad depended not only on physical appearance but also on other cultural signs of a "civilized" as opposed to "barbaric" or, more often, plebeian status.[27] Spanish colonial societies were also structured according to social estates or *estamentos*. These estates corresponded to the principal orders of ancien régime European society: nobility, clergy, peasantry, and militias. In colonial Venezuela, a number of factors—origin, education, occupation or profession, and juridical status—determined one's social estate.

In terms of calidad, Venezuelans recognized three basic socioracial groups: whites, Indians, and African blacks. Considered the bearers of Spanish values and the European "civilizing" culture, whites were at the top of the social hierarchy and exercised power over the rest of the society. This group was also divided in three subgroups: Spaniards (known as *blancos penisulares*) who were born on the Iberian peninsula and were living temporarily or indefinitely in the province; creoles (known as *blancos criollos*) who were born in the Americas but culturally identified themselves with Spanish values; and *blancos de orilla*, who were born in the Canary Islands but because of their humble origin, artisanal occupation, and poor education occupied a lower stratum than Spaniards and local creole whites.

Indios (Indians) was the name given by the Spanish colonizers to the diverse communities of natives who originally inhabited the American territories. Since the early colonization of Venezuela, most of these communities, but not all of them, were integrated into colonial society and were forced to work as members of quasi-fiefdoms called encomiendas,[28] to live and work in religious missions, or to occupy *pueblos de indios* (Indian towns) established by the Spaniards and strategically located near the haciendas where indigenous labor was required.[29] By the end of the eighteenth century and as a consequence of the abolition of the encomienda system in Venezuela, indigenous communities were divided into "tributary Indians," who paid tribute, and "free Indians," whom the colonial government exempted from the tribute. Most of the tributary Indians were located in two large areas of Venezuela: along the central Valleys of Caracas and in the highlands of Nueva Segovia, at the western edge of the Province of Caracas.[30]

The black population, represented by African slaves and their descendants, was located at the bottom of the social hierarchy. Depending on their legal condition, blacks were either "slaves" or "free," and they could also be *bozal* or *criollo* depending on their place of birth—bozales were born in Africa, and criollos were born in the Americas. Most of the black population, enslaved and free, worked in the cacao haciendas and in the mines, but some worked as domestic servants and skilled workers in the urban centers and port towns.

During the colonial period, a large and heterogeneous group—a product of ongoing relations among the three basic groups—became increasingly visible. These people of intermediate "quality" were known as pardos and, in theory, included all people perceived as mixed-race: *mulatos, zambos, tercerones, cuarterones, quinterones*, etc. The category of pardos was, and still is, difficult to define. For example, pardos and mulattos were both understood to be products of relations between whites and blacks, but sometimes the term "pardo" was used to refer to educated mixed-race people of slightly fairer skin, while the term "mulatto" denoted darker and less-educated mixed-race individuals.[31] Zambo, on the other hand, referred to the children of unions between Indians and blacks, and they were despised as a "bad race" because they supposedly distilled the worst aspects of Indians and blacks and completely lacked the desirable characteristics of whites.[32] Although some whites would refer to a zambo as a kind of pardo, there were pardos who would strongly argue that zambos did not possess the same calidad as pardos because zambos lacked *blancura* (whiteness).[33]

Frédérique Langue argues that in Venezuela the word "pardo" was regularly used for all "non-whites," understood in both anatomical and cultural terms. But historians Alejandro Gómez and Luis Pellicer believe that this definition merely echoes the views of local whites, who tended to lump pardos with other mixed races. Pardos, for their part, had a different perception of their status: they believed themselves superior to other mixed-race groups because only those who had some portion of European blood (such as cuarterones or "quadroons") could be considered pardos.[34]

By the end of the eighteenth century, the population of Venezuela numbered approximately 800,000. Almost 50 percent—close to 390,000 people—inhabited the Province of Caracas. According to historians Manuel Lucena Salmoral and Eduardo Arcila Farías, at the beginning of the nineteenth century, mixed races (pardos, zambos, and others) represented almost 38 percent of the population of the Province of Caracas, while enslaved people and mostly free blacks represented more than 24 percent. This means that people of African descent constituted over 60 percent of the population of the Province of Caracas in the period under discussion here. Barely 25 percent were listed as whites (peninsular Spaniards, creoles, and islanders), and 12 percent were labeled as Indians (see table 1).

The overlapping of categories of calidad and social estate gave shape to four main social groups in colonial Venezuela, each with internal divisions and distinctions. At the top were the *personas principales* (leading people), a white elite who represented the highest stratum of society. This group included local nobles, planters, and hacendados who had made or inherited important fortunes and enjoyed social privileges due to their lineage. High-ranking officials and authorities of the Crown—the captain general, governors, and magistrates or *oidores* of the audiencia—and church representatives also belonged to this group. Members of this group of "leading people" were usually known as *mantuanos* or, in the case of landowners, as *grandes cacaos*.[35] Not of the same rank as nobles and landowners but important enough to be considered members of this group were rich, white Spanish and creole *comerciantes* (merchants), who participated in international commerce and whose lifestyle was similar to that of nobles and landowners.

Table 1. Population of the Province of Caracas (1800)*

SOCIORACIAL GROUPS	NUMBER OF INHABITANTS	%
Pardos	147,360	37.9
Whites	99,642	25.6
Slaves	60,880	15.7
Indians	47,605	12.2
Free blacks	33,632	8.6
Total	389,110	100

* Lucena Salmoral, "La sociedad de la provincia de Caracas," 158–61; and Arcila Farías, El régimen de la encomienda en Venezuela, 70. Unfortunately, there is not one reliable source for demographic data of Venezuela during the colonial period, and different studies have produced different numbers. For a discussion of these historiographic incongruences, see Pérez Vila, "El gobierno deliberativo," 36–38.

In a middle stratum were the *personas de condición* (people of standing), who included white Spaniards, white creoles, and a limited number of educated pardos. This category included those individuals who had sufficient education to be members of the lettered body—university or seminary professors—or to have a profession. The whiter portion of this group usually assumed bureaucratic posts; their number also included medical doctors, lawyers, justice officials, and, in lesser degrees, notaries, secretaries, scribes, public accountants, and highly skilled artisans. Small merchants who played a significant role in local commercial networks were also considered members of this group. Some educated pardos who became savvy merchants and businessmen, and who possessed sizeable fortunes and maintained ostentatious lifestyles, were considered personas de condición, but they were nonetheless never seen as the equals of white individuals, because they lacked the necessary calidad and purity of blood.

In the lowest stratum—a heterogeneous group, in terms of calidad—were the *personas de baja condición* (people of lower standing). This group included local poor whites and blancos de orilla from the Canaries, pardos, Indians, and free blacks who dedicated themselves to artisanal or mechanical activities (carpenters, tailors, shoemakers, silversmiths, bakers, butchers, and tailors); people who performed services (petty surgeons, muleteers, masons, cooks, laundresses, healers, and barbers); and small merchants (shopkeepers and hardware traders). In the rural areas, pardo and mulatto peasants and free blacks working on plantations and haciendas were also part of this group. Below this category were, of course, enslaved blacks. Of the sixty thousand slaves who lived in the Province of Caracas, almost 70 percent were concentrated in a relatively small area near the coast, the Costa de Caracas, where the majority of cacao plantations and haciendas were located. In the main cities and ports like Caracas, La Guaira, and Puerto Cabello, there was a large number of slaves who did not perform agricultural tasks but instead worked as domestic servants, fishermen, sailors, muleteers, or skilled artisans.

During the eighteenth century, the relationships among and within these different social groups became increasingly strained due to changing political, bureaucratic, and economic circumstances. In theory, in Spanish America peninsular Spaniards held political positions that were not accessible to white creoles; however, this was not strictly true in Venezuela where, as Ann Twinam argues, until the mid-eighteenth century "Caraqueños [the white creole elite] experienced Spanish Administration—'light'"[36] and enjoyed certain political autonomy and authority. Increasing Bourbon administrative control and restrictions in the political realm created, nonetheless, new tensions between Spanish administrators and the creole elite, who continued challenging colonial authorities. In addition, the considerable expansion of the captaincy's economy allowed newly prosperous white creoles to continue gaining access to important institutions, such as the town council and the Real Consulado (a colonial institution created to protect and promote commercial activity throughout the captaincy general), and to exercise some pressure on the Spanish political elite. By the end of the eighteenth century, white creoles and some pardo families openly challenged colonial institutions such as the royal audiencia, and even disobeyed royal orders that went against their economic interests.[37]

On the other hand, the growing number of pardo elites (often called *pardos beneméritos*) exacerbated tensions with whites. White Spaniards and creoles played important roles in the clergy, government, and military academies, and these positions were regarded as unsuitable for pardos, who were despised by Spaniards and local whites as an inferior group. Their African blood and their link with their enslaved ancestors, the brown color of their skin, and their supposedly bastard origins coalesced into a stereotyped image of inferiority, which led to various forms of social, spatial, and legal segregation.[38] White elites depicted pardos as illegitimate children with no traceable genealogy. A document written by members of the Caracas city council stated: "Pardos, mulattos, and zambos have the defect of illegitimacy, because it is rather rare to find a pardo, mulatto, or zambo with legitimate parents."[39] In colonial Venezuela, as in other provinces of Spanish America and the Caribbean, pardos did not have access to education in public schools or universities, could not be ordained as priests, could not occupy any public office, and could not carry certain arms. Sumptuary laws forbade pardas (pardo females) from wearing certain clothes and accessories, including pearls, silk, and gold. In Caracas, pardos were not allowed to sit in certain sections in churches, in government offices, or at public ceremonies.[40]

However, by the end of the eighteenth century, pardos—especially the lighter-skinned, educated, and wealthy elite—had devised legal strategies to gain access to positions from which they had traditionally been excluded. Among these was a royal edict—known as the Real Cédula de Gracias al Sacar—which could bestow on the wealthiest pardos a "dispensation of color" (*dispensa de calidad*), granting them honorary white status.[41] White creoles ferociously opposed such edicts, arguing that they violated the Crown's policy against social mobility. Multiple documents recording this debate reveal the passion with which white creoles defended their perceptions of racial order and honor, depicting them as fundamental values of the colonial social structure. In a letter presented by the Caracas city council to the king of Spain at the end of 1796, white creoles insisted that the honor of whites could not be extended to pardos, because honor and tradition depended on "proper order and subordination." In 1796, for example, members of the same cabildo pleaded for the king to continue "guarding the honor of their ancestors and the thoughts of their elders, saving them from the outrage of having to mix with pardos favored by a Royal Decree that promises elevation for them, and that announces equality, disorder, and corruption."[42]

These social tensions recorded in hundreds of eighteenth-century Venezuelan documents have fueled debate regarding Venezuelans' acceptance of or opposition to the status quo in the late colonial period. While traditional historiography has focused primarily on studying political conflicts and rebellions, characterized in this period as particularly tense and conflictive,[43] a more recent historiography that concentrates on everyday life and economic growth describes this time as the "golden years" of colonial Venezuela, a period in which the province expanded economically and reached an unprecedented political maturity.[44] This newer narrative suggests that conflicts expressed in rebellions and conspiracies were not reactions to contradictory interests between the empire and the province, nor were they responses to the unequal access to power by different social groups, but rather these were processes of adaptation to the new administrative transformations triggered by the Bourbon reforms. Twinam argues that, depending on the kinds of sources scholars use, historians may come to one interpretation or the other, but certainly there was a combination of factors in Venezuela—a substantial presence of free blacks and pardos, significant social mobility, and intense repression by the white elite—that created a tense atmosphere ripe for confrontations and power struggles between different social groups.[45]

Although calm on the surface, eighteenth-century Venezuela was a society founded on social privileges and differences that constantly created tensions within distinct social groups and stoked anxiety among the ruling elites. Lower social groups used multiple strategies to challenge a social system that they perceived as unclear and unfair, yet also flexible enough to allow some gains and a modicum of participation.[46] In the final decade of the century, revolutionary events exacerbated social tensions and disrupted this "tense calmness"; ideas of liberty and equality from the American and French Revolutions reached Venezuela. The rising tide of political turmoil in the Caribbean, which included calls for abolition and equality, certainly increased political anxiety and socioracial struggle.

Reading and Circulation of Books in a Province with No Printing Press

Even before French revolutionary events impacted Europe and the Antilles, some local whites and educated pardos began to challenge Venezuela's social, political, and educational systems. These challengers were not exclusively inspired by French Enlightenment ideas. Instead, they were more clearly influenced by Spanish intellectuals who articulated the fundamental precepts of Spanish reformism, such as the critique of the "lazy and unproductive" nobility, the promotion of education and literacy among artisans and laborers, and the inclusion of agricultural laborers and merchants in the political sphere. In Spanish America, these social changes sowed tensions between the Crown and the provincial governments, and more specifically between Spaniards (*peninsulares*) and white creoles, dividing individuals along the lines not of calidad or estamentos but in terms of ideological groups such as "conservative" and "modern."

Foreign visitors noticed these ideological changes. Describing men from Caracas, for example, Alexander von Humboldt noted that "a change of ideas" had recently produced two kinds of men: those tied to old uses and customs, and those open to new ideas "but so contaminated by foreign influences that they often lose the appropriate path for achieving happiness and social order."[47] Another foreign visitor, François-Joseph de Pons, a French agent who traveled to various Venezuelan cities between 1801 and 1804, noticed a peculiarity in the education of white youth:

> Aware of the insufficiency of their education, [they] endeavor to supply what is lacking, and peruse with avidity the works of foreign authors. Several of them attempt, with the aid of dictionaries, to translate and speak the French and English languages, particularly the former. They do not think, like their fathers, that geography is a superfluous science, or that history is a useless study. Commerce has begun to be less despised than formerly. Although the mania in favour of rank and distinction continues as great as ever, it is natural to suppose that it must yield in its turn to the progress of reason.[48]

Some of these young, white creoles supported Venezuela's pardos in their plea for access to universities or their petitions to open pardo schools; others tried to establish educational institutions for pardos, while inviting pardos into their homes to discuss books and ideas. These young creoles contributed to the creation of networks of information and books that would gradually expand literacy beyond the traditional socioracial boundaries envisioned by the government and the white elite. What do we know about Venezuela's literary world? What do we know about the books and reading tastes of Venezuelans?

Although little attention has been paid to the study of literacy in late colonial Venezuela, a few studies do provide some information about private libraries and the importation of books into the captaincy general during the eighteenth century. These studies can be used to shed light on reading practices and literary tastes in late colonial Venezuela, when the first written materials on political and social upheavals in France and the Caribbean started to circulate in the Atlantic world.[49] We need to bear in mind that such studies, which rely entirely on sources such as inventories of private libraries and ships' cargoes, do not allow us to draw definitive conclusions about literacy in Venezuela. If, for example, we examined the number of wills in the

Province of Caracas that contained library inventories, we might infer that by the end of eighteenth century almost 13 percent of the population of the province possessed books and knew how to read them.[50] We should be aware, however, of some methodological difficulties: first, not everyone who possessed books left behind a postmortem inventory; only the elites (*personas principales* and some *personas de condición*) typically had the means to leave wills. Second, not all books or printed matter proved valuable enough to be itemized in a will; and third, not everyone in possession of a library necessarily knew how to read. To form a clearer understanding of literacy at the time, we must therefore consider additional sources, such as marriage registers' signatures and censuses.[51] Private library inventories and ships' manifests are sources, however, that allow us to pinpoint certain broad characteristics about the social composition of the Venezuelan readership, the progressive transformation of literary tastes, and the secularization of private libraries toward the end of the eighteenth century.

Testaments, postmortem library inventories, and shipping lists suggest that the clergy, followed by the local nobility, government authorities, and landowners, possessed the largest percentage of libraries. In Caracas, for example, the clergy possessed almost 20 percent of the private libraries registered in postmortem inventories, while the white nobility and planters together possessed another 25 percent. Together, the two groups possessed almost 70 percent of all books registered in private libraries between 1770 and 1810. People dedicated to commercial activities—merchants, petty traders, and shopkeepers—held 14 percent of registered libraries. Other social groups, such as "men of letters" (lawyers, and seminary and university teachers) and government functionaries (official secretaries, tax agents, and scribes), possessed 10 percent of the libraries registered in Caracas's inventories.[52] Some poor whites had small libraries, but I have found only one record of a library possessed by a pardo woman and no records of libraries belonging to free blacks or slaves. It is important to note, however, that very few inventories were drawn up for pardos and none for free blacks or slaves.[53] The question, then, is whether this absence of documentation implies that pardos, free blacks, and slaves were illiterate or did not have access to books and other written materials. We will return to this problem later.

From 1760 until 1810, several ships loaded with books arrived every month in the port of La Guaira, where first the Caracas Company and later private merchants sold new volumes to avid readers, shopkeepers, and owners of pulperías. The last three decades of the eighteenth century witnessed a significant increase in the number of books brought from Spain to Venezuela.⁵⁴ As an extreme example, there is the case of the commercial company La Viuda Irisarri e Hijo (The Widow Irisarri and Son), which in 1764 exported sixteen boxes of books from Cádiz to La Guaira and which, by 1774, had commercialized a total of fifty-five boxes of books; the number continued increasing during subsequent years.⁵⁵ The number and size of private libraries in the cities of the province—especially Caracas and La Guaira—also increased annually. For example, the average number of titles per library almost doubled in twenty years, from twenty-five titles per library in the decade 1770–1780 to forty-nine titles per library in the decade 1800–1810.⁵⁶

The books that came from Spain to Venezuela during the last decades of the colonial period were quite diverse. During this period, new genres first appeared in Venezuelan libraries, suggesting an important transformation in local literary tastes. Venezuelan readers continued buying seminal religious texts, such as the Bible, breviaries, catechisms, mass books, the "lives of saints," and theological literature; but by the end of the eighteenth century there was a clear increase in nonreligious literature. Ship inventories reveal that, during this time, the importation of religious books had decreased considerably, while there was a growing interest in books about politics, government, history, law, administration, commerce, education, agriculture, mathematics, and military and naval engineering. Also popular were dictionaries, with an increasing presence of Spanish-French ones, plus manuals for artisans.⁵⁷

Similarly, an analysis of Caracas's private libraries shows that the proportion of religious books drastically decreased from almost 54 percent in the decade 1770–1779 to 26 percent in 1800–1809, while other fields such as education, agriculture, mathematics, geography, military arts, politics and administration, and belles lettres (plus dictionaries) practically doubled or tripled (table 2).⁵⁸

This new configuration of Caracas's private libraries meshed with the reformist discourse that sought to promote progress in Spanish America through scientific study of the region and its natural resources, the diversification of labor, an efficient administration, and new commercial developments. More interestingly, this transformation of Caracas's libraries shows that there was a process of secularization of books and reading practices evolving, a process that had been slowly developing in Europe and other Spanish American regions throughout the mid-seventeenth and the entire

Table 2. Thematic Distribution of Books in Caracas's Private Libraries (1770–1779, 1800–1809)

1770-1779	NO. OF TITLES	%	1800-1809	NO. OF TITLES	%
Agriculture	0	0.00	Agriculture	10	1.05
Belles lettres	14	2.55	Belles lettres	56	5.86
Classics	4	0.73	Classics	14	1.46
Dictionaries	16	2.91	Dictionaries	55	5.86
Education	9	1.64	Education	40	4.18
Grammars	16	2.91	Grammars	25	2.62
History	17	3.09	History	84	8.79
Law	40	7.27	Law	120	12.55
Math	2	0.36	Math	11	1.14
Medicine	14	2.55	Medicine	25	2.59
Military arts	0	0.00	Military arts	15	1.57
Philosophy	16	2.91	Philosophy	25	2.59
Politics	12	2.18	Politics	45	4.71
Religion	295	53.64	Religion	253	26.22
Not classified	95	17.27	Not classified	187	19.38
Total	550	100	Total	965	100

eighteenth century but that in Venezuela occurred rather abruptly during the last decades of the eighteenth century.

Multiple factors might have caused this transformation of literary tastes in late colonial Venezuela. It is clear that during the second half of the eighteenth century, Venezuela's economic growth and stability increased the purchasing capacity of local residents—especially families related to productive and commercial activities—who imported more objects and luxury goods (including books) from Europe and who refurnished their houses and haciendas. In addition, a more solid and structured commercial network initiated by the Caracas Company in the middle of the eighteenth century had also provided Venezuelans with a stable offer of imported European goods, allowing the expansion and diversification of local markets. There is no doubt that French Enlightenment ideas and Spanish reformist ones found their way into Venezuelan society. Venezuelans not only followed European fashions and tendencies but also integrated new objects and created new forms of socialization in their everyday lives. It was precisely at the end of the eighteenth century that Caracas's wealthy residents began to create more specialized spaces in their houses, like reading and coffee rooms, bureaus, and libraries. They also had expensive wooden bookshelves built, which were rapidly filled with new editions.[59]

The crucial question, now, is how Venezuelans bought new books in cities with no printing presses or bookstores. Although it has not been possible to identify a printing shop or a single bookstore in any of Venezuela's main cities, it is clear that a more stable, structured, and vigorously expanding market for books emerged by the end of the eighteenth century. Every year, an increasing number of people in Caracas and La Guaira ordered books from Cádiz merchants through friends and family members.[60] Some merchants of the port of La Guaira also offered new titles and editions to a selected clientele in their homes or shops. In fact, two residents of the port town, don Gerbasio Navas and the Captain Antonio Romero, sold new and used books in their shops in Caracas and La Guaira. Romero, for example, left a will that listed 209 volumes and 1,200 cartillas or primers that remained in his shop.[61] Regular bodegas and pulperías also offered hundreds of inexpensive printed materials, such as *librillos* (pamphlets) on saints' lives, religious catechisms, and cartillas, to a growing public.[62] Public auctions (*remates*) also offered buyers an opportunity to acquire a variety of titles at accessible prices. Afraid of losing books—and money—to the menace of moths and humidity, heirs and heiresses were usually interested in selling the entire libraries of their deceased family members, and people in the urban centers learned by word of mouth about titles and prices offered at public auctions and attended them frequently.[63]

New titles were publicized by diverse groups of people who gathered in taverns, pulperías, barbershops, and the street markets to talk not only about what they were reading but also about European news and Atlantic politics.[64] Concerned city dwellers often denounced semipublic political debates to government officials, priests, or officers of the Inquisition. Reports from the Real Audiencia and the Real Intendencia to the captain general of Venezuela suggest that people were reading prohibited texts and were commenting on them "in public," often in front of people of lower condition. In October 1795, the intendant or regional Crown official of Caracas issued a report expressing his concern about the dissemination of French ideas in public settings, where pardos could easily become contaminated. These denunciations and the subsequent investigations reveal another complex network that connected readers and expanded the literate sphere: the network for lending books.[65]

During the two decades from 1790 to 1810, officers of the Inquisition frequently visited the homes of individuals suspected of possessing forbidden books in order to confiscate them. During the month of April 1806, for example, these officers visited the houses of more than twenty-five people in Caracas to investigate reports of the possession of prohibited texts. In response, the readers offered the same excuses over and over: "I used to have the text but I loaned it and I cannot remember to whom," or, alternatively, "I read the book but gave it back to the owner or someone else." Benito Prada, an agent of the Holy Office, asked don Domingo Díaz if he possessed a copy of the forbidden title *History of the Revolution*. Díaz said that "he remembered reading the first volume, but that he had lent the book to don Francisco González de Linares." When the officer asked don Gabriel Ponte if he had *La Jáira* by Voltaire, don Gabriel answered: "That book is normally *running freely* and, today, I don't know where it is. I gave it to someone, but I don't know whom."[66]

The practice of lending books was so pervasive that it is not uncommon to find notes at the end of a postmortem inventory clarifying that there were books out on loan that had to be returned to the original owner before the final appraisal.[67] Priests and university professors regularly lent their volumes to curious students or invited them to read at their homes, and members of extended families and neighbors circulated their recently acquired books and shared their impressions. Library inventories show that priests and professionals (lawyers, doctors, and professors) were particularly prone to borrow books from members of their literate communities.[68]

The same book could spend weeks going from one home to another, and many readers were interested in making their own copies, partial or entire, of the same book. In fact, the lack of a printing press and the existence of this informal web for printed materials encouraged practices of hand-copying and translating books. Caracas's and La Guaira's private libraries contained not only printed but also many manuscript books. The library of Governor Pedro Carbonell, for example, contained a "manuscript on painted paper about the use of Arms and other military tactics." The library of priest and professor José Ignacio Moreno, dean of the University of Caracas, included a hand-copied version of a text entitled "Treaty of Philadelphia," among other handwritten copies of foreign materials.[69] In Caracas and La Guaira, many readers became copyists and translators of particular excerpts of texts containing ideas they wanted to preserve after they had returned the book to its owner or passed it on to another reader. These practices ended up transforming the texts themselves, changing their typography and material conditions, often mutilating and fragmenting them. As a result, these texts were converted into new texts, and their copyists—and translators—into authors themselves.[70] Seminary and university professors offered their books to students, who copied part of them and studied with their handwritten notes, which they also shared among classmates. For example, the university professor don Baltasar de los Reyes Marrero used to invite his students to his home to transcribe texts, a practice whereby he also avoided the risk of having his precious books stolen or lost.[71]

Colonial officials and members of the Inquisition were especially concerned about this practice of copying and translating texts that subversive individuals could use to disseminate forbidden texts. Numerous denunciations to the secretary of this institution claimed that certain individuals possessed handwritten copies of prohibited books. A note in the Inquisition Notebook reads: "Don Rafael Lugo has mentioned 'the Raynal' several times; in past days he showed me a hand-copied paragraph translated by him. This same paragraph, don Rafael Mexias told me, was given by D. F. Montillas to don Diego Urbaneja and to others."[72]

By the end of the eighteenth century, the establishment of a more stable book market and the popularity of public auctions had brought readers (and listeners or potential readers) closer to printed materials. The number of libraries, their sizes, and the diversity of their titles had also increased dramatically, reflecting an ongoing process of secularization of written knowledge. In short, reading in the urban centers of Venezuela was no longer perceived as an exclusively religious practice but as an educational and even recreational activity that also facilitated—and required—social interaction. The lack of printing presses and bookshops did not prevent readers in Venezuela from accessing books; instead, it encouraged them to connect with other readers and to create networks for sharing and transcribing books. Venezuelan readers quickly realized that in order to follow recent European publications and news, they needed to rely on social networks of friends, neighbors, family members, teachers, classmates, and acquaintances. As we will see, this practice of sharing texts ultimately made possible the creation of public spaces for discussion and debate. Interestingly, these diffuse networks of readers and listeners largely escaped the control of colonial state and religious institutions. Priests and colonial officials suspected their existence but could do little to eradicate them.

Prohibited Books and the Social Control of Literacy

During the entire eighteenth century, the church was the institution formally entrusted with the task of finding and confiscating prohibited books and seditious papers in the ports and urban centers of Venezuela.[73] After the events of the American and French Revolutions, the Spanish Crown and local governments became increasingly concerned about the expansion of revolutionary ideas on the South American mainland and undertook, along with the church, the job to censor, ban, or confiscate potentially dangerous texts.[74]

The church and the Spanish Crown, however, had concerns about French ideas long before the events of the French Revolution. By mid-eighteenth century, both the Spanish Crown and the Inquisition prohibited the entry into Spanish territories of several French titles that challenged the moral order, Christian principles, or the monarchical state. In 1772, however, the Crown attempted to take more control over censorship when King Charles III issued a royal decree declaring that the inquisitor general could not prohibit particular books without royal permission.[75] However, concerns about the circulation of French philosophical ideas continued and required a collaborative effort by the state and the church. In 1778, Spanish priest and writer José Francisco Isla wrote: "Voltaire, Rousseau, and other leaders of modern impiety had invaded the most distant corners of Spain."[76] Other priests and officials likewise bemoaned the avid interest of Spanish readers in acquiring and reading French books that threatened the social and moral orders.[77] In 1784, the Crown responded to this menace by banning the sale of any foreign book, in any language and on any subject, without the authorization of the Council of Castile.[78] By 1789, when revolutionary ideas had begun to circulate in the Atlantic world, long-standing institutional tensions between the Crown and the Inquisition eased, and Spanish council members and Inquisition agents shared the responsibility of reading, examining, censoring, prohibiting, and controlling written texts of any kind that threatened subordination, vassalage, obedience to the king, or the respect of Christian precepts.[79]

The king of Spain, Charles IV, was deeply concerned about the effects of the French Revolution and its propaganda on Spain's American territories. In September 1789, he was informed that members of the National Assembly of Paris were trying to smuggle into Spanish America a seditious manifesto that could "shake the power of Spanish dominion among its inhabitants." Immediately, the Spanish minister, the Count of Floridablanca, sent a royal decree to the governors of the Spanish provinces in America ordering them to guard against the importation and diffusion of any texts that could "promote Independence and anti-religion." From 1789 to 1790, the Spanish monarch issued several royal decrees restricting the entry of French books and papers, prohibiting those whose content was considered dangerous to religion, proper subordination, and the social order.[80] In September and October 1789, respectively, the Crown issued two royal orders prohibiting "the entry of any illustration, printed or handwritten papers, boxes, fans or any other object alluding to the French Revolution. If authorities find any of these items, they were to be sent directly to the Secretary of State."[81] Likewise, in 1790, the Council of Castile prohibited the introduction of several French newspapers, revolutionary catechisms, and books related to the French Revolution.[82]

In December 1790, the captain general of Venezuela wrote a report in which he stated that "within the last four months, several newspapers, journals, and broadsides from Paris, but printed in the French islands, had been introduced in Tierra Firme,"[83] adding that these might cause serious harm to the population. Likewise, several official reports from all the provinces of Spain—including the American territories—decried that, despite governmental efforts, French books and papers were making their way into the hands of curious and avid readers. In response, the monarch issued another royal decree on September 10, 1791: "The introduction of any letters or seditious papers contrary to the principles of public fidelity and tranquility is strictly prohibited." Those who flouted this decree were to be prosecuted for the offense of disloyalty. Local authorities were responsible for controlling the circulation of these materials and sending copies to the council in Madrid.[84] The French Revolution had evidently compounded official anxieties over local reading practices, and the church cooperated closely with the royal government in its attempts to promote vigilance.

The Spanish Inquisition's regulations and edicts arrived regularly in Venezuela. Approximately twenty-six "Edicts of Prohibited Books" were read aloud after the Sunday Mass and pinned to the outside walls of churches of

Caracas and other towns between 1762 and 1807; twenty-one (or about 80 percent) of these edicts were published after 1789.[85] Priests and Inquisition commissaries (regional representatives who reported to the Holy Office in Cartagena) visited several private homes in Caracas and other cities with the purpose of collecting prohibited French books and delivering them to the Inquisition See.[86]

Between 1789 and 1810, the church relied on denunciations to uncover banned printed material. People in Venezuela were encouraged to report any forbidden books they had seen in private homes or heard mentioned in any conversations. Not only were people to be on the lookout for prohibited books; they were also expected to listen in on conversations in order to identify "seditious ideas." Don Gabriel Josef de Lindo, an agent of the Inquisition, kept a notebook in which he recorded all the denunciations made by the people of the Province of Caracas. These notes provide a window on public discussion and interpretation of books at the time. One note reads: "In 1797, don Francisco Carreño heard from a child named Marcos Torres that 'he believed that Hell existed' but that 'another child told him that it did not exist because he read it in a book.'" Another note says: "Josef Bernardo Aristiguieta told me that he has permission to read prohibited books, and that for this reason he had many of these in French." Another Inquisition agent, don Miguel Castro, wrote in 1806: "I know that don Francisco Guerra, doctor, has the *History of America* by [William] Robertson, because he has made reference to several paragraphs that I found in it."[87]

Prohibited titles registered in private libraries' inventories, as well as in records of the Inquisition between 1789 and 1810, show the ease with which prohibited books made their way to the peripheries of the colonial world.[88] French books and papers were secretly introduced into Spain through a number of conduits. Papers were rolled up and put inside boxes of items such as hats, clocks, and musical instruments, and books were hidden in heavy crates that were dropped overboard when the Inquisition official boarded the ship, to be retrieved later.[89] In Venezuela, where inspections were less comprehensive, it was not necessary to employ such creative methods; boxes of French books frequently entered the ports of La Guaira and Puerto Cabello unnoticed. In addition, smuggling webs could have helped introduce foreign forbidden books and gazettes that found their way to urban centers.

Readers in the cities of Caracas, Cumaná, La Guaira, and Puerto Cabello owned prohibited French texts such as Rousseau's *The Social Contract* (plus his pieces *Abelard and Heloise* and *La Julia*); Voltaire's *Philosophical*

Dictionary (and his novel *La Jáira*); Jacques Delille's poetic works; Jean le Rond d'Alembert's writings on philosophy, literature, and history; and *Theory of Social Laws* by J.-F. Dauray de Brie. According to several anonymous informants who made denunciations, readers in La Guaira and Caracas had, among other items, the forbidden texts of the Abbé Condillac, the Abbé Raynal, William Robertson, Pedro Montengón y Paret, Thomas Paine, the Marquis of Condorcet, Montesquieu, and Gaetano Filangieri.[90]

Agents of the Inquisition found most of these prohibited books in the libraries of white priests, rich hacendados, military officials, and merchants, whose family members always found an excuse to justify the presence of the dangerous texts in their homes. The majority of these elite readers regarded reading and writing as practices reserved for those of a certain social status; they believed that they were entitled to read any book, because their educational background and social condition had equipped them with the "right understanding" (*buen entendimiento*) to comprehend complex or pugnacious texts.[91] For example, an Inquisition agent wrote in a notebook: "Don Marciano Echeverría told me that he could read prohibited books about State matters, because he is an enlightened subject who does not suffer the danger of perdition."[92]

Most of these readers firmly argued that books (and prohibited titles in particular) should not be read by inferior social groups such as pardos, free blacks, slaves, and Indians, who lacked the intelligence to differentiate good books from bad, or fiction from nonfiction. They believed that the content of a given text could alter common people's attitudes toward the political regime, their own economic circumstances, or the broader social order.[93] Colonial agents likewise believed that reading might sow "erroneous ideas" among pardos, free blacks, and slaves, encouraging them to challenge the institutional order, the authority of the local government, and even the sovereignty of the Crown. These fears of ideological contagion of lower-status groups reached a peak during the years of the Haitian Revolution (1791–1804), which helped to spread information about racial confrontation, the abolition of slavery, freedom, and equality throughout the Atlantic world.[94] But did pardos, free blacks, and slaves in Venezuela have ready access to written materials? And if they did, how did they come into contact with them? The literate world of Venezuela, as in other provinces in Spanish America, was a complicated one. Communities in the main urban centers of the province such as Caracas, La Guaira, Valencia, and Puerto Cabello were mostly "semi-literate" communities: different socioracial groups had only partial or mediated access to the written word and used different media to spread information and engage in debates.

Spanish Reformism and Plebeian Literacy in Venezuela

Not all whites in Venezuela believed that access to print should be restricted to the elite. Some educated white creoles (merchants, priests, and teachers), inspired by Spanish reformism or infused with the republican values of equality and fraternity, believed that pardo artisans and skilled workers—who were not allowed to attend public schools, religious seminaries, or universities and were generally seen by the elite as people who did not need literacy—should learn to read and write in order to improve their own condition and contribute to the country's progress.[95]

By the mid-eighteenth century, traditional views of society and education had undergone an important transformation in the Spanish territories. In an effort to eradicate perceived ignorance, vice, and idleness among the population at large, Spanish reformists promoted literacy and education for all. In fact, several editions of books by Spanish reformists, such as Pedro Rodríguez de Campomanes, Gaspar Melchor de Jovellanos, Fray Benito Jerónimo Feijóo y Montenegro, Gerónimo de Uztáriz, and Bernardo Ward, among others, arrived in Venezuela during the final decades of the eighteenth century.[96] All of these authors extensively discussed the need to reform the Spanish monarchical system and its administrative and legal structure in order to achieve agricultural and commercial development, while also seeking to produce changes in the public sphere, largely through education, labor reform, and social progress. They championed public education as an antidote to illiteracy and ignorance, and argued in favor of creating schools to teach peasants, artisans, and urban laborers to draw, read, and write in order to transmit their knowledge to others. They also argued in favor of a more educated society that could use *ciencias útiles* (useful sciences) for the progress of Spain and its territories.[97] At the same time, they emphasized the importance of intra-imperial trade and the development of locally produced alternatives to imported goods. As Aguilar Piñal asserts: "Every thoughtful step of these enlightened thinkers would be preceded by words such as 'public benefit' and 'usefulness,' magic words that would change the face of the country."[98]

In his *Teatro critico universal* (1781), which turned up in many Venezuelan private libraries,[99] Fray Benito Jerónimo Feijóo y Montenegro criticized the laziness and vanity of the nobility, and the ignorance and superstition of the common folk or *pueblo*. The solutions proposed by Feijóo for both groups emphasized the value of education and hard work. In fact, the main goal of his eight volumes was to eradicate false ideas and common "vices" that impeded good or rational understanding (*buen entendimiento*) among individuals. Throughout the work, Feijóo not only proposes concrete suggestions but also traces the process whereby he arrived at them. Convinced that anyone, regardless of social status or background, could read his essays, Feijóo sought to introduce a large reading public to his ideas and new methods, and firmly defended the social expansion of literacy and education.[100]

Another Spanish writer, Pedro Rodríguez, Conde de Campomanes, dedicated his entire book *Discurso sobre la educación popular de los artesanos y su fomento* (1775) to analyzing the importance of education for all social groups, especially artisans and laborers. "Artisans," he wrote, "should live according to the general laws that rule society, and not apart from them." As artisans and laborers perform essential social roles, they require formal instruction from a young age: "Apprentices should not be treated as serfs or *criados* by their masters, nor should they be occupied in other labors different from their occupation." According to Campomanes, even shoemakers, tailors, carpenters, masons, and smiths should learn to draw, read, and write in order to transmit their knowledge to others through the written word and to improve their skills. Moreover, he argued, artisans should receive religious, moral, and civic education, which would instill in them a sense of social values and a commitment to their occupations.[101] Also widely read in Venezuela was the work of don Gaspar Melchor de Jovellanos, whose *Memorias de la real sociedad económica de Madrid* emphasized the importance of educating the peasantry. "Society," he wrote, "wishes that they become literate: that is that they learn to read, to write and to count. What a huge space this sublime but simple knowledge would open to man's faculties of perception!"[102]

Although none of these Spanish authors particularly addressed the need to educate the indigenous population or people of color in the Spanish Indies, when translated into the local context, their ideas had a different effect than in Spain. In Venezuela's social reality, the reformists' proposals meant that pardos and free blacks, the majority of the rural peasants and urban artisans, should become literate and partake of this well-needed social and cultural change. In fact, some Venezuelan instructors enthusiastically adopted the

Spanish reformist model that promoted literacy and formal education for the common people.

Following this reformist impulse, concerned teachers in Caracas advocated for improving the quality of public schools—traditionally attended by whites—and for creating schools for pardos (*escuelas de pardos*) in the cities of the province.[103] In 1786 and 1794, respectively, two white creole teachers, José María Buñuelos and Simón Rodríguez, advocated for the creation of these schools; they proposed their ideas to the cabildo, but no one seemed interested in pursuing the project. Their accounts suggested that, although some wealthy pardo families could afford to hire private tutors who taught students to read and write in their homes, surprisingly, the vast majority of the "semiliterate" pardo population learned to read and write at the shops of barbers and shoemakers, or thanks to the assistance of priests, artisans, carpenters, and musicians, who informally offered their educational services to pardo children.

Given the impossibility of enrolling their children in public schools, wealthy pardo families of Caracas—like the Landaetas and the Mexías Bejarano—had no option but to hire private teachers. These privileged pardo children not only learned to read and write but also were encouraged by their parents to continue more advanced studies such as theology, law, and medicine. In the meantime, their fathers engaged in the complex and contentious process for a petition of "dispensation of color" (*dispensa de calidad*) so their sons could access the Caracas seminary or the university.[104] Other, less privileged pardo families offered their children a modest education that allowed them to become recognized artisans, such as musicians (the brothers Juan José and José Luis Landaeta, and Lino Gallardo), painters (like Juan Lovera, Blas Miguel Landaeta, and Francisco José de Lerma y Villegas), and silversmiths.[105] There were many other pardo families who did not have the means to pay for private teachers but had connections with priests or teachers who were happy to educate their offspring. This was the case of the Olivares family, a pardo family in Caracas who were very close to two well-known priests, Father José de Osío and Father Pedro Palacios Sojo. They taught the Olivares brothers, Juan Manuel and Juan Bautista, how to play and compose religious musical pieces, and how to build and play musical instruments (violin and harpsichord); and they probably introduced one of them, Juan Bautista, to advanced studies in Latin, rhetoric, philosophy, and theology. Later, Juan Bautista Olivares established a strong relationship with the priests of the temple of San Felipe de Neri, with whom he continued a clandestine instruction in theology.[106]

The vast majority of the poor pardo and moreno populations of Venezuela struggled to get an education. Historical sources suggest, however, that many of them—especially those who lived in urban centers—had access to a rudimentary instruction that afforded them access to literacy. In 1786, teacher don José María Buñuelos alerted the city council to the pitiful state of primary education in the city of Caracas. He deplored the "scarce number" of primary schools: "Many schools are reduced to barbershops, beauty salons, shoe stores, and other places of mechanical occupations, where it is impossible to pay attention to this primordial matter."[107] According to Buñuelos, the majority of pardo children learned to read thanks to elder artisans who taught only basic grammar and pronunciation, with a cartilla or simple primer as their textbook.[108]

The Caracas teacher don Simón Rodríguez, with whom I opened this chapter, wrote a long account in 1794 entitled *The State of Primary Education in Caracas*. In it, he described a similar situation.[109] Like Spanish reformist teachers, Rodríguez emphasized the need to expand literacy by educating artisans and peasants, occupations that in Venezuela were performed mostly by people of color: pardos, morenos, and mulattos. About the large population of pardos, he wrote:

> The mechanical arts are linked, in this city and elsewhere in the Province, with pardos and morenos (free blacks). They do not have anyone to teach them, they cannot attend the school for whites, and poverty limits them from childhood on. They therefore learn through practice, but without technique; lacking this, they proceed in everything by improvisation. Some become teachers of others without ever having been students, with the exception of those who with an extraordinary vigor have achieved their formal instruction thanks to painful efforts.[110]

Rodríguez believed that pardos needed education as urgently as whites did; society, in turn, would benefit from the education of both groups. To this end, Rodríguez proposed to found a school for pardos. Rodríguez reported that in order to receive some education, pardo children attended beauty salons and barbershops, but these places, he argued, were not appropriate venues for schooling. Moreover, barbers and artisans lacked the comprehensive knowledge and the pedagogical training of effective educators: "These improvised teachers do not even know who their students are and how they have progressed." In these improvised classrooms, Rodríguez complained, children learned at once "to read and to comb their hair, to write and to shave."[111]

Rodríguez's account provides a detailed and also highly opinionated picture of the poor state of popular education in Caracas: students learned in inappropriate settings and on irregular schedules from "instructors" who were not trained to teach. Rodríguez underscored that these children who attended the improvised schools learned to read narratives "in dialogue"; as a result, they did not "learn to read all the discourses; they learn only through answers and questions." As adults, they therefore struggled to understand more complex forms of language. Interestingly, this practice mirrors the use of catechistic formulas to impart religious knowledge to children. The genre took the form of a conversation: an "ignorant" person (usually a child, a woman, an Indian, or a black man) asks questions of a wise interlocutor (father, teacher, or other white male) whose primarily role is to instruct the other.[112]

Rodríguez sought to expose the multiple problems that plagued this informal and uncontrolled education system, and at the same time his report represents a unique ethnography of the education of pardos and the social spaces in which it took place. It is clear now that, despite official prohibition, there was a middling group of people of color who collaborated in developing an alternative system of education to provide their children with basic skills in reading, writing, and counting. In short, the prohibition of attending public schools did not mean that pardos and morenos were illiterate or were not educated in basic matters.[113] These groups clearly had members who received a basic, improvised, and austere education, and they probably took part in a semiliterate culture where brief written texts intermingled with images, dialogues, songs, and performances.

Moreover, barbershops and beauty salons were not merely underground schools; Rodríguez describes them as dynamic spaces for socializing where teaching, exchanging knowledge, and debating ideas took place. For example, there were barbers and artisans in the city who would read and write letters in exchange for money or other services. Nonliterate neighbors visited these "literate artisans," who would read aloud their private correspondence or any papers or pamphlets that had fallen into their hands.[114] More sophisticated entrepreneurs offered translation services from English to Spanish, or from French to Spanish.[115] In urban spaces and ports, barbershops were also places where people of different social groups (professionals, merchants, militiamen, students, and artisans) met to play board games, chat with friends, read aloud, and share ideas. As we will see in the following chapters, these spaces of socialization fostered a variety of literary practices that in the end contributed to the emergence of an incipient sphere of public opinion open to diverse socioracial groups with different interests and political ambitions. It was clear, then, that Venezuelans did not need a printing press or a bookstore to access printed materials, and their *tertulias*[116] did not take place in exclusive coffee shops or pubs but rather in more socially heterogeneous spaces, such as barbershops and pulperías, where literacy and the written word were accessible to all.

CHAPTER 2

The Spread of the "Revolutionary Disease"

News, Pamphlets, and Subversive Literacies

↠ IN DECEMBER 1789, THE JUDGES OF THE AUDIENCIA OF CARACAS MET to discuss the Código Negrero of 1789, a royal decree that sought to regulate and control the treatment of slaves by their Spanish American masters.[1] In the opinion of the court, the masters of the Captaincy General of Venezuela treated their slaves well; indeed, the slaves' condition could hardly have been improved. Certain slaves had risen up against their masters, the audiencia concluded, merely because they had never been properly disciplined.[2] In such a case, applying the Black Code was not the best solution, because, as the audiencia reasoned, "improving the lives of slaves would give them greater hope of freedom and incite them to rebellion."[3] The members of the Caracas city council, for their part, warned that if they were to apply the Black Code,

> the economy would perish, slaves would definitely lose all respect and consideration for their masters, and it would not be surprising if a general uprising occurred, because [the Code] would awaken in them a sort of independence and libertinage that would lead to a general uprising in the Province, with the killing of all the whites, and with the slaves becoming masters of the country.[4]

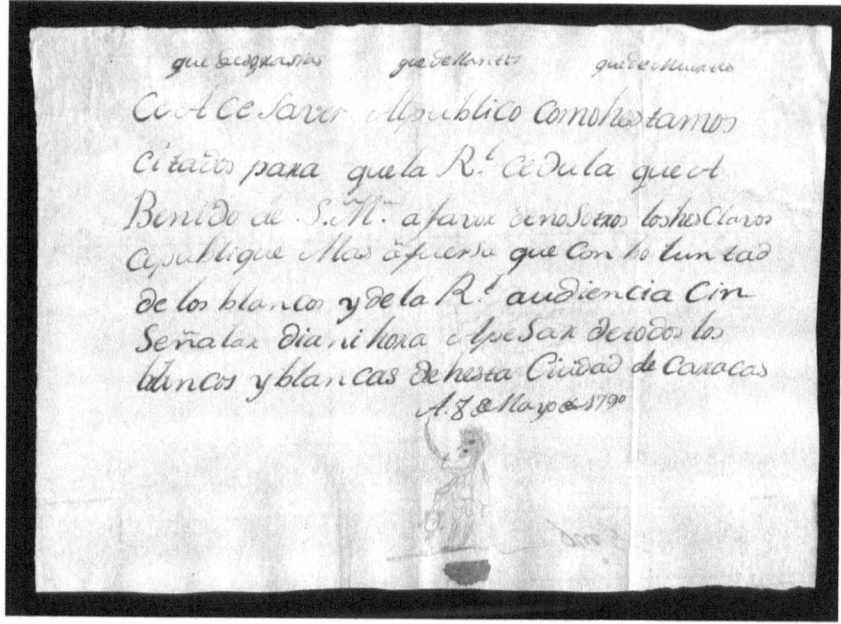

Figure 1. Pasquinade found in Caracas, May 8, 1790. "Representation de la Real Audiencia al Rey sobre la Real Cédula de tratos de esclavos de 1789," Archivo General de Indias, Caracas, 167. Courtesy of Archivo General de Indias, Ministerio de Educación, Cultura y Deporte, Spain.

The overwhelming rejection of the Black Code of 1789 by Caracas elites reveals their dependence on their slaves and their resistance to altering the social and economic status quo. The audiencia ultimately decided to apply this royal decree, "but without any hurry, and making use of measures capable of slowly calming the ardent spirits."[5]

Six months later, in June 1790, it became evident that these spirits had not cooled, as four incendiary pasquinades were found affixed to the walls of the central square of Caracas (fig. 1).

The four pasquinades all bore the same message, written in a clumsy handwriting:

> Oh Sorrows, Oh Cries, Oh Deaths!
>   We announce to the Public that we are summoned on the
> Royal Decree that has come from Our Majesty in favor of us, the

slaves. This [royal decree] will be published more by force than by the willingness of the whites and the Royal Audiencia, which has not indicated day or hour, to the disgrace of all the white men and women of this city. May 8, 1790.[6]

The pasquinades also contained an illustration of a black man with a machete in his right hand, and a white man's head—dripping blood—in his left. By the time the officials found the papers, people had already begun to discuss their meaning in public. Horrified by this anonymous threat to the social order, local officials debated the authorship of the broadsides and wondered whether they had been written by blacks or by "idle and evil white people insistent on provoking a black uprising, on sowing mistrust where none should exist."[7] Officials never managed to identify the author or authors of these papers, nor the person responsible for posting them in public.

It is interesting to note that these pasquinades began circulating a year before the first slave uprisings erupted in Saint-Domingue. Their imagery of violent rebellion reflects pervasive tensions between masters and slaves in Venezuela—and more generally between whites, free blacks, and mixed-race pardos. It seems that the notion of a slave uprising, even a revolution, was far from unthinkable in such a context: indeed, white masters imagined a scenario in which slaves rebelled, exterminated all whites, and became "masters of the country," and their fears were regularly compounded by anonymous threats of rebellion.[8] The events of August 1791 in Saint-Domingue would only reinforce these violent images in the minds of whites, blacks, and mixed-race pardos, compounding already extant tensions.

These broadsides did not merely reflect tensions between social and racial groups and growing awareness of Atlantic abolitionism and amelioration; they also served as important instruments for communication. Pasquinades such as these sought to overcome the mnemonic limitations of oral culture and to circumvent the restrictions of a literate world largely controlled by the white elite and the state. Pasquinades, then, became a medium comprehensible to all, especially to the large population of Caracas that participated in semiliterate networks of communication, in which only a few members could read and write, others could read but not write, and the large majority was nonliterate. Messages were then regularly transposed from one medium to another: written messages (letters, newspapers, pamphlets, and pasquinades) were read aloud and even transformed into poems or songs, while oral messages were recorded in writing and/or represented in images. Although some historians of late colonial Latin America have insisted that low literacy rates and the absence of printing presses in certain regions restricted the scope and limited knowledge transmission,[9] here I argue that in late colonial Venezuela widespread illiteracy did not necessarily make written texts inaccessible to the majority of the population. On one hand, reading was widely perceived as a public and shared practice, and curious listeners frequently accompanied readers. On the other hand, the written word did not depend on printing presses, as many texts circulated largely, or even exclusively, in manuscript form. The previous chapter examined the presence of manuscripts in Venezuelan private libraries as well as the practice of copying and transcribing books; this practice was also applied to other texts such as pamphlets, pasquinades, and newspapers.[10]

Ephemeral texts—newspapers, broadsides, pasquinades, and letters—were perhaps the most important media for late colonial Venezuelans who relied on mediators and semiliterate practices to access the written word. In a society with no printing press, and with limited access to books, these papeles sueltos (loose papers) facilitated the exchange of ideas and information among underprivileged groups. Thanks to their accessibility and ease of distribution, and also to their ephemeral character—it was difficult to identify where they were produced or how they were distributed—many of these texts eluded attempts at control and censorship by both the state and the church.[11] Those who were not afforded a formal education used these texts to participate in an emerging sphere of public opinion, where ideas about abolitionism and republicanism were debated and the Spanish monarchy was openly criticized.[12]

From 1789 to 1808, revolutionary texts from Europe and the Americas—in particular, France, Saint-Domingue, and Trinidad—appeared in the coastal towns of Venezuela. While these newspapers, pamphlets, and broadsheets horrified local officials and elites, they aroused the curiosity of the common people, who, regardless of race, education, and status, did not hesitate to read them—or to listen to their contents—and to put them in circulation. This chapter analyzes the content of some of the most popular texts—those that surprisingly survived the hardships of time and the archive—and shows how their accessibility brought Venezuelans closer to the Caribbean revolutionary struggles and the republican values that enforced them.

Periodical Publications, News, and Letters

One night in June 1794, a British captain named William Gisborne went to the house of the captain general of Venezuela, don Pedro Carbonell, to report that, upon his arrival with a "load of 100 African blacks" in the port of La Guaira, a port official had visited his ship and asked whether he was carrying any newspapers or written materials. Captain Gisborne provided the inspector with one English gazette, which the official promptly confiscated. The captain's translator asked the official to return the gazette, explaining that he had no intention of sharing it with the locals, but the official refused and left his ship.

After hearing Gisborne's account, Carbonell decided to inquire into the destiny of the gazette and ordered the commander of La Guaira to find out who had confiscated it, "and to collect it immediately, along with all the copies that could have been made of it."[13] Days later, the commander found out that the official in question was don Juan Josef Mendiri, a resident of La Guaira, royal interim accountant, and guard of the port. Mendiri returned the gazette, claiming that he had not copied it. Although Carbonell was suspicious of Mendiri's claim, the desire to maintain "tranquility and calmness" ultimately prevailed, and the captain general made no further inquiries.

Three years later, in July 1797, a republican conspiracy led by a group of white creoles and pardos was uncovered in the city of La Guaira. Juan Josef Mendiri was among the group of people who had collaborated with this movement for "liberty and equality" and the "Rights of Man," for the abolition of slavery, and for the establishment of a republican government.[14] Indeed, it was Mendiri, the main guard of the port and the person tasked with confiscating any arriving contraband and controlling the entry of dangerous papers, who stood accused of creating an archive of gazettes and of sharing news about republicanism and abolitionism to galvanize the other conspirators.

Venezuela did not possess the technology for printing newspapers or gazettes until 1808. Prior to this date, all newspapers, journals, and gazettes circulating in the region came from Europe, North America, or other Spanish American provinces. The strategically located and frequently visited port of La Guaira, where numerous ships loaded with both goods and information stopped daily, allowed Mendiri and others to collect foreign newspapers. They then shared these papers with circles of readers and listeners in La

Guaira, and some of these texts were copied and translated in order to expand their reach among the local population.

According to Andrew Pettegree, in the eighteenth century a new generation of newspapers and political journals extended the range of political commentary and reflection in Europe and North America: "For the first time, newspapers played a vital role not only in recording but in shaping political events."[15] During the eighteenth century, European countries such as Prussia, Bavaria, the Low Countries, Great Britain, and France saw the development and expansion of a commercial news market, which played a decisive role in shaping popular opinion in these regions. This explosion of new media transformed the reading public. The way they consumed news and opinion changed, as did their patterns of political participation. Several studies have analyzed the role of newspapers and political journals in the revolutionary eras of the United States (1763–1783) and France (1789–1798). In the case of the American Revolution, it has been argued that local newspapers and pamphlets began to focus on American, as opposed to European, affairs, thereby increasing public awareness of local political issues and fostering a newfound sense of community around "colonial grievances."[16]

In the case of the French Revolution, the explosion of newspapers, broadsheets, and pamphlets in Paris was even more impressive: the capital went from publishing 4 journals in 1788 to publishing 335 in 1790. As Pettegree comments: "Paris was suddenly awash with a flood of exuberant, passionate, committed newssheets." The great majority of these papers were entirely devoted to politics; many described in careful detail the endless heated sessions of the National Assembly, while others encouraged readers to participate actively in revolutionary politics.[17]

Spanish reformism promoted the growth of periodical publications that sought to provide potential readers and listeners with access to erudite knowledge, and many writers talked about the benefits of these publications. The Abbot Langlet, for example, commented in 1763: "Few [people] have time to devote themselves to reading entire books. . . . On the contrary, the small paper is easy to read, and contains, in its narrow limits, the same matters that are extensively written in the vast boundaries of a masterpiece."[18] A Spanish newspaper editor, Julián de Velasco, commented on the benefits offered by such publications:

> The daily events that are happening in the particular matters pertaining to the Arts, the Sciences and health literature: Are they contained in

Masterpieces already written? The discoveries of [William] Herschel, so important to Astronomy, or the discoveries of vaccination, so useful to humanity, etc: By which media were these to be rapidly spread if not by the newspapers of all Europe?[19]

It was clear that newspapers, gazettes, and journals offered multiple benefits for the expansion of knowledge: they were inexpensive, they were produced rapidly and regularly, and their subjects were presented succinctly.

King Charles III of Spain firmly favored the spread of newspapers in Spain and in the American territories, as he saw newspapers as an important vehicle for the forms of knowledge and critical thought that Spanish reformism promoted. However, aware of the danger of "excessive Enlightenment," the monarch also encouraged the Council of Castile to monitor the content of periodicals printed in Spain and its provinces. Newspapers and journals could easily promote antimonarchical or blasphemous ideas, instilling confusion in their readers. Many periodicals and gazettes of Madrid, for example, copied extracts and ideas from French literary pieces that expressed critiques against the monarchy and the nobility. These extracts often passed unnoticed by government censors. For this reason, Charles III asked his ministers to carefully control the kind of materials that were printed in Spain's local periodicals.[20]

Newspapers and periodical publications favored the development of more flexible and extensive circuits of communication between Europe and America. Information circulated quickly and freely from one province to another, and from one country to another. Travelers to Spanish American cities and ports frequently carried several European newspapers and gazettes in their baggage. These newspapers contained European court gossip, military and diplomatic reports, political and moral essays, news about the ships and the goods arriving from America into the European ports, articles on fashion, scientific findings, poetry, and lists of new printed editions and book recommendations.[21] Spanish American newspapers printed in Mexico City, Bogotá, and Lima, for example, devoted most of their space to news copied verbatim from Madrid newspapers, thereby bridging the geographic and cultural divide separating the outlying population from the metropolitan center. But over the course of the eighteenth century, local publishers in Spanish America began to emulate publishers elsewhere in Europe by adapting the content, format, and style of their periodicals to local communities.[22]

A close look at Caracas's and La Guaira's inventories of private libraries and travelers' baggage reveals the important presence of newspapers and other periodical publications in late colonial Venezuela. Approximately 18 percent of the postmortem inventories in Caracas (1770–1810) mentioned newspapers, journals, and/or periodical publications such as *semanarios* (journals). If one takes into consideration the low value of newspapers and journals and the little importance they should have had in a testament, this number seems strikingly high. In most of these cases, the owners had amassed entire collections of periodical publications, which had often been bound together and archived in specific sections of their libraries. The library of Juan Vegas Vertodano, a hacendado and property owner in Caracas, contained an entire shelf of manuals and "diverse scattered papers, gazettes, and journals" that he had collected and classified over the course of decades. The merchant Juan Josef Mintegui also possessed a rich library that included dictionaries; books of history, politics, commerce, and administration; and several gazettes and newspapers from Spain and the Caribbean. In 1797, the merchant Manuel Montesinos y Rico, who owned houses in Caracas and La Guaira and was accused of participating in the conspiracy of La Guaira, left a similarly impressive library, where he kept "forty-three volumes of gazettes, nine packets of *mercurios* [like a gaceta; a generic newspaper title], and several numbers of the *Gaceta de Madrid* and the *Gaceta de México*." In 1809, the hacendado and merchant Miguel Carmona left a collection of "thirty-six Spanish periodicals from the years 1797, 1798, and 1799" [23]

It was certainly more common to find newspapers and journals in travelers' luggage than in commercial cargo. In 1770, don José Carlos Agüero, who traveled to Caracas to serve as governor of the province, carried several boxes of books: religious texts; volumes on politics, law, administration, and governance; and several issues of the *Gaceta de Madrid* and the *Mercurio Histórico-Político*.[24] In other cases, individuals requested specific newspapers from the peninsula. In 1775, for instance, don Pedro Martín de Iriarte and don Juan de Argaín asked don Jorge Araurrenechea in Cádiz to send them more than sixty books and several "*Gacetas, Mercurios* and *Guías de Forasteros*." [25]

Readers in Caracas, Puerto Cabello, La Guaira, and Cumaná had access to a diverse array of newspapers and journals. Periodicals such as the *Semanario Erudito* (Madrid), *Semanario Económico* (Madrid), *Mercurio Histórico-Político* (Madrid), *Semanario de Agricultura* (Madrid), *Gaceta de Madrid*, and *Gaceta de México* (Mexico City), among others, were frequently found in local private libraries and the personal belongings of travelers arriving in Venezuela. In addition, foreign newspapers such as the *London Gazette*, the *London Journal*, the *Pennsylvania Gazette* (Philadelphia), and various French periodicals were found during government searches of baggage and homes in the province.[26] Many of these newspaper provided Venezuelan readers with detailed information about international politics during the Age of Revolutions.

In his popular *Teatro crítico universal*, Spanish writer Fray Benito Jerónimo Feijóo y Montenegro alerted readers to the dangers of blind trust in newspapers and gazettes. "Political dishonesty," he wrote, "brings evil into this world.... As long as wars exist among the powers, the gazettes of each Kingdom will exaggerate the advantages of their realm, while minimizing their losses."[27] Despite this inherent unreliability, Feijóo believed that Spanish gazettes could be useful for readers because they were more trustworthy than other European newspapers. The *Gaceta de Madrid*, in his opinion, was more reliable than the *Gaceta de Barcelona* and the *Gaceta de Zaragoza* because it had not been thoroughly contaminated by foreign newspapers. Usually printed twice a week after being approved by the Spanish Crown, the *Gaceta de Madrid* was a well-known newspaper in Caracas, Mexico City, Havana, Lima, and other major Spanish American cities.

Like many other European journals, Madrid's *Gaceta* could not avoid recounting the events of the Atlantic revolutions. In several issues, for example, the *Gaceta* reported on the American Revolution and the political climate of the young republic. Perhaps because Spain had aided US independence, the newspaper presented these changes in a positive light. Most of this reporting was done in Philadelphia. For example, one issue included a two-page summary of George Washington's address to the citizens of Philadelphia on December 9, 1790. In his speech, Washington discussed the economy of the fledgling republic and emphasized the need to achieve economic independence and political stability. In another issue, published in the same year, the *Gaceta* reported: "Agriculture and commerce, industry and maritime commerce are all making important progress in [the United States]. The great number of goods produced in these States that are offered to European markets is clear proof of this."[28] At the end of 1791, the *Gaceta* informed readers that the United States had paid off all its war debt and that individual states were using their excess revenue to "build roads and canals, make rivers viable, and establish important industries."[29]

The publishers of the *Gaceta de Madrid* may have thought that a favorable depiction of the United States aligned well with the basic precepts of Bourbon reformism in Spain, which emphasized agricultural activities and liberal commercial policies. From the perspective of Spanish American readers, however, these reports might have had a different meaning: the economic progress of the United States could easily have been understood as the direct result of the American achievement of full independence from the British. The political message contained in Spanish periodicals, then, could be interpreted in vastly different ways, depending on the reader's geographic location and sociopolitical background. Spanish publishers (and censors) seemed unaware of this possibility despite regular warnings by colonial officials that this influx of information could have unexpected outcomes in the American territories.[30]

After the events of 1789 in France, the Spanish Crown prohibited the importation of any newspapers, written texts, and even objects into Spanish territories that alluded to the revolutionary events, including coins, fans, clocks, engravings, and paintings.[31] Spanish-language newspapers published in France, in particular the *Correo de París* and *Publicista Francés*, were banned from all Spanish territories because they contained "falsity and aimed to disturb the fidelity and tranquility that must exist in Spain."[32] These regulations not only affected the importation of texts from France and other European nations but also restricted the use of information from or about France in Spanish periodicals.[33] It was a common practice among Spanish publishers to include extracts, news, and reports from French newspapers, journals, and literary pieces in their periodicals. However, in June 1793, at the height of the war between Spain and France, the Council of Castile prohibited the printing of any news about revolutionary France.[34]

In December 1789, Venezuela's captain general, don Juan Guillelmi, warned the authorities in Madrid that, since the month of August, "gazettes, dailies, and supplements from or about France, providing news about current events in Paris, have entered Venezuela." According to Guillelmi, the "evil designs" of these texts represented a danger to the captaincy; he was therefore ready to use all possible means to prevent revolutionary contagion.[35]

The governor of the island of Trinidad, don José María Chacón, took more drastic steps. In January 1790, Chacón condemned to exile the French writer and printer of the *Gaceta de Trinidad*, Jean Bautiste Vilaux, because he had "copied and printed diverse articles of public foreign papers related to the current Revolution in France, in which there were many subversive phrases, contrary to the good order of our Constitution."[36] Apparently, the printer—who passed unnoticed on this peripheral island—had not foreseen the consequences of his actions.[37] In his report, Chacón added: "It was my intention to prevent the evil or to eliminate it at its origins, without alarming the public or provoking its curiosity about the reasons for my decision. ... Different news would make people talk about themes that are better left in silence."[38] Chacón's report embodies the general attitude of local authorities toward the circulation of revolutionary information: above all, they sought to impose a climate of silence.

Such restrictions, however, were not uniformly respected in the Spanish territories, where many newspapers reported on the Atlantic revolutions. Printers and publishers knew that news of the revolutions sold well, and official bans only served to increase the sales of newspapers.[39] While most of these periodicals adopted a negative view of the revolutions in France and Saint-Domingue, they nonetheless provided precise information and detailed descriptions about the main political debates, events, and protagonists.[40]

The *Gaceta de Madrid*, in particular, continued publishing articles on the revolutions taking place in France and, later, in Saint-Domingue. Indeed, many Spanish American readers learned about the French Revolution through the pages of the *Gaceta*.[41] Between 1790 and 1793, for instance, this periodical published details of the king's mounting difficulties and the potential eruption of a new political order. After the execution of Louis XVI in January 1793, and despite the abrupt interruption of communication between France and the rest of Europe, the *Gaceta* dedicated a significant number of pages to the revolution.[42] The *Gaceta* described the chaos that reigned in the Paris Convention, "where any plebeian—including women—could raise their voices and make the most insane demands." Violent republicans, the *Gaceta* claimed, proposed the "most abominable and bloody measures," declaring death to all those who dared oppose the revolution and threatening to redistribute the riches of all nobles among the *pueblo*.[43] Although the *Gaceta* insisted on presenting the French Revolution as one of the darkest episodes in France's and Europe's history, it nonetheless spread information about the important political outcomes of the revolution, such as the Declaration of the Rights of Man and the new constitution.[44]

The *Gaceta de Madrid* also offered detailed information about the events unfolding in Saint-Domingue. The first news about slave uprisings in Saint-Domingue appeared in an issue published in November 1791. The news traveled from Jamaica via London, and then to Madrid. People in Jamaica heard

Figure 2. First page of the *Gazeta de Madrid*'s issue reporting news on the Saint-Domingue rebellions. *Gazeta de Madrid*, no. 94, November 25, 1791, 856–57. Gazeta: Colección Histórica del BOE, 1661–1959.

about a significant slave insurrection in the north of Saint-Domingue thanks to a letter written by a French official who implored British colonial officials for help to control the movement. The article noted that more than 360 armed blacks had "set fire to all the masters' houses, and destroyed sugar and coffee plantations. . . . More than 200 plantations were reduced to ashes, and nearly 300 whites were killed."[45] At the end of 1791, the *Gaceta* announced, "the colony of Saint-Domingue has been shaken by the crimes and atrocities committed by the slaves, many of whom are still hiding in the mountains." The newspaper added that French island colonies such as Martinique, Guadeloupe, and Saint Lucia were also experiencing insurrections and general disorder.[46]

Between 1791 and 1793, the paper offered detailed information on the black rebels, their military campaigns against plantations and masters, and the proclamations of the revolutionaries.[47] Later, it also offered news about the abolition of slavery by the French National Assembly in 1794, and about the movements and decisions of revolutionary black leaders such as Toussaint Louverture and André Rigaud. In subsequent years, the *Gaceta* continued offering information on developments in Saint-Domingue. These included detailed accounts of the expedition of Napoleon's commissioner, Victor Emmanuel Leclerc, who attempted to overthrow Louverture and reestablish slavery.[48] In October 1804, the *Gaceta* announced: "On January 1 the Generals and Chiefs of Saint-Domingue proclaimed Jean-Jacques Dessalines perpetual Governor of the island.... All the Generals swore to resist France, and to die before submitting themselves to its domination."[49] Therefore, it is clear that despite the Spanish Crown's warning regarding the publication of news about the republican revolutions, Spanish gazettes continued offering information and details about their outcomes, and readers in different regions of Spanish America had wide access to these Spanish newspapers.

Newspapers and journals were by no means the only available source of news in late colonial Venezuela. Complementing the information available in newspapers was a more traditional source of news: letters. Since the 1600s, Spanish American Crown officials and colonial elites had learned about the main events in Europe and other regions of the New World through letters that messengers, family members, and colonial officials carried to Spanish American towns.[50] In the 1700s, Bourbon reforms sought to reorganize the mail system in order to shrink the vast Spanish Empire, strengthen the bureaucratic chain of command, and streamline colonial administration.[51] As Rebecca Earle argues with regard to late colonial New Granada: "Letters continued to form the backbone of the Spanish Administrative structure."[52] With a reformed mail system, letters became even more significant as tools for spreading word of current events. In the case of Venezuela, it takes only a brief glance at archive indexes to see that the circulation of letters between Spanish and local officials increased notably in the second half of the eighteenth century. It could be argued that this increase reflected the growing economic importance of Venezuela, a traditionally peripheral region, within the empire. Nonetheless, it is clear that the postal reforms made possible a more direct and constant communication between Caracas and Madrid, Trinidad, Puerto Rico, Santo Domingo, and Havana.

After the French and Haitian Revolutions, communication between colonial authorities in the Spanish Caribbean and Venezuela became more frequent. Officials throughout the region perceived Saint-Domingue as a source of revolutionary contagion and frequently apprised one another of the local political climate in their respective territories. Because of their proximity to Saint-Domingue, the governors of Cuba, Spanish Santo Domingo, and Puerto Rico had frequent communication with the authorities in both Spain and nearby provinces, including Venezuela. In fact, of all the provinces in the mainland, the Venezuelan authorities seemed to be the only ones included in this Spanish Caribbean correspondence network.[53]

During the final decade of the eighteenth century, the flow of news about the revolutionary Atlantic, especially about Saint-Domingue, was constant. As Ada Ferrer argues, however, the information was incomplete, ambiguous, repetitive, and largely composed of anecdotes and personal impressions. Ferrer suggests that there was a particular discourse for describing the Haitian Revolution—alarmist and dramatic—that was repeated over and over again, regardless of the local context or of the unfolding events in Saint-Domingue.[54] From the beginning, officials and members of the elite decontextualized Saint-Domingue, using it as a generic trope for black insurrection, material destruction, rape, and wanton violence. This "troping" or stereotyping of Haiti has often been read by historians as an act of silencing, since this was the strategy that the colonial powers and local elites used to evade the intellectual and historical particularity of the revolution.[55] However, not all the information about Haiti was imprecise and vague; certain sources—pamphlets, leaflets, and broadsides—provided readers and listeners in Venezuela with concrete ideas about republicanism, emancipation, abolition, and equality. Colonial officials did everything they could to control the spread of these texts, but many of them nevertheless made it into the hands of radical whites, pardo militia members, free blacks, and even slaves.

Foreign Leaflets and Broadsides

As soon as news of the rebellion in Saint-Domingue arrived on the shores of Venezuela, colonial officials redoubled their efforts to control the increasing influx of both people and information. Local authorities devised strategies for monitoring ports, scrutinizing arriving passengers and their belongings, spying on foreign visitors and their neighbors, confiscating prohibited books and gazettes, and even forcing local clergy to provide information about their congregants' reading habits.[56]

The execution of Louis XVI and the beginning of the War of the Pyrenees in 1793 only intensified this paranoia. In August 1793, members of the Council of the Indies issued a royal order to the governor of Caracas warning that, "due to the current circumstances of war with France, dangerous books, papers, and news could enter our territories, jeopardizing the purity of our

Religion, public tranquility, and subordination."[57] The council's statement reflected the widespread idea that papeles sueltos were quietly diffusing subversive ideas throughout the province and required increased vigilance on the part of local officials. For months, authorities searched for these texts and debated the extent of their diffusion and what danger they posed to the captaincy. Many of the texts mentioned in the colonial records could not be found in the archives. In most cases they were destroyed. A few of these texts, however, have survived, and their contents allow us to explore the kinds of news and ideas about turbulence in the French colonies that reached the mainland.

At the end of 1793, Josef Luis Aleado, a cadet in one of Caracas's pardo militias, found a document entitled "Excerpt of the Manifesto that the National Convention made for all Nations."[58] Historian Clément Thibaud has recently identified the document as a loyal translation of the "Résponse de la Convention nationale aux manifestes des tyrans ligués contre la republique, propose par Robespierre au nom du comité de salut public, et décrété par la Convention dans la séance du 15 frimaire (an II, 5 décembre 1793)."[59] The text, widely seen as the first antimonarchical document to reach the mainland, summarized the arguments that the National Convention of Paris, an institution that helped to foment the French Revolution, made against the monarchy. The document defended the republic as an ideal system that opposed neither belief in God nor belief in the Catholic faith. The text discussed the need to spread the revolution to the rest of Europe; to eliminate the old, corrupt, and despotic monarchies because "Kings are exquisite creations of human corruption."[60]

The document was distributed by navy captain and La Guaira merchant Juan Xavier Arrambide, who translated it into Spanish with the help of, among others, Tomás Cardozo, a local pardo pharmacist. Capitan General Carbonell chose not to punish the translators and readers of the text in order to avoid attracting the attention of neighbors and to "maintain the tranquility of the province," and also because he was unsure of the penalty Arrambide and Cardozo should receive. Nonetheless, he ordered port officials to redouble their efforts to control the circulation of these texts by examining all people and documents that entered the mainland.[61]

Port agents largely followed these orders. At times, however, the authorities came to suspect the very agents who were supposed to guard against the entry of subversive materials. Such was the case of Juan Josef Mendiri, mentioned earlier, who, although entrusted with the task of confiscating revolutionary texts, became a collector and distributor of them. Like Mendiri, Arrambide and Cardozo became participants in the conspiracy of La Guaira.[62] Why Carbonell did not punish these readers more severely remains unclear. A number of possibilities might be entertained. First, it seems that by this time Carbonell was concerned more with hiding the evidence of subversion in the province than with imposing punishments that might well have brought more public attention to the issue. Second, these three distributors of seditious papers—Mendiri, Arrambide, and Cardozo—were educated professionals; perhaps Carbonell subscribed to the common notion that educated men should be allowed to read all kind of materials because, unlike Indians and blacks, they were intelligent enough to differentiate falsehood from truth and were thus immune to ideological contagion. The conspiracy of La Guaira, uncovered in 1797, would finally put this idea to rest.

Rumors of the circulation of prohibited texts in Venezuela continued to swirl over the following years. In May 1796, the audiencia met in order to discuss the circulation of a "dangerous" document entitled "Instructions that shall serve as rules for the French interim agent, stationed on the Spanish side of the Island of Santo Domingo," written by Philippe Rose Roume de Saint-Laurent. Roume was appointed French agent in Spanish Santo Domingo in order to organize the civil administration on the Spanish side.[63] According to Caracas's audiencia judges, the document contained several ideas "capable of causing harmful impressions among the simple people, especially the slaves who, in this province alone, represent more than one hundred thousand souls."[64]

The document contained recommendations concerning the French occupation of Santo Domingo. It put forward a program of promoting love and respect for the nascent republic: "It is important, above all, to make all new citizens love the Republic, and to try to preserve all that precious population which belongs to the Island."[65] The author identified two principal enemies of the republican cause: English invaders and royalist Spaniards. Roume represented Spain as a reactionary nation that ignored the advantages of republicanism and lived without its glory. He encouraged French agents and officials to do their utmost to win over the Spaniards, emphasizing the need to unite not only both sides of the island but both populations and "nations." Roume writes: "The difficulty then is . . . to prove to the entire world through an intimate union with the Spanish Chiefs how easy it is to establish a perfect harmony between both nations, taking advantage of the existing difference between the political principles (of both nations)."[66]

Roume also briefly narrated the history of Santo Domingo and highlighted its importance and centrality in the colonies. The document described Spanish attempts to comply with the Treaty of Basel (1795) and predicted how the Spanish monarch would transfer the administration of the island to the French. The author foresaw that the transfer of authority could provoke massive emigration among the Spanish population, and, in consequence, he encouraged French officials to "persuade and convince all these citizens of the falsity of ideas that may have been impressed upon them about the French Revolution, and to calm their spirits regarding any suspicions they may have about the free exercise of their religion."[67]

According to the author, French agents would have to provide Spanish Santo Domingo's inhabitants with information about the French republic, thereby dispelling their false notion of an opposition between Christianity and republicanism. He contended that Spaniards had mistakenly confused revolution with "anti-religion," whereas the revolution and the republic in fact recognized the independence of political and religious institutions. The emergence of the republic therefore did not threaten the status of Christianity but rather fostered a perfect harmony between church and state.

Interestingly, the author contended that French officials would have to defend their ideas with the constitution in hand; advocating for the abolition of slavery, he wrote:

> If the constitutional act annihilates the horrible right of slavery of one man over another equally endowed with a rational soul, it is clear that this article cannot be seen as an infraction of colonial property rights, except by people preoccupied with their own interests or inspired by a vile interest. And this objection should have even less weight among Spaniards, who in addition to having fewer slaves than other European nations, have always treated them with a humanity capable of turning them into friends. The new humane and generous settlers should then expect that, once free, their slaves will not abuse their freedom, but on the contrary will always be devoted to them and, like true children, will never abandon them.[68]

Contending that the republican constitution rejects the "horrible" system of slavery, the author strongly criticizes the law and practices of the Spanish colonies. According to him, only people motivated by "a vile interest" could consider the enslavement of a rational being as a "colonial property right."

However, along with criticism of the institution of slavery, Roume also seems to offer praise of Spanish "leniency"; he seems to think that abolition will be easier in Spanish Santo Domingo as a result of a "less harsh" system and a more affable relationship between Spanish masters and their slaves.

This idea of liberty represents the optimistic rationalism of many French abolitionists: the author insists that, once freedom is granted, the ex-slaves would not "abuse their liberty." Only manumission could guarantee the tranquility of the former slaves, preventing them from fomenting political discord. Granting slaves their liberty meant keeping them content and passive. The author thus expressed a paternalistic and conservative view of abolition as a necessary "sacrifice" on the part of the French republic in order to preserve social and political harmony on the island. More interestingly, he does not equate abolition with equality between blacks and whites; on the contrary, he asserts that freed blacks will continue to depend on their former masters, as children depend on their fathers.

Members of the Audiencia of Caracas were particularly concerned by the abolitionist message of the document and its potential effects on the "common people of color" in the province. Although the paper was addressed to French officials in Santo Domingo, they believed that it could easily have harmful consequences in "all the Americas." "Anywhere it was read," they concluded, "it would be understood in the same way."[69]

On July 24, 1796, Venezuela's captain general sent an order to the authorities in other provinces instructing them to confiscate this "hazardous" document. The governors of Trinidad and Barinas and the lieutenant of Coro answered that they would forward any confiscated copies to the captain general. The governors assured him that they would proceed with "wisdom and care, not letting anyone know about the inquiries."[70] Various copies of the document were found in the city of Caracas, the cities of Valencia and Coro, and the distant village of Obispos, in the Province of Barinas.[71] Although the governors managed to collect a few copies of the document—using "the greatest discretion"—they never discovered who had first introduced it into Venezuela, who had read or discussed its contents, or how many copies remained in circulation. The governor of Trinidad, José María Chacón, insisted that he was guarding against the entry of the text, but that he was concerned that it could enter Trinidad or the mainland directly from Saint-Domingue. The administration, he concluded, simply lacked the capacity to monitor the entire coast of Venezuela.[72]

Indeed, the text circulated widely in La Guaira and Caracas. A year later, don José Ignacio Moreno, a priest in Caracas, mentioned the effects of the document in a long essay on the causes of the 1797 conspiracy of La Guaira. Moreno contended that, since 1793, "the venom of liberty had assumed one thousand forms in order to introduce itself into the innocent hearts of the people." Written texts had been among these. French revolutionaries, he continued, "talk and write papers, like the one written by Mr. Roume and brought from Saint-Domingue and Guadeloupe, . . . in which they try to mask their government, and perturb our Holy religion, our tranquility and our happiness."[73]

Rumors that the Spanish mainland was flooded with "seditious papers" from the Antilles required a more determined response on the part of the royal government. On August 5, 1796, the audiencia met again in order to respond to the appearance of more "menacing and dangerous" printed materials from France and, in particular, Saint-Domingue. They ordered the governor and the interim commander to conduct an investigation into the character of these materials and their introduction into the province. They also instructed the captain general to alert other local authorities in the region to the matter.[74]

The members of the audiencia met again six days later. This time they had three new texts in hand, all of them from Saint-Domingue. The first was an unsigned document brought to their attention by the white hacendado don Gerónimo Winderoxhul. It was an untitled paper of two or three pages that began: "After receiving the news, I am delighted," and ended, "join us for the benefit of France, and European and American Spain." The president of the audiencia also presented two other papers. One began: "Encyclical Letter of the Bishops of France to their brothers, and other Bishops" and ended: "The signatures of Five Bishops follow," and the third document began: "Paris October nineteen, year of Our Lord one thousand seven hundred and ninety-five, and fourth of the Republic" and ended: "Gregorio, Bishop of Le Loire and member of the National Convention of France."[75]

According to the members of the audiencia, the anonymous author of the first letter sought to "produce a general hatred of Spain and the Spaniards on the part of the inhabitants of the Spanish part of Santo Domingo."[76] Although the other two letters were deemed ultimately innocuous, they were nonetheless judged sufficiently "bad, ambiguous, and confusing" for the audiencia to prohibit their circulation. Consequently, in August 1796,

Venezuela's captain general sent decrees to the governors of the provinces, and the bishop and ministers of the church, ordering them to collect all circulating copies of these documents. Again, the captain general was particularly explicit when instructing local officials to do so with utmost secrecy, and "with the greatest possible wisdom and care."[77]

At the end of August 1796, Captain General Carbonell sent a letter to the Spanish prime minister, don Manuel Godoy, along with copies of the four documents. He suggested that unknown French persons had brought several copies of these documents into the province. Carbonell assured Godoy that he was exercising extreme vigilance to prevent their diffusion throughout Venezuela, adding that they represented an "extreme evil that we must fear."[78]

It is worth mentioning that both the "Instruction addressed to the French Agent" and the "After receiving the news, I am delighted" missives were written after the Treaty of Basel (1795), which had ceded the Spanish part of Santo Domingo to France while prohibiting France from publicly intervening in other Spanish colonies. Due to a lack of economic resources, France would not act on this clause; the occupation took place later, in 1801, when Toussaint Louverture assumed control of the Spanish half of the island. The central theme of the letter "After receiving the news, I am delighted" was the occupation of Spanish Santo Domingo by the French, as well as the problems that occupation might provoke. Although the exact date of the papers is unknown, they appear to have been written during 1795–1796. We do know, however, that the "Instruction" circulated before the paper with the heading "After receiving the news, I am delighted," as the former piece was quoted in the latter. This seems to show how popular the first piece became in the Caribbean region.

In "After receiving the news, I am delighted," the author compares the French republic to Spain's monarchical regime and concludes that "the new political and economic order of the republic would make all the families of Santo Domingo happier than ever."[79] The author contends that the French Revolution should not be confused with other "unfinished events that have on occasion moved the history of the World." Rather, the French Revolution was a unique event in human history. The author compares it to a tree that spreads its fruits throughout the world, and argues that the events of Saint-Domingue reflect this fruitful expansion. This statement clearly makes reference to "L'Arbre de la Liberté" (the Liberty tree), a well-known revolutionary symbol of emancipation and liberation originally inspired by Thomas Paine's poem and then used in both the French and Haitian Revolutions. In

Saint-Domingue, celebrations of the anniversary of the abolition of slavery took place around large trees, and the image was also used in pamphlets and paintings and even as a watermark on printed stationery.[80]

The author also shows respect and admiration for the Treaty of Basel,[81] which, he argues, would benefit all the inhabitants of Santo Domingo. It permitted them to leave the island with all their possessions while protecting any possessions left behind, allowing those who chose to emigrate to bequeath these possessions to their heirs. Perhaps most importantly, the treaty granted French citizenship to Spaniards who chose to stay. At the same time, however, the author condemns the Spanish monarchy for having betrayed the people of Santo Domingo by ceding the island to the French. He refers to the many times that the Spaniards of Santo Domingo fought in the name of their king and emphasizes the comparative ease with which this loyalty was forgotten:

> The Spanish [Prime] Minister, awakening from his terror and panic, forgot about all the blood that you so many times shed in the Valleys, Plains, and Mountains of Haiti, after the more than three hundred years that you fought for the glory and usefulness of the Monarchy; whether it was against the ancient Indians, legitimate owners of the Island, or against the English . . . or finally against the fearless filibusters. He no longer remembered your Expenses, your exhaustion, your work and intrepid courage in the discovery and the conquest of the Islands and the American continent.[82]

While asserting that the Treaty of Basel would provide favorable conditions for the entire island and its inhabitants, the author depicted the Spanish monarchy as deceitful and ungrateful to its subjects. The author encourages the inhabitants of Santo Domingo to forget about Spain and instead embrace the "glorious" French republic, as "France will dedicate itself to providing you with all the good you deserve, and to consoling you for all the ingratitude and insult you have received."[83]

The author is particularly animated in encouraging the people of Santo Domingo to remain on the island, to join the glorious and victorious republic, and, more importantly, to accept the abolition of slavery. With certain slyness, he asks: "Are you going to regret the new rights of blacks, while you are prisoners of a more humiliating and hateful tyranny?"[84] According to him, slavery and monarchy alike were systems based on arbitrariness and despotism. The author even argues that a master treats his slaves with greater consideration than the Spanish monarchy had treated its vassals: "You live with your slaves. You manage them. You feed, and dress, and take care of them, and you have never treated them with as much neglect and barbarism as the Spanish government has treated you!"[85]

It is rather curious, then, that the author insists he does not seek to promote hatred toward the Spanish but rather to encourage unity between the two nations. He claims to desire this unity "for the benefit of France, as well as the European and American Spaniards." This assertion, of course, seems cynical, as the rest of the document proclaims that the republic is an ideal system and strongly criticizes the Spanish monarchy. The text was obviously prohibited in Venezuela because it called into question the legitimacy of the Spanish monarchy and slaveholding in general. Local authorities soon began to equate the word "Republic" with political chaos, disorder, and "anti-religion." Freeing slaves and promoting equality among whites and people of color implied both the collapse of the economy and the disruption of the social order.

How were these texts first smuggled into the Spanish South American mainland? Records reveal that several circumstances facilitated the entrance of these materials into Venezuela's urban centers and ports. Foreigners brought books, gazettes, and papers to coastal towns and cities and shared them with locals in private meetings and discussion groups. The record of denunciations made to the Inquisition reflects the commonly shared idea that foreigners spread subversive documents. When people were asked how they had come across a certain prohibited book or document, they would frequently answer that a foreign visitor had given it to them. Don Domingo Díaz admitted that he once had volumes of *History of the Revolution* in his house in Caracas, but insisted that he had returned them to the captain of an American ship who was offering them for sale. Doña Manuela Ybarra confessed that she had *Abelard and Heloise* but explained that the volume was a gift from her nephew, a priest from Chile. Captain Juan Vicente Bolívar averred: "I had *La Julia*, but it was not mine. A foreigner lent it to me and I have returned it."[86] Of course, it was easier for these readers to blame an outsider than to accuse a family member or friend, or to admit guilt for their own part in the circulation of forbidden materials. But such excuses were often deemed credible, as the government was invested in the notion that foreigners were responsible for the sudden expansion of "the revolutionary disease" on the mainland.

Colonial authorities were obviously concerned about the circulation of revolutionary information among the local population, and Venezuelan readers tried to avoid responsibility by accusing a foreign source or by using insatiable curiosity as an excuse. In several of their confessions, readers mentioned that they read prohibited texts because they needed to learn about the current state of events in Europe and the colonies, but that these readings never perturbed their loyalty to the Crown or to the religious institutions; what really concerned colonial authorities is that these readings could reach a larger audience and incite them to rebel. The governor feared that a popular rebellion inspired by revolutionary precepts would go against social order and harmony, respect for figures of authority—the clergy, colonial authorities, the fathers of families (*padres de familia*), and the masters—and ultimately the monarchy.

Officials came to believe that, in meetings and tertulias, foreign texts were not only read aloud but also transcribed and reproduced manually. In fact, many of the copies that were collected by the authorities were manuscripts produced locally. In 1793, for example, Captain General Carbonell criticized the governor of Cumaná, don Vicente Emparan, for having allowed a French visitor, Antoine Arteman, to visit his district from the island of Trinidad. The governor believed that Arteman was "infused with perverse ideas, with hateful maxims that he intends to spread among locals." He also believed that Arteman had brought seditious papers from the French colonies on his trips to the mainland and was transcribing copies of others that commonly circulated in the region.[87]

Venezuela's coast was wide open to the Caribbean Sea, and government agents found it extremely difficult to guard against the entry of smugglers as well as fugitives, maritime maroons, and other subversive characters who might carry prohibited books or papers. Many of the gazettes, newspapers, and pamphlets that entered the mainland came from the nearby islands, including Trinidad, which was occupied by British forces in 1797 and formally ceded to the English Crown in 1802.[88]

Some months after the English occupation of Trinidad in 1797, Cumaná's governor, Vicente Emparan, expressed his concerns to the captain general about the smuggling activities of English ships all along Venezuela's eastern coast. He had heard that "Spaniards from Trinidad" were exchanging cattle and other livestock, leather goods, and tobacco for European goods. Emparan even mistrusted his "subalterns, who never mentioned a word about this irregularity," and expressed his frustrations over the impossibility of controlling contraband and illegal commercial activities in his jurisdiction, where, "for every door I close, three or four are opened."[89]

In the same letter, Emparan comments that many seditious texts were circulating in Cumaná and nearby towns. Most of these papers, he concludes, came from Trinidad and had been brought to the mainland by smugglers. He also describes one man who was suspected of spreading "seditious texts" in Cumaná: don Antonio Valecilla, a soldier from the Trinidad battalion. Valecilla had supposedly been living in Cumaná but, after receiving the governor of Cumaná in his house and hearing that he was under suspicion, had escaped back to Trinidad.[90]

The circulation of contraband texts between Trinidad and the mainland continued throughout the first decade of the nineteenth century. In 1807, for example, a traveler visiting the city of Cumaná described the ubiquity of politically sensitive documents:

> Having one day entered the store of a grocer in that town [Cumaná], I found him occupied in making paper bags and wrappers from the Declarations of the Rights of Man, copies of the Social Contract, and the bulls true or false of Pope Pius VI, which excommunicated the French nation. I inquired how those papers had come to his shop; the following was his answer: "I made a voyage to Trinidad after the peace of Amiens: the Mr. gave me a bale containing five hundred copies of these writings, and as many by a Peruvian Jesuit, who has long resided in London, by which he encouraged us to renounce our allegiance to our sovereign, and promised the assistance of England. Such bales are given to all traders who frequent the ports of Trinidad. As for me, I took mine to the governor, after having reserved some copies for making bags, &c."[91]

Frequently, foreign merchants and local traders brought boxes of prohibited books, pamphlets, and leaflets, and introduced them secretly into the Venezuelan mainland, where they always found curious and avid readers. Venezuela, with its vast coast, represented an easy target for republican propagandists. Even the port authorities were not completely loyal to the Spanish government and frequently used their official position to collect and spread subversive documents.

Forbidden Texts and Readers of Color

Spanish political elites and white creoles felt threatened by the circulation of these texts, which could promote political agitation among pardos, free blacks, and slaves, together representing more than the 60 percent of the population. In May 1796, the governor confessed that his "greatest fear was the spread of loose papers, and the political instruction that *gentes sencillas* [simple people] might receive from them, especially the slaves who in this Province [Caracas] alone number more than 100,000."[92]

It has been difficult to determine the precise reach of these seditious texts among Venezuelans of African descent, who, fearing punishment, likely read and discussed these texts only in absolute secrecy; it is extremely hard to find historical evidence for activities that people intentionally hid. However, the identification of even a few individual readers could provide us with some sense of the circulation of these texts among lower-status groups. There is some evidence that these groups did in fact have access to prohibited papers and gazettes. It was shown earlier that Josef Luis Aleado, a veteran of the pardo militia, found a copy of the pamphlet "Extract of the Manifest That the National Convention Made for All the Nations" and gave it to the captain general. Months later, he found another paper that "seemed to be a translation of some paragraph proceeding from a French Gazette," which he judged "prejudicial and seditious, especially because it could create confusion among the simple people."[93] On several occasions, Aleado demonstrated his loyalty to the Crown and the local government by turning over copies of such texts. However, he never revealed how he had come by these documents originally, giving neither the names of the people who provided him with the documents nor the places where he collected them. Although we do not know how he came across these texts, if we take into consideration Aleado's social status and professed calidad, it seems plausible that he obtained them from people from his own social group. In other words, these papers may have circulated among pardos and people of African descent.

It has been possible to identify some white creoles and Spaniards who shared political documents with people of color. There were also a few pardos and blacks who managed to acquire a basic education without the assistance of whites and used their literacy to share ideas with others of their class.[94] The first group could be defined as dissident elite readers: white Spaniards and creoles—planters, merchants, officials and militiamen, and others—who participated in the conspiracy of La Guaira in 1797 and spread republican ideas among the colored population. We know that certain individuals, like the port official Juan Josef Mendiri, helped to collect written materials and gazettes, while the creole merchant Juan Xavier Arrambide copied and translated documents that ultimately circulated among La Guaira's various sociracial groups. One of the leaders of this conspiracy, Juan Picornell, a Majorcan who was sent to the prison of La Guaira for participating in the San Blas conspiracy (uncovered in February 1796), even produced texts to help others understand the principles and ideals of the republican movement, and provided literary training to the pardo barber Narciso del Valle on how to write similar texts. These cases will be explored in more detail in chapter 5.

To exemplify the second group—the lettered plebeians—there is the extraordinary case of Juan Bautista Olivares, a pardo musician who was accused by the Venezuelan captain general of "being a subversive and arrogant pardo, capable of encouraging the people of his own class to shake off the yoke of obedience and vassalage."[95] In 1795, two documents ("Extract of the Manifest That the National Convention Made for All the Nations" and "Sermon from the Constitutional Bishop of Paris, Mr. Embert") were found in the hands of a group of pardos in Caracas. Apparently Olivares had been reading these papers to morenos and mulattos in the city. Olivares was also accused of writing and circulating letters containing "arrogant and seditious phrases" against colonial authorities. To the captain general, these accusations suggested that Olivares's intent was to "spread the seed of equality among mulattos."[96]

Increasing socioracial tensions between whites and people of color and the political forces emerging from the Atlantic revolutions had turned Juan Bautista, a literate pardo, into an extremely uncomfortable character for local authorities. Olivares perceived himself as an exceptional individual of color who, despite local social restrictions and limitations, found ways to receive education in theology and religious studies, directed a religious chorus, and participated with his also literate brother, Juan Manuel Olivares, in the creation of a well-known music school in Caracas. Although Juan Bautista recognized that he could never enroll in a public school or the university due to his "quality," he found ways to educate himself: he probably learned to read and write with the help of his father, a mulatto silversmith, and his older brother Juan Manuel, but later he found support from two white priests, Father José de Osío and Father Pedro Palacios Sojo, who offered a formal education to the Olivares brothers. With them, Juan Bautista discovered his desire to become a priest. He borrowed books from friends, asked some professors and priests to privately hold intellectual debates with him, and even took exams in secret.[97] No one seemed to be concerned about Juan Bautista's exceptional path until he asked permission to take the Holy orders. With this, he seemed to have pushed limits too far.[98]

In August 1795, the Council of the Indies in Madrid decided to investigate the charges of insubordination made by the captain general against Olivares. First, the judges in Cádiz inquired about Olivares's correspondence: they asked him if he had written a letter to a mulatto named Lauro in which he had stated that "the powerful of this world triumph over the humble" and concluded that "they will be favored while the dark times last." He admitted that he had written the quoted sentences but insisted that his intentions had not been evil, as he had taken the phrases directly from Father Juan Eusebio Nieremberg's book *Diferencia entre lo temporal y lo eterno*. By "dark times," he added, "I meant the time of mortal life, nothing else." Olivares was making clear that his notion of light and darkness was by no means related to the Enlightenment perception of "Light" as the republican system and "Darkness" as the monarchical system. His idea of light and darkness was profoundly Catholic: "Light" represented the immortal life with God, and "Darkness" the mortal time of humanity on Earth.[99] In addition, Nieremberg's book was one of the most popular religious books in colonial Venezuela. Olivares had quoted a well-known and widely accepted reference, proving that his statements were neither antireligious nor antimonarchical but profoundly pious.[100]

The judges then asked Olivares whether he had read and explained to another mulatto named Victor Arteaga a sermon attributed to the archbishop of Paris. The response was:

> Although he [Olivares] knows a mulatto carpenter named Victor Arteaga, he had never read in front of him that sermon, nor any other writings. What did occur was that, on one occasion, a friend of his named Pedro de Silva or Arrecheguera brought to his house another mulatto known by the name Acuña, with the purpose of reading a manuscript sermon that was said to be by the Archbishop of Paris, and that in fact it had been read by Acuña himself. He read the sermon and Acuña immediately took it [the sermon] with him and he had not seen it again, because although he asked Acuña to lend it to him so that he could copy it, he learned afterward from a Priest of San José de Chacao Parish, called José Antonio García Mohedano, that the sermon was forbidden.[101]

Clearly, Olivares tried to disclaim responsibility for having read "seditious" papers to others, but the truth is that his account allows us to imagine a complex scenario in which he and other pardos and mulattos met to read, copy, and circulate papers. When asked if he knew that the archbishop of Paris's text was infused with maxims of freedom and equality, he answered: "Although it is true that I wanted to copy it, it was only to feed my curiosity; I have always detested these maxims."[102] Olivares was then asked if he had read, copied, or circulated other documents on the French Revolution or other revolutionary topics. He answered that he had not read any other papers regarding this issue, except for "the *Gaceta de Madrid* and the testament of the King of France."[103]

Olivares sought to prove that the captain general and Audiencia of Caracas had sent him to Cádiz not because he was a subversive pardo but because he was anxious to join the clerical order, and his petition had created significant discomfort among the colonial church authorities. During his time in prison, Olivares wrote a revealing letter in which he clearly explained his circumstances and presented himself as a fervent Catholic and loyal vassal of the king.[104] The letter provided the Council of the Indies with a clear description of the "misfortunes" and discrimination regularly experienced by pardos in the province, where they were not allowed to pursue an education, attend seminary, or be ordained as priests. Finally, the king and council realized that the case against Olivares was not as serious as the authorities in Caracas had argued, and in December 1795 he was set free. Olivares was even granted permission to return to Caracas on the condition that he behave with utmost prudence.[105] Madrid's decision enraged Captain General Carbonell, who complained that Olivares's return would encourage "the pardos to challenge the proper order in a province covered by pestilent poison." He concluded: "They [pardos] always try to present themselves as the equals of whites by any imaginable means."[106] In 1796, Olivares returned to Caracas, where he resumed work as a musician, directing a religious chorus in the cathedral.

While the increasing popularity of subversive texts among the white population aroused the concern of colonial officials, the circulation of such texts among the black population was seen as downright dangerous. Thus, Venezuela's highest authorities did not hesitate to send Juan Bautista Olivares to Cádiz for being a "subversive subject," even as they ignored the misdeeds of Mendiri and Arrambide, both white creoles who were found to have possessed and translated forbidden texts. Olivares's case thus speaks to the racialized anxieties of white elites, who felt that the very social order of colonial society was threatened by republican ideas.

Seditious papers and books continued to circulate in the Province of Venezuela throughout the first decade of the nineteenth century. In 1809, the Inquisition of Caracas issued another "Edict of Prohibition of Papers and Books," apparently the final such order issued during colonial times. This edict denounced several texts that proclaimed "insurrection, subversion, and insubordination to the Legitimate Powers." The inquisitors concluded:

> In all times, experience has taught us of the injuries that the reading of certain evil books and papers causes to Religion, to the State, and to the tranquility of the conscience.... Unfortunately, we now see how many have been seduced by the freshness of this bad seed; [we see] that many persons are enchanted by the novelties of these days, produced by insurrections, by false decrees and manifests, who are not capable of recognizing the consequences of this terrible danger.[107]

CHAPTER 3

The Power of the Voice

Imperial Anxieties and Rumors of Revolution

ON THE BREEZY EVENING OF JULY 25, 1797, A MULATTO BOY WAS suddenly arrested by officials in the port city of La Guaira. The officials demanded that the little boy—the slave of a white creole from the island of Curaçao—repeat the French songs he had been singing on the bridge. The boy, named Josef, dutifully complied.

According to the official report, all of Josef's songs had the same chorus: "Long live the Republic, long live Liberty, long live Equality."[1] Little Josef, who was likely around eight years old, innocently commented that his master frequently sent him to houses of friends and family in La Guaira to sing to them, and that he had even sung for the port's royal mail administrator. Little Josef added that two other Curaçaoan slaves, Marcos and Domingo, regularly performed similar songs in the port as well.

Astonished and enraged, the officials decided to transcribe, word for word, the lyrics of the songs. Although the officials did not manage to translate all the lyrics, it was quite clear to them that the boy was singing French revolutionary anthems.[2] The songs contained rather damning lines: "The Republican 'sansculotte' is a friend of Liberty"; "Long live the French Republic, French Liberty, and Equality"; "Let's go, French Citizen, form your troops, and march with our cannon"; "Come and die for your homeland France."[3] The officials believed that little Josef did not sing "with evil intentions," but they considered these songs politically dangerous anthems that might incite the local population to revolt against the Spanish monarchy. They therefore decided to hold the little boy in custody until they were able to locate his master.

When Venezuela's captain general, don Pedro Carbonell, learned about little Josef, he ordered the immediate exile of the three slaves: Josef and the two he had named as fellow singers. He also fined the owner of the slaves, don Francisco Hernández, who frequently traveled between Curaçao and La Guaira, 1,000 pesos for illegally bringing foreign slaves to the Spanish port and, moreover, for ordering them to sing these "dangerous songs" in private homes and, even worse, in public spaces. He ordered officials to visit each of the houses where Josef had sung and demanded that the master of each house pay a fine of 50 pesos.[4]

The captain general also reminded the people of Caracas and La Guaira that "reading and circulating texts containing ideas offensive to Religion and to the Government" was strictly forbidden. He ordered local authorities to affix "posters in every public space visited by people" commanding neighbors in possession of books or printed materials containing revolutionary ideas to surrender them to local authorities. People would be fined 50 pesos for every prohibited book discovered in their possession. Finally, Carbonell encouraged governors, commanders, and officials to guard against songs, poems, or verses that contravened "good manners and proper respect for the Legitimate Authorities—the Clergy, the Fathers of Family, the Masters, the Magistrates, and the King." The punishments meted out in such cases would depend on the quality (calidad) of the transgressors.[5]

The authorities' close attention to French revolutionary songs suggests that they knew all too well just how effectively lyric formulas could disseminate information. Because of their mnemonic force, songs represent effective media for spreading ideas; lyrics, governed by rhyme and meter, had powerful advantages in a society that was largely semiliterate.[6] People could easily memorize a song and repeat it over and over again. Little Josef, who was only eight years old, was a vivid example of the power of the voice.[7] Colonial authorities did not underestimate this power; on the contrary, they assiduously monitored the spread of information through oral channels.

Only five days after Josef's performance, port authorities put him, his mother, María, and the two other slaves on a ship back to Curaçao. In the case of little Josef and his fellow singers, the solution seemed easy, yet limited: expulsion. But what if others who had heard the songs had memorized their lyrics? What if they were repeating them to others, again and again? How could the officials stop the spread of these powerful songs? The truth is that they couldn't.

Although officials considered the little boy innocent, Josef's story proved that songs with "dangerous revolutionary contents" could reach anyone regardless of age, race, or education. Even more frightening was the ease with which listeners could reproduce and disseminate these messages; orality was an incredibly effective medium of communication. In late colonial Venezuela, controlling people and their voices proved much more difficult and exhausting for the authorities than controlling books, ephemeral broadsides, newspapers, and pasquinades. Oral information was far more accessible for people of lower status.

Beginning with Julius Scott's important 1986 study on Caribbean networks, historians of the revolutionary Atlantic have recognized the importance of studying the complex web of commercial, social, and political relations that connected port towns and cities during the Age of Revolutions.[8] The myriad revolts and social movements in the Caribbean islands mobilized people of diverse social statuses, races, and political tendencies across the Americas. This mobilization altered, in turn, the social dynamics, political perceptions, and even economies of each region.[9] This chapter amplifies this view and offers a detailed analysis of how the oral dissemination of information shaped local understandings of emerging transatlantic republican ideals in Venezuela.

The chapter attributes considerable importance to the agents of these processes. People from the revolutionary Atlantic had an important effect on Venezuela's political culture during the years of the French Revolution, Guadeloupe's political turmoil, and the Saint-Domingue rebellions. Despite attempts by the local government to impede the entrance of foreigners into the ports and urban centers of Venezuela, between 1790 and 1808 several hundred individuals from France and the Caribbean islands nonetheless entered the mainland. Their reasons for travel and their political dispositions were widely divergent, as were their interactions with local inhabitants and their understandings of recent events in France and its colonies. The foreigners who entered the port towns and cities of Venezuela were diverse: there were French visitors, who were often accused of speaking about the revolution in public spaces, and sailors and maritime maroons who brought reports of increasing political instability. Also, there were slaves brought by refugee families, French royalists, and African militiamen, who sometimes incited political agitation and other times offered their services to the royalist cause. Together, temporary visitors and local inhabitants of Venezuela constructed ideas and images that contributed to different understandings of the Atlantic revolutions but that also responded to local anxieties, fears, and hopes.[10] This wave of rumors and images sowed anxiety among Venezuela's official authorities, who found it very hard—if not impossible—to control the oral transmission of information. Officials were well aware that this information affected local perceptions of monarchy, racial hierarchy, colonialism, and slavery; such information could lead to political unrest, social tension, and even panic.

In late colonial Venezuela, speaking about the French or Haitian Revolutions was a grave act of transgression. The "search for the truth" about revolutionary events had to take place outside official channels and without any means of formal verification. The paucity of official information only hastened the emergence of informal, uncontrollable, and transgressive networks of communication based on rumors.[11] It is extremely difficult to determine where and when oral information about the revolutions emerged (and vanished) in Venezuela, or to identify the agents who put it into circulation. Nevertheless, verbal enunciations and rumors constitute valuable historical evidence because they speak to the motivations, desires, and tensions of the social groups that spread them; at the same time, they reveal the concerns, fears, and anxieties of colonial agents.[12]

What kind of "revolutionary" rumors circulated in Venezuela? Who was privy to these rumors? How did the colonial state try to control the oral dissemination of political ideas? Based on a rich mix of documents, this chapter chronicles what people in Venezuela said about revolutionary events in the Caribbean and how an anxious colonial state attempted to control the flow of people and verbal information, the channels of rumors, and the venues of expression. These factors created a cloud of gossip and hearsay punctuated by occasional bolts of intentional sedition—a political climate ultimately precipitated by the Caribbean tides of revolution.

Throughout this chapter, speech is approached through writing. I look at official reports, colonial agents' letters, and other documents produced by colonial authorities and members of the colonial elite. These documents speak to the fears and anxieties of the groups in power; at the same time, their stylistic features—repeated phrases, subtle changes in tone, the adoption of discourses and rhetorical strategies—hint at a gradual transformation of the social and political atmosphere of Venezuela, where the words "revolution," "equality," and "abolition" became more familiar and malleable. The documents presented here record the anxious efforts of a colonial state trying (and largely failing) to "catch up" with the "revolutionary contagion." Ample evidence shows how an initial concern about the presence of a few unwelcome, particularly vocal French subjects gradually became a shared preoccupation with all forms of speech—the circulation of an imaginary decree emancipating all slaves, or the exchange of ideas between French and Caribbean prisoners and members of plebeian social groups, or the familiarity with which locals began to talk about equality and freedom.

Although local agents, provincial governors, the captain general, and Spanish ministers avoided mentioning revolutionary vocabulary and references, their official communication was crisscrossed with everyday voices and impressions that official prose alone could not contain. These powerful figures reacted to an increasingly unstable climate of change in which far-flung republican ideologies kindled long-standing tensions among the local population. Official letters and reports allow us to trace agents' reactions to this climate and their efforts to control, silence, persuade, and resist the revolutionary cause.[13] In this sense, I follow Ann Laura Stoler's claims that colonial archives are "condensed sites of epistemological and political anxiety rather than skewed and biased sources"; and, as such, they are "both transparencies on which power relations were inscribed and intricate technologies of rule in themselves."[14]

The cases presented here dramatize the role of outsiders from the revolutionary Caribbean in sharing information and fomenting political unrest among the inhabitants of Venezuela, while showing the several strategies that the colonial state designed to conceal, contain, and restrain those voices. By the end of the period, however, agents of the colonial state were convinced that ideological contagion was imminent and unavoidable, and that locals from different socioracial groups were actively engaged in political debates that put the monarchy, the social order, and the system of slavery into question. Based on rumors and oral enunciations, this chapter shows the gradual process through which colonial agents lost not only control over the political information that Venezuelans put in circulation but also their confidence in the population's loyalty and obedience. As a consequence, officials needed to create new ways of engaging with the local population, especially groups of color, and reduce any risk that they could rise against the government and the ruling elites.

A Colonial State Imposing Silence

A few months after the start of the French Revolution, King Charles IV of Spain and his ministers voiced their concerns about the influence of revolutionary ideas in the Spanish domains, especially in their remote Spanish American territories. In September 1789, the king was informed that some members of the National Assembly of Paris had a strong interest in introducing seditious manifestos into Spanish America that "could shake the power of Spanish dominion among its inhabitants."[15] Immediately after receiving this warning, the Spanish prime minister, the Count of Floridablanca, issued a royal order to the governors of the Spanish provinces in America that instructed local authorities to guard against the introduction and diffusion of any text that could "promote Independence and anti-religion." In this same order, Floridablanca clearly acknowledged that written materials were not the only source of information that could contaminate the Spanish territories "with evil principles of liberty." Visitors, specifically those from France, could spread seditious ideas very efficiently by word of mouth.[16]

Some months later, in May 1790, the Crown issued a royal decree to Venezuela's captain general repeating the order to control the diffusion of "dangerous papers" from France. The decree also reinforced the "urgent need to control the entry into the Province of black fugitives coming from the foreign colonies," specifically warning that "slaves or black fugitives, as well as persons of other colors coming from the French islands, could influence our vassals with ideas that are prejudicial to their due subordination."[17] It thus became imperative that colonial authorities dedicate themselves to monitoring visitors from the French islands—a task that would soon prove well-nigh impossible.

In a December 1790 letter to Floridablanca, Captain General Carbonell underlined the direct connection that he believed existed between the revolution in France and the nascent instability in the French colonies. In Guadeloupe, the captain general recounted, struggles between the monarchists—who refused to obey equal rights for free blacks—and the republicans had recently led to a conflagration that destroyed one-third of Pointe-à-Pitre.[18] The letter warned that the proximity of the French islands posed a particular danger to Venezuela, the "gateway to the Spanish American mainland." In fact, throughout the eighteenth century, colonial authorities were persistently concerned about Venezuela's geographic location and the danger of contamination. Venezuela was often depicted as an

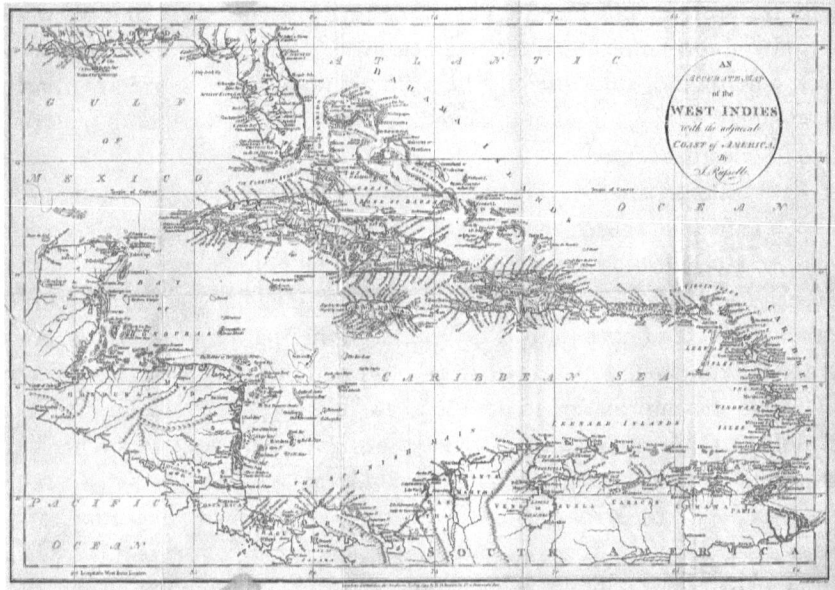

Figure 3. "An Accurate Map of the West Indies with the Adjacent Coast of America," by J. Russell (London: H. D. Symonds, 1794). Courtesy of the John Carter Brown Library, Brown University.

"open country" (*país abierto*) with an extensive and accessible Caribbean coast; it was unusually vulnerable to foreign influences. The captaincy's coastal topography facilitated both maritime trade and smuggling, and its many rivers, stretching from the shore deep into the interior, allowed unwelcome Atlantic visitors to circulate and spread information about current events[19] (fig. 3).

In addition, the captain general expressed his concerns that a great number of black fugitives from the turbulent islands would soon enter Venezuela, where they could spread ideas about abolition and equal rights by word of mouth. He assured the minister that he would do everything he could to keep local slaves "entertained with work and with other quotidian matters." At the end of the letter, he added that news relating to the situation in the French colonies should not be disseminated in Venezuela by any means, written or verbal.[20]

The initial attention to the French Revolution and its propaganda was quickly superseded by a serious preoccupation among Crown authorities with the eruption of violence in France's Caribbean colonies. Officials worried that information and ideas could easily travel from the Caribbean basin to the mainland, since merchants, sailors, and travelers moved regularly from one port to another and inevitably brought with them both material and intellectual cargo.

Local authorities' first course of action was to attempt to silence and prohibit any form of speech about the events in France and its Caribbean colonies. In fact, most official documents about the political upheavals in the French Caribbean carried the same heading: "To be handled with extreme care and in the utmost secrecy." In a letter to the Spanish minister, the governor of Trinidad, José María Chacón, expressed the need to control the flow of people and information to the island and lamented the varied difficulties of doing so in secrecy, so that "society does not learn about the events." In regard to French immigrants who were moving to Trinidad, the governor expressed: "I have arranged to expel certain suspicious French subjects. I have done this with care and circumspection, trying to prevent the news from reaching the public. I made people disappear [by expelling them], and the rest of society should not suspect that the government had a reason to have done this." [21]

With the arrival of news about the violent slave rebellions in Saint-Domingue in August 1791, official concerns about revolutionary contagion in the Spanish territories reached fever pitch. To prevent the circulation and proliferation of French and Franco-Caribbean revolutionary ideas, local authorities scrutinized traffic into and out of the ports, organized censuses of coastal cities, and spied on foreign visitors and residents who served as their local contacts.[22] The very act of speaking—or, in the case of little Josef, singing—about the revolutions of the day represented a palpable threat to the social, economic, and political stability of Venezuela. Paradoxically, the silence imposed by the colonial state created the perfect climate for an uncontainable torrent of rumors. During 1789–1804, local authorities produced an unprecedented number of reports about the oral circulation of revolutionary information in the province. It seems that, given the violent crisis in the French colonies, the scarcity of reliable—or at least official—sources of information, the absence of a printing press, official censorship, and the fear of revolutionary contagion encouraged even more the proliferation of oral information.

Such information about the French and Caribbean revolutions traveled quickly and efficiently throughout Venezuela. It was whispered in public squares, pulperías, markets, and taverns; outside churches; and, above all, in private homes. Soon, political rumors became a mirror onto which the population projected their social, racial, and political anxieties. Rumors do not necessarily reflect social reality, but they do capture a collective need to understand and clarify an obscure and incomplete image of that reality.[23] The colonial state, of course, became aware of this proliferation of oral information and employed all available means to dampen the curiosity of the public. Oral news and rumors traveled effectively throughout the Caribbean, and, as Stoler argues, "state secrets excite expectations."[24] The surreptitiousness of the colonial state may well have made Venezuelans more attentive to revolutionary events in the Caribbean.

The First Seeds of Contagion: Suspicious French Visitors

In the Crown's eyes, revolutionary movements in France and its colonies seriously challenged the pillars of the monarchy, the Catholic Church, and the most essential concepts of an obedient and harmonious society. In Spanish and Spanish American newspapers, the French Revolution was depicted as a "terrifying" movement—an endless litany of violent murders, fires, parricide, and self-immolation. Above all, it was painted as the destruction of the basic principles of political, religious, and social order. The most frightening aspects of the French Revolution were regicide, attacks on religion and the Catholic Church, the climate of general anarchy and lawlessness, and, above all, the Terror. Spanish authorities perceived the regicide as a barbarous act that cast into doubt the principle of divine right; in consequence, the execution of Louis XVI was seen as a sacrilege committed in the most atrocious manner.[25] Establishing a "sanitary cordon" in the Spanish peninsula and the overseas Spanish territories required the implementation of numerous strategies. The first course of action was to prosecute those individuals who were perceived as opponents of the monarchical system, the Catholic Church, and the social order. As a result, colonial authorities developed strategies to control the entry of foreigners, specifically French individuals, who might spread "the revolutionary disease."

In Venezuela, some restrictions on the presence of foreign visitors had been in place well before the French Revolution. For decades, however, the geographic location of the province encouraged not only the development of profitable smuggling networks but also the entry of fugitives and "possible invaders." Colonial authorities eventually came to suspect every Dutch, English, or French ship navigating close to the Venezuelan coast and mobilized troops accordingly. However, after August 1789, the authorities directed their attention not only to maritime traffic but also to individual foreigners.

In 1792, for example, Captain General Juan Guillelmi ordered local governors and regional lieutenants to investigate foreigners living in their jurisdictions: "who they are, the lifestyle and customs of each one of them, their occupation or profession, and the reasons for their presence in the Province."[26] Likewise, the lieutenants were instructed to determine whether these foreigners, especially French, had made suspicious statements on paper or verbally. Guillelmi also added that any foreigners without royal authorization to live in the Spanish territories were to be sent to Caracas "along with all their papers and books" for further investigation.[27] Immediately, information about the presence of suspicious Frenchmen began to circulate throughout official channels. At the end of 1792, in the town of Siquisique—an indigenous community approximately 110 miles west of Caracas—a Frenchman named Jerome was prosecuted for allegedly expressing opinions against the sacred dogma in public. In the town of El Tocuyo, a French doctor known as Pedro Deo (possibly Pierre Diu) was also under suspicion and investigation for "speaking or writing against the State, in accordance with the spirit of Independence that is found in France."[28]

The execution of Louis XVI in January 1793 and the onset of war between France and Spain months later led the Crown and the church to further clamp down on the diffusion of French propaganda. The Crown asked colonial authorities to be on the lookout for any sign of French influence, however minimal, in the Spanish American territories. In 1793, another French doctor, Víctor Droin, was accused of declaring in the main square of Guanare—a small town located approximately eighty-five miles southwest of Caracas—that the "French people did well in killing the King of France." The local priest of the town, don Pedro Hurtado, accused Droin of "being opposed to the Spanish King in the War against France, and for revealing and expressing in public attitudes contrary to the Monarchy, and even against Religion."[29] This accusation corresponded to the common characterization of revolutionaries as antimonarchical, anticlerical, and atheistic.[30]

When colonial authorities questioned Dr. Droin about these serious accusations, he denied them all. He claimed that, because he did not speak the Spanish language very well, locals had probably misunderstood him. Droin was married to a white creole woman and even had two daughters with her, the three of them living in the town of Coro (on the western coast), but, as he did not have royal authorization to live in Venezuela, he was summarily expelled from Guanare. In Caracas, Droin solicited a pardon and brought five witnesses, all French, who stated that he was a person of sound moral principles and honorable occupation. Once the Audiencia of Caracas learned that he was working as a doctor without the appropriate authorization, however, it ordered his immediate expulsion from the captaincy.[31]

Initially, Droin recognized the weakness of the original accusations. In a colonial province flooded with dubious information about seditious foreigners, he could easily claim that he was not an agent of French revolutionary propaganda but merely a victim of linguistic confusion and local rumor. The authorities, however, were not convinced by Droin's arguments. He had been living in Venezuela for more than eight years, he certainly had a good command of the Spanish language, and he fit all too well the official characterization of a French instigator. However, the colonial authorities clearly sought to disguise the fear and anxiety that his presence and his ideas evoked; they preferred to use the anodyne "lack of royal authorizations to live and to work in the Province" as a legal argument to expel Droin from Venezuela. In such expulsions, colonial authorities did everything possible to hide what actually drove their decisions: the power of the voice and the fear of ideological contagion.

The Council of the Indies closely followed the case of Víctor Droin and, in 1795, decided to definitively expel him from all Spanish territories. They believed that his "dangerous statements" betrayed his revolutionary ideas; Droin was a "harmful example to all who could hear him." However, the council was also concerned by another aspect of Droin's case: "It should not be overlooked that it seems that in Venezuela, and particularly in its ports, foreigners are being allowed in, especially the French, because Droin found enough witnesses (five) from his nation to support him and speak on his behalf."[32] Therefore, the council warned the local authorities: "It is prohibited by Law for all foreigners to enter the Indies and to settle in them unless authorized to do so by a royal naturalization and license." Further, it instructed: "All the Viceroys, Audiencias, and Governors shall procure to *cleanse* the Kingdoms of them [the foreigners]."[33]

This mandate fueled counterrevolutionary animosity toward all French people in the Spanish territories—a collective anxiety that, by the end of the eighteenth century, had devolved into outright Francophobia. Instigated by state officials, the local population began to pay more attention to the actions and words of their French neighbors and shared this intelligence among themselves and with the authorities. On different occasions, colonial authorities arrested some of these French suspects and sent them to Cádiz. They often depicted them as persons who challenged both colonial authorities and the church, twin pillars of social order and harmony.[34]

Cases of alleged French agitators led to considerable anxiety at the Spanish court. In March 1796, the king issued yet another royal decree ordering colonial officials to guard vigilantly against the entry of foreigners who could hold "seductive or dangerous *conversations* with my loyal vassals." This time, the king also recognized that his vassals were not altogether invulnerable to revolutionary contamination. In the same order, he decreed that *"any person who in words or actions expresses attachment to the hateful maxims of a misunderstood liberty, or tries to persuade another person, shall have a judicial process opened."* [35]

Revolutionary ideas and information were thus detached from their original French or Caribbean sources, because officials believed that the "revolutionary disease" could poison anyone who had been exposed to it, regardless of origin, status, or race. Whereas early concern focused on the diffusion of specific information about the events of the French Revolution (battles, terror, regicide) and the Caribbean political upheavals (racial violence and massacres), in later years officials widened the scope of their vigilance: any form of ideological contamination could incite the populace to insubordination.

Many of the French visitors who arrived in Venezuela during the 1790s came from those islands of the Caribbean that had sheltered hundreds of French families escaping from the "horrors of Saint-Domingue," and the "disorders in Martinique and Guadeloupe." Afraid of losing their lives and their slaves, some of these families fled to Trinidad, a province of the Captaincy General of Venezuela, because the island offered good prospects for recent arrivals.[36] According to historian Rosario Sevilla Soler, these waves of immigrants to Trinidad contributed to the much-needed demographic growth and economic development of the island during the last years of the eighteenth century.[37] Governor Chacón, commented:

> A great number of French royalists have escaped from the persecution of the republicans. Among them, there are many prominent individuals from the most respectable families; most of them bring blacks and many

instruments for agricultural labor, but there are others that need aid in order to survive.[38]

The governor drew attention to the political orientations of recently arrived white Frenchmen, but he did not seem concerned—at least not yet—that their slaves might become agents of political contagion. During the first years of political struggle in Guadeloupe and Martinique and of the Saint-Domingue rebellions, more whites than free blacks and slaves arrived in Trinidad. In subsequent years, however, this trend reversed: by 1795, slaves represented 58 percent of new arrivals.[39] Governor Chacón became aware of the political consequences of this demographic trend, and in several communications he alerted the captain general to the danger of ideological contagion, drawing his attention to the frequent visits of some of these blacks to the mainland and the possibility that Trinidad could be invaded by a foreign power.[40]

The governor of the Province of Cumaná, Vicente Emparan, was particularly wary of undesirable visitors to his region, which was separated from Trinidad by only fifteen miles of sea. In 1795, missionaries in the region told Emparan that a suspicious visitor coming from Trinidad was "spreading seditious maxims in the *pueblos de indios* [Indian towns], with the terrible consequence that the Indians even ceased to pay tributes"; in some regions, "Indians abandoned the towns and fled to the mountains, with serious consequences for the fields."[41] In light of these circumstances, Emparan suggested that the captain general reduce the amount of Indian tributes, because "no other time is less inappropriate than the present to raise taxes, or introduce any novelty that could be burdensome."[42] The captain general responded by reversing his previous order to increase the tributes. He also decided that Indians could pay tributes in goods, as they had done before the reforms.[43] In this way, both the governor of Cumaná and the captain general of Venezuela recognized the vulnerability of the local population: a foreigner had indeed influenced some of the indigenous communities of Cumaná, whose inhabitants had decided to stop paying their tributes and abandoned the towns. Rumors effectively led to disobedience and political unrest, which in turn stalled the implementation of new revenue schemes.

A witness who had met the unknown instigator told Emparan that he had heard him saying in perfect Spanish that:

Someday these lands are going to be ruled by other people, and the poor people will finally be able to breathe, and they will, with help, make progress; they will see more haciendas and sugar mills, and commercial activities free of duties and taxes. Soon, everybody will be rich and powerful.[44]

The anonymous *forastero* (stranger), who never revealed his name, concluded his speech by announcing that a change was needed because "the Spanish King has tyrannized this land." According to different testimonies, the foreigner did not have any luggage; his only possessions were a hammock and some notebooks and pages of writing he frequently read out loud to curious listeners. Another witness, the priest Vicente Blasco, sent a report in which he mentions that he had met the visitor in person. After drawing out his "truly dangerous ideas of liberty," Fray Blasco accused the stranger of behaving like a "Frenchman." The man contested that he was Spanish but had been raised in France; he had lived in Mexico and then moved to Trinidad, where he currently lived. He traveled occasionally to Venezuela to sell mules and certain products. He added that he was up to date on all the news about the situation in the French Antilles. When Father Blasco protested that a good vassal of the king would obey his father and certainly would not engage in sedition, the visitor replied: "It is true, but sometimes they [the Crown] want to pull the cord so tight that it snaps."[45] Fray Blasco ordered the man not to talk about these issues with the common people (*el pueblo*), but he later heard that the stubborn visitor was giving public sermons to large crowds in different towns of the Cumaná region.

The Audiencia of Caracas met to discuss the case of the mysterious visitor. According to the various written testimonies received in the court (the letter from the governor of Cumaná and some other letters written by missionaries in the town in Barcelona), the visitor was a moving target. He traveled all over the eastern region of Venezuela, spreading dangerous ideas that "impressed people," "especially the Indians and blacks who are always inclined to follow the perverse example of the wayward French." The governor immediately ordered the suspect captured.[46] He reasoned that this kind of individual took advantage of the "simplicity of the Indians, who are easily persuaded by these stories, and currently may produce serious consequences for the public order, and [disrupt] the happiness of vassals."[47]

The priest insisted on characterizing the instigator as French, though this assumption was not based on origin, appearance, or language. Rather, it rested on the kind of information and ideas that the suspect apparently spread among the population. This insistence speaks to a desire to classify—and thereby contain—sedition as foreign, a product of revolutionary France and/or the Caribbean colonies. Accordingly, sedition was cast as conceivable only outside the Spanish territories; contamination occurred when foreign instigators and innocent people came into contact. The foreign visitor, the instigator, was a deceitful person who sought to lure the most vulnerable among the local population, the subordinated groups, taking advantage of their innocence, blindness, or gullibility. Indians and blacks were seen as especially susceptible to false information and rumors. In the officials' and elite's eyes, the perceived "ignorance" or simply "lack of intelligence" of these subjects prevented them from differentiating between truth and falsehood, rendering them especially vulnerable to manipulation.[48] In this dichotomous scheme, oral information and rumors were seen as effective media for manipulation and persuasion—tools for promoting suspicion, inciting disobedience, and organizing rebellion.

Colonial authorities thus believed that disobedience and outright rebellion were products of external factors. Indigenous peoples and blacks were perceived as "simpleminded," incapable of thinking politically for themselves.[49] Authorities and church representatives believed that inciting others to disobedience or sedition was scandalous, but if one's audience consisted of subordinated subjects, the crime of incitement was considered even more serious.[50] Two fears thus intersected here: the fear of revolutionary contagion and the fear of popular disobedience and rebellion. The latter was clearly based both on recent Spanish American and Caribbean experiences of insurrection—the Túpac Amaru (1780–1782) and Comunero (1780–1781) rebellions in the Andean region, plus the recent slave revolts in Saint-Domingue and other Caribbean locations—and also on the emergence of recent local revolts and popular movements.[51]

Caribbean Blacks and Rumors of Emancipation

In "The Common Wind," Julius Scott shows how events in Saint-Domingue and the political turbulence of other Caribbean islands catalyzed political movements and insurrections throughout the Atlantic world. According to Scott, African-descended communities in the Atlantic basin were bound together by a network of communication that gave momentum to the cause of emancipation. Slaves and free blacks moved from place to place, spreading news of liberation and brewing political unrest throughout the Atlantic world of the eighteenth century.[52]

Given the menace this network represented, both Spanish and local authorities soon worked hard to seal themselves off from it. In November 1791, as the news of the slave uprisings in the north of Saint-Domingue began to spread, the Spanish king restricted the slave trade and the entry of French ships into Spanish American ports. In February 1792, for example, Venezuela's captain general wrote confidential letters to the governors of the Provinces of Cumaná, Guayana, Maracaibo, Trinidad, and Margarita and to the commanders of the ports of La Guaira and Puerto Cabello reminding them to prohibit the entry of any French ship that arrived "with the intention of selling slaves."[53]

But these restrictions on the slave trade would seriously endanger the agricultural development and economic growth of Spain's Caribbean domains, and Spanish and white creole planters were well aware of the negative economic consequences.[54] Three months later, the king succumbed to mounting pressure to eliminate the restrictions; a royal decree issued in June 1792 permitted "controlled" entry of French ships exclusively carrying *bozales*, recently enslaved Africans who had not been exposed to the new brand of dangerous "French ideas."[55] The governors and commanders of Venezuela, with the exception of the governor of Trinidad, followed these orders strictly.[56] In October 1792, the commander of the militia in Cumaná, don Antonio de Sucre, reported that he was not allowing the entry of French ships with loads of "creole slaves" into his ports and that he had already rejected several of them.[57]

In November 1792, however, the king issued another royal decree in which he expressed his concern over the declining number of slaves that had been sold in Spanish territories during the preceding months. "In almost three months, only 3,307 slaves have been introduced," he wrote. "This reduced number doubtless accounts for the bad situation of agriculture."[58] The king ordered planters and landowners to discuss more efficient ways to promote the slave trade in Venezuela without affecting the tranquility of the region, but Venezuelan planters simply decided to avoid problems by curtailing slave importation. Historians Federico Brito Figueroa and Peter M. McKinley have shown that, unlike other regions in the Caribbean, by 1795 the importation of slaves into Venezuela drastically decreased, a surprising fact since this was just when the economic situation began to improve. Although the authors did not explore the reasons for this sudden drop in slave imports, both agreed that hacendados seemed more comfortable employing free *jornaleros* (day laborers) than holding slaves, most haciendas being too small to require a great number of slaves.[59]

A recent study by historian Alex Borucki confirms that the arrival of slaves in Venezuela decreased drastically in the period 1795–1811. In the previous decade, 1784–1794, approximately 1,551 slaves arrived per year, whereas in the roughly fifteen-year period 1795–1811, an annual average of only 120 slaves arrived in the captaincy. Borucki argues that economic factors (lack of capital and credit, rising slave prices in the British Caribbean, and lack of long-distance commercial networks) represent just one possible explanation for this sudden decrease. He believes that political factors, such as Atlantic warfare and the eruption of slave revolts in the Caribbean, may have played a more significant role. Venezuelan masters seemed mortified by the eruption of violence in the Caribbean, and these uprisings may have discouraged them from importing additional slaves. According to Borucki, between 1795 and 1800, "no other major Spanish American region was more affected than Venezuela by the combined threat of French privateers, unrest among black troops, and British invasion, as well as slave and republican conspiracies."[60] Although Venezuela's slave trade decreased drastically after the Saint-Domingue rebellions, it was clear that the king and local officials were willing to promote the slave trade while banning slave ships from the French islands.[61]

Although colonial authorities and elites tried to control the slave trade, there was another major problem: the presence of maritime maroons. Throughout the eighteenth century, slaves fled from the Antilles to the vast and unpatrolled coast of Venezuela. A royal decree of 1750 manumitted all slaves fleeing foreign colonies who agreed to convert to Roman Catholicism. From that point on, hundreds of maritime maroons from the Caribbean felt driven to flee to Venezuela to gain their freedom.[62] The policy changed abruptly when in May 1790 the captain general of Venezuela, Juan Guillelmi, received a royal order forbidding the entry of foreign slaves to the captaincy.[63] In July 1790, he issued an order to Venezuela's several governors:

> It has been observed that creole slaves or slaves educated in foreign colonies are harmful for these Provinces, where there is no opportunity for providing occupation for the fugitives. The King has therefore decided to suspend the application of the Royal Decree that conferred freedom on them. Consequently, no purchased black or fugitive slave from foreign colonies will be allowed to enter the Province.[64]

Although the provincial governors and captain general restricted the entry of fugitive slaves, the clandestine immigration of fugitive blacks from the Caribbean continued.[65] According to Ramón Aizpurua, during the eighteenth century there were three different regions through which foreign maritime maroons could enter Venezuela: the southeast, where slaves from Dutch Essequibo entered the Spanish province of Guayana; the east, where slaves from English and French colonies, such as Grenada and Trinidad, entered the region of Cumaná; and the west, where slaves from Curaçao came ashore, mostly in the Province of Coro.[66]

The suspension of the 1750 royal decree that granted freedom to foreign slaves fed the hopes of planters from nearby islands who visited Caracas to demand the return of their slaves. In 1791–1793, for example, white masters from Curaçao repeatedly asked the captain general to return the slaves who had escaped from their plantations to Venezuela. Interestingly, some of them even demanded the retroactive application of the order, asking the governor to return "all the slaves who had escaped from his and other people's lands in Curaçao from the year 1751."[67] Although Guillelmi promised to work to return seven slaves who had recently fled to Venezuela, he claimed that he could not return the rest, as "it would be very difficult to reduce to slavery again the great number of blacks who have lived freely for years in the towns of the Jurisdiction of Coro." In his opinion, this would awaken in the slaves a rebellious anger that could only be dangerous for the region.

Colonial authorities not only feared that slaves from Curaçao, like little Josef, would spread information or songs about the revolutionary events of the French islands; they were also concerned that among the arrivals would be slaves from Saint-Domingue who had experienced firsthand the violence against white planters and who had been emboldened by the cry for emancipation. In a communication to Venezuela's regional governors, the captain general commented that some Saint-Domingue slave-owning families had escaped to Curaçao, some taking their slaves with them. It was these slaves, now in Dutch territory, who subsequently spread news about the insurrection to the local population.[68]

Under these circumstances, Venezuelan authorities began to regularly repatriate maritime maroons who had arrived from Curaçao. In January 1796, for example, local officials in Coro captured and returned eight slaves to Curaçao. To encourage this form of cooperation, the governor of Curaçao added that he would readily return any runaway Venezuelan slaves to their rightful owners.[69] Several communications issued by local white planters from 1794 to 1797 reveal the presence of former slaves from Curaçao living in what were then known as the *luango* communities of Coro and Barlovento.[70]

There is little historical evidence regarding the kind of stories and rumors shared by these fugitive slaves from the Antilles, but we do know that their presence provoked increasing discomfort and fear among the political and social elite of the region.[71] According to several official reports, one rumor became increasingly popular among local slaves—that emancipation had been, or would soon be, decreed by the king, and that local authorities and whites were concealing this royal order. Between 1789 and 1794, this same rumor circulated throughout Venezuela, that the king of Spain had granted freedom to the slaves and that local authorities and planters were hiding and suppressing this royal decree. As noted in the previous chapter, in December 1789, the Audiencia of Caracas received Spain's revised Black Code, the laws governing slaves and slave owners under Spanish rule. Venezuelan officials had focused mostly on what they perceived as the negative consequences of executing the new code, and thus they decided to implement it slowly and progressively, in response to the reactions of local slaves and free blacks.[72] Rumors of the concealment of the 1789 royal decree by the audiencia circulated among slaves and free blacks, who not only produced threatening pasquinades but also spoke of an (ultimately imaginary) "decree of emancipation."[73] Once more, secrecy on the part of the colonial state fed suspicions and rumors of revolutionary change; furthermore, these rumors coincided with the circulation of rumors of slave emancipation elsewhere in the Caribbean.[74]

As early as August 1789, rumors circulated in the French Caribbean islands (specifically in Martinique, Guadeloupe, and Saint-Domingue) that the French king had ordered the emancipation of the slaves and that local authorities were actively concealing the news. Several anonymous letters and broadsides supported these rumors, but they also circulated by word of mouth among slaves. As Laurent Dubois and David Geggus demonstrate, these rumors were in fact prophetic, as they became important stimuli for large-scale slave revolts in these regions. Dubois argues that, as the struggles between French royalists and revolutionaries unfolded in subsequent years, slaves in both Saint-Domingue and Guadeloupe began calling not on the king but on the young French republic to deliver them from bondage.[75]

Gradually this discourse made its way to Venezuela. When Governor Chacón of Trinidad heard the rumors of a general emancipation decree, he accused both royalist and republican French militiamen of carelessly spreading false information. In a letter written in February 1791 to both the captain general of Venezuela and the Spanish secretary of state, Chacón commented that there were "everyday fights and disagreements among men of both parties, in which they repeat the same phrases loaded with the flame of rancor and hatred." According to Chacón, both groups produced and reproduced false testimonies that were heard, believed, and repeated by the naïve public of the island. Among these rumors was one claiming the existence of a suppressed royal decree offering freedom to "slaves who join the royal troops and kill patriot whites"; as a consequence, "slaves in several haciendas are confronting their masters and asking them to grant them freedom, asserting they will kill anyone who opposes them."[76] Chacón was particularly worried about the effects of these false rumors throughout the territory; he recognized that misinformation could ignite the most ferocious of rebellions. In this report, Chacón mentioned that although Trinidad had largely benefited from the migration of hundreds of French families and their slaves, the "disorders in the French Islands keep me in a perennial unrest." Clearly the circulation of rumors represented a stark menace to the tranquility of the island and to other Spanish territories in America. Recognizing that he could not control the large and growing number of foreign masters and slaves, Chacón feared ideological contagion and political unrest.[77]

By 1794, news arrived in Venezuela that the National Assembly of France had declared the abolition of slavery in all French territories. It soon became clear that emancipation had become a definitive republican prerogative. Colonial officials worried that emancipated slaves from the French islands would carry the news to local slaves, sowing "confusion and consternation in our territory."[78] Several official dispatches spoke to the need to sever all connections between the islands of Margarita and Trinidad and the mainland in order to disrupt the flow of communication and prevent "contagion." In a revealing document, the War Office magistrate of Trinidad, Josef Damián de Cuenca, argued that any form of communication between Trinidad and mainland Venezuela presented a serious threat: "The Island is close to those French islands of Martinique, Guadeloupe, and Saint Lucia, and its inhabitants are mostly French; the island does not have forts or enough troops; the number of foreign slaves is excessive; Trinidad is clearly exposed to the fire of the revolutionaries." In addition, he argued that if French insurgents were to take control of the island, they would also assume de facto control of the eastern coast of Venezuela—in particular the Gulf of Paria. French republican ideas would

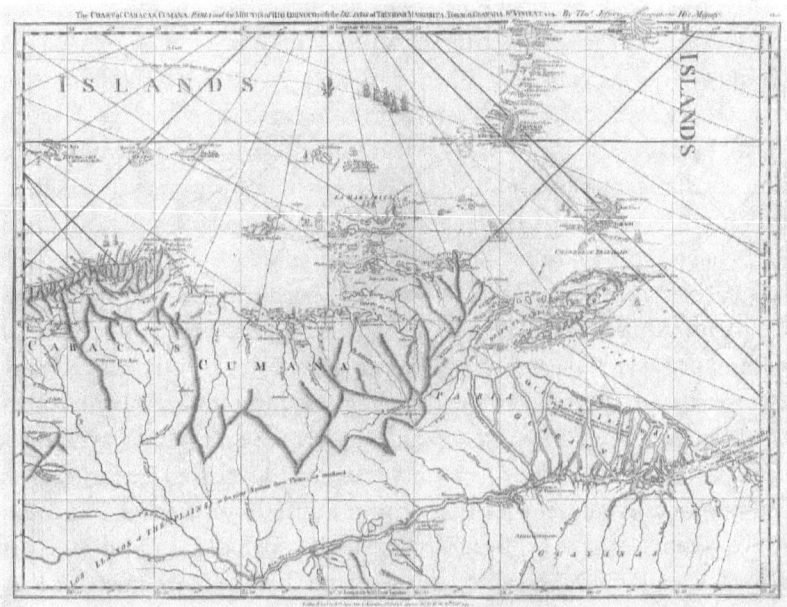

Figure 4. "The Coast of Caracas, Cumaná, Paria, and the Mouths of Río Orinoco," in Thomas Jefferys, *The West Indian Atlas* (London: Sayer and Bennett, 1775). Courtesy of the David Rumsey Historical Map Collection.

thus spread along "the huge rivers of Orinoco, Guarapiche, and El Tigre and the infinite numbers of streams"; the "contagion of rebellion" would soon spread to "the Provinces of Cumaná, Guayana, Barinas . . . and as far as the Kingdom of Nueva Granada"[79] (fig. 4).

On several occasions, Venezuelan governors warned that they did not have enough troops to guard their own coasts from Caribbean smugglers and instigators. They therefore could not possibly afford to supply troops to protect neighboring islands. The 1797 invasion of Trinidad by the British did not come as a surprise, and it decisively cut off all official communication and connections between the island and the mainland. However, the presence of maritime maroons from Trinidad in Venezuela, specifically in the region of Cumaná, plus ongoing contraband trade continued to provoke anxiety among local authorities and elites. In fact, the governor of Cumaná expressed his concern that the Trinidadian maritime maroons might share stories of emancipation with locals.[80]

The presence of maritime maroons was not the only source of official anxiety; the control of local runaways was another matter of great concern. Colonial authorities not only asked masters to prevent slaves and free blacks from coming into contact with foreign visitors, including fugitive slaves from abroad, but also sought to prevent fraternization between local slaves and members of maroon communities.[81] The presence of runaways, in fact, worried Venezuelan authorities and elites during the Age of Revolutions because they believed that maroons provided encouragement and material support to potentially rebellious slaves. Seen by the authorities as vaguely anarchic black communities where vice and chaos prevailed, *cumbes* and *palenques* had long provided refuge for fugitive slaves.[82] Colonial officials commonly characterized maroons as robbers, smugglers, and criminals who helped to free other slaves, provided shelter and support to recent runaways, and carried on contraband trade with pirates. Hacendados feared Venezuela's scattered cumbes, as residents of these communities on the fringes of colonial society often stole crops, firearms, agricultural tools, and animals from nearby haciendas.[83] White elites also assumed that the maroon communities contributed to slave uprisings by providing them with material resources such as weapons, food, livestock, or money.

The rumors of an emancipatory decree that spread throughout Venezuela between 1794 and 1798 encouraged yet more slaves to flee their masters. For this reason, the captain general decided to establish squadrons made up of soldiers and civilian residents throughout Venezuela to monitor slaves, dismantle maroon communities, and "reestablish order among the colored population in the rural regions."[84] Venezuela's merchant guild paid for some of these semiprofessional squads, while others were financed by the hacendados themselves. Between 1794 and 1797, for example, the merchant guild created fifteen patrol squadrons of approximately twenty-four soldiers each to monitor slaves in the Province of Caracas.[85]

These squadrons succeeded in infiltrating and dismantling many such maroon communities on the coast of Caracas. The procedures followed by colonial authorities were surprisingly measured in their relative absence of violence. Colonial authorities asked members of the squadrons to search for maroon communities, visit them, and perform censuses.[86] Officials identified and interrogated runaways and then sent them to jail in Caracas, where they were kept for several months in order to allow authorities to conduct further interrogations and to decide on final sentences.[87] Colonial authorities assigned different punishments to these runaways: some were whipped in jail, others were delivered to their masters with permission to whip them, and yet others were assigned to new masters. Interestingly, many of these maroons perceived the authorities' treatment to be more bearable than that of their masters.[88]

Many members of the squadrons who captured the maroons did not agree with the judges' decisions, which they considered mild. According to the slave catchers, these individuals had fled not merely for the freedom to live on their own but to "produce tumults, shaking off the yoke of subordination."[89] Squadron members alleged that runaways deserved "severe bodily punishments in public and even the death penalty" so that "slaves could see what would happen if they try to escape." Royal authorities, however, disregarded such suggestions. The judge in Caracas maintained that, in the current fragile circumstances, his decision was final, adding that he could not sentence fugitive slaves to death based only on "rumors and suspicious accusations."[90] Colonial authorities considered that, above all, it was crucial to keep order and tranquility in the province. It was clear, then, that tensions with the black population prevented authorities from imposing the harsh penalties that had previously been common.

At the beginning of 1798, a slave conspiracy was discovered by Spanish authorities in the town of Cariaco, in the Gulf of Paria. Slaves from multiple haciendas in Cariaco had planned to rise up on the morning of January 10, when most of the whites would be attending mass. A free mulatto, Francisco Villaviciosa, heard that slaves had been holding suspicious meetings and revealed the plans of the revolt to a local hacendado. According to Villaviciosa, the insurgent blacks intended to "take control of the city, declare war and kill all the whites, and announce their freedom."[91] Venezuela's captain general appointed Captain Luis Mejía and his troops to control the situation in the east. Within a short time, Mejía successfully apprehended the alleged ringleaders and defused the rebellion. In the opinion of the captain general, this conspiracy was inspired by blacks who traveled between Trinidad, now controlled by the British, and the west coast of Cumaná[92] (fig. 5).

In subsequent years, the British governor of Trinidad, General Thomas Picton, sent several letters to Venezuela's captain general to request support in capturing and returning fugitive slaves of Trinidadian planters. In exceptional cases, creole slaves moved back and forth between the Spanish mainland and foreign-held Caribbean islands. In February 1800, two local hacendados in Cumaná, don Antonio Sotillo and doña Rosa Alcalá, asked the governor of Curaçao to help them locate and return eighteen slaves, who, persuaded by two Dutchmen, had escaped in a British vessel from the coast

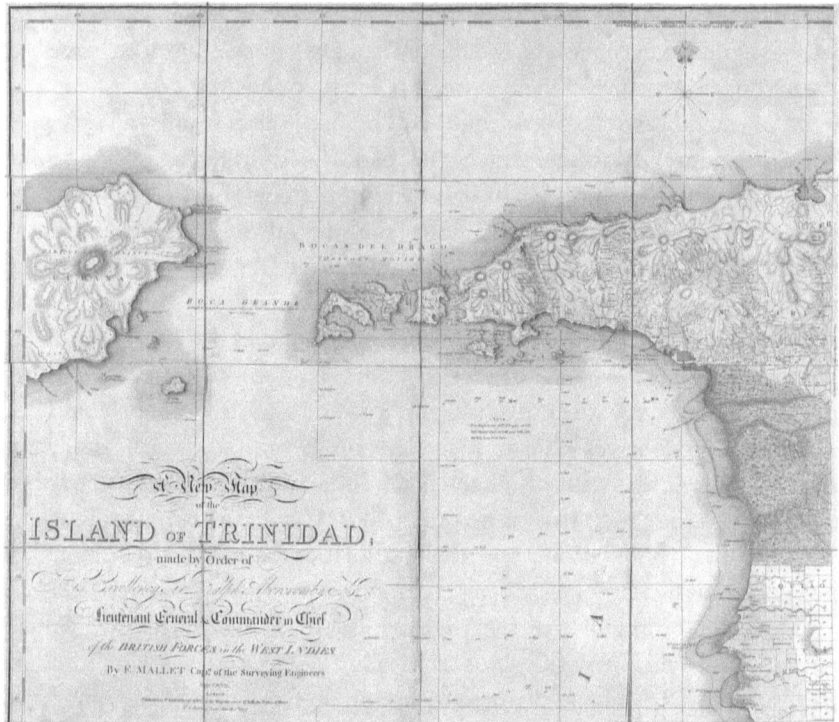

Figure 5. "North Western Trinidad and the Coast of Venezuela," in W. Fanden, Geographer, to His Majesty and to H. R. H. the Prince of Wales (London: Charing Cross, 1802). Courtesy of the John Carter Brown Library, Brown University.

of Cumaná to Curaçao.[93] Local slaves who traveled to the islands of the Caribbean may well have heard and shared news about the revolutions in France and Saint-Domingue; once back in Venezuela, they also could have spread the news to local blacks.

No matter how many regulations Venezuelan authorities put in place, the steady entry of people who had experienced the political tensions of the Caribbean was impossible to control. At the end of the eighteenth century, many families from Spanish Santo Domingo migrated to various port towns in Venezuela as well. Following the laws of hospitality for inhabitants of Spanish territories, local authorities helped them settle in Venezuela or relocate to other regions.

With the signing of the Treaty of Basel in 1795, the Spanish Crown ceded its half of Hispaniola to the French republic in exchange for the evacuation of Spanish territory occupied by French troops on the Iberian Peninsula. That same year, the French government appointed a commission to take over civil administration of the Spanish portion of the island. Among these men was Philippe Rose Roume de Saint-Laurent, who, as mentioned above, originally was the French agent in Spanish Santo Domingo. Above Roume were General Étienne Lavaux, who was the existing governor of the French section of the island, and General Jean-Baptiste Rochambeau, who was named to a similar post on the Spanish side, assisted by General François-Marie Kerversau. The official cession of Spanish Hispaniola was nevertheless delayed, as France lacked the military force and economic resources needed to replace Spanish military personnel. In the end, thanks to France's weak position on the ground, it proved unable to formalize the handover dictated by the Treaty of Basel.[94] Although the cession never happened, many Spanish inhabitants left eastern Hispaniola because, for them, it was evident that there was no going back to a situation that benefited primarily them. By this time, many wealthy Spanish proprietors and merchants had fled with their goods and their slaves to other Spanish American destinations. Some families reached the coast of Venezuela in 1796 with the intention of settling and setting up businesses there.[95]

Fearing that their slaves might become a source of revolutionary contagion among other slaves and free people of color, Venezuelan colonial authorities were reluctant to accept the presence of these refugees from Santo Domingo on the mainland. In a report to the Crown, General Esteban Fernández de León advocated creating "some difficulties" for the Spanish Dominicans who wished to settle in province and dissuading other families from coming to Venezuela. He argued that these refugees would "bring slaves contaminated with the ideas of freedom, especially after the French agent Mr. Roume arrived." These ideas, in turn, "could cause a terrible impression in this country, as the population is made up in large proportion of slaves and people of color."[96] In short, the colonial authorities were wary of the arrival of these refugees and their "contaminated slaves" on the beachhead of the Spanish Main, where ideas could spread more easily and quickly to the rest of the continent.

In 1796, the captain general sent a confidential letter to the commander of La Guaira ordering him to be vigilant regarding the entry of slaves from Spanish Santo Domingo. He wrote: "Among the slaves who arrive or are sent by the immigrants from Santo Domingo, there may be some who are French or raised and educated in the French colonies."[97] Three days later, La Guaira's commander responded that he had not yet identified any French slaves among the arrivals from Santo Domingo. Additionally, he mentioned that he had visited Juan de Andueza, a town shopkeeper, and had asked him to share any news of foreign slaves in the port town.[98] The *bodeguero* (shopkeeper) seemed like the right person for this task, since his job put him in daily contact with travelers in the port.

Authorities tried to monitor not only the numerous slaves and maroons from the French Antilles; there were also rumors about "literate French blacks" who represented yet another menace to the public order.[99] In 1797, the captain general encouraged his officials to look for and arrest a group of "educated" French blacks and mulattos living in the city of Caracas. One of these men, the so-called black Ballegard, was described as "a protagonist of the first movements of the colony of Guarico and later in Martinique." According to testimonies of some residents, along with a Trinidadian "mulatto" named Constant and two others, Ballegard had allegedly organized gatherings for local free blacks, where they "infused them with maxims opposed to our system of Government."[100] Although the governor ordered their immediate arrest and expulsion from Venezuela, these visitors were never found. Indeed, their very existence was never corroborated and remained just a rumor. On different occasions, colonial officials and members of the elite circulated rumors of ex-slaves and rebels from Saint-Domingue visiting the province and spreading subversive ideas among local blacks. In most cases, however, these rumors could not be verified. Even when colonial officials were able to identify a suspect, they could not link him to the turbulent events in the French Caribbean.[101]

All the cases above revolved around anxieties over unauthorized French-speaking refugees and black visitors in Venezuela—in particular, the threat to local politics and social order that these visitors were seen to pose. The news and rumors of these visitors certainly awakened the curiosity of Venezuelans, but it was ultimately the influx of prisoners and militiamen from the Caribbean that forced Venezuelans to confront the broader region's new political reality.

French and French Caribbean Militiamen and Prisoners on the Coast of Caracas (1793–1796)

Between 1793 and 1796, more that one thousand French militiamen, prisoners, and slaves from Saint-Domingue, Martinique, and Guadeloupe reached the Spanish mainland of Venezuela. They brought stories of republicanism, black insurrection, the abolition of slavery, and equality, which spread rapidly among the local population. People in Venezuela responded differently to this new wave of oral information. Having absorbed the profound Francophobia of colonial elites, some locals avoided the new arrivals and questioned their presence in Venezuela. They worried that their stories, whether true or fabricated, might incite people of the lower social groups to rebel, following the model of what they called the "French Laws." Others responded by opening spaces for discussion of these new ideas. Some attempted to adapt radical ideas to the local context, even planning insurgent movements. Just as this new wave of oral information was diverse and ambiguous in meaning, the reactions it evoked were highly heterogeneous.

In January 1793, a squadron of four ships with a large number of French passengers from Martinique arrived in Port of Spain, Trinidad. The commander of the squadron, Monsieur Rivière, presented himself to Governor Chacón and asked that his passengers be admitted to the Spanish territories. He also offered to help the Spanish Crown combat the French revolutionaries, whom he saw as a great menace to the whole Caribbean region.[102] According to historians Ángel Sanz Tapia and Alejandro Gómez, a total of 145 militiamen—52 officers, 34 subalterns, and 59 rank-and-file marines—arrived in Trinidad. While Rivière waited for a response to his petition from the Spanish king, he traveled back to Guadeloupe and Martinique in order to investigate the political situation in the French islands and to persuade their inhabitants to support Spanish rule.[103] In May 1793, he received news from the governor of Trinidad that, with war declared between Spain and France, the king had offered royal protection to his squadron and militiamen and had requested that he proceed to Puerto Cabello in Venezuela.[104] Rivière returned to Trinidad with 2,500 more colonists fleeing Martinique; "among them, there were soldiers from the garrison regiment of Martinique and neighboring islands, and also a group of marine officials who had been at the service of the royal family."[105]

In August 1793, Rivière arrived in Puerto Cabello, along with another French royalist, Joaquín Fressinaux, who was named commander of the 181 immigrant French officers who came with them. In Puerto Cabello, they met with don Gabriel Aristizabal, admiral of the Spanish squadron. Aristizabal informed the group that 59 of these 181 French marine officers would be incorporated into his squadron; the remaining 122 were to remain in Puerto Cabello at the disposition of the governor and captain general of Venezuela.[106]

After some months living in Puerto Cabello, Commander Fressinaux complained to the captain general about the vicious inactivity of his militiamen and their living conditions in the port. In his opinion, the town of Puerto Cabello did not offer favorable climatic conditions for his men; it was too hot and humid, and the military barracks were "extremely unhealthy, because they are surrounded by humid marshlands and swamps." The rate of illness among the men increased dramatically; worst of all, the townspeople treated his men with contempt, even "charging them incredibly high prices for drinking water."[107]

The captain general suggested that Fressinaux and his soldiers go to Caracas, where they would find better living conditions. Most of the men moved to the port town of La Guaira, and from there to Caracas.[108] But the problem persisted; the discourtesy of the local population made the lives of these French militiamen unbearable. Apparently, people in Venezuela's small towns and ports did not accept the presence of these French royalists and snubbed them. Fressinaux commented that he was treated contemptuously by the people of La Guaira: "There," he said, "the word 'French' is a pretext for refusing us entry to any place to eat and drink." Disappointed, he commented: "I have done nothing to deserve this kind of misfortune in a friendly country; I see myself forced to seek from Your Lordship, the protection the King of Spain has granted us, and to entreat you to order this intolerable humiliation to cease."[109]

It seems that the Spanish Crown's own counterrevolutionary discourse had created strongly negative images of the French, even French royalists, among Venezuelans: "French" became synonymous with "atheistic," "anarchistic," and "evil." Locals did not tolerate the presence of French people in their towns and openly expressed contempt for them. In some places, French royalist militiamen reported that they were not even allowed to enter the church or linger in public spaces. In a letter addressed to the king, the captain general explained some of the reasons for this general rejection on the part of locals. He stated that although he could not corroborate the accusations of disorder, excess, and antireligiosity that had been directed at these Frenchmen, "some of them lack modesty, and show freedom and moral laxity, and [also] little respect for our religious ceremonies have been observed."[110] Colonial officials worried that the presence of these French royalists exacerbated local political tensions because many of them seemed ambiguous in their political positions; they often maintained open and public discussions, speaking too freely about religion and politics.

In December 1793, an extraordinary meeting (*junta*) was held by the captain general, the quartermaster general, various members of the audiencia, and church leaders to discuss the influence of these royalist militiamen in Venezuela. There were rumors that the foreign officers displayed irregular conduct regarding politics and religion; their example was thought to be scandalous, likely to have dangerous consequences and to upset the tranquility and security of the province. The resulting report asserted: "Of the 122 militiamen, only 8 are Catholics. In addition, there is no confirmation of their preferred political system or their attitudes toward the current Revolution in France, and there are some strong indications that some of them are even antiroyalists.[111]

For all of these reasons, the members of the junta agreed on the necessity of sending these military officers to Europe. Disagreement between authorities and transportation difficulties delayed the expulsion of these French militiamen, but the captain general believed that their presence in Caracas was harmful because they were promoting social disorder in the city, so he ordered their immediate transfer back to La Guaira and, then, to Puerto Cabello while they waited for their definitive exit from Venezuela.[112] The officers waited several more months, and after facing many additional problems with the local population, they finally departed in different ships during the summer of 1795. The last French militiaman left Venezuela in November 1795.

During their stay in Venezuela, the royalist officers seemed to have established better relations with high-ranking officials, such as the governor of Trinidad and the captain general of Venezuela, than with the population at large. In general, people distrusted the foreigners, whose intentions and political positions were never made clear. The captain general asserted:

> Since these 122 officers and immigrant French sergeants arrived in the city, I noted by regularly observing them, and also by information that I received from different trustworthy persons, their lack of moderation and modesty with respect to religious, moral, and political matters. I proceeded to reprimand them verbally with little result.... [T]he evil continued and grew, the scandal increased, and I noticed that the immigrants had differences among themselves, and shared declarations capable of gravely questioning the true system, as well as the reasons for their immigration.[113]

The truth is that this was a heterogeneous group made up of colonial regiments (Guadeloupe and Martinique) and other regiments originating from diverse parts of France (Forez, Aunis, Bassigny, and Touraine). They maintained contrasting positions and engaged in open discussions that did not go unnoticed by Venezuelans. In fact, in different reports, members of the junta stated that they were not sure if these officers should go to Santo Domingo, because some of them did not display clear royalist inclinations. On occasion, some expressed preference for republican regimes.[114]

However, there was another factor working against the harboring and maintenance of these militiamen in Venezuela. As will be seen, by the time of their arrival in the province, more than seven hundred prisoners and slaves from Santo Domingo had been relocated in La Guaira, where they were eliciting strong reactions from the white population, who feared the ideological contagion of local pardos and blacks.

In August 1793, the governor of Santo Domingo, don Joaquín García, sent 538 French prisoners to La Guaira. All of them were placed in the dungeons and a hospital of the port city; according to the terms of their capitulation, the officials received four reales (half a peso) daily, while sergeants and soldiers received one and a half reales for their expenses. From the very beginning, the presence of this substantial number of Frenchmen from Saint-Domingue was considered disruptive and extremely dangerous for the harmony and tranquility of Venezuela. Thus, on November 2, 1793, colonial authorities held a junta, presided over by the captain general, to discuss the problem posed by the presence of these men in the province's most important port town.

Members of the junta shared with white elites and port authorities the perception of French prisoners and slaves from Saint-Domingue as "people infused with pernicious maxims and doctrines, who desperately seek to extend their ideas among local slaves, free blacks, and mulattos."[115] They also explained that residents from La Guaira, Caracas, and other nearby towns were becoming increasingly anxious; since the arrival of these prisoners, local slaves and free blacks were misbehaving, "showing an unacceptable arrogance toward their masters and employers."[116]

The report produced by this first meeting of the junta included a number of references to the contemptuous and at times seditious attitude of local slaves and free blacks. For example, a customer in a bakery in La Guaira heard two slave bakers "cheering each other up while kneading the bread dough, saying—confident that no one was hearing—that within a year they would be as free as those [slaves] in Guarico."[117] Another witness reported that he had heard one slave saying to another: "This is the right moment to shake off slavery and the authority of the Spanish, in the same way the blacks of Guarico had shaken off the authority of the French."[118]

These rumors, in the form of denunciations, were clear indications of anxiety about ideological contamination among elites and colonial officials. The sources of contagion, however, were no longer only the French who traveled to the communities and port towns of the province, or the maritime maroons who brought ideas of emancipation, or the hundreds of prisoners and slaves from Saint-Domingue who shared information about revolutionary events. Now the revolutionary phrases seemed to come from local free blacks and slaves, who allegedly referred to the "brave blacks of Saint-Domingue" and publicly announced their ambition to march down the same revolutionary path.[119]

Other denunciations in the report did not refer directly to the Saint-Domingue rebellions but nonetheless showed how the ideological and political tenets of the rebellion were applicable to local contexts. A Spanish official, for example, commented that he had heard a black French officer saying to a local slave in the street that "no man should be the slave of another."[120] Likewise, a white lady in La Guaira complained that, after offering a domestic job to a free mulatta, the colored woman airily responded that "there was no inequality between the two of them except for their color. As for the rest they were equals."[121]

The report described all three groups of militia—prisoners, slaves, and French officers—as "irreligious, immoral, and politically dangerous." The officers were accused of not respecting religious ceremonies, turning their backs on sacred ornaments, and using their time in church to look the ladies up and down, showing disrespect and causing distractions. Many of them were accused of being overtly atheistic. For their part, the prisoners and slaves from Saint-Domingue were cast as people who "break all the limits of good behavior, [who] blaspheme against the most sacred, insulting our government and lauding the fact that they are free men now."[122]

The report also contended that seditious ideas about liberty and equality had spread far beyond the "frontiers" of the port of La Guaira, where the majority of the French prisoners were held:

> In the Valleys of Aragua, and particularly in the city of Valencia, many slaves and people of color have been contaminated with dark expressions related to the imagined equality and liberty that these prisoners wanted to preach.[123]

The report clearly emphasized and exaggerated the effects of orally transmitted information in a province where 60 percent of the population was of African descent. The recently reported misbehavior and general disobedience of these groups of people were seen as evidence of revolutionary contagion. The authorities had long tried to monitor itinerant foreigners who might spread the "seed of revolution" throughout Venezuela; by this point, however, the menace was clear and tangible: the presence of a crowd of people (538 prisoners) from Saint-Domingue who had brought "to life... desires for equality and freedom" among slaves and free blacks alike.[124]

The members of the junta asserted that conditions at the fort and the hospital of La Guaira, where the prisoners and some officers were being held, were not sufficiently controlled. Local officials could not silence the "dangerous voices of the prisoners that had pierced the thick walls of the dungeons."[125] The junta nonetheless believed that it was not feasible to send the prisoners to Europe. They decided instead to send them to Havana, where the governor would try to sell some as inexpensive labor to local planters or use others for public service:

> These prisoners and many others may remain in the Castle of La Cabana or in other [forts] that defend the city and the island [sic] of La Havana, for the time that Your Majesty desires, comfortable enough and with absolutely no communication with the population; from there, not even if they yell will their pernicious way of thinking be heard, nor will they be able to escape, nor will their influence be feared as it is in this province and mainland.[126]

According to the report, Havana offered two important advantages that La Guaira and Caracas did not. In first place, Venezuela was a vast mainland where the prisoners could easily escape, while the island of Cuba seemed to have a more "controllable" geography. On the other hand, Cuban planters seemed more open and interested in buying these as slaves at advantageous prices than Venezuelan hacendados.

While the authorities discussed what to do with the 538 prisoners, another group of prisoners and slaves from Saint-Domingue arrived in La Guaira on November 3, 1793. This time, there were 431 people—188 white French prisoners of war, 220 slaves for sale, and 14 black prisoners.[127] The French prisoners were supposed to join their countrymen in the fort, whereas the slaves were to be offered for sale on the open market to Venezuela's landowners and planters. At this point, local authorities felt that the situation was spiraling out of their control. A total of 969 people from Saint-Domingue were living in La Guaira. This number represented more than 10 percent of La Guaira's total population of just under 7,000 souls. In the face of these demographic facts, authorities felt obliged to restrict the influence of the French and francophone prisoners by any means necessary—even expulsion.

At first, local authorities thought that this overwhelming concentration of foreigners in La Guaira would be temporary. They assumed, for instance, that the slaves would soon be sold to local planters, or perhaps even disbursed among other cities and ports of Spanish America. However, it soon became clear that local planters did not want slaves from the French Antilles or, even worse, slaves "who had seen and experienced the atrocities that blacks committed against whites in the rebellions of French Sto. Domingue."[128] Local planters insisted that they would never buy such slaves, as "no one will bring the stimulus of insubordination, the lack of religion, and the corruption of good habits into his home."[129]

At the end of November 1793, the Audiencia of Caracas met once again in an extraordinary session to discuss the most recent wave of foreigners—slaves and prisoners—to arrive on Venezuela's shores. The court's report contended that the slaves and prisoners were uneducated and disobedient: they often challenged local authorities and disturbed the local order. In addition, the report lamented that the fortifications, hospital, and dungeons in La Guaira were too small to house all these foreigners; officials simply could not control "the bad example and the dangerous doctrines of these desperate and uncontrolled men,"[130] who on occasion were seen walking freely on the streets of the small port city. The prisoners regularly interacted with locals, including jailers and soldiers, barbers, doctors and nurses, shopkeepers, laundresses, and street vendors. The presence of these foreigners was real, significant, and unavoidable.

After two years of trying—and largely failing—to control such daily interactions, colonial authorities managed to expel most of the foreign prisoners by the end of 1795. At first, the captain general and quartermaster general expended considerable effort to find the most convenient ways of deporting the unwanted men. Letters exchanged with governors of various Spanish islands make clear the local authorities' sheer desperation to rid Venezuela of these interlopers. They sent several letters to the governor of Santo Domingo, the governor of Cuba, and the governor of Puerto Rico. More than seven hundred prisoners of war were ultimately sent to Havana, where the dungeons and fortifications could at least accommodate their numbers. Moreover, Caracas's highest-ranking officials believed that there was less danger of ideological contamination on the "isolated" island of Cuba than in Venezuela.

The fate of the 220 slaves from Santo Domingo was less clear. At first, the Venezuelan authorities believed that they could send the slaves to Puerto Rico, but the quartermaster of that island refused to accept them for fear that they would endanger public order.[131] Finally, in December 1794, the king of Spain decreed that the slaves be sent to Cuba: "As it is not possible to send the slaves to Puerto Rico, nor to other foreign islands, your Lordship should send them to the Island of Cuba where, if they are not bought by private individuals, they could be employed in Public Service."[132]

Ridding Venezuela of the "unwanted immigrants" proved a very difficult task, compounded by the need to quell the social unrest that had been sparked by their presence. In January 1795, don Antonio López Quintana, the interim quartermaster of Caracas, sent a letter to Spain in which he mentioned some measures taken to prevent possible uprisings. He argued that, after a year and a half of "contamination," he had become aware that revolutionary doctrines had influenced the population of color, "especially the pardos, whose uncontainable need to emulate the whites and characteristic haughtiness, continue to increase apace."[133] For this reason, colonial authorities in Caracas decided to prepare two and a half companies of white militia to squelch potential uprisings, thereby guaranteeing the security of the province. They had also decided to establish neighborhood magistrates (*alcaldes de barrio*), who were responsible for monitoring rumors among the population and for keeping track of suspicious gatherings. He believed that close supervision by colonial authorities would prevent the spread of any "perverse plan," but he warned that Venezuela could not "count on a true security until all these prisoners and immigrants get out of the Province."[134]

Throughout 1795, ships carrying French slaves and prisoners departed from La Guaira, bound for Havana. In April 1795, 220 imprisoned slaves and 4 "free French men" left La Guaira for Batabanó, also in Cuba. Of these 220 slaves, 160 were men and 60 were women or children.[135] Also included in that group were four white French officials, who were sent first to Havana and later to Europe. With the departure of each of these ships, colonial officials experienced profound relief. Gone was the economic burden of providing food and shelter for these prisoners; gone, too, were their "dangerous ideas of liberty and equality." However, as we will see in subsequent chapters, these foreign captives and slaves had permanently altered the social and political environment of La Guaira. "The seed of disobedience and haughtiness" had indeed spread among local pardos, free blacks, slaves, and even some white creoles.

The hope that someday slaves would be free and equal to whites certainly remained in the minds of some Venezuelan slaves and free blacks. In July 1797, for example, a violent fight broke out between a black slave, Luis Alejandro, and a white man, Josef Bustamante. Bustamante accused Luis Alejandro of having claimed that "whites and blacks were all equal."[136] Apparently, Luis Alejandro had gone to Bustamante's warehouse in order to weigh some cacao. Bustamante demurred, as he was busy; the slave replied that he must weigh the cacao. Don Josef thundered that no slave could rule in his house, that they were not "equals." Furious, the slave took his steelyard scale and left, proclaiming: "My master, we are all whites."

The witnesses agreed that those were the exact words Luis Alejandro used—"My master, we are all whites"—but Luis himself reported them differently: "We are all white because no one black enters the Court of God." In his confession, the slave ascribed a religious meaning to this sentence: in order to enter into the court of God, all men must be white, or "equals." However, all the witnesses—including other blacks—believed that Luis Alejandro had imbibed the revolutionary maxims of freedom and equality that were circulating among the population of La Guaira. He was finally sentenced to two years of hard labor.[137] Apparently, the echoes of republicanism were resounding not only in the minds of elites and officials but also among free blacks and slaves.

These cases trace the emergence throughout Venezuela of socially diverse spaces where revolutionary ideas spread through oral channels. In both towns and surrounding villages it was possible to perceive, in the words of a concerned official, a "revolutionary humor" that shaped local expectations and motivations.[138] In the case of La Guaira, the presence of almost a thousand immigrants from the French colonies could not pass unnoticed; indeed, it was believed to be one of the reasons why an important republican movement erupted there a year later.

Colonial authorities and white elites tried through various measures to limit the expansion of the "revolutionary disease." Ultimately, none of these efforts silenced the voices of the hundreds of visitors, and the local population continued to absorb and transmit oral information about the French Caribbean. Colonial authorities recognized the impossibility of controlling the circulation of revolutionary information that efficiently traveled through oral channels. Rumors of conspiracy and insurrection made whites begin to see the threat of insurrection in even the most innocent expressions. Everyday sights, such as a conversation between two slaves, a song, the sound of drumming at night, or an opinion critical of whites, became evidence of imminent tumult. Colonial authorities, then, had no option but to begin using different strategies to prevent people of African descent from rebelling.

Fear of black insurrection had seemingly paradoxical effects. On one hand, this fear was used as a justification to increase control over local free blacks and slaves—through the creation of maroon squadrons, the enforcement of white militias, the establishment of neighborhood magistrates, among other methods. On the other, this same fear was used as a strong reason for granting free blacks and slaves better living conditions and trying to keep them contented. Historical records show that Venezuelan masters had no problem in limiting the number of slaves they imported. Likewise, Crown officials moderated taxes in some regions and showed their willingness to "listen" to people of color, including runaway slaves.

In September 1796, the Venezuela's captain general heard rumors of a possible rebellion in the Valleys of Aragua and gave orders to Juan Agustín de la Torre to undertake an investigation into the current state of relations between whites, free blacks, maroons, and slaves in the region. Torre traveled to the plantation zone and found no sign of black insurrection; instead, he expressed concern about the general living conditions of slaves and free blacks.[139] He stated that slaves and free blacks in greater Aragua lived in a "disorder of customs" (*desorden de costumbres*): there was an evident lack of authority and control on the part of the whites. Some slaves, for example, escaped from one hacienda to work on another just like any free worker. Furthermore, landlords did not control their workers and employed blacks regardless of their condition, without even asking for a card of liberty (*carta de libertad*) and without inquiring into their origins. In Torre's opinion, the blacks of Aragua lived in "general disorder and responded with insolence," though he held local whites responsible for this disorder.[140]

Even as he recommended that masters establish stricter control over their slaves, Torre suggested that masters should listen to their slaves and grant them certain concessions to keep them contented and calm. In his opinion, the happiness of the slaves ensured the tranquility of the province. He suggested, for example, an increase in government control over local shopkeepers (*pulperos*) who abused poor blacks and slaves by overpricing their products or not measuring them correctly. Torre noticed that the slaves who went to nearby towns to buy certain products felt frustrated by the abuses committed by shopkeepers. These shopkeepers, Torre explained, bought agricultural products from maroons at very low prices and sold these same products to slaves and free blacks at high prices, "gaining more than 50 percent of the value of the product." Likewise, these shopkeepers "did not use measures or weights, and sold everything just the way they wanted." Therefore, it was the government's task to control these merchants, making sure they didn't continue with their abuses. He also suggested creating new routes to bring good-quality meat from the plains to the coastal regions so slaves could improve their diet, and he went so far as to criticize masters for not providing their slaves with sufficient, good-quality tobacco.[141]

Free and enslaved blacks alike were well aware of these inclinations to appease them on the part of the authorities and began to employ different maneuvers to get what they wanted. In December 1797, the free blacks and slaves of Curiepe sent a letter to Venezuela's captain general denouncing their miserable treatment at the hands of white hacendados and the *justicia mayor* (local magistrate) of Curiepe, José Anís. They also complained that commercial taxes were too high. Immediately, the captain general sent a letter to Anís alerting him that "in the current circumstances" he was "not to oppress or allow anyone in town to oppress the blacks of the region."[142] Enraged, Anís answered that all the denunciations in the letter were "lies made up by a group of blacks who don't want to work and who live miserably because they do not accomplish their tasks." He added that local blacks did not show any respect for his authority, "believing that they depend directly on your Government and Captaincy."[143] Anís was referring specifically to Juan Pablo Castellanos, a black man from Curiepe, who in 1797 made a trip to Caracas to express his dissatisfaction directly to the captain general. Obviously, Anís felt threatened by local blacks like Castellanos, who could directly approach the captain general. Anís acknowledged the importance of keeping blacks contented but insisted that he could not control the "malicious intentions" and rumors of some of the blacks, who, "in order to provoke fear, stir up hotheads and spread false rumors that seriously damage the population."

Swirling rumors of insurrection and political unrest in the Caribbean connected elites and popular groups of color in Venezuela. Colonial officials and elites feared the revolutionary impulse brewing in the French Caribbean, while some pardos, slaves, and free blacks recognized and exploited this fear to express their anger and make new economic and political demands. Common spaces of communication reveal processes of imposition, contestation, negotiation, and transaction through which these social groups engaged with new strategies to struggle for power and improve their lives.

PART 2

Movements

CHAPTER 4

The Shadow of Saint-Domingue in the Rebellion of Coro, 1795

LEARNING OF THE DAMAGE THAT BLACK REBELS HAD WROUGHT AT San Diego, her sugar hacienda in the mountainous region of Coro in Venezuela, doña Felipa Caro could not believe her misfortune. Just months after the rebellion of Coro, at the end of 1795, doña Felipa had left Santo Domingo for Caracas with her son and daughter. The recent cession of Spanish Santo Domingo to the French had led her to abandon her comfortable life, possessions, and slaves in search of safety on the mainland.[1] Her only hope lay in the productive sugar hacienda left to her by her late husband, José Antonio Zárraga. The Coro rebellion, however, soon left her with nothing: rebels severely damaged her hacienda—the fields and the house were reduced to ashes, the agricultural tools destroyed—and local authorities soon executed eleven of her hardworking slaves.[2]

The political and social turbulence of the late eighteenth-century Caribbean had twice deprived doña Felipa of economic security. Desperate, she asked the king of Spain for a pension of 600 pesos to support her suddenly destitute family. Like many others, Felipa became convinced that a revolutionary contagion was inciting slaves and free blacks everywhere to rebel, jeopardizing the tranquility and integrity of Spanish America.

Doña Felipa's woes began on the night of May 10, 1795, when the free zambo José Leonardo Chirino led a group of about 350 rebels comprising free blacks, slaves, and a few indigenous persons into the city of Coro to present their political intentions directly to the local government. The rebellion started on the hacienda of La Macanilla, located in the Serranía de Coro, also known as the sierra of San Luis, a mountainous area in northwestern Venezuela that was largely devoted to cattle ranching and the production of sugarcane during the colonial period. The rebels sought not only to abolish commercial and transport taxes (*alcabala*) and to reduce Indian tributes but also to free the slaves and to found a "republic" based on what they referred to as the "Law of the French." Before presenting their demands to the government, the rebels sacked and burned the houses of local whites, beat and killed white males, set fields on fire, destroyed agricultural tools, and assaulted travelers and tax collectors.

The Coro uprising, like many other slave revolts throughout the Caribbean, was met with overwhelming force by the colonial state: white colonial authorities and elites captured, tortured, and summarily executed most of the participants. In 1796, Chirino was finally arrested and sentenced to death. After he was hanged, his body was mutilated and decapitated; his head and hands were displayed publicly as a warning against insurrection.

By the end of Venezuela's long struggle for independence in 1830, the Coro rebellion had been largely effaced from public memory by Venezuelan authorities. The nineteenth-century political elite—still entrenched in the racist discourse of colonial times—inherited a fear of racial war and social confrontation that led them to erase this event from narratives of the country's struggle for independence and from national historiography.[3] It was not until 1910 that historian Pedro Manuel Arcaya presented the first academic work on the Coro rebellion, and even so it was published only in 1949.[4] Since its "rediscovery" in the mid-twentieth century, the rebellion has become a symbol for diverse political and social movements in Venezuela. It has served as a blank canvas onto which different social groups have projected their demands, their frustrations, and their political ideals. Today, more than eight African-descended cultural organizations in the northern sierra of Coro commemorate the rebellion and celebrate the memory of its leader. These organizations challenge traditional understandings of the movement as a local political revolt that fed on ideologies imported from the French and Haitian Revolutions. Instead, they argue that the rebellion was an organized movement for social justice—a reaction to an oppressive colonial system and, in particular, a rejection of the abuses of colonial tax agents.[5]

Traditional histories of the Coro insurrection suggest that the discourse of the black and mixed-race rebels reflected the influence of the Haitian

Revolution and that the rebel leaders explicitly sought to model their movement on Haiti. Venezuelan historians Pedro Arcaya and Federico Brito Figueroa have argued, for example, that the circulation of "French" revolutionary ideas in the province, as well as the visits of some of the rebellion's leaders to Saint-Domingue, catalyzed the insurrection.[6] More recent works, however, suggest that the Coro rebellion's goals were obscured by a paranoid colonial discourse, which was only echoed by the later national historiography. Historian Ramón Aizpurua, for example, argues that the rebels were primarily concerned with solving socioeconomic challenges—through exoneration from taxes, for example—rather than with establishing a republic or replacing the colonial system with the "Law of the French."[7] Aizpurua suggests that the French and Haitian revolutionary models were not directly invoked by the rebels; rather, the connection was drawn by an increasingly apprehensive colonial elite. Other historians such as Pedro Gil Rivas, Luzmila Bello, Luis Dovale, and Javier Laviña have deepened Aizpurua's interpretation, reopening the debate surrounding the motivations of the rebels.[8] They trace white elites' influence on historical accounts that describe the rebellion as a local reaction to hemispheric ideological forces—that is, as yet another instance of imported French republicanism and anticolonialism. These historians have thus encouraged scholars to pay closer attention to the local colonial order and the slave system as it existed in Venezuela, particularly in Coro.[9]

Slave revolts and conspiracies in the Americas reached a peak in the 1790s, the most significant ones occurring in the two decades after the Saint-Domingue uprising of 1791.[10] Historians of slavery in the Americas would agree with David Brion Davis's contention that the Haitian Revolution "marked a turning point in the history of New World slavery."[11] Nevertheless, scholars differ on the nature of the connections that linked Saint-Domingue and slave rebellions elsewhere in the Americas.[12] Perhaps a more nuanced notion of influence should be used to understand the effects of Saint-Domingue throughout the Atlantic world. In recent works, Sibylle Fischer and Ada Ferrer refer to "repercussions" instead of influence, because Saint-Domingue became a focal point or symbol in a discourse that was put to diverse uses by distinct social groups in different regions of the Atlantic world.[13]

The historiography of slave conspiracies and rebellions in the Atlantic world poses important questions about the discursive artifices and methodological difficulties that historians face when dealing with events that are entirely recorded by those in power.[14] When describing slave conspiracies and rebellions, elites and colonial authorities exaggerated accusations, fabricated evidence, and demonized the actors in order to justify blunt repression. Recently, historian Jason T. Sharples has raised questions about the significant incongruities between the portrayals of violence by local authorities and the violence that actually occurred during various Caribbean rebellions.[15] Nevertheless, Sharples shows that elites could not completely control evolving discourses. "The conspiracy findings," he argues, "did not originate with just one group but were a product of unequal co-authorship between Africans and Europeans." Sharples shows how the knowledge produced during the 1692 Barbados conspiracy, for example, depended on analogies between ideas from many overlapping discourses—European theories of rebellions and conspiracies, African notions of war and confrontation—added to the local Barbadian sociohistorical context.[16]

Like many other black rebellions, the rebellion of Coro has been represented through a multilayered and fragmented set of discourses, deployed by different social and political groups with divergent agendas. Surprisingly, the debate about whether the rebels' motivations were primarily economic or political is much older than historians have recognized. Indeed, it began just four months after the rebellion. In September 1795, Captain General Carbonell called an extraordinary session of the Audiencia of Caracas to discuss the French invasion of Spanish Santo Domingo and its governor's petitions for aid. Members of the audiencia, the War Committee (Junta de Guerra), and other important colonial authorities like the royal intendant, Esteban Fernández de León, were at the table when Carbonell described the delicate circumstances experienced in Spanish America, in particular by Venezuela. Carbonell argued that expressions of discontent reported in several Indian towns, as well as towns of free blacks and slaves in different regions of the captaincy, reflected the "the indiscreet vigilance of the tax agents," whose overzealous enforcement of recent tax laws he blamed for the recent uprisings.[17]

Fernández de León defended himself, first orally and then in writing. He argued that he had rigorously implemented the tax regulations established by the royal decree of 1792 and confirmed in 1793. Those regulations, in his opinion, did not increase the burden of Indian tributes on the local population; in fact, they decreased the amount of tributes and excused Indian women from paying them. As for the Coro rebellion, he disputed the contention that the tributes were to blame, as free blacks and slaves did not have to pay them. Instead, he argued, the rebellion had erupted in response to a false rumor about the king's emancipation of the slaves and, more generally, "to all the seditious news of liberty and equality spread by the French, and because of the bad example promoted by the insurrection of slaves in the French colonies."[18] This early postmortem debate shows how not even well-informed colonial authorities agreed on the causes of local rebellions or the slaves' motivations. Some blamed unfair tax practices, whereas others pointed to foreign ideological influences and the government's lack of political control.

The available sources on the rebellion reveal a complex reality: in Coro, the demands of the rebels, such as the elimination of taxes and indigenous tributes, responded mainly to local economic and administrative circumstances, but these demands were accompanied by revolutionary calls for the abolition of slavery and, in some cases, the reversal of colonial socioracial hierarchies. These more radical demands allowed colonial officials to imagine connections between Coro and Saint-Domingue and, as a result, to justify radical measures to eradicate the movement. In this chapter, I disentangle this intricate set of discourses in order to reveal the threads—imagined or real—that connected Saint-Domingue with the Coro insurrection in Venezuela. While I do not intend to diminish the importance of local circumstances of oppression and economic pressure in motivating free blacks and slaves to rebel, I argue that Saint-Domingue remained a powerful image for the people of Coro, a familiar point of reference that allowed them to imagine different political scenarios. Saint-Domingue had many different meanings: for colonial officials, it referred to republicanism; for the white elite, it represented the extermination of white planters, the destruction of their haciendas, and the establishment of a new sociopolitical order. For local blacks, however, Saint-Domingue may well have exemplified the possibility of presenting their demands and negotiating with colonial authorities.

As previous chapters have shown, news and rumors of revolutionary events in the Caribbean circulated widely in Venezuela, especially along the coast. White elites read and talked about Haiti, as did pardos, free blacks, and slaves. The distance between these social groups did not prevent slaves from hearing—and conveying—elites' rumors and anxieties. Information about Saint-Domingue, then, was almost certainly transmitted across different socioracial groups: white elites feared the example of Saint-Domingue, a fear undoubtedly recognized by local blacks, who soon adopted the image of Saint-Domingue to express their discontent. Here, I show how "Saint-Domingue" thus functioned as a term of contention, a powerful reference that set the parameters of the political struggle and negotiation between opposing socioracial groups in Coro.[19]

The most significant compilation of documents to emerge from the Coro rebellion is the *expediente*, or case file, produced by the Caracas Audiencia from 1795 to 1797. The compilation comprises several dozen reports issued by colonial authorities in Coro to the captain general of Venezuela, hundreds of letters from inhabitants of Coro to the justicia mayor of Coro and the captain general in Caracas, reports from the captain general of Venezuela to the Spanish monarch and his ministers, and letters written by local authorities to their subordinates. The file also contains several testimonies of direct and indirect witnesses from all social groups and ethnicities.[20]

The Audiencia of Caracas expediente, however, lacks one significant category of evidence: the testimonies of suspected and accused rebels. Unfortunately, when the audiencia began to hear these cases, many of the black rebels had already been executed by Coro authorities, who failed to record testimonies or hold formal trials. From the very beginning, then, colonial authorities silenced the rebels' voices, not even allowing them to defend themselves or to argue their motivations in public.[21] The available historical sources on the Coro rebellion thus do not include any testimonies from the rebels; their desires and motivations remain largely a matter of conjecture, based on the representations collected, shaped, and promulgated by colonial officials and white elites.

It is known, however, that José Leonardo Chirino, the leader of the rebellion, was captured months after the uprising, and his testimony was recorded by colonial authorities in Coro and later by the audiencia in Caracas. Pedro Arcaya was the only historian to study these sources at the beginning of the twentieth century, but Chirino's testimony mysteriously disappeared from the public record soon thereafter.[22] Historians, local chroniclers, and African-descended activists continue to search for these sources in hopes of rescuing the voice of a rebel leader whose material traces have been all but effaced.

Local Tensions, Foreign Connections: The Serranía of Coro in 1795

The Coro insurrection took place in the Serranía de Coro, a hilly region to the south of the city of the same name.[23] In 1770, a foreign traveler described the area as unique for its "pleasant and healthy" climate and its fertile soil: "These soils are apt for cultivating appetizing and tasty fruits. The soil is good for everything, except for cacao. There are some *haciendas de trapiches* [small sugar plantations] in the region, including: San Joaquín, San Diego, Santa Lucía, El Carmen, Macanillas, and Curimagua."[24] Of all the haciendas of Coro, only two were of particular economic importance: the Hacienda de la Caridad and the Hacienda de la Concepción de los Güeques. The rest were smaller operations devoted to the production of sugar.[25] Other areas of the province, such as the outskirts of the city of Coro and the northern haciendas, were known for producing a diverse array of crops, including rice, manioc, corn, coffee, plantains, and a variety of root crops. These areas were also known for livestock breeding and ranching.

During the early phases of colonization, in the sixteenth century, the lands of Coro were used mostly for raising cattle. At the end of the seventeenth century, agriculture was introduced, and, by the eighteenth century, the serranía was considered the most productive agricultural area of the Province of Coro due to its notable production of sugar and cacao. The Coro Province also became an important center for the raising of cattle, goats, and mules, and for the production of milk, cheese, and leather. In addition, Coro was an important center for the exchange of goods between the hinterland and the coast. It possessed a number of tracks and paths for the transportation of goods between the western inland regions of Venezuela and the coast.[26]

Coro also served as a significant node in the smuggling networks that linked the mainland to the Caribbean islands, especially Curaçao. Because of its location, Coro was an important port for the exchange of goods between the Caribbean and the mainland. Cattle and mules from the distant plains of Guanare and San Carlos, as well as cacao, tobacco, and hides, thus made their way to the Caribbean islands, including Saint-Domingue, Jamaica, Curaçao, and Aruba, where they were sold by Dutch corsairs and Caribbean merchants.[27] Historians Ramón Aizpurua and Linda Rupert have traced the significant economic and social links between Venezuela and Curaçao in the seventeenth and eighteenth centuries. Coro and Curaçao, in particular, maintained strong economic and social ties for a number of reasons. These included the Spanish Main's proximity to Curaçao, the local authorities' general tolerance of illicit commercial activities between the two regions, and strong interest among Curaçaoans in Venezuelan commodities such as tobacco, cacao, salt, leather, cattle, and mules. For their part, the people of

Coro sought an array of Dutch manufactured goods such as textiles, semi-processed foodstuffs, and alcoholic beverages.[28]

The Valley of Curimagua in the Serranía de Coro was a particularly fertile region, "rich in desirable crops and inhabited by some landowners, their slaves, free colored workers (creoles and *luangos*) and some indigenous communities."[29] During the eighteenth century, the region included twenty-three small towns, some of which were home to a mixed population whereas others were inhabited exclusively by Indians or free blacks. A 1795 census of these twenty-three towns shows that the jurisdiction of Coro had a population of approximately 26,390.[30] Around 30 percent of this population was identified as "Indian,"[31] while almost 55 percent was labeled "black" (43 percent were free blacks and about 12 percent were enslaved) and 14 percent were whites.[32]

This proportion of free blacks, slaves, and Indians allows us to imagine the hybrid nature of labor in the region. The haciendas of the sierra were originally cultivated by Indians and black slaves, but over the course of the eighteenth century an increasing number of free blacks began to participate in field labor. By the end of the eighteenth century, the free blacks working in the fields notably outnumbered the slaves.[33] This situation raises important questions: who were these free blacks? Were they manumitted ex-slaves from non-Spanish colonies? Were they local maroons? These questions have not been fully answered, and a closer study could shed new light on the socioracial composition of the Coro rebellion.

Historians have convincingly argued that the increasing number of free blacks in the region reflected the immigration of former slaves from Curaçao.[34] The economic links between the two regions would have facilitated this sort of movement. Commercial relations and smuggling activities between Coro and Curaçao required constant communication and a general sense of trust between agents in both locations. A diverse group of smugglers—men and women of varying socioracial backgrounds and political beliefs—facilitated the transit of goods, thereby bridging the geographic and cultural distance separating Curaçao from Tierra Firme, or the Spanish mainland.[35] "Maritime marronage" likewise contributed to increasing social and cultural bonds between the two regions.[36]

During the eighteenth century, slaves from Curaçao fled to the region of Coro, where they were automatically granted freedom. Various sources suggest that Curaçaoan slaves frequently built or stole small boats and crossed the sea that separated the island from the mainland. Once in Coro, these ex-slaves were free to settle, work small plots of land, and even participate in contraband trade.[37] For decades, Coro's local authorities showed no particular interest in repatriating slaves from Curaçao, as their presence in Venezuela helped to mitigate the region's chronic labor shortage.[38] These fugitive slaves, commonly called *luangos*, *minas*, or *curazaos*, thus became important for the economic development of the region, although their presence created some tension with other local groups.[39]

Slaves and free blacks in the Serranía de Coro had similar responsibilities. Slaves worked a predetermined number of hours each day on their masters' plantations, sometimes finishing their work early in order to spend afternoons and weekends working small subsistence plots (*conucos*). Masters provided their slaves with these plots as a way of avoiding maintenance expenses. Slaves even sold their produce in the markets of local towns, enjoying thus a certain measure of economic independence from their masters.[40] Free field workers performed the same tasks as slaves but received payment for their services and were not subject to the same restrictions in terms of permissions and social control. Although this situation must have created tensions between free blacks and slaves, frequent intermarriage blurred the lines between these two groups.[41] The leader of the Coro rebellion, José Leonardo Chirino, a local free zambo, was, for instance, married to an enslaved woman, María Dolores. Their three children were condemned to live in the same condition as their mother, since the colonial judicial system held that children of enslaved mothers were slaves. Their fate may well have contributed to José Leonardo's desire to challenge the system of slavery.[42]

Despite the social and cultural bonds between local free blacks and slaves, Afro-Curaçaoans formed communities apart from local free blacks and slaves. Under the leadership of a charismatic individual, the luangos frequently struggled against both whites and local blacks for land, resources, and economic opportunities.[43] Javier Laviña claims that while free blacks in Coro generally cultivated the haciendas of white families, luangos worked on the royal lands of Macuquita.[44] Hacendados and royal officials, who were politically invested in dividing the free black population, emphasized differences between creole free blacks and luangos.[45] In fact, some white inhabitants of Coro were wary of the luangos' presence on royal land, as they feared that local blacks would resent the privileges given to the luangos. Indeed, the luangos' situation created significant tensions. Many whites questioned their privileges, whereas local free blacks and slaves came to believe that they themselves deserved similar dispensations from the Spanish Crown.[46]

According to census records, almost 14 percent of the population of Coro was white. Among these whites were many poor families that ran small businesses and stores or worked as artisans. Roughly twelve rich white families, representing less than 1 percent of the total population of the region, controlled the economy of Coro as well as the city council and its most important public offices. These families possessed important sugar plantations in the serranía and benefited significantly from the economic growth of the region in the eighteenth century.

Coro's powerful white families, however, experienced their own tensions as they competed for control of the local economy. Two elite clan groupings in particular entered into a thorny conflict with each other: on one side was the Zárraga-Zabala family, and on the other, the Tellerías, Chirinos, and Arcayas. The Zárraga-Zabalas arrived in Coro at the beginning of the eighteenth century as agents of the well-known Compañía Guipuzcoana, or Royal Caracas Company, and their control over the commercial operations of Coro allowed them to rapidly achieve a privileged position in local society. More established and traditional families of Coro, such as the Tellerías, the Chirinos, and the Arcayas, however, were wary of the sudden incursion and increasing power of the Zárraga-Zabalas.[47]

One of the conflicts between the Zárraga-Zabalas and Coro's other white families revolved around the occupation and use of uncultivated lands in the serranía by the luango communities. The Zárraga-Zabalas engaged in a territorial dispute with certain luangos who were using the Macuquita lands. The Zárraga-Zabalas claimed that the luangos had taken over lands that belonged to their family.[48] Yet the luangos fought back. Represented by their leader, José Caridad González,[49] and supported by the Tellería and Chirinos families, who paid for a trip González made to Madrid, the luangos in 1792 obtained a royal decree declaring the land to be *realengo*, or royal land, set aside for the use of the luangos, beneficiaries of freedom by royal grace.[50] With the royal decree in hand, the luangos continued cultivating the Macuquita lands, incurring the resentment of many local white families and local officials. Indeed, this very resentment prompted González to attempt to establish a luango militia in Coro, although he ultimately failed to secure the captain general's permission for the project.[51]

The black population of the serranía, both free and enslaved, owned or rented plots of land where they cultivated crops for sale in towns and cities. They were required to pay taxes (known as *derechos de alcabala*) for the transportation of agricultural commodities at checkpoints on local roads, in the customshouses of the region, and at the main entrances to the towns. During the last decade of the eighteenth century, a new tax collector, don Manuel Iturbe, was assigned to the Province of Coro. Prompted by the impulse behind the Bourbon reforms, Iturbe argued that the local tax system was disorganized and poorly administered. To remedy this inefficiency, he decided to exert more rigorous control over Indian tributes, to reestablish old alcabalas, and to impose new ones in the serranía. This decision, of course, provoked great displeasure among everyone trading agricultural goods, but small merchants—mainly Indians, free blacks, and slaves—bore the brunt of these new measures.[52] In determining alcabalas, Iturbe's tax agents evaluated the crops to be sold and charged an anticipated tax, which, in many cases, exceeded the price at which the products were to be sold. As a result, small merchants and produce sellers in the serranía, especially Indians, free blacks, and slaves, perceived customs agents as corrupt and arbitrary officials who abused their power and extorted money from the people to enrich themselves. Some of the serranía's Indians and free blacks claimed that they had to resort to paying these duties with their own clothing and agricultural produce. Regarding the abuses of Iturbe's collectors, Josef Tellería, the master of rebel leader José Leonardo Chirino's wife, reported in 1794:

> The poor farm laborer or rancher was the target of his shots; his things, and crops were taken at each step: only these officials were the transgressors of the law, they are the authors and instigators of contraband; they torment [the poor] with whippings, and inhumane punishments; and while the ostentatious illegal rider advanced with impunity, those poor men were dragged to prisons and jails, and this brought misery to their families, caused by the confiscation of their goods.[53]

This situation must have produced great discontent among Coro's Indians and blacks. According to Tellería's report, on at least one occasion José Leonardo discussed the terrible consequences of unfair taxes on the black population and asked for Tellería's help in opposing these measures. Nonetheless, Tellería could do little to quell Iturbe's determination.

It was in this tense atmosphere that a wave of rumors about a royally mandated emancipation of slaves began to circulate. According to several witnesses, some months before the rebellion a black healer named Cocofío, who traveled freely from plantation to plantation in the serranía, spread the news that the king of Spain had declared freedom for all the slaves of the province but that local authorities and masters were hiding the proclamation from the enslaved population. According to witness Manuel Carrera, the same story was told again and again, "causing [the slaves] erroneously to believe that they had been made free."[54] Cocofío's optimistic claim may well have derived from the same wave of rumors regarding the "imaginary decree of emancipation" that circulated in the Caribbean and other parts of Venezuela, but in the Coro region this rumor seemed particularly plausible in light of the Crown's recent decree granting luangos the right to settle on the royal lands of Macuquita. As Carrera argued in the aftermath of the Coro rebellion, this decree "must have confused local slaves, who believed that the same proclamation had granted them freedom."[55]

By 1795, friction between socioracial groups—whites, free blacks, luangos, and slaves—and rumors of emancipation had compounded the tensions created by the new tax system. Nonetheless, royal officials and colonial elites did not expect a slave rebellion, and the news sparked an animated debate about the causes. Ultimately, whites interpreted the Coro rebellion through an analogy with the racial war in Saint-Domingue—which, in turn, provided a convenient justification for blunt repression.

Official Narratives of the Rebellion: The "Law of the French"

Early in the afternoon of May 11, 1795, residents of Coro heard the "terrible news": slaves and free colored people of the serranía had risen up against their masters with firearms and machetes, sacking their houses and setting fire to their fields. Don Manuel Urbina, a young white man who had managed to escape when the insurgents arrived at his family's hacienda, offered a detailed story of the events. While setting fire to his parents' house, the rebels called repeatedly for Urbina, but he hid in the bushes with some *criados* (domestic servants). From his hiding place, he heard the rebels yelling that "they will put an end to the alcabalas, *estancos* [liquor and tobacco monopolies], and other royal demands, they will grant freedom to the slaves, they will kill all the white men and marry the women."[56]

That afternoon, Lieutenant Mariano Ramírez Valderrain, Coro's highest official, wrote an urgent report to don Pedro Carbonell, Venezuela's captain general. Ramírez had learned, some four hours earlier, of a black and mulatto rebellion in the Serranía de Coro: "The rebels have killed white hacendados and have sacked and burned their houses." He mentioned that "slaves were clamoring for their freedom, accompanied by some free blacks and mulattos," and finally he concluded that the insurgents sought "to damage all the plantations and to go to the city of Coro in order to demand freedom and tax exemptions."[57] Complaining about the lack of military protection, Ramírez asked for arms and troops to help him save the city. In the meantime, he had ordered *vecinos* (mostly whites but also some pardo residents) to prepare to confront the rebels. Ramírez explained that some Indians in the region had likewise responded to his call to arms and were prepared to defend the city.

On May 15, 1795, Ramírez wrote a second report to the captain general announcing that the rebellion was under control. On the night of May 11, he had sent a group of soldiers to one of the customshouses of the city to search for nearby rebels. The soldiers found the bodies of three guards, presumably killed by the insurgents. With this intelligence in hand, Ramírez gathered a militia of "householders, whites, mulattoes, and some non-tributary Indians who came from the town of Carrizal" and lay in wait for the rebels. At seven o'clock on the morning of May 12, as Ramírez's motley band of troops was about to retire, 350 men appeared on the plains: "They waved their flag and sent an envoy declaring that freedom should be granted for the slaves, as well as exemption from the alcabala and other taxes, and that they would do no harm if the city was given to them."[58] Local officials answered with a cannon shot, and the Indians of Guaybacoa sent innumerable arrows in the direction of the rebels, who quickly began to flee. The battle ended in a bloodbath: twenty-five blacks were killed on the battleground, while twenty-four more were wounded and then beheaded that very afternoon; still others were sent to prison to be interrogated before their execution.

The lieutenant explained that, due to time and space constraints, testimony from the accused was taken only orally (*a la sola voz*). He reported that imprisoned rebels had quickly supplied the names of their two leaders: the luango chief, José Caridad González, and a free black (later described as zambo), José Leonardo Chirino. The interrogators were also told that "a Real Cédula ordering freedom for all slaves had come from Spain and had been concealed by local officials in order to maintain slavery."[59] This information, according to Ramírez, was "used by the leaders to convince [the slaves] to rise up and rebel."[60]

Apparently, Chirino was to lead the rebellion in the countryside, while González was charged with organizing the movement within the city. At this point, however, there had been no uprising in the city. That very night, José Caridad appeared at the armory of the city of Coro, offering his support and twenty of his men to Ramírez to assist in the fight against the rebels. Ramírez, who suspected that José Caridad was one of the rebel leaders, refused his offer and arrested him, along with other luangos. The lieutenant claimed that after José Caridad was officially declared a suspect and sent to prison, he tried to escape during the night and was killed alongside two other luangos. Ramírez never furnished any written testimony giving voice to José Caridad or any other luango or slave. At the end of his second report, Ramírez concluded:

> This same day, the fifteenth, I beheaded nine of the prisoners, confirmed as criminals, with no trial other than an oral one, as this is what was called for because last night the women of the luangos tried to bribe the jailer and because there is a great deal to be done. I acted based on the known truth without any form of written trial.[61]

In response, Carbonell congratulated Ramírez and his troops on their decisive action and the "favorable" outcome they had achieved. However, he encouraged Ramírez to follow standard judicial procedure and to send along copies of the testimonies of the accused, the number of executed and sentenced blacks, and the number of those who were still in prison, in order to "further clarify the events."[62] Carbonell knew all too well that Ramírez was not fulfilling the requirements of the law. A 1774 royal decree compelled authorities to "allow those sentenced to give evidence and present a legitimate self-defense."[63] Even after receiving Carbonell's order, Ramírez failed to transcribe the testimonies of the accused; indeed, he continued to sentence and execute suspected rebels without even recording their fates. Instead, he asked other white witnesses to send their testimonies to the captain general.

In a third report, the lieutenant confirmed that he had quashed the rebellion and that he needed no additional troops, as he already had more than six hundred men, divided between the city and the mountains, who were charged with patrolling the region. In the following days, Ramírez sent further reports on the arrest of suspects and their subsequent executions. Still, he never provided the governor with any written documentation of the rebels' testimonies. He simply added that he was sure that the captured blacks represented the most "furious and atrocious of the region," reiterating that the haciendas were in a pitiful state, the houses all burned and sacked, and the animals killed, because "those men had not even respected the sacred ornaments of the religious chapels on the plantations."[64]

Twelve days after the uprising, Ramírez sentenced fifty more people, including free blacks, slaves, and Indians, to corporal punishment, exile from the Province of Coro, or death. Ramírez justified these irregular sentences by claiming that the local prison was overcrowded and that there were not enough people to guard it.[65] By sentencing the accused to exile or death without trial, the lieutenant presumably sought to prevent the prisoners from escaping and orchestrating an even more serious uprising in the province, or from questioning his authority.

Ramírez specifically sentenced twenty-two free blacks to death because they allegedly participated in the burning and sacking of houses, or in the beating and killing of white men. He added that these rebels intended to "take the city and execute their plans to kill all the whites, eliminate tax payments, take control of the entire city, and follow the 'Law of the French.'"[66] For the first time, Ramírez introduced the idea of the "Law of the French." While it is not clear what exactly he meant by this phrase, it seems that he believed this law sanctioned killing white people, eliminating taxes, and taking control of the city. Here, nevertheless, it is possible to identify an important shift in Ramírez's perception of the rebels' motivations: in earlier reports, the lieutenant identified their main demands as manumission and exemption from taxes. Only after he was chastised for failing to follow legal protocol did Ramírez mention the lure of the "Law of the French."

Why did Ramírez change his account of the rebels' motivations? One might argue that he merely sought to convey to a distant audience the terrible threat posed by the rebels. The killing of whites and the burning of fields evoked the stories of Saint-Domingue that circulated throughout the Atlantic world. If the behavior of the rebels in Coro and in Saint-Domingue was similar, Ramírez seemed to imply, then their final designs must be the same. For the white elites, the shadow of revolutionary republicanism loomed over Coro, and the failed rebellion soon took on revolutionary proportions. At the same time, we should bear in mind that Ramírez had no respect for judicial process. Anxious to restore order, he took justice into his own hands. Having achieved his immediate ends, he may have sought to explain his extrajudicial measures by exaggerating the rebels' political intentions.

In this report, Ramírez introduced a second novel claim about the rebels. In the first report, he had characterized them as slaves supported by some free blacks, but in his second report he named José Caridad González, the chief of the luango community, as one of the principal leaders of the rebellion. José Caridad had obviously become an uncomfortable figure for some white families with important properties in the serranía. Implicating him in the rebellion may have been an astute political move to get rid of the luangos' prerogatives, or at least to restore the traditional socioracial hierarchy of the region.

There is no conclusive evidence regarding the participation of José Caridad in the Coro rebellion. Ramón Aizpurua, for example, demonstrates that the number of luangos captured in the rebellion was minimal: "Primary sources show that two hundred luango men lived in Macuquita. If José Caridad González and José Leonardo Chirino were allied, why would José Leonardo rebel without the direct collaboration and participation of these luango men?"[67] Most of the luangos who were executed without testimony were captured in the city along with González, and their participation in the rebellion is highly doubtful.[68] José Caridad was a free black man who, just years earlier, had successfully obtained a Gracia del Rey (favor of the king) to live and use land in the serranía; as a result, he was well positioned in local society, and this may explain his decision to offer his support to the lieutenant. José Caridad's name was probably mentioned by captured rebels who knew about the conflict between local white families and the luango leader and sought to use him as a scapegoat, or by white members of the elite who wanted to get rid of the luangos because they represented a menace to the socioracial order of the region. Ramírez remained uncertain about the participation of luangos in the rebellion; at one point, he quipped: "Although they are not confirmed criminals, I don't take them for saints."[69]

Official records attribute the rebellion largely to external forces: the influence of Saint-Domingue and "French Law" on the one hand and the leadership of a foreign free black like José Caridad on the other. These characterizations indicate a political and military campaign that emphasized foreign ideological and political factors and gave far less attention to local conditions.

One month after the rebellion, Carbonell sent a report to the Spanish war minister on "the insurrection of the black slaves and free people of Coro, who intended to *create a republic* and receive exoneration from royal tributes."[70] In this new narrative, Carbonell gave special attention to the image of a republic in order to portray the rebels as ideological radicals; exemption from taxes became a secondary concern, although it, too, could have been read as an implicit rejection of vassalage.[71] By presenting these two demands as the fundamental purposes of the Coro rebellion, Carbonell drew attention away from the irregularity of Ramírez Valderrain's legal procedures.

In his report, the captain general provided a detailed description of the rebellion, recounting the actions of his officials in order to control the uprising: the provision of troops from Caracas and Puerto Cabello to Coro, and the brave, decisive actions of Ramírez. Particularly interesting is his version of the lieutenant's confrontation with the rebels outside the city. At this point, according to Carbonell, the rebels demanded freedom for slaves, exoneration from taxes and "other benefits for the free people," and, above all, control of the city, where they intended to establish a republic. Carbonell implies that, at the moment of the confrontation, the rebels were already clamoring for the formation of a republic.

The captain general's narrative was based, albeit not exclusively, on the previous reports of Ramírez. Thus, we should ask: Did Ramírez mention the creation of a republic as a fundamental demand of the rebels? The lieutenant did allude to the "Law of the French," but he did not explicitly mention the establishment of a republic as a main goal of the rebellion. When he did mention it, he described it merely as a possible outcome, not as a demand made by the rebels.

It is instructive, then, to compare Ramírez's account with Carbonell's. On May, 15, 1795, Ramírez described the confrontation to Carbonell:

Three hundred fifty men, even more, appeared on the plain, [and I] quickly turned back, marching quietly with the campaign cannon and approaching them at a prudent distance. [The rebels] waved their flag and sent an envoy stating that freedom should be granted for the slaves, as well as exemption from the alcabala and other taxes for free men, and that they would do no harm if the city was given to them.[72]

On June 12, 1795, Carbonell wrote to the Spanish war minister:

More than three hundred fifty men appeared on the plain, and waving their flag, they sent an envoy demanding freedom for slaves, and exemption from alcabala and other taxes for free men. They wanted to take the city in order to establish the republic that rudely and criminally they imagined in their minds, and procured with the atrocity of their hands, stained with the blood of their masters and other whites, already destroyed by the fury of their ignominy.[73]

Here we can see the captain general's transformation of Ramírez's account. Carbonell added a dramatic touch to the story with the image of the bloodstained rebels' hands. He also added the phrase "creation of the republic" to the list of the rebels' demands. At the end of his narrative, Carbonell concluded: "If Ramírez had not acted in this manner, immediately punishing such criminal and disgusting offenses, his tolerance would have had dreadful and ruinous consequences for the Province."[74]

As this discursive transformation suggests, official narratives inevitably interpreted the Coro rebellion by analogy with the rebellion in Saint-Domingue as a movement that sought to establish a republic accompanied by the abolition of slavery. This analogy, in turn, provided local authorities with a convenient justification for their blunt repression of the rebellion. Official narratives, in other words, transformed both the events and the discourses produced during the rebellion and forced them to fit their own image of republicanism as a system that, in their view, produced chaos, destruction, and violence.

Other White Narratives: The Fear of Extermination

If official accounts of the rebellion dwelled on the rising tide of seditious French ideas, local whites inevitably emphasized the rebellion's *exceptional* character: the sheer size of the rebel force, the comparatively small number of whites, and the "atrocities" that rebels had committed and their "violent nature." The whites of Coro did not necessarily mention the rebels' political aspirations—the creation of a republic, or the establishment of a new political order. Rather, they saw in the rebellion a deep-seated desire for racial revenge, the inversion of socioracial hierarchies, and the rejection of colonial rule.

Some days after the rebellion was put down, a *corregidor de indios* (chief magistrate of Indian towns), don Hilario Bustos, told Carbonell that during his captivity he had heard the rebels "proclaiming freedom for slaves, the extermination of white males, the servitude of white women, exemption from royal rights, universal pillage, insolence, outrage, and invasion of the city of Coro."[75] Among this flurry of claims, it is possible to identify concrete demands (manumission and tax exemptions) and imagined threats ("pillage and insolence"). Between these two extremes was "the destruction of white males and the servitude of white women"—a threat that expressed a supposed desire to take revenge on white men and invert social hierarchies. Don Andrés Manuel de Goribar, a local resident who participated in the capture, interrogation, and execution of rebels, emphasized this tendency toward violence, writing that the goal of the rebels was simply to "take the city and kill all the whites."[76]

Another witness, don Juan Hilario de Armas y Castro, affirmed that, on the night of May 11, a motley band of blacks and zambos, slaves and free people, and even a few Indians terrorized local haciendas, killing white males, holding their wives and children captive, and sacking and burning their houses. He added that, on the morning of May 12, "425 militiamen arrived *en son de Batalla* [intending to fight] at the gates of the city. They sent an emissary to announce that they would do no harm if we rescinded the alcabalas and gave freedom to the slaves; we answered with a cannon shot."[77] Armas y Castro's testimony suggests that, despite the violence of the preceding day, the rebels intended to negotiate with local officials. The violence would continue, then, only if the rebels were not granted their demands. According to this witness, the rebels' ultimate goals were to obtain freedom for the slaves and exemption from taxes, and also to "kill all whites and colored [mixed-race] people, in order to be left with their women, and to apply the 'Law of the French.'"[78]

On June 2, don Manuel Carrera, another local hacendado who helped to capture the rebels, wrote a detailed report on the rebellion. Don Manuel commented that, in the course of "committing their atrocities," the rebels had espoused different goals. Nevertheless, all of them had demanded "absolute freedom for slaves, tax exemption, the elimination of the tobacco monopoly and suppression of commercial taxes, [and] the death of all white males regardless of age or name," and expressed the desire "to take their white wives in order to marry them."[79] Carrera's report raises the possibility of overlapping demands: some rebels sought to exterminate the white population and take control of the city, whereas others used a discourse of violence in hopes of obtaining political ends—freedom and tax exemptions. The murder of all whites and the possession of their wives represented a powerful discourse of racial violence that played into, and was perhaps even conceived in response to, whites' anxieties stemming from Saint-Domingue.

To the local white population, these images of the elimination of all white men and the possession of their wives to serve or to marry them—there is no explicit mention of rape—represented not merely a form of racial violence but a complete inversion of the social order. Anxiety around this sort of inversion was not without precedent. In his work on slave conspiracies in the Americas and the Caribbean, Winthrop Jordan traces the trope of the rebelling slave as a potential rapist to the seventeenth century. In the intervening two hundred years, this image had been used repeatedly throughout the Americas to demonize subordinated rebels. In most cases, there is little if any evidence that such rapes actually occurred during the rebellions.[80] Such accusations fit into a broader paranoid colonial discourse—frequently unspecific and repetitive—that sought to dehumanize enslaved and indigenous peoples throughout the Atlantic world.[81] During the events of the Haitian Revolution, these images of socioracial inversion came to embody the larger sociocultural fears of local whites. Accounts of cruelty and barbarism among the rebels in Saint-Domingue filled the pages of travelers' diaries, witnesses' testimonies, and newspapers. A set of topoi—an impaled white child, the violated womb of a pregnant woman—was repeated obsessively in the wake of the rebellion.[82]

The accounts of Saint-Domingue that circulated throughout the Caribbean inevitably emphasized sexual rivalry and racial vengeance. Numerous eyewitness testimonies included stories of the rape of white women by rebels, or of black rebels who proclaimed that they wanted to murder white males and to impregnate white women.[83] This trope soon traveled throughout the Atlantic world, igniting anxiety among white planters—especially fathers and husbands—and colonial authorities.[84] In Coro, whites used this imagery to link the rebellion to recent events in Saint-Domingue; the rebels' celebration of the "Law of the French" only cemented this connection. At the same time, this was not merely a discourse. The rebels in fact killed and wounded white men, burned houses and fields, captured women, and threatened to kill any slaves who opposed the rebellion.

For local whites, it soon became clear that the black rebels had long planned on exterminating the white males of the region. Francisco Jacot, a captain appointed by Carbonell to lead troops in Coro, relayed a conversation with Father Pedro Pérez, a priest in the region. According to Father Pérez, some weeks before the uprising, local blacks had attended *zambas* (dances), where they had danced "a thousand obscenities" and sung "dishonest verses." The priest recounted that one of the revelers had proclaimed: "A black with *placa* is worthier than a white's head: flame up, flame down, bring out the *machaca*, cut off his head, the vultures eat, drink the *aguardiente*."[85] According to historian Josefina Jordán, *placa* was a word used to refer to certain coins from the Netherlands, so the song could have implied that a black man with money was worthier than a white. *Machaca* was an instrument used to cut or smash, and the song was enunciated as an order: use the machaca to cut the white's head off; while vultures eat the white man's body, blacks celebrate by drinking rum.

Another resident of the region, Nicolás Coronado, reported to Jacot that he had heard similar songs. Although he could not understand some of the lyrics, certain lines caught Jacot's attention:

> Flame down, flame up, death to the white, life to the black: and Josef Leonardo with his gang, gathers the blacks at La Macanilla, and with his *volero* made of "royal palm," death to the white, black for the seed: white dig, black remain for the seed, the ones who live will see.[86]

La Macanilla is the name of a hacienda located in the Serranía de Coro where Chirino worked and where the rebellion first erupted, and a *volero* (in current spelling, *bolero*) is a hat made of palm fiber. In the verses, the word *candela* ("flame" or "fire") could have been used to refer to the uprising itself. This second song explicates an uprising with recognized participants like José ("Josef") Leonardo—as a leader—and his people. The verses may also have contained geographic references to the serranía ("flame up") and the city of Coro ("flame down"). Jacot explained that free blacks customarily danced during religious festivities, and that they normally had permission from the magistrates, who sent officials to maintain order.[87] One official confessed that he was particularly concerned by the phrase "black for the seed," and that it was only after the uprising that he understood "that with this expression the blacks wanted to say that they would try to extend their offspring through white women."[88] In this case, white women were not only the vehicles of male honor and dishonor; they also represented the most valuable facet of a man's identity—the ability to reproduce himself. In colonial societies, this ability was understood as crucial to the maintenance of social order. From the perspective of whites, the threat of miscegenation evoked the specter of a new social order: an entire society of pardos and mulattoes.[89]

Contrary to the official accounts, these songs did not mention exemption from taxes, manumission, or the creation of a republic. They dwelt instead on blacks' desire for revenge through the reversal of the socioracial hierarchy and the establishment of a new social order based on "French Laws." It is clear that local whites reinterpreted the songs retrospectively, in light of the rebellion. That said, it was easy to draw such connections, not only because many witnesses said that they had heard rebels repeating that they would "exterminate whites, keep the women for themselves, and establish the Law of the French," but also because the rebels did precisely that, insofar as they were able: they killed or wounded every white man they encountered, they imprisoned women and children in a house guarded by slaves, and they marched to the city, where they would present their demands to colonial authorities.

Narratives from Below: Saint-Domingue as a Term of Contention

In August 1795, the Audiencia of Caracas decided to initiate a formal investigation into the events at Coro. In order to clarify the sequence of events, the audiencia's panel of judges asked witnesses from Coro to travel to Caracas to testify or, alternatively, to send written testimonies. The audiencia solicited the testimonies of previously silenced actors: white women, free blacks, Indian headmen, and even female slaves who had witnessed the events. These "narratives from below" convey a more complex view of the uprising and its participants. Some witnesses contended that not all the region's slaves were involved in the rebellion, or that some had been forced to join under threat of death. Others reported that they had been aware of a general sense of discontent among the black population but that they had had no premonition of what was to come.

On September 7, 1795, doña Nicolasa de Acosta, widow of don Sebastián de Talavera and a survivor of the rebellion, wrote her account of the events. She stated that on the night of May 11, a group of blacks came to her house and called her name, asking her to open the door. When they did not receive a response, they set fire to the house. Don Josef María Manzano, a friend who was with her that evening, went outside to find out what was going on. The rebels immediately killed him. One rebel smashed one of the windows of the house in order to provide an exit for his sister, one of Acosta's household slaves. Through that very window, all the women of the house escaped from the fire. When the enslaved woman asked her brother why they were rebelling, he affirmed that "no white male will remain, not even his seed, that white women would have to adapt to their 'new laws,' that slavery was over and so were the alcabalas."[90]

It seems that before the confrontation with government troops, some rebels had already proclaimed that "new laws" would be established, including freedom for slaves and exemption from taxes. This rebel's statement likewise seems to confirm that "killing white men" was part of the rebels' plan. Doña

Nicolasa survived with the help of some domestic slaves who assisted her and other women in escaping. None of these women were sexually abused. Colonial guards erroneously arrested five of doña Nicolasa's slaves and three free blacks who worked on her hacienda because they were suspected of collaborating with the rebels, when in truth they had helped their mistress escape.[91] On several occasions, doña Nicolasa tried to defend her slaves, but Ramírez ignored her petitions and sentenced them to death without taking testimony or holding trials.[92] Two of her female slaves confirmed doña Nicolasa's account. Indeed, a state of confusion reigned in the serranía in the days that followed the rebellion; many slaves and also luangos were mistakenly taken as prisoners and even sentenced to death, even as many slave owners argued that their slaves had been forced to join the movement.

Some accounts by free blacks and slaves confirmed the climate of general discontent among the population of Coro in the wake of the new taxes and rumors of emancipation. On September 23, the audiencia judges interrogated María Dolores Chirino, slave of Josef Tellería and José Leonardo Chirino's wife. After explaining in detail her encounter with the rebels in the house of her master, she affirmed that she had not known about her husband's plan, which had "taken her by surprise." She recounted hearing her husband drinking and fighting outside her master's house. When she warned him that her master was nearby, he answered: "Come on, this is a joke, this woman doesn't know what is going on."[93] Later, she testified, Chirino and his allies began to fight with other slaves; when white men came out of the house to see what was going on, the rebels murdered them all, including María Dolores's master.

María Dolores confessed that she had heard some slaves in her neighborhood express their discontent, saying that they would demand freedom and exemption from taxes, but she insisted that she did not know about the planned uprising: "This all came as an unexpected situation," she said.[94] Like María Dolores, other black women were aware of the rising discontent among male slaves, but they claimed ignorance as to the precise plans of the rebels, probably to avoid suspicion of complicity.[95]

Two days after the rebellion was put down, an Indian headman or cacique from the town of Pecaya appeared before the city council of Coro. In his hand was a letter that José Leonardo Chirino had sent to him the day the rebellion erupted:

Dear Señor,
I am working hard to put an end to these hardships that are killing us. I

ask you to give me some of your people so we can all present our demands in Coro, to see if we can catch them and receive relief. With this done you won't pay *demora* [overdue tributes]. This is what I can offer for now. I ask God to guard you for many years.

From your dearest servant who kisses your hands,
José Leonardo Chirino[96]

José Leonardo had dictated the letter to a white soldier, Manuel Josef de Guero, who had been apprehended by the rebels and then forced to write what they told him. Manuel had been driving the carriage of don Josef Tellería and don Francisco Rosillo, both killed by the rebels, when the rebels captured him. He was taken to the rebels' headquarters (at La Macanilla), where Chirino spared his life, asking him to write a letter and take it to the chief of the Indian town of Pecaya. Terrified, Guero complied and took the letter to Pecaya, although he later escaped and soon notified two white hacendados about his ordeal.[97] Instead of addressing José Leonardo's petition, the chief of Pecaya took the letter to the Coro city council and offered to help capture Chirino in exchange for tribute exemption. The city councilmen agreed and conceded the exemption to the tributary Indians of the town of San Luis de Pecaya.[98]

What exactly was José Leonardo Chirino proposing to the Indian headman? First, he mentioned that he was working to eliminate the hardships that were oppressing blacks and Indians alike, ostensibly referring to taxes. Then, he asked for recruits to join him in his march to the city to "to present their demands." At no point did he mention establishing a republic or overthrowing the colonial system, or even killing white males; he seemed more concerned with enlarging the ranks of his movement in order to push the authorities to fulfill their demands. Finally, he mentioned that, if the movement succeeded, the Indians would be freed from belated tribute payments. Here, Chirino's intentions seem less radical than pragmatic. It is important to remember that, for months, José Leonardo had asked his wife's master, Josef Tellería, to intercede with the local government in order to reduce taxes, and although Tellería had sent a letter asking for consideration, he did not succeed. The failure of this first attempt apparently did not discourage Chirino from seeking ways to continue negotiating with the authorities. In a second attempt, he decided to organize a larger movement in order to present his demands directly to the local government.[99]

For three months, the government searched for José Leonardo Chirino. He was finally found in the town of Baragua, approximately sixty miles south of the sierra of San Luis, at the end of July 1795. On August 1, 1795, Chirino was taken to Coro and imprisoned in the house of Lieutenant Ramírez, where colonial authorities interrogated him. Although his testimony is lost and can only be deduced from the early study by Pedro Arcaya, we have the testimonies of others who were directly informed of José Leonardo's declarations, and it is possible to identify some commonalities between the sources. One of these witnesses was don Gerardo Tinoco, a white militiaman appointed by Venezuela's captain general to investigate the causes of the rebellion and the involvement of the indigenous population. Tinoco's account is particularly interesting because he was very critical of the local government of Coro: he denounced the abuses of tax collectors and accused Ramírez of not following legal procedure and deciding cases arbitrarily.[100] In his report, Tinoco commented that he was in Coro when colonial authorities began interrogating Chirino. Apparently, Chirino immediately confessed that he had organized a movement with the support of three white men in Coro: his wife's master, Josef Tellería; a foreign friend of Tellería named don Josef Nicolás Martínez; and the lawyer Pedro Chirino. Pedro Chirino, according to José Leonardo, had been in contact with some Frenchmen ("los franceses") and was willing to give the city to them.[101] Tinoco mentioned that local authorities were scandalized by Chirino's confessions. In fact, during the twenty days Chirino was imprisoned in Ramírez's house, Coro's judges, secretaries, and even two priests tried to persuade José Leonardo to change his harmful declaration, but José Leonardo insisted on implicating the three white men in the rebellion. He repeated his testimony to judge Antonio Flores, who had come to ratify his declaration.[102]

According to Arcaya, once in Caracas Chirino declared that there was great anger at tax collectors in Coro, whose abuse of power had impoverished local producers and muleteers.[103] José Leonardo discussed the situation with his wife's master, Josef Tellería, who, with the support of the Coro city council, presented a formal report to the captain general.[104] Apparently, Tellería had had several conversations with José Leonardo and sympathized with his frustration. Chirino also recounted that in 1794 a Mexican visitor named Josef Nicolás Martínez had spent several months at Tellería's hacienda, where José Leonardo and his wife worked. José Leonardo apparently first learned about the French Revolution and the slave rebellions in Saint-Domingue in conversations with Tellería and Martínez, who talked openly about the end of the ancien régime in France and of new laws that proclaimed equality and freedom for the whole population. Apparently, the people of the serranía also shared rumors and fantasized about the French invading Coro, bringing their ideas and their new laws to the mainland.[105]

Discontent over new taxes and the royal tax agents' abuses, a rumored decree of emancipation, and talk of revolution on foreign shores compounded the sense of injustice among slaves and free blacks in the Serranía de Coro. Together, these factors probably motivated José Leonardo Chirino and others to plan an insurrection that would begin with a dance on the night of May 10 at La Macanilla. According to Arcaya, after the initial insurrection at La Macanilla, Chirino followed a careful plan to distribute his leaders (*cabecillas*) among the other haciendas of the region, where they would invite other slaves to rebel. As part of the plan, José Leonardo asked another leader, Juan Cristóbal Acosta, to take some of the rebels to the city. Meanwhile, he would continue gathering more rebels in the serranía and would join Acosta later to confront the colonial government.[106]

According to Arcaya, Chirino delivered an eloquent defense of his actions before the royal audiencia, insisting that he had never condoned violence toward whites and that the slaves' goal was merely to "present their demands to the authorities." In short, he depicted the social movement as an act of negotiation. He apparently added that blacks were not the only ones angry with the Spanish government; he had heard many white masters—including his wife's master—criticizing the local government and its abuses. The rebels had indeed committed crimes, José Leonardo admitted, but violence was by no means the primary intention of the movement.[107]

Other elements of Chirino's actions seem to support this rendering of his testimony. Did the Coro rebels really want to create a republic? This was not what José Leonardo proposed to the chief of Pecaya. On the other hand, had the rebels been interested in forming a republic right away, they would hardly have sent an emissary to negotiate or present demands. Instead, they would have confronted the troops directly in order to take control of the city from the first moment. None of the firsthand witnesses testified to the rebels' desire to create a republic, and yet it is clear that the rebels sought a fundamental restructuring of society: one in which they could be free and would not pay taxes.

If we read the witnesses' testimonies alongside the remaining traces of José Leonardo Chirino's declaration, a new relationship between Coro and Saint-Domingue begins to emerge. It has little to do with the creation of a republic, or with racial warfare and violence; it is grounded instead in the vast space for negotiation that rebellions opened for free blacks and slaves in Saint-Domingue. Anyone familiar with the history of the Haitian Revolution knows that from August 1791 until the emancipation decree of 1794, and perhaps even later, until the declaration of independence in 1804, black rebels in Saint-Domingue sought to negotiate with almost every figure of power they encountered: French colonial authorities, French commissioners, and Spanish and English supporters. Laurent Dubois notes that, from the very beginning of the insurrection, rebels presented their demands to the authorities in terms of an exchange: "One group approached a French officer and told him that they would surrender if 'all the slaves should be made free.'"[108] Such processes of negotiation took place over long periods of time, often overseen by different insurgent leaders such as Jean-François Papillon, Georges Biassou, Charles Belair, Jean Guyambois, and Toussaint Louverture. French commissioners, including Léger-Félicité Sonthonax and Étienne Polverel, knew all too well that they had been sent by the National Assembly to negotiate with black leaders. Although the terms of the negotiations changed over time and depended on several factors, it was ultimately clear that the insurrection had permanently opened new spaces for communication and negotiation between blacks and whites, slaves and free men. Indeed, insurgents soon began to phrase their demands in the language of republican rights enshrined by the French Revolution.[109] While the whites of Coro saw in Saint-Domingue an image of wanton violence and destruction, free blacks and slaves may have perceived something quite different—a window for negotiation and a framework for contention.

It remains unclear whether any whites were implicated in the rebellion. By mentioning them in his testimony, however, José Leonardo emphasized yet another connection between Coro and Saint-Domingue: it was with these white men that José Leonardo first learned about the French Revolution and the rebellions of Saint-Domingue. Moreover, these men were supposedly sufficiently discontented with the local administration that they were willing to support him with the "help of the French." As in Saint-Domingue, many blamed the insurrection in the serranía on irresponsible white planters who had spread the ideals of the French Revolution among their slaves. If revolutionary ideals had brought whites and blacks together in Saint-Domingue, would they not have the same effect in Coro?

The documentary sources on the Coro rebellion, fragmentary though they are, reveal a palimpsest of overlapping discourses. On the one hand, an "official discourse" highlighted the rebels' intention to create a republic under the banner of the "French Laws." On the other, the narratives of white witnesses characterized the rebels as violent hooligans hell-bent on exterminating white men and possessing white women. Finally, the accounts of other witnesses, mostly disinterested third parties, suggest that the uprising was part of a larger plan that would involve negotiation with the local government to eliminate taxes and abolish slavery. All of these narratives, however, emphasize the connection between Coro and Saint-Domingue, albeit in very different ways. It is clear that slaves and free blacks in colonial Spanish America had sufficient reasons to resist power and oppression, but the information they used to rebel was as important as the actions they took.[110] Throughout this chapter, I have shown that rebels could have used the reference of Saint-Domingue to reimagine their relationship to whites, to conceive of themselves as political agents and ultimately as forceful negotiators.

Lasting Effects: Repression, Control, and Fear

Venezuelan colonial authorities used representations of "violent black insurgents" as grounds for repressing the rebellion and punishing its instigators: they systemically tortured the rebels and dismembered and decapitated their bodies. On the morning of December 17, 1796, José Leonardo Chirino was publicly executed in Caracas. After he was hanged, his hands and head were removed from his warm body and placed in separate boxes. The head was packed in salt in an iron cage and displayed on the road between Caracas and Coro. Chirino's hands were sent to officials in Coro and displayed at sites where whites had been murdered and where blacks could see the terrible consequences of insubordination.[111] The execution of the rebel leader thus became a public spectacle that symbolized the power of the colonial state to punish and instill fear. The dismemberment of Chirino's body symbolized the brutal dismemberment of the rebels' imagined political body and served as a warning to all those who dared to challenge the Spanish king and the colonial government.

Relatives of the rebels were also targets of state violence. Chirino's wife, María Dolores, and his sister were publicly flogged and expelled from the Province of Coro. Chirino's daughter and two sons were separated from their mother and sold to different masters. Sixty-four free blacks were sentenced to naval imprisonment for a period of ten years. Several dozen free and enslaved blacks and indigenous people were sentenced to hard labor, while others were exiled to different provinces throughout Venezuela.

By brutalizing and dismembering the bodies of the rebels and humiliating their relatives, Spanish officials expressed the sovereign's power to not only restore order but to literally dismantle the political aspirations of the insurgency. Chirino's mutilated body became an immediately recognizable image, intended to evoke feelings of abhorrence and fear among the local population.[112] After the rebellion, colonial officials redesigned the crest of the city of Coro: three decapitated black heads were placed above the image of the city's patron, Santa Ana de Coro. The royal emblem was thus visually transformed so people in Coro would never forget the abominable acts of these black insurgents. In these ways, white elites and officials began to strategically shape how the event was to be remembered. In addition, the colonial state forbade locals from memorializing the executed rebels and even prohibited the inhabitants of Coro from mentioning the rebellion in public.[113]

In a letter addressed to the Audiencia of Caracas in December 1796—one and a half years after the rebellion—Venezuela's governor proclaimed that the real cause of the Coro rebellion had been "the negligence of the masters of the Haciendas of the Valley, who have not provided slaves with the necessary Christian and political education and care." "Abandoned to their passions," the slaves of the region "violently razed to the ground everything they encountered."[114] To prevent similar uprisings, the governor recommended that the Crown vigilantly guard against the spread of seditious ideas from the revolutionized Atlantic that lapped at Venezuela's shores; he also suggested strategies for monitoring—through a subtle form of "education"—the local black population.

In fact, the authorities and the elites of greater Coro did take measures to prevent conspiracies among the black population. White elites soon lost trust in their slaves, leading to a decrease in voluntary manumission. In the period 1750–1810, there were 289 cases of manumission in Coro; 47 percent of these cases were "manumission by testament."[115] Between the years 1795 and 1799, however, there was not a single case of manumission in the region. Clearly, whites had either lost confidence in their slaves or sought to punish them for their rebelliousness.[116]

Colonial authorities also established a new military command in the region of Coro and enacted new laws regarding the functioning of haciendas, the treatment of slaves, and the presence of the church in the serranía district. By the end of October 1798, a royal decree made Andrés Boggiero the new commander of Coro, the official responsible for maintaining the military, political, and civil order of the region. This same decree contained forty-seven articles, each directed at different members of the community, from shopkeepers to heads of household, overseers, hacendados, free blacks, and slaves. One of the articles restricted the festivities of blacks, "who every Saturday night and even on weekdays get together to dance and sing." If given permission by the commander to congregate, the slaves were to "talk and sing in our language, which is well known by them."[117] Another article ordered the establishment of a Catholic church in the Valley of Curimagua, where the insurrection took place, and frequent visits by priests to say Mass and teach the Christian doctrine to the local black population, so that the communities "might live in order and appropriate subordination." Likewise, the royal decree suggested that masters restrict meetings between slaves and free blacks in the region, especially if they were not married, and encouraged free blacks to live in the recently founded town of Caburo, "where there is a Church, and whence they could go every day to the Valley in order to earn their *jornales* [day wages]."[118] Finally, the decree contained a warning: "The Commander will take all the necessary measures to prevent free mulattos, zambos, and blacks from perverting the slaves of this region, over whom they have had great influence until recently. This influence was the main cause of the black insurrection of 1795."[119]

Colonial authorities understood that they needed to increase their vigilance over Coro's black population. However, there was another group of measures directed at controlling the authorities of the region, especially tax collectors, administrators of the royal treasury offices, and lawyers. These articles ordered tax collectors to collect only the commercial taxes, tributes, or duties (*aranceles*) approved by the king. The articles also charged the commander with preventing abuses on the part of tax collectors. Several articles sought to reform judicial procedures, giving a central role to the Audiencia of Caracas, which was tasked with ensuring that the local court followed appropriate legal procedures, especially in criminal cases. In particular, the decree emphasized the importance of written records: "Secretaries must take down written testimony of any civil or criminal case, and the report should be sent directly to the Royal Audiencia." All these articles suggest that the new captain general, Manuel de Guevara y Vasconcelos, knew about the extrajudicial measures taken by Lieutenant Ramírez during the rebellion.

The rebellion deepened feelings of mistrust while increasing friction between whites and blacks in Coro. For years, people in Coro silently remembered its effects and remained aware of any sign that could evoke an insurgent movement. Coro was profoundly impacted by the rebellion of 1795; the white population remained immersed in a deep fear of racial war. In February 1801, don Agustín Yraola, a serranía hacendado, reported that the news of Toussaint's invasion of the Spanish part of Santo Domingo had spread to Coro, and that local blacks joyfully repeated refrains about Toussaint and his triumphs.[120] A month later, this same hacendado expressed his worries to the governor of Coro: "Slaves and colored people in the serranía were joyfully celebrating the invasion of Santo Domingo by black Tussain [sic]."[121] As a result, white families of the serranía fled to the city in fear.

In April 1806, Francisco de Miranda, a Venezuelan who had fought in both the American and French Revolutions, attempted to land on the Venezuelan coast near Ocumare with a small multinational force that he called "the Colombian Army." His idea was to enter the South American mainland through Venezuela in order to begin a movement to liberate the continent from Spanish oppression and to establish a republican government. A spy from Trinidad had warned colonial authorities in Venezuela about Miranda's plans, and officials strategically deployed two Spanish coast guard vessels, which repelled Miranda's expedition. Three months later, Miranda landed with his forces in the port of La Vela de Coro and marched twenty miles inland until they reached the city of Coro. When Miranda and his forces reached the city's outskirts, they found it abandoned, the inhabitants apparently having fled for fear that republican heretics would rob and kill them.[122] Coro remained profoundly impacted by a slave rebellion that had left the white population terrified of "French Laws" and racial war, and the population of color beaten down by colonial state repression.

During Venezuela's independence movement, Coro remained a royalist holdout: between 1810 and 1821, *corianos* repeatedly declared their loyalty to King Ferdinand VII. Coro's royalism during the wars of independence should not lead us to deny the impact of Saint-Domingue and its revolutionary narratives on the region. On the contrary, this continued desire for Crown protection and authority is one reason why we need to critically revisit the slave rebellion of 1795, its effects, and the contrasting revolutionary narratives that emerged from it.

CHAPTER 5

A Revolutionary Barbershop

Rumors, Texts, and Reading Networks in
the La Guaira Conspiracy of 1797

ON JULY 13, 1797, THE CAPTAIN GENERAL OF VENEZUELA, DON PEDRO Carbonell, first heard the news about an evolving republican movement in which hundreds of people from Caracas and La Guaira were supposedly implicated. Rumor of the conspiracy traveled through circuitous—and often surprising—channels. Manuel Montesinos y Rico, a merchant in Caracas and a participant in the movement, told his barber, Juan José Chirinos, who was also a pardo soldier, that a group of people in La Guaira and Caracas were planning a republican movement based on the principles of equality and liberty. Inviting his barber to join the movement, Montesinos provided Chirinos with a handwritten copy of a republican song, the "Soneto Americano," encouraging him to copy it and pass it along to others who might join the movement.[1] The song's lyrics are as follows:

The Whites, the Blacks,
Indians, and Pardos,
Let's admit all
That we are brothers,
That we are all united
With a common interest

To make war against Despotism.
Long live our Pueblo.²

What Montesinos did was not particularly risky. In the port town of La Guaira, the movement had a significant number of supporters, and barbers and artisans were among the social groups most attracted to such a political project. Montesinos probably thought that the pardo barber in Caracas would be eager to share the news with those of his class and status. Unfortunately for him and his collaborators, Montesinos was absolutely wrong.³

Chirinos immediately shared the rumor of insurrection with two other barbers and militiamen, Francisco Javier de León and Juan Antonio Ponte. Ponte passed the news along to Fray Juan Antonio Ravelo, a priest in the convent of San Francisco. That very afternoon, accompanied by the three barbers, Ravelo went to the house of the priest Juan Vicente Echeverría, former dean of the University of Caracas, and told him about the planned insurgency. Echeverría recommended that they keep the rumor secret, while he would communicate the news to the governor, who would decide on a course of action. However, Chirinos also shared the information with another priest, don Domingo Lander, who together with Echeverría and Ravelo went to the bishop's house. There, the three priests told the bishop everything they knew about the conspiracy and the danger it represented to the Catholic religion, the Spanish monarchy, and the people of the captaincy. They ultimately decided to relay the information to Governor Carbonell.⁴

The night of July 13, Carbonell received the "terrible news." Concerned about the danger represented by this republican movement, he conferred with some of the highest colonial authorities—the king's lieutenant, don Joaquín de Zubillaga; the regent of the Audiencia of Caracas, don Antonio López Quintana; and the audiencia judge, don Juan de Pedroza. Together, they decided to arrest Montesinos and begin a formal inquiry in order to root out the conspiracy's participants, and to elucidate their origins, ideals, and procedures. Several members of the audiencia and other colonial authorities formed what was known as a Real Acuerdo, a group of judges (*oidores*) and commissioners responsible for overseeing the inquiry. Members of the Real Acuerdo soon discovered that the movement had three leaders: a Spanish prisoner named Juan Picornell, plus two white creoles: don José María España and don Manuel Gual. In an early report, the commissioners ascribed the popularity of the movement to several factors, including the French and

American Revolutions and the " terrible political confusion" sown by recent revolts in the Caribbean region.[5]

Soon, the Real Acuerdo discovered that the conspiracy had its origin in the port of La Guaira, thereby confirming the suspicion that the Venezuelan coast had been ideologically contaminated by the constant flow of people and ideas entering the port. In fact, members of the audiencia placed particular blame on the significant population of foreigners from different regions of the Caribbean who had reached La Guaira between 1793 and 1796. They contended that these foreigners spread ideas of liberty and equality, thereby fostering a permissive and liberal environment in which revolutionary voices were frequently heard on the streets and in public spaces. Furthermore, they claimed that written texts from France and Saint-Domingue had helped to spread these "false seeds of equality and liberty . . . introducing an anarchy, which promised an imaginary happiness that seemed real to all simple-minded people." For the colonial authorities, it was clear that the flexible and liberal atmosphere of La Guaira was fertile ground for the emergence of a movement that followed the French model and went against "the monarchical system, slavery, and the harmony and order of society."[6]

The main goals of the republican movement were diverse. They included the establishment of free trade, the abolition of slavery with compensation to slave owners, the elimination of Indian tributes, and the abolition of taxes (especially the estanco, taxes imposed on foodstuffs, and commercial alcabalas). The movement also sought to foster harmony among races: whites, pardos, Indians, and blacks were seen as "brothers in Jesus Christ." Although they were white creoles, both Gual and España obtained remarkable support from many pardos and poor whites, small merchants, royal officials, soldiers, and artisans from La Guaira and Caracas.[7]

Historical studies of the so-called Gual and España conspiracy abound. However, as Ramón Aizpurua has recently argued, many of these works have unduly simplified the conspiracy by depicting it as a pre-independence movement, more radical and republican than the successful independence movement of 1811.[8] Studying the republican movement of La Guaira only in light of the subsequent independence movement, however, obscures and simplifies not only its real motivations and achievements but also its original social composition and its leaders' strategies for disseminating information among popular groups. Venezuela's independence movement was organized mostly by white creoles who struggled to convince various popular groups to join them; traditional studies of the La Guaira movement have sought to connect its white creole leaders with the subsequent leaders of Venezuelan independence without analyzing the unique social composition of the movement and its strong connections to the French Caribbean.

More recently, Venezuelan historians have analyzed some of the artificial threads linking the Gual and España conspiracy to the independence struggles of 1811, providing a more cautious, detailed, and fair-minded interpretation of the movement itself.[9] It seems impossible to understand Venezuela's turn toward independence in 1811 without analyzing the social composition, political implications, and effects of the La Guaira conspiracy, precisely because discursively the movement offered something that the long and bloody process of independence found very hard to offer: racial equality and the abolition of slavery. Here I provide an analysis of the distinct ways in which different actors participating in the La Guaira movement shared a political language and common networks for the transmission of information that sought to integrate a divided society. To this end, I analyze the texts, discursive formulas, and communication strategies used by these actors in order to recruit people of different races, social statuses, and educational backgrounds—and to keep them united by way of a common political cause.[10]

The official records of the inquiry reveal that, while planning their movement, the La Guaira insurgents used a variety of sources and media to spread political information and create a dynamic social network of communication. Revolutionary texts and newspapers from France, Spain, the United States, Trinidad, and the French Caribbean colonies circulated among different groups of people involved in the conspiracy; these same groups also produced a considerable number of texts designed to instruct their followers in the republican principles of the movement. Among these documents were proclamations of insurrection, poems, stories, songs, and translations and adaptations of the "Declaration of the Rights of Man." These texts provide a helpful vantage point for analyzing the insurgents' diverse strategies for imparting political knowledge and galvanizing their supporters.[11] This chapter analyzes the rebels' strategies for disseminating information and their attempts to produce a common language for political opposition. In particular, I show how the leaders of the movement, who frequently met at a barbershop, repurposed political ideas from the revolutionary Atlantic to support their cause and designed original strategies to recruit followers from different races and social strata. Insurgents created texts that sought to adapt republican ideas to local social and economic circumstances, and through innovative narrative strategies made them accessible to a semiliterate population of color. In this context, I argue that the La Guaira movement's social networks developed around multimedia sources of information that were crucial to the formation of an emergent public sphere. This public sphere, which escaped the control of elites and colonial authorities, was built not upon printing shops or local newspapers controlled by white creoles but upon effective circuits of reading and sharing manuscripts, stories, and songs among socially diverse participants arranged in their own networks.

Centered on an analysis of local practices of reading and information sharing—and not merely of printed texts or newspapers—this chapter offers a new means to understand the emergence of the public sphere in colonial Latin America. Many studies of Latin American independence have argued that the demand for information about the crisis of the Spanish monarchy of 1808 and its reverberations triggered the proliferation of public spaces for political debate. François-Xavier Guerra, for example, explores the emergence of an early form of public opinion in different cities of Latin America between 1808 and 1814, a period that witnessed the promulgation of the free press and that was characterized by the proliferation of newspapers in the region.[12] This chapter provides an array of evidence that, years before the independence movement, an early public sphere emerged in Venezuela, which responded to the original dynamics of information sharing and the circulation of texts that allowed the formation of social spaces where people openly debated ideas of revolution, equality, liberty, loyalism, and republican principles, questioning the status quo and the local structures of power.[13]

In examining the texts produced by the La Guaira insurgents, this chapter also analyzes the movement's political base. My goal is to demonstrate how reverberations from political events in France and also the French Caribbean emerged in the La Guaira movement. Most Venezuelan historians assume that the movement's white leaders—Juan Picornell, Manuel Gual, and José María España—were directly and exclusively influenced by French revolutionary ideas; these same historians have paid little attention to the pardos and free blacks who participated alongside them, to their sources of information, and to their previous interactions with French and Franco-Caribbean visitors, prisoners, slaves, and refugees.[14] These equal instigators of the La Guaira movement offered a radically new view of racial and social equality dependent on the emergence of a civic corpus that integrated the whole population, and this original view of a multiracial, united society was deeply influenced by political events developing in the Caribbean, where promulgations of racial equality were so central. Manuscripts, adaptations and translations of the "Declaration of the Rights of Man," short stories and dialogues, oral readings, and revolutionary songs performed in an overcrowded barbershop were far more important than any French or American revolutionary text. These locally produced texts helped the people of La Guaira to envision a possible future for themselves, a future without a tyrannical king and without social privileges, "where people could elect the judges themselves and live in liberty and equality as brothers in Jesus Christ"[15]

A Revolutionary Port: Caribbean Connections

Bathed by the Caribbean Sea and not far from Caracas, La Guaira became one of Venezuela's most important ports during the seventeenth century, when cacao exports grew rapidly. At the beginning of eighteenth century, the Compañía Guipuzcoana set up shop in La Guaira. As part of a Bourbon experiment, the company was granted a monopoly on shipping and commercializing cacao in the Spanish market. It was also expected to curb contraband trade, long prevalent in Venezuela.[16] During the company period, the port of La Guaira became an important trading center through which manufactured European goods, cloth, and wheat entered Venezuela and from which tropical agricultural products such as tobacco, indigo, and cacao were sent overseas. The influence of this resource-intensive economy was impressive, as it transformed the port of La Guaira into the most dynamic trading center in the region. This key role persisted after the company's fall, as trade between Spain and La Guaira represented 90 percent of the legal commercial activity of Venezuela during the last decade of the eighteenth century.[17]

As noted in chapter 3, La Guaira was also a major site of social interaction between people of different origins, "qualities," occupations, and nationalities. People from different regions of the Atlantic world arrived in La Guaira to trade or to settle in the Captaincy General of Venezuela. During the eighteenth century, La Guaira was a place where diverse merchandise and captive Africans were traded, and where people of different backgrounds, origins, and statuses met and exchanged information and ideas.

Like many other Caribbean port cities, La Guaira expanded not only as a result of its central position in Venezuela's legal trade but also because of its military role in the defense of the Spanish Main. In the wake of attacks by buccaneers and by English, Dutch, and French naval forces, La Guaira was

Figure 6. De la Guayra, on the Spanish Main, by G. T. Richards (1808), etching, aquatint, work on paper, 14.5 × 24.9 centimeters. Colección Mercantil. Courtesy of Mercantil Arte y Cultura, Caracas. Image by Walter Otto.

transformed into a heavily fortified and walled city. As a major gateway to the South American interior, La Guaira played a fundamental role in the military protection of the region, and the commanders of Puerto Cabello and La Guaira were among the highest-ranked military posts in Venezuela. Fortifications were not entirely new. Early in the seventeenth century, colonial authorities recognized the importance of protecting La Guaira from possible invasions and of combating smuggling by buccaneers and pirates. Between 1660 and 1700, various fortresses were built in and around the town, among them Catia La Mar, Del Peñon, El Colorado, El Zamuro, and El Gavilán.[18]

The eighteenth century was marked by major new investments in the fortification of La Guaira. Royal fort-building projects provided employment to hundreds of local workers and artisans and necessitated the purchase of many slaves. In 1764, Governor and Captain General José Solano wrote: "The port of La Guaira is defended by several batteries on the shore, and these are connected by a wall to two more batteries on the hills above town." Between 1790 and 1799, approximately eight hundred militiamen (infantry and artillery officials, noncommissioned officers, and paid soldiers) served in La Guaira.[19]

The French visitor Jean-François Dauxion-Lavaysse visited La Guaira during the first decade of the nineteenth century and described it as a "badly built town, but tolerably well fortified." He mentioned that La Guaira was the commercial port of the city of Caracas, "separated from it by a distance of five leagues that could be pleasantly traveled in a single day." According to Dauxion-Lavaysse, in 1807 the town had a population of approximately seven thousand souls, and a garrison of eight hundred men.[20] The British merchant and traveler Robert Semple spent some days in La Guaira in 1810. He wrote: "The population of La Guaira is reckoned to be about eight thousand, of all colors. Of these, comparatively few are Europeans, or even white creoles, a far greater proportion being people of color."[21]

During the last decades of the eighteenth century, the population of La Guaira mirrored the social composition of the rest of Venezuela's central coast: free people of African descent (pardos, morenos, and mulattos) made up an important proportion, approximately 50 percent; a little more than 20 percent were black slaves; approximately 10 percent were Indians; and some 15 percent were whites (Spanish and creoles). The relative size of the free and enslaved populations varied between rural regions and urban centers. Cacao haciendas among the coastal valleys had a larger proportion of black slaves, whereas in urban centers the proportion of whites and freemen of mixed race was greater.[22]

Most of the elite white householders of La Guaira devoted themselves to supervising their haciendas in the nearby countryside, while they actively participated in the commercial activities of the port. In 1780, once the Compañía Guipuzcoana had ceased its operations and free trade was established, the number of Spanish immigrants and white creoles participating in commercial activities increased dramatically. With the establishment of free trade, many of these white men, former employees of the Basque company, gained economic independence and political power and sought to control the operations of the port, establishing a decisive military influence.[23]

A significant population of free blacks produced marketable goods, worked as sailors, and provided diverse services in La Guaira. There were artisans—mostly blacks, pardos, and zambos—who worked as carpenters, masons, tailors, shoemakers, and barbers. Some were small merchants and shopkeepers (pulperos and bodegueros), and all participated in the economic activities of the town. There were also independent peasants, sharecroppers, and muleteers who transported fruits and vegetables from nearby haciendas to La Guaira. Many also transported goods and people from La Guaira to Caracas and back. There were free black women who worked as domestic servants, laundresses, and seamstresses. Enslaved men, women, and children worked on nearby haciendas, or as domestic servants, builders, petty traders, fishermen, or stevedores.[24]

As in other urban centers in Venezuela, tensions emerged among these diverse social groups. Frictions often emanated from their differential influence on political decision making. Much of the political tension of the late eighteenth century can be ascribed to a colonial social order based on status inequality. Outside influences could exacerbate the situation. As seen in previous chapters, the presence of almost one thousand prisoners, refugees, and slaves from Martinique, Saint-Domingue, and Santo Domingo during the years 1793–1795 did not pass unnoticed among the inhabitants of La Guaira. Townsfolk frequently held discussions regarding events in the French colonies, taking every opportunity to express their discontent with their own system and emphasizing the need to change it. Other observers emphasized the potential danger represented by visitors from France or Saint-Domingue. Such visitors threatened the tranquility of the port and made revolutionary contagion imminent.[25]

Once Gual and España's political movement was unmasked in 1797, the connections between discontented locals and uninvited Franco-Caribbean visitors became even clearer. A report sent by the Audiencia of Caracas to Spain in August 1797—three weeks after the conspiracy was uncovered—stated that La Guaira was threatened by the presence of "more than nine hundred" prisoners and slaves who had been sent by the governor of Santo Domingo. The report argued that, despite their isolation, these captives were in regular contact with local Spaniards: "Some of these [Spaniards] loved them, and the words and phrases of these prisoners highly influenced them, especially the young population of both sexes and from all classes."[26] José María Reina, La Guaira's official port accountant in 1796, noted that it was necessary "to control the vices so typical of port towns, where the diversity of nationalities promotes corruption, disorder, and insubordination." He observed that colonial rule was already flexible and permissive, "but what ended up opening the floodgates of popular passion was the arrival of more than nine hundred French republican prisoners from Santo Domingo, who, despite [official] vigilance, had relatively free relations with the general public."[27]

In 1797, the priest and dean of the University of Caracas, José Ignacio Moreno, wrote a long report about what he thought were the real motivations of the "Conspiracy of 1797." He recommended measures to prevent future insurgencies. Moreno argued that the prisoners and slaves sent from Santo Domingo to La Guaira fanned the fires of sedition among the population of the port, which since 1794 had been receiving news of revolution from France and the turbulent French colonies. In his report, Moreno decried the supposedly royalist Frenchmen who now could not contain their liberal ideas:

> The Frenchmen who came to the Spanish lands told their stories and whined about them, but in their private conversations they vomited fire against our Gospel, mocking and degrading the right subordination of our slaves and of the common people.[28]

Numerous witnesses confirmed the significant influence of French refugees, prisoners, and slaves on the people of La Guaira between 1793 and 1796. Spaniards, white creoles, and pardos attested that people in La Guaira were in fact in continuous contact with the French prisoners and were receptive to their political ideas. Witnesses declared that some people in the port even had close friendships with the prisoners. José Manuel del Pino, a pardo tailor and soldier accused of being involved in the conspiracy, declared that Narciso del Valle, a pardo barber (and soldier) implicated in the movement, was friends with two French officials who were imprisoned, "one Monsieur Franquá and another one named Rouseau, or Rossel."[29] Another pardo, José Cordero, declared that Valle commented that some of the French prisoners intended to provoke a revolution in the province. In a revealing testimony, the accused José María España asserted that when the French prisoners of Santo Domingo arrived:

> They started talking favorably about the Republican government and the new system adopted by the French, about the articles that emanated from the convention, and consequently they showed their hatred for our constitution. In this way, they expressed themselves to the pueblo, but particularly to those who were in direct contact with them, such as Narciso del Valle, José de Rusiñol, don Joaquin Sorondo, don Manuel Gual, don Josef Antonio, and myself.[30]

In this confession, España mentioned the names of those individuals who were part of the frequent meetings and discussion circles focused on political matters: people who attended readings, shared manuscripts, copied and circulated texts, and became involved in the planning of the insurgent movement. José de Rusiñol, a sergeant in the Caracas Battalion stationed in La Guaira, who was accused of being one of the leaders of the movement, commented that he saw a "general inclination of the people of La Guaira to embrace the maxims of liberty and equality, observing that people talked openly and without any caution about the establishment of a Republic."[31] Narciso del Valle also declared that Sergeant Rusiñol used to go to his barbershop, where he always talked about political matters, stating that "citizens should have the power to legislate and appoint judges . . . and that these were inalienable rights given by the Supreme Being."[32]

A unique feature of the La Guaira political movement was its socially diverse composition: Spanish officials and port authorities, white creole merchants and hacendados, white and pardo shopkeepers and artisans, pardo and free black workers; all joined the movement.[33] What in such a hierarchical colonial society could have made these people come together to plan a "republican movement for all"?[34] Certainly, the republican ideology and effective strategies of circulation of ideas might have helped people from different and contrasting social groups find a common political and social cause, but the large presence of a multiracial group of people from the French Caribbean in La Guaira and their daily interactions might have also offered a vivid example of what equality would look like. A local pardo carpenter and soldier named José Antonio Noguera, for example, declared that in his free time he used to visit Narciso del Valle's barbershop. One day, he was standing at the door of the shop with the pardo sergeant José Cordero when they saw a group of French and Franco-Caribbean men pass by. They both noticed with surprise that some of the whites were "tied" (*engarzados*), meaning they were walking arm in arm, with the mulattos. Cordero praised these fraternal physical expressions among Frenchmen of different "qualities," while Noguera disclosed his skepticism and asked: "How many mulattos have been appointed as presidents in France?"[35] Despite the differences of opinion between these two Venezuelan pardos, this episode shows how the simple presence of Franco-Caribbean individuals in La Guaira and their daily interactions produced reactions among the population, even provoking debates about the notions of equality and fraternity, allowing locals to imagine possible scenarios for themselves. On many occasions, colonial authorities showed great concern about the presence of Franco-Caribbean visitors in La Guaira and the "harmful impressions" they caused among the residents of the port.[36]

Social Networks, Reading Circles, and the Planning of a Conspiracy

According to historian Casto Fulgencio López, there were two main groups supporting the La Guaira movement: one in the port city itself, led by José María España, and another in Caracas, led by Manuel Gual. However, a closer look at court records reveals a more complex web of social relations upon which the movement was built. Aizpurua's study of La Guaira's social networks provides us with a clear idea of how the different social groups came together, the threads that connected them, and their roles in the political plan. Aizpurua argues that the groups corresponded not only to geographic areas, such as La Guaira and Caracas, or particular leaders, such as España or Gual, but to other criteria like occupation, calidad, education, and family connections. Traditional social bonds were initially important forces of synergy among potential participants, but innovative ideas that challenged the colonial order made their way into these meetings, where whites and mulattos shared the same table and discussed the need to "end the fanatic custom of considering one better than another, because there is no better distinction than that of one's own merit, and we need to treat ourselves as brothers."[37] From the beginning, participants in the La Guaira movement made clear that in order to build a true republic, they needed to eradicate absurd social distinctions and privileges and recognize the inherent brotherhood that transcended calidad and status.

High-ranking white Spanish and creole officials, along with certain hacendados and merchants, rallied around José María España, a white creole who was born in La Guaira in 1761 but had lived in Bayonne, France. España was himself a royal official, serving as corregidor of the small town of Macuto, near La Guaira. He owned and administered several cacao and coffee haciendas in Naiguatá and possessed several houses in the towns of Macuto and La Guaira. He was recognized as an educated and enlightened person with a copious library and diverse intellectual interests.[38]

España brought together a group of people who met to read and lend each other books and documents, and who frequently held discussions about the French and the American Revolutions and about the turbulence in the French colonies. Don Agustín García, commander of La Guaira, attended these meetings until his promotion to the rank of lieutenant colonel. Juan Josef Mendiri, the interim accountant and chief guard of the port, attended the meetings as well and brought European gazettes and newspapers he had collected in the port to share with the group. Patricio Ronán, an Irish lieutenant of the Royal Corps of Engineers and commander-extraordinaire in La Guaira, and Juan Lartigue de Condé, a Frenchman who was also a Corps of Engineers captain in La Guaira, also confessed to having attended these meetings.[39] José de Rusiñol declared that, in these gatherings, they read diverse foreign texts, from newspapers and history books to political proclamations and military manuscripts. Among the texts he listed were *Rights of Man* by Thomas Paine, Edmund Burke's *Reflections on the Revolution in France*, an account of the death of Louis XVI, a history of the revolution in North America, the "Declaration of Independence of the Thirteen United Provinces of America," and the Constitution of the State of Pennsylvania. They also shared several manuscripts produced locally and that successfully spread throughout La Guaira.[40]

Lower-ranking military officials also attended the meetings and contributed to the movement by recruiting people and connecting different groups' leaders. One example was José de Rusiñol, a native of Catalonia and second sergeant of the Caracas veteran battalion stationed in La Guaira. Others included Bonifacio Amezcaray, second lieutenant of the Royal Armada, and Joaquín Sorondo, an employee of the port's royal treasury office.[41]

The white creole Manuel Gual attended some of these meetings and exchanged information and news between the city of Caracas and La Guaira. Gual had been a captain of the veteran battalion of La Guaira but had retired from military service in order to dedicate himself to the administration of a hacienda in Santa Lucía, in the Tuy Valley some twenty miles from Caracas. Gual was also in charge of supervising, along with Patricio Ronán, the construction of forts in La Guaira. He made frequent trips between his hacienda, Caracas, and La Guaira, and was in part responsible for establishing communication networks between the Caracas reading cluster and the one in La Guaira.[42] In Caracas, he met with other white elite families to discuss texts and revolutionary ideas. Gual and other white creoles such as don Juan Manuel Salas, Doctor Luis Peraza Ayala, don Nicolás Ascanio, and don Vicente Estrada clandestinely met in the tavern Los Traposos in Caracas and in the house of a white lady, doña Ana María de Castro.[43] In those meetings, declared a witness, the "attendants openly talked about matters of revolution and liberty, and the formation of a new republican government."[44]

In addition to these high-ranking militiamen in La Guaira, there were other groups of white people who had family or professional connections to the leaders of the movement. Some were merchants, like Juan Xavier Arrambide, Francisco Sinza, Martín Antonio de Goenaga, and the Montesinos y Rico brothers; others were professionals, like Doctor Pedro Canibens (España's brother-in-law), Doctor Juan de la Tasa, the pharmacist Tomás Cardozo, and Domingo Sánchez, an employee in the royal treasury (also España's brother-in-law). All of them attended the meetings and social gatherings that España and Ronán arranged in La Guaira. The location of these meetings varied; sometimes they met in the homes of Ronán and España, while on other occasions they went together on walks to the river, where they had lunch and enjoyed the fresh air. José María Salas confessed that he attended some of these meetings, in which "we talked about news in Spain and France brought by the gacetas and papers that came from Spain and Trinidad."[45]

Another La Guaira–based group of people met to read political texts and discuss recent events in the Atlantic world. They were primarily pardo artisans and soldiers who met at the barbershop of Narciso del Valle, also an official of the pardo battalion of La Guaira. Valle's barbershop, located close to the main church and across the street from the pardo military barracks, was very popular. In his shop, common folk (*gente común*), including people of African descent, read diverse texts and listened to readings about recent events in Europe and the Caribbean colonies. Ten of the sixteen pardos who confessed to involvement in the movement stated that they had ultimately been recruited by Narciso del Valle in his barbershop. José Cordero, a sergeant of the pardo militias, belonged to this circle and was also responsible for establishing close relations with José de Rusiñol, the leader of a group of veteran white militiamen. A diverse group of officials in the local pardo battalion—tailors, carpenters, masons, and soldiers—attended meetings at the barbershop, taking turns reading aloud "papers provided by Rusiñol and Serrano in which the governments of North America or France were praised."[46]

Narciso del Valle also established a close relationship with Lorenzo Acosta, a free black shoemaker and lieutenant of the free blacks in the town of Carayaca, whom Valle even paid to recruit people to the revolutionary cause. According to Acosta, Valle told him that they were planning a republic to "get rid of the sales taxes, the restrictions on selling tobacco, the fees for burials and baptisms, and that everyone will be equals, like they are in

France, they will be ruled by judges elected by themselves, and they will get rid of those who are evil."⁴⁷ Acosta spread the news of a planned revolutionary movement among the people of Carayaca, but he failed to persuade them to travel to La Guaira and join the movement.

In calling the 1797 La Guaira movement the "Gual and España conspiracy," historians have emphasized the planning roles played by these two white creoles, thereby minimizing the important voices and participation of lower-ranking officials and people of African descent.⁴⁸ Aizpurua argues that participants from a diverse array of social backgrounds were brought together thanks to the efforts and connections of six leaders: the pardos Narciso del Valle and José Cordero, the Europeans José de Rusiñol and Patricio Ronán, and the white creoles José María España and Manuel Gual. All of these men encouraged people to read and circulate revolutionary texts, recruited people to attend their meetings and discussions, and opened networks of communication with the purpose of articulating a common political plan. They envisioned a radical movement that would bring much-needed political change to the Captaincy General of Venezuela, erasing racial differences and eliminating unjust social inequalities.

Yet an outsider, the Spanish prisoner Juan Bautista Picornell, also became a key actor in the planning of the movement. On December 3, 1796, Spanish authorities sent Picornell to the already tumultuous port of La Guaira. A member of various scientific and literary societies in Spain, a teacher, and a prolific writer, Picornell had led a group of plotters in a revolutionary movement in Madrid earlier that same year on San Blas Day (February 3). Unhappy authorities referred to the movement as the San Blas conspiracy. Like many other Spanish academics of his time, Picornell had ties to the Freemasons, who had inculcated him in the philosophy of the French Revolution. Thanks to their influence, Picornell soon began to criticize the rule of Charles IV and the absolutist government of his prime minister, Manuel Godoy.⁴⁹

The San Blas conspiracy aimed to overthrow the Bourbon monarchy and establish a republic in its place. The movement was planned with the assistance of other professionals and students such as Manuel Cortés de Campomanes, Juan Manzanares, Sebastián Andrés Aragón, and José Lax. All of them produced texts to encourage people to unite, arm themselves, and join the revolutionary cause. Apparently, by the beginning of 1796, more than three hundred people in Spain had joined the movement. Their plans, however, were uncovered in February 1796, and the insurgents were soon condemned to die in the gallows.⁵⁰

The Spanish government later decided to send the accused, one by one, to the American colonies in order to prevent further ideological contagion on the peninsula. Juan Picornell arrived in La Guaira in December 1796, and Captain General Carbonell ordered him imprisoned and held incommunicado until he could be sent on to Panama. The rest of the conspirators (Sebastián Andrés Aragón, José Lax, Manuel Cortés, and Juan Manzanares) arrived in La Guaira over the course of the next year. By May 1797, the key San Blas agitators had been reunited in the colonial port.[51]

In prison, Juan Picornell was glad to discover that he was not an unwelcome visitor; his jailers became his friends and confidants, and they held frequent conversations about republican and liberal ideas. Seen as victims of Spanish government persecution, the insurgents of San Blas won the trust of local officials who accorded them special treatment, including the privilege of communicating freely with the people of Caracas and La Guaira. Rusiñol, for example, was the one responsible for escorting Picornell from portside to prison cell when he arrived, and, after this initial contact, Rusiñol remained in regular contact with him. He even invited his own friends to visit the illustrious prisoner.[52] Don Pedro Canibens, a doctor at the hospital in La Guaira and España's brother-in-law, also visited Picornell under the pretense of examining him, and he frequently brought his assistant, Juan de la Tasa. Sergeant José Cordero was also allowed to visit Picornell on various occasions, as did Narciso del Valle, ostensibly in order to shave him.

By the beginning of 1797, as Casto Fulgencio López puts it: "Picornell had been interviewed in his jail by almost everybody involved in the conspiracy."[53] In these visits, the locals learned about Picornell's revolutionary ideas. According to those who met with him, Picornell stated that Spain had tyrannized and economically exploited America, that slavery was an outrageous imposition, and that a new, more egalitarian government would liberate America from Spanish oppression. Under the new government, all Venezuelans would be considered equals, and commerce would be open to all nations.[54]

Given the political environment of La Guaira, Picornell possibly realized that the locals were by no means unaware of Atlantic revolutionary ideas, yet he still had to confront the particularities of the Spanish colonial world. The political and economic circumstances in the colonies, particularly in Venezuela, were different from those on the peninsula, as were the social divisions and racial tensions. Picornell was a savvy revolutionary writer, but he was ignorant of local political and social conditions; he had much to learn from his local visitors, and therefore he needed to exchange ideas and information with them. They soon apprised him of their political, social, and economic grievances.[55] Together with his friends in La Guaira, Picornell transformed his prison cell into a revolutionary workshop where the first insurgent texts were outlined, drafted, and revised. These texts soon made their way to Valle's barbershop, España's and Ronán's houses, and the conversations and minds of the avid readers and listeners of La Guaira.[56]

Literary Contagion: The Books of the Conspirators

After identifying the main leaders of the movement, members of the investigative commission, or Real Acuerdo, visited their homes in Caracas, La Guaira, and Santa Lucía in order to seize all texts that might offer additional clues about the planned insurgency. On July 17, 1797, royal official Francisco Espejo and his secretary went to the house of José María España, who had escaped from La Guaira the night before, and began to search for documents and texts in his desk and his library. That same day, the judge, don Antonio Fernández de León, and his secretary searched the house of Manuel Gual in Santa Lucía. Having discovered that Gual had left his hacienda two days earlier, they decided to look for documents and papers. Fernández ordered his officials to seal all the chests found in the house and carry them to Caracas. At the bottom of one chest, in a secret compartment, were some of the most relevant texts of the conspiracy.

Colonial authorities soon discovered that the conspiracy had been no mere improvisation. Numerous documents showed that a group of people had been planning the movement for months. For the authorities, the La Guaira conspiracy seemed to have been devised by people inspired by Enlightenment literature from France and by manuscripts from the French and American Revolutions. New sources, however, showed that for months La Guaira—lacking a printing press or a bookstore—became a center for the exchange of revolutionary information and the production of texts written by Spaniards, white creoles, and pardos who were moved by their own passions, concerns, and political interests.

Both José María España and Manuel Gual were literate and highly educated white creoles who possessed impressive libraries. España had one of the "most notable" libraries in La Guaira, comprising approximately ninety-one titles in two hundred volumes.[57] During a second inspection of España's library on August 8, 1797, Espejo found that the books were kept on cedarwood shelves, clean and neatly organized. The list of books included titles in Spanish, English, and French. The library contained several books written by popular reformist Spanish authors, including the eight volumes of the *Teatro crítico* and the *Cartas eruditas* by Fray Benito Jerónimo Feijóo y Montenegro. On the shelves they also found several books on geography, mathematics, and agriculture, such as *Descripción geográfica de la region magallanica* by Francisco Saija, *Relación histórica del viaje a la América meridional* by Jorge Juan and Antonio de Ulloa, *Diccionario geográfico* by Lorenzo Echard, *Manual de trigonometría* by Pedro Manuel Cedillo, *Naturaleza y virtudes de las plantas* by Francisco Ximénez, and *Tratado del cultivo de tierras* by a French author. There were many books about naval sciences and maritime subjects, and many others on the geography of America and the Antilles. Seven volumes of the famous *Histoire philosophique et politique des établissements et du commerce des européens dans les deux Indes* by Abbé Guillaume Raynal were found there, alongside thick dictionaries of Spanish, French, and English. Of the ninety-one titles, thirty were in French, including books about French politics and the French Revolution. Espejo immediately seized all these books and sent them to Caracas.

In all, España's library looks very similar to the libraries of his contemporaries in the Americas, with several books about politics, economics, commerce, and "useful subjects" such as agriculture, mathematics, and geography, as well as dictionaries. French titles figured significantly among his books; this did not necessarily indicate an inclination toward revolutionary ideas but rather the owner's taste for French literature and Enlightenment themes, very common among colonial elites.[58] With the exception of Raynal's *Histoire philosophique*, none of these books were prohibited by the Spanish Crown or the Inquisition.

A second list, compiled by Espejo and other officials, shows the prohibited books seized by colonial authorities, including those found in the libraries of white conspirators such as España, Gual, the Montesinos y Rico brothers, and Salas. Other individuals, like Juan Josef Mendiri—the port official—collaborated in the collection and dissemination of written materials and gazettes in the port, while Arrambide and Cardozo copied and translated texts and documents that circulated among La Guaira's various social groups. This list not only catalogs the books possessed by some of these leading insurgents but also indicates the kinds of texts that colonial officials considered dangerous.

In September 1802, the Audiencia of Caracas sent a wooden box to Spain containing thirty-eight seditious volumes (see the appendix) in addition to sixty-two copies of a Spanish translation of the "Declaration of the Rights of Man and of the Citizen." Commissioners Antonio Fernández de León and Francisco Espejo had collected these books in the houses of the conspirators during the months of July and August 1797.[59] The list contains eighteen titles. All of the books, with the exception of the sixty-two copies of the "Declaration of the Rights of Man," were written in French and covered diverse fields such as history, politics, agriculture, travelers' chronicles, marine engineering, and philosophy.

The sixty-two copies of "Derechos del hombre y del ciudadano" represent one of the first Spanish translations of the famous "Déclaration des droits de l'homme et du citoyen," written during the French Revolution and adopted by the French National Assembly as a foundational document of the revolution.[60] According to the Audiencia of Caracas, the "Declaration" had the appearance of a small notebook (*librejo* or *cuadernillo*) printed in Trinidad or Guadeloupe, of "the type that commonly circulated in the French colonies and was introduced in Venezuela through Trinidad."[61] According to the text, "the natural and undeniable rights of man" include "liberty, property, security, and resistance to oppression." The declaration called for, among other things, the destruction of aristocratic privileges, freedom, equal rights for all men, and access to public office based on talent. The monarchy was to be limited, and all citizens were to have the right to take part in the legislative process. Colonial authorities believed that this text corrupted the most sacred values of society, and, "through its artificial, weak, and dangerous arguments, confused the reason of men."[62]

The list of volumes seized by the authorities reflects the kind of knowledge that officials saw as the sources of inspiration for the movement. Fernández de León and Espejo declared that they had seized "books prohibited by the State and others that deserve to be prohibited because they contain maxims contrary to our government."[63] However, a close look at the list shows that, by the time authorities seized the volumes, a wider set of concerns had arisen. First, we can perceive a sort of Francophobia whereby any book written in French became a potential source of revolutionary contamination. Resistant to the idea that the movement could have been inspired by local circumstances, officials desperately looked for evidence that could help connect the conspirators to the French revolutionary movement. The sixty-two copies of the "Declaration of the Rights of Man," the works of Jean-Jacques Rousseau, *Histoire philosophique and politique* by Raynal, and *La police de Paris dévoilée* by Pierre Manuel were philosophical texts, which, in words of Roger Chartier, "held up morality and politics, beliefs and authority, to critical examination,"[64] and authorities pointed at them as evident sources of French revolutionary contagion. However, the *Oeuvres choisies* of Jean-Baptiste Rousseau, *Recueil de pieces galantes* by Henriette de Coligny de la Suze and Paul Pellison, and *Histoire de Pierre du Terrail* by Guillaume-François Guyard de Berville were by no means revolutionary texts. Rather, they were works of eighteenth-century French literature on popular "enlightened topics," some of which promoted favorable views of France and the French people, and these positive depictions must have caused concern among the Spanish authorities.

The officials also collected books on topics such as American geography, agriculture, technology, commerce, and administration. These books were seized not because they were considered "revolutionary" but because they broached sensitive topics, such as slavery, labor exploitation, free trade, and taxes. *Bibliothèque phissico economique instructive et amusante* by Jean-Baptiste Bory de Saint-Vincent, *Dictionnaire de la marine françoise avec figures* by Charles Romme, *Bibiothèque amusante et instructive* by Jean-Pierre Nicéron and François-Joachim Duport du Tertre, and *Nouveau voyage aux isles de L'Amerique* by Jean-Baptiste Labat are in this group. The last of these titles in particular contained a section describing the Caribbean islands, the production of sugar and other crops, the slave trade, and the everyday lives and hardships of free blacks and slaves.

The volumes seized by the colonial officials reflected a simple pattern: they were all written in French. Only a few contained information about the French Revolution and its principles (such as the texts of Raynal, Rousseau, and the "Declaration of the Rights of Man"), while the rest were simply about general topics in literature, theater, and agriculture. Some of these French books contained information about the agricultural exploitation of America and indirectly denounced the slave system, but not to the extent that they could be considered abolitionist tracts. Pardos such as Narciso del Valle and José Cordero also possessed some French books—borrowed from others or bought in the port—and asked the French hairdresser André Renoir to help them translate some of them.[65] Nevertheless, these pardos represented rather an exception: pardos and free blacks generally had access to only brief texts, newspapers, pasquinades, and local manuscripts.

Although colonial authorities tended to emphasize the influence of French revolutionary books in the La Guaira movement, surviving sources indicate that their presence was minimal and irrelevant compared to the numbers of local manuscripts and brief texts that were produced by the insurgents. Written in a simple narrative and adapted to the circumstances of the province, local manuscripts were far more popular and accessible to readers and listeners of La Guaira than the works of Rousseau and Raynal, which could be found only in a small number of libraries owned by whites. The insurgents of La Guaira had produced their own body of literature: stories, dialogues, songs, instructions, constitutions, and political plans that articulated an original and complex republican movement.

The Conspiracy on Paper: Picornell's Instructional Writings

On several occasions, written and oral testimonies mentioned a series of texts produced by Juan Picornell during his imprisonment in La Guaira. Picornell was in fact a prolific writer. Before planning the San Blas movement in Spain, he had written educational books, civil catechisms, and guidebooks for parents in which he stressed the importance of education and rational thinking if children were to reach perfection and become useful to their fatherland (*patria*).[66] Later, during his years as an insurgent in Spain, he authored short revolutionary texts and *libelles* with his collaborators. In 1795, Picornell wrote two important political texts: *Instrucciones* and *Manifiesto*, in which he expressed the importance and benefits of adopting a republican system, and how this system took into consideration the rights of the common citizen and of the pueblo of Spain. His texts also talked about the need to implement a true Hispanic patriotism, with citizens who really cared and worked for the improvement of agriculture, industry, and commerce in the country. His pieces provided instructions on rebel organization, communication strategies, respect for leadership, camaraderie among rebels, and leadership posts. He made clear that the republican movement needed to recruit peasants, artisans, and working people.[67]

In La Guaira, Picornell needed to draw upon local information. He collected stories from friends like Rusiñol, Valle, Canibens, and Cordero in order to produce appropriate texts, adapted to the local political and social contexts. Picornell's manuscripts offered La Guaira's readers and listeners something no other revolutionary texts had offered before: a reflection on their own reality. With no printing press of their own, Venezuelans frequently complained about the seeming irrelevance of peninsular books,

French treatises, and North American proclamations to their geopolitical situation.⁶⁸ For some followers, Picornell's writings ended the agony of misrepresentation, speaking directly to local concerns. His texts offered an acute picture of colonial conditions: the lack of justice, an unfair social system, the tyranny of monarchical rule, and the absurdity of racial differences. His pieces were particularly appealing to Venezuelans of African descent, in part because they were written in a style appropriate for reading out loud and making use of catechistic formulas of answers and responses that made reading easier in a context of semiliteracy. They also used familiar and easy-to-memorize narrative formulas such as epistles, dialogues, and stories for more effective oral transmission.⁶⁹

One of these texts, entitled *The Life of the Admirable Bitatusa*, narrates the story of Bitatusa (an anagram of Picornell's middle name, Bautista), a young soldier in the service of the king of the *ñapoleses* (an anagram of "españoles," Spaniards), who, influenced by the ideas of a philosopher named Dadver (an anagram of *verdad*, truth), abandons his military career and dedicates his life instead to reading and study. Bitatusa learns that in order to stop bowing down before the king, he would have to educate himself and embrace the light of reason. The lesson was clear: Venezuela's common people, the pueblo, needed education in order to embrace reason and secure true liberty.⁷⁰

Another text, entitled *Revelation of Fray José María de la Concepción*, tells the story of a priest who receives a visit from the spirit of José Leonardo Chirino, the leader of the black rebellion of Coro of 1795 who is now in heaven because he died a martyr. In the story, Chirino's spirit appears to the priest to convey that "in the name of the Father, Americans must recover their liberty and that they may count on the support of Almighty God." The priest runs to the bishop to tell him about the miraculous apparition, but he ends up in jail because his report is seen as seditious. Desperate, the priest asks God for help and miraculously receives pen and paper. Inspired, he begins writing "Exhortation to the Americans," which presents the "Rights of Man" and the benefits of abolishing slavery and of enjoying liberty and equality.

This story challenged the commonly held idea that republicanism was an antireligious movement, as Chirino is canonized and speaks in the name of God, who supports the new republican system. Instead of representing José Leonardo Chirino as a disloyal and treacherous black rebel, the story portrays him as a martyr whose body suffered torture and brutal death. The body of Chirino, then, went through a symbolic healing, with the subsequent resurrection of his ideals of freedom and justice. In this sense, Picornell's political argument was made trenchant through an emotional appeal to the recent memory of black insurrection.[71]

In *Letter from a Grandfather to his Grandchild*, Picornell switches to a different format. Here, he offers an imaginary epistle from a grandfather in Cádiz to his grandchild, who lives across the Atlantic in America. The old man describes the difficulty of life in Spain, where "bad government" oppresses the poor people and where agriculture, commerce, and the arts are devastated by the tyranny of the king. He comments that Americans, too, have experienced oppression and misery, but that he has heard that a new political movement will soon liberate them. He exhorts his grandchild to join this imminent revolution that will take place on American soil.[72] With this text, Picornell sought to foster a sense of empathy between peninsular and American Spaniards, both of whom could be seen as oppressed by the monarchical system. He optimistically placed his hopes of change in the American territories, inviting Americans to rebel, take up arms, and be the protagonists of their own political destiny.

Another of Picornell's texts, *A Dialogue between a Black Lieutenant Colonel of the French Republic and a Black Spaniard, His Cousin*, took the form of a dialogue with questions and answers, following a catechistic narrative formula, very popular among novice readers. The author tells the story of a black Spaniard who encounters his cousin dressed up as a French officer. Surprised at his cousin's regal French uniform, the black Spaniard soon learns that in France all men are equal and free, and as such they can attain both military and political positions.[73] This text sought to convey how the republican system, based on the prerogatives of liberty, equality, and fraternity, erased arbitrary racial distinctions and benefited people of African descent.

These texts fostered an awareness of how the Spanish king and his colonial officials oppressed subjects in the Americas. What was to be done? Picornell insisted on the argument that education and reason were necessary to responsibly defend the American fatherland (*patria Americana*), and he legitimated the idea of rebellion as a space within which to link revolutionary equality and fraternity with Christian love for others.[74]

These texts became relevant media for transmitting knowledge about revolutionary movements in Europe and America, and about the republican system. It is difficult to determine the effects that Picornell's texts achieved in the port city. After all, the majority of the population was nonliterate or semiliterate. However, Picornell's familiar discursive formulas—epistles, dialogues, tales, and stories—facilitated reading out loud, making them accessible to less-educated groups. Thus, by using popular rhetorical and narrative strategies, Picornell and his collaborators created a mirror in which Venezuelans could see themselves as both agents and beneficiaries of revolutionary political change. Picornell's visitors collected these writings, then copied them by hand and distributed them in private homes throughout La Guaira. They also read them in gatherings and tertulias that took place in bodegas and at Valle's barbershop. Witness testimonies confirm that many visitors and clients read these manuscripts at the barbershop. In fact, Rusiñol, Cordero, and Valle appear as the main agents in charge of spreading these texts through their own social networks. The physician Juan de la Tasa, for example, commented that he had read "the one about Bitatusa, the sermon of the Friar, and another song that a friar from Santo Domingo gave to him."[75] The pardo José Manuel del Pino also declared that at the barbershop he had read a "paper about the apparition of the spirit of José Leonardo to a priest, and the letter from the grandfather to his grandchild," and that Rusiñol had given these papers to Valle. Pino also commented that he had seen the text about the "black cousins" in the hands of the merchant José Montesinos y Rico, but that this copy was later burned, along with the writings that Narciso del Valle had provided to him.

Several declarations allow us to appreciate the care that some of the participants of the conspiracy took with these texts. Narciso del Valle—who received them from either Rusiñol or Picornell—circulated them in his barbershop, but, afraid of them being spotted there, he gave them to José Cordero, who then kept them in a drawer in his house. However, once the news broke that the conspiracy had been discovered and that authorities had arrived in La Guaira, Cordero gave the writings to another conspirator named Miguel Granadino with instructions to bury them. Terrified, Granadino decided to burn the papers; infuriated, Cordero told him that he had "acted badly, because this was a job that had taken don Juan Picornell six months of work."[76]

Valle's barbershop was an ideal place to share and discuss these readings: it was a place for socialization where people of different social statuses, education, and ethnic backgrounds got together and shared ideas. As discussed in the first chapter, in Venezuela, barbershops sometimes served as improvised primary schools for pardo children who were not allowed into the public educational system. Barbers were informal teachers who also offered literary services to common people (such as reading out loud and writing personal letters). Valle's barbershop became a place where people did more than simply read newspapers, share impressions, and get their hair cut. Here, visitors learned political lessons and made decisions on whether or not to join in the conspiracy. Everyone, regardless of color, occupation, or status, had equal access to the barbershop and to the heated discussions that took place inside.

As a teacher, Picornell had clear ideas about how to capture the attention of different kinds of readers (and listeners). His communication strategies were effective, and he even instructed others in how to achieve similar results. Following Picornell's example, Valle wrote a text to recruit the black people of Curiepe, exhorting them "to unite in order to achieve in this province what the French and the British Americans had done in their countries." He also talked about "natural equality and the other rights of men." Apparently, Valle had previously sent his composition to Picornell and to Manuel Gual, both of whom agreed that the letter should be modified because "its style ... was more elevated than the intelligence of these men, and ... they should be addressed in a more comprehensible way."[77]

Picornell's success in producing a number of instructional texts for the ordinary people of La Guaira encouraged the organizers of meetings and reading circles to ask the incarcerated Spaniard to help them plan an insurrectionary movement in Venezuela. The same people who were in complicity with the prison guards where Picornell was being held helped him escape from jail on June 3, 1797.[78] The complex and diverse group of insurgents also worked closely with him in the elaboration of a political plan, which included the production of a number of documents to organize the rebellion and to map out Venezuela's first republican government.

Planning a Republic: *Instrucciones* and *Ordenanzas*

The chests that royal authorities confiscated from Manuel Gual's hacienda in Santa Lucía outside La Guaira contained several revealing documents. One was a text in French entitled "Instructions on the Civil Constitution of the Clergy" by a certain Mr. Mirabeau, written in January 1791. It detailed the adjustments the church and clergy would have to make upon the establishment of the new republic and its government by assembly. Next was "The Declaration of Independence of the thirteen United Provinces of America presented to the General Congress, July 10, 1776." Third was the "Letter of don Miguel Rubín de Celis, a Spanish official living in Bayonne who wrote to [fellow Spaniards] on the [Iberian] Peninsula, in November 1792," in which the author criticized the monarchical system and praised the values of liberty and equality.[79] However, Venezuelan royal authorities also found a number of manuscripts they had not seen before. These included letters, lists, and papers containing instructions, recommendations, proclamations, songs, and illustrations related to the planning of a republican government. At that moment, colonial authorities understood that the conspiracy in La Guaira was not an improvised or spontaneous movement. Rather, a tight-knit group of people had been working together for months to produce a body of documents designed to give shape to a genuinely new government in Venezuela.

Spaniards and creoles, including Juan Bautista Picornell, Manuel Cortés de Campomanes, and Manuel Gual, collaborated actively in the circulation of republican ideas and values among the population of African descent. They expended considerable effort to produce a body of texts to help others understand the republican movement's principles, motivations, procedures, and plan of action. In fact, agreeing to help lead the conspiracy, Picornell began producing two sets of texts, some of them addressed directly to his collaborators and others aimed at the population in general. Some of these texts were written in jail and others while he was in hiding in a house in La Guaira. Three texts in particular are worth mentioning: the "Ordenanzas" (or "Constituciones"), the "Instrucciones," and the "Exhortación al Pueblo." Several drafts of these documents circulated among the leaders of the movement, and on various occasions individuals copied these texts, distributed them, and even produced different versions intended for specific audiences. Nevertheless, the substance of the documents remained the same.[80]

The "Ordenanzas" contained forty-four articles setting forth the principles for "the revolutionary commanders in the Province of Tierra Firme in order to restore liberty to the pueblo Americano." In general, these articles encouraged revolutionaries to follow an organized plan of government that preserved tranquility and social order while promoting unity and loyalty among individuals. The "Ordenanzas" lent particular importance to respecting the church and the clergy as well as all religious buildings, ornaments, and images. The document also clarified that priests and nuns should receive the same payments that they received before the revolution, but, should they act against the "general happiness," they were to be treated as traitors.

The "Ordenanzas" emphasized the importance of following a plan while forming a government board (Junta Gubernativa) that would take possession of public offices, buildings, and documents and would determine the responsibilities and salaries of the new public posts. Regarding the election of the Junta Gubernativa, the seventh article of the "Ordenanzas" said: "Only those residents and Hacendados who beforehand have proven their constant patriotism, love for the poor, and knowledge in matters of Government may be elected to this Board."[81] The following article stated that every citizen would be invited to submit their written vote for the member of the junta they considered best suited to serve on the board.

The "Ordenanzas" also contained several articles about the collection of taxes. They proclaimed the end of restrictions on the cultivation and commercialization of tobacco, and the abolition of taxes on food (specifically rice, bread, fruits, vegetables, and root crops). Taxes on other items were to be automatically reduced by 25 percent while the new government reached its definitive decisions on such matters. Likewise, the text abolished commercial taxes paid by shopkeepers and all the alcabala taxes that muleteers, hacendados, and small cultivators had to pay to transport their produce. With these articles, the 1797 La Guaira leaders responded to a ubiquitous grievance of eighteenth-century popular movements in Spanish America: numerous and rising taxes. Taxes were widely regarded as an expression of monarchical oppression and the cause of many of the miseries of the common people.[82]

Articles 32 through 36, on the other hand, spoke to the value of natural equality in society. Peace and liberty were only possible if individuals experienced the benefit of equality. Article 32 says:

> Natural equality among all the inhabitants of the Provinces and Districts is declared: and it is mandatory that the greatest possible harmony prevail among whites, Indians, pardos, and morenos, who shall treat each other as brothers in Jesus Christ and equals before God, and shall establish distinctions between one and another only on the basis of merit and virtue, the only real basis for distinguishing between one man and another.[83]

Unlike other texts such as songs, dialogues, and tales, in which authors explicitly mention the word "blacks," this text does not mention "blacks" but just "morenos." The term "moreno" was frequently used to refer to free blacks, but it was also used to allude to the mixed offspring of whites and blacks. Considering that this document was primarily addressed to white people and pardos, who probably wouldn't accept full equality between whites and blacks, it seems that "moreno" was used as a euphemism for "black."[84]

The principles of equality and fraternity were thus enshrined in La Guaira's republican "constitution," but they were transformed and adapted to fit local social and political contexts. As mentioned earlier, revolutionary texts were transformed in two ways: in their discursive or narrative strategies and in their contents. Many of the texts produced locally reframed revolutionary writings as epistles, dialogues, songs, and tales—forms considered appropriate for teaching revolutionary principles to the common people. In fact, some of the concepts expressed in the "Declaration of the Rights of Man" were woven into Picornell's dialogue between French and Spanish black cousins, his *Revelation of Fray José María de la Concepción*, and the "Ordenanzas," where liberty and equality played fundamental roles.

The contents of these texts, too, were adapted to respond to American social realities. In Venezuela, equality meant not only eradicating status distinctions but also eliminating the socioracial differences that had been imposed on the people by the colonial state and propertied elites in order to maintain order, and to reinforce a social hierarchy that had little to do with economic standing.

One of the La Guaira movement's collaborators, the white Spaniard Manuel Cortés de Campomanes, was responsible for composing and adapting lyrics from revolutionary songs for a Venezuelan audience. One of his songs, "Soneto Americano," extols the brotherhood that would prevail between people of the new republic, to be composed of whites, blacks, Indians, and pardos. The lyrics are as follows:

> We are all interested
> In pursuing this goal,
> So let's unite as good brothers.
> Friendly fraternity,
> Embrace the arms of
> The new neighbors:
> Indians, Blacks, and Pardos,
> Long live one sole Pueblo.[85]

Proclaiming total equality implied not only the application of the same laws to peasants, professionals, and merchants, as it did in revolutionary France, but also the application of the same laws to whites, pardos, Indians, and blacks. In "Carmañola Americana," another song translated and adapted by Cortés from the revolutionary French song "La Carmagnole," poor people and people of African descent are called "the shirtless ones" (*descamisados*) and are directly compared with the French revolutionary sansculottes—people who have been tyrannized and forgotten by the monarchy and the nobility.[86]

If anyone wants to know
Why I am shirtless,
It is because with his tributes
The King has undressed me.
The Shirtless ones are already Dancing!

The French sansculottes
Have shaken the world,
But the shirtless here
Would hardly be less successful.
The Shirtless ones are already Dancing![87]

The song proclaims that equality and fraternity among men of all races will prevail. Equality in this case refers not only to social status but also to calidad and purity of blood. The principal aim of these texts was to gain the support of the pardos and free blacks who represented the two largest oppressed social groups in Venezuela. In this way, the discourses of the French and the Haitian Revolutions that had arrived in La Guaira during the previous years were adapted in ways that reflected the highly racialized nature of local political tensions. In both songs, "Soneto Americano" and "Carmañola Americana," Manuel Cortés adds, to the well-known French revolutionary pillars of liberty, equality, and fraternity, other values such as unity and justice. The songs express that only united would the Pueblo Americano prevail against a tyrant regime, and they clarify that a new government will administer justice equally among all Venezuelans.[88]

Such bold declarations of equality among the entire population implied the elimination of two important colonial institutions: slavery and Indian tributary taxes. Social equality and the abolition of slavery were important distinguishing features of the movement, whose leaders hoped to attract the vast majority of local people of African descent to the movement. Article 34 of the "Ordenanzas" declared the abolition of slavery, which was denounced as a "system contrary to humanity." The text made clear, however, that masters would be compensated for the loss of their slaves.[89] Other articles also reflected general concerns regarding the occupation of the newly liberated slaves. Two solutions were proposed: the new black citizens could join the military, or they could continue to work as hired day laborers in order to further the agricultural and commercial development of the region. The new government would also eliminate the payment of Indian tributes, which "a tyrant government has imposed on the land they have stolen from them";[90] this same article established that the new government would grant Indians ownership over their land or over any other land they considered useful, making certain that indigenous groups received resources so "they could be as happy as the other citizens."[91]

While the "Ordenanzas" represented a plan for the establishment of a new republican government, the "Instrucciones" outlined twenty-two guidelines—or articles—that should be followed by the insurgents while taking control of the entire Province of Venezuela. These included, for example, the proclamation to be announced in public spaces: "Long live the Law of God, long live the American People, Death to Bad Government."[92] The same refrain was to be pronounced when taking possession of public offices and buildings, when forming patrols composed of the inhabitants of each town, and in announcing the formation of the Junta Gubernativa.

The "Instrucciones" differed in some respects from the "Ordenanzas." Regarding the election of the Junta Gubernativa, the "Instrucciones" declared that all citizens would belong to a neighborhood (barrio), and that the inhabitants of each barrio would elect two persons to serve on the neighborhood board, which, in turn, would appoint the Junta Gubernativa. "Everyone," the document reads, "will give his vote to persons known for their affection to the fatherland, for being particularly enlightened and prudent, without regard for their color or for any other feature that could have the most minimal influence."[93] Here, unlike the "Ordenanzas," there is no allusion to the hacendados or landowners as the social group best suited to government service. This omission begs the question: why this fundamental discrepancy between the two documents? Picornell wrote the "Instrucciones" before the "Ordenanzas," and despite his clear call to establish an egalitarian republic, he may have had to make concessions to the political interests of white creole hacendados, who would not have been comfortable with the idea of appointing poor whites, pardos, or free blacks to the junta.[94]

Two articles of the "Instrucciones," Articles 14 and 15, reflect the importance attributed to the abolition of slavery in the movement, if not to the role of the slaves themselves in achieving it. Article 13 declares that, after the Junta Gubernativa has been established and sworn in on the main square of the town, the slaves living in town will present themselves in the square, two by two: "They will have on their arms an easily removable chain, together with any other symbol of their enslavement, and their masters will present a brief written report on them."[95] Then, a person would remove the symbols of enslavement and, embracing each freed slave in turn, "the secretary will announce in the name of the fatherland, the president, and the other individuals that they are free and will be recognized as citizens."[96]

Here, the abolition of slavery is represented in a ritualized act in which the united American people or pueblo americano are not just witnesses but rather actors—benefactors who grant liberty to the slaves. At the same time, the slaves are depicted as passive characters, as grateful recipients of their liberty. They are not allowed to remove their own chains but must passively wait for someone (probably white) to remove their fetters. Here, the abolition of slavery is depicted not as the result of the slaves' own struggle—as it would have been in the case of Coro and as it was in Saint-Domingue—but as the consequence of the determination of a mixed-race government to eradicate the system of slavery.

It is true that rumors, news, and texts coming from the turbulent Franco-Caribbean colonies permeated the environment of the Province of Venezuela and, in particular, the port of La Guaira, where they gained true significance as social spaces for political debate opened up. At the same time, the reluctance to use the word "blacks" in some texts generated by the conspiracy's leaders, the uncertain position of black citizens in the future government, and the vision of slaves as passive recipients of a freedom granted by someone else force us to ask: What kind of example was the revolution of Saint-Domingue for the 1797 movement of La Guaira?

Depending on the social context, Saint-Domingue was invoked either as feared or as a model to follow. Several testimonies show that some white participants feared succumbing to the fate of Saint-Domingue and ultimately joined the conspiracy because they feared that free blacks would follow the lead of their counterparts in Guarico (Saint-Domingue). Manuel Montesinos y Rico, for example, declared that Manuel Gual had persuaded him to convince other friends to join the movement because "if they do not accept, they could become the victims of blacks and zambos." Another participant of the movement, Martín Antonio de Goenaga, said that, in a meeting at España's house, he heard someone say: "If we don't unite with the people of color, we will die as victims of their fury." Likewise, Jean Lartigue remembered a conversation in which Gual asserted that "it was necessary to abolish slavery to prevent events as unfortunate as those of Guarico, where whites were victims of the people of color." [97] As the conspirators' plans developed, many whites also expressed the concern that the revolution would incite violent reprisals by slaves and people of color against all whites.

Here and in previous chapters I have presented evidence that pardos, free blacks, and slaves of La Guaira, Caracas, and Coro looked at the revolutionary movement of Saint-Domingue with hope, as an example to be followed on the South American mainland, where they were victims of inequality and discrimination. However, pardos and blacks who participated in the conspiracy of La Guaira mistrusted some of their white coconspirators, as they had doubts about the ultimate success of the movement and feared that, in case of failure, "the whites will remain free, and will put all the blame on us." [98]

An understanding of the specific political and social conflicts in Venezuela reveals how representations of the French and Haitian Revolutions refracted and reformulated events and ideologies. Neither revolution was conceived of in terms of a monolithic political structure, but rather, each represented a malleable framework within which different social groups articulated their own desires, anxieties, and beliefs, which found expression in the possibility of leading a revolutionary movement. Liberty and racial equality in the Atlantic revolutions were seen by some conspirators (some radical whites, but mainly pardos) as a model to follow, while others (especially whites creoles) perceived these as disastrous scenarios that could be avoided only by their assuming leadership of the movement themselves and providing some modest benefits to Venezuela's people of African descent. [99]

The La Guaira movement ultimately failed, but the case shows that revolutionary ideas and experiences from the Caribbean traveled to the mainland, where individual actors received, interpreted, and reproduced words, ideas, and practices through particular social networks. In La Guaira, authors and diffusers of written revolutionary texts had to deal with the ambiguity that the example of Saint-Domingue represented. They tried to offer the promise of a "multiethnic" political movement for the population of African descent while guaranteeing political control and social order to white elites. Even so, those social groups that were not controlled or led exclusively by literate white creoles might have interpreted the texts differently. Local people of different socioracial groups, statuses, and occupations sought to create a new political movement, but their divergent agendas ultimately complicated the unity of the plan.

The emergence of a dynamic public sphere for political debate was not necessarily or exclusively linked to a literate elite or a printing shop, nor was it a direct consequence of the expansion of northern Atlantic political ideals. Here, the configuration of regional social networks and the circulation of local manuscripts represented a crucial base for the emergence of a public sphere. In these new spaces, public and semipublic political debates developed at the margins of colonial state vigilance and control. This sphere of independent political action was still in an incipient phase, but the conspirators and their many followers certainly complicated the Venezuelan political landscape. In the following years, Picornell, Gual, España, Cortés, and other insurgents hiding on nearby islands continued to introduce revolutionary texts and written pieces into Venezuela with the hope that they would continue nurturing Venezuelans' political debates.

In July 1800, the new captain general of Venezuela, Manuel de Guevara y Vasconcelos, expressed his concern over the many seditious papers that circulated from Trinidad to the west coast of the captaincy. These papers, he said, "contain the most energetic expressions capable of persuading the people that our government oppresses them and restricts commerce and agriculture."[100] The captain general was afraid that the escapees from La Guaira were now receiving support not so much from France or Saint-Domingue but from British officials in Trinidad. Like others before him, he lamented the lack of military forces sufficient to guard the long Venezuelan coastline, exposed as it was to all kinds of enemies. He emphasized: "These vast coasts cannot be sealed off from our neighbors, not even with a multitude of men who sometimes driven by necessity or convenience side with the enemies."[101] It was clear to him, then, that other changes would need to be introduced in the province in order to satisfy local expectations and guarantee the sacred loyalty of Venezuelans.

CHAPTER 6

The Fear of Foreign Invasion

Black Corsairs in Maracaibo and
Other Stories of Black Occupation

◈ AFTER THE EVENTS OF CORO AND LA GUAIRA, COLONIAL OFFICIALS were haunted by the specter of an invasion led by revolutionary Frenchmen somewhere along the Spanish Main. Officials complained in particular about suspicious ships lurking near the coast, which seemed to represent an imminent danger to Spanish American territories. This fear, however, was not the product of mere paranoia. There is evidence that, in the last decade of the eighteenth century and especially between 1794 and 1800, several ships captained by black corsairs traversed the Caribbean Sea, spreading revolutionary ideas and inciting rebellion in numerous black communities.[1]

Since 1791, the Spanish Crown had been alerting colonial authorities about the need to avoid any contact between local inhabitants and French foreigners, or at least to strictly control such contact. A royal decree of November 1791 instructed viceroys, captains general, and governors of all the Spanish American territories to remain neutral with respect to the struggle between "blacks and whites in the insurrection of Guarico [Saint-Domingue]." However, the decree added that, if groups of bandits (*malhechores*) or pirates were to attack coastal communities of whites from the high sea, Spanish authorities were to act in accordance with the "rules of Humanity," providing aid to the white refugees "but being careful to prevent the contagion of the insurrection in the Spanish possessions."[2] Contact between Spanish soldiers and French people had to be avoided at all costs, and officials were instructed to redouble their efforts to prevent fugitive blacks from the French colonies and other "suspicious" foreign visitors from entering Venezuela.

Piracy, like smuggling, had long been a fact of life in the Spanish Caribbean, but a new maritime menace seems to have emerged in 1793, when the French National Convention encouraged French corsairs to conduct raids on enemy ships. In the Caribbean, this decree gave rise to what David Geggus calls the "revolutionary war at sea."[3] In 1794, the convention also sent French troops to the Antilles under the leadership of civil commander Victor Hugues. Immediately after arriving in Guadeloupe, Hugues liberated the local slaves and declared whites and mulattoes equals; he then formed a battalion of more than two thousand black and mulatto militiamen and black corsairs. These corsairs were authorized to attack enemy ships as well as merchant vessels suspected of trading with the British.[4] By 1795, Hugues had "turned Guadeloupe into the main base for French Privateering in the eastern Caribbean."[5] Black and mulatto seamen were largely responsible for orchestrating these attacks, which terrorized local shipping agents and port officials. By the mid 1790s, Guadeloupe-based privateers had captured more than seven hundred ships. Records indicate that some five hundred British Caribbean vessels, the principal target of these corsairs, were attacked yearly in the period 1703–1805. Ships flying the flags of neutral nations, including Denmark and the United States, were likewise targeted.[6]

The black corsairs authorized by revolutionary France sailed throughout the Caribbean Sea and visited several ports, where they spread news of their freedom and extolled the benefits of the republican system. While republican leaders such as Victor Hugues in Guadeloupe, and Jean-Joseph Lambert and Gaspar Goyrand in Saint Lucia, supported rebels in Grenada, Saint Vincent, and Dominica around 1795, many other rebellions in the region were orchestrated entirely by Guadeloupe-based black corsairs who acted on their own.[7]

By 1798, however, many of these black corsairs had abandoned inciting revolution in favor of simple piracy. Political changes in Guadeloupe (including the removal of Hugues in 1798) and in the larger Caribbean region (a stronger British naval presence) left the black corsairs without a commander. Without clear orientation and guidance, and with no support from republican governments, these corsairs felt free to act on their own, attacking neutral ships and raising the concerns of French, Spanish, and British authorities in the Caribbean. The colonial government of Guadeloupe, led now by General Étienne Desfourneaux, tried to restrain the corsairs, although this ultimately proved an impossible task.[8]

Colonial records show that these same Guadeloupe-based black corsairs frequently visited Venezuela's vast coast, capturing small ships and destroying British vessels.[9] The 1796 military alliance between Spain and France had ushered in a period of relative peace between these two nations, and during this time Spanish colonial authorities in Venezuela even allowed corsairs flying French colors to enter Spanish waters. After the La Guaira conspiracy in 1797, however, the fear of revolutionary contagion brought an end to these practices, reviving a climate of mistrust between the two nations. Once again, colonial authorities in Venezuela prohibited the local population from engaging in any sort of dealings with French blacks.[10]

From 1798 to 1800, military commanders and governors of Venezuela's western provinces (mainly Puerto Cabello, Coro, and Maracaibo) frequently reported the presence of French corsairs near the coast and asked for military reinforcements. In some cases, they specified the exact number of ships captained by "French blacks" that had been seen "visiting" their communities and detailed their suspicious practices; other times they reported wholesale attacks on coastal towns. For Spanish colonial authorities, it seemed evident that these black corsairs, imbued with revolutionary ideas, sought to incite sedition and destabilize the region. Plunder was a secondary concern.[11]

The contagion was allegedly widespread, penetrating neighboring districts. During Holy Week, 1799, the pardo corporal Manuel Yturén denounced a slave conspiracy in the heavily fortified port city of Cartagena, New Granada. Apparently, a group of French slaves, recently bought by naval officers, had allied with local blacks and conspired to rebel against their masters. The main goals of the movement were to kill all the whites, including the governor; to seize the city's fortresses; and to plunder the city. The French slaves supposedly had convinced a local black militiaman to join their movement. He had then helped them to procure and hide arms and ammunition in the area. The group had also tried to recruit Yturén, along with his pardo militia unit, although Yturén promptly reported the conspiracy to the governor of Cartagena, don Anastasio Zejudo.[12] Zejudo acted immediately, arresting six French slaves and securing the port. Two conspirators, however, managed to escape and set fire to a hacienda near the city. A week after the discovery of the plot, Cartagena's governor announced that he had arrested all those who had been implicated. At the same time, he asked for additional military support from Spain to reinforce the Cartagena coast guard, which remained, in his opinion, extremely vulnerable to attacks by French black corsairs.[13]

A month later, in May 1799, a similar movement was uncovered in the port of Maracaibo, in Venezuela. This movement was likewise denounced by a militiaman who reported that black French corsairs, the leaders of the conspiracy, had encouraged local pardos, mulattoes, and slaves to "introduce into the city the same system of freedom and equality that has reduced to total ruin . . . the French ports of the island of Saint-Domingue."[14] As in Cartagena, the authorities in Maracaibo acted quickly, arresting the main suspects and securing the region. Inevitably, colonial officials—not only in Cartagena and Maracaibo but also in the inland capital cities of Bogotá and Caracas—linked the two alleged conspiracies. They expressed great concern about the influence of French blacks in these coastal communities, both of which were populated mostly by people of color and Indians.

But could these corsairs really incite local blacks and Indians in Cartagena and Maracaibo to rebellion? In the case of Cartagena, historian Aline Helg argues that, although colonial officials feared a possible alliance among foreign slaves, local slaves, free blacks, and unconquered Indians, this union never materialized due to socioracial and ethnic tensions.[15] Although similar reasons may have precipitated the failure of the conspiracy of Maracaibo in May 1799, I argue that it was probably the lack of solid social networks among foreigners and locals, the absence of effective webs of communication and information, and an effective official campaign against Frenchmen that ultimately doomed the Maracaibo conspiracy. Like other colonial cities in Venezuela, Maracaibo had a society structured upon socioracial privileges and differences in status. Class tensions created frictions within socioracial groups, and the even stronger socioracial divisions separating whites, pardos, free blacks, and slaves could not be easily erased by imported ideologies. In addition, we have to bear in mind that over the course of the preceding decade the colonial state had mounted an effective political campaign against French revolutionary ideas, instilling fear in the population and a general contempt for the French. The difficulty of overcoming these ingrained suspicions about foreigners (especially French blacks) further weakened the plot.

In this chapter, I examine the failed Maracaibo rebellion of 1799, arguing that a lack of organization on the part of the corsair interlopers, weak participation of the local pardo and black populations, and a general suspicion of French corsairs largely explain the movement's failure. It seems clear that the organization of any such movement required the active participation and involvement of local actors, individuals not likely to take orders from foreigners. Venezuelans may have shared inspiring narratives about these seaborne Francophone rebels, but accepting their presence and leadership in their own communities was a completely different story.

Tales of the brave Toussaint Louverture in Saint-Domingue certainly awakened the curiosity of the general population, but this did not mean that people in Venezuela wanted Toussaint to rule their provinces. The image of Toussaint Louverture definitely changed in 1801, when a new wave of rumors circulating in the region in response to Toussaint's invasion of Spanish Santo Domingo spread extremely negative images of the black leader as someone who wanted to expand racial hatred, insubordination, and chaos to rest of the Americas. This chapter also analyzes the impact of rumors of Toussaint's invasion of Santo Domingo among Venezuelan communities in the early nineteenth century. Hundreds of Dominican refugees who arrived in Venezuela circulated oral stories that depicted Toussaint as an irrational, vengeful, and violent leader willing to import unruliness and horror. Fear of a racial war, along with the presence of foreign agitators, made local elites suspicious of all blacks, enslaved and free, undermining the fragile social and political stability of Venezuela. As Captain General Pedro Carbonell commented in 1798, in the aftermath of the events in Saint-Domingue and the tumult in the French colonies, for elites and authorities it was clear "that whites cannot trust blacks anymore."[16] The general concern about a potential foreign invasion led officials and elites to increase their vigilance over the local African-descended population. Authorities, however, not only demanded more local control; they also encouraged masters to moderate their punishment and use rational methods to discipline their slaves, and to even negotiate some of the slaves' demands in order to "keep them contented" and maintain the region's tenuous peace.

Black French Corsairs in Maracaibo, 1799

Only four years after the Coro rebellion, the Venezuelan elite's fears of invasion were confirmed. On May 6, 1799, two French corsair vessels landed in

Maracaibo, the most commercially vibrant and strategically significant port in western Venezuela. The ships hailed from Port-au-Prince in Saint-Domingue, carrying a total crew of approximately sixty free black men. It was not an attack; the vessels entered the port of Maracaibo with the excuse of hauling in an English ship that had been suspiciously surveying the Venezuelan coast. Local authorities allowed the two French ships to exchange goods with local merchants and to stock their vessels with foodstuffs and other commodities.

Twenty days after the ships' arrival, a local soldier denounced the black corsairs to the governor of Maracaibo, claiming that they were conspiring to kill the city's wealthy whites, to overthrow the local governor, and to follow "the same system they [had] established in Saint-Domingue." They had ostensibly planned to recruit some two hundred pardos and free blacks. The pardo commander, Sublieutenant Francisco Xavier Pirela, was accused of serving as the local leader of the conspiracy. That very day, Pirela confessed the whole plan to the governor of Maracaibo. The governor acted rapidly, capturing and jailing sixty-eight suspects and launching a comprehensive investigation aimed at uncovering the intentions of the political movement and identifying all local supporters.

Only recently has this abortive movement, often referred to as the Pirela conspiracy, received careful attention from historians. Most researchers have connected the episode to other similar events in the Caribbean—Cartagena, Cuba, and Curaçao—where French corsairs likewise threatened to topple colonial regimes.[17] Historians still debate the motivations of the French corsairs in Maracaibo, inadvertently echoing colonial discussions and speculation. Some modern scholars contend that these black Frenchmen were genuinely seeking to promote a republican uprising, while others argue that the improvised character of the visit and the poor organization of the conspiracy suggest that the corsairs were more interested in piracy than politics. For this latter group of historians, the corsairs' primary intent was merely to steal money from the government and local rich families, along with arms and ammunition from the royal artillery.[18] The question of the French interlopers' intentions aside, it is clear that the conspiracy failed because it did not attract sufficient local support. The population was likely reluctant to follow foreign leaders. Indeed, the failure of the plot convinced local authorities that Venezuelans were not inclined to join conspiracies or rebellions led by foreigners. Change, if it were to come, would have to be orchestrated from within.

Maracaibo: Venezuela's Western Gateway

In 1777, Maracaibo, a province of New Granada since the days of buccaneer Henry Morgan, became part of the Captaincy General of Venezuela. Authorities in Madrid argued that the distance between Maracaibo and Santa Fé de Bogotá (the capital of the Viceroyalty of New Granada) was much longer than that between Maracaibo and Caracas. Thus, they believed that royally appointed officials would be better placed to administer and defend the region if Maracaibo were reassigned to Caracas. The transition was not so easy, as colonial officers in both Maracaibo and New Granada resisted this Bourbon shuffling. Even so, they couldn't change the king's mind nor those of his advisers.[19]

By the late 1780s, Maracaibo was one of the most important provinces in the western region of Venezuela, mainly because the port city became a significant center of commercial exchange for a portion of northern South America. The vast Lake Maracaibo provided safe harbor as well as efficient communication with the Caribbean; moreover, several rivers connected the port with inland cities and towns, reaching the Andes and the southern llanos (plains).[20] Maracaibo was the center of a large commercial network in which local produce (cacao, sugar, indigo, cotton, wood, leather, hides, and mules), and goods from the Antilles, Spain, and the United States (textiles, flour, liquor, agricultural tools, and prepared foods such as salted meat and biscuit), were exchanged.[21]

With a busy commercial life, Maracaibo was vulnerable to contraband traders hailing from both non-Spanish and Spanish ports. By 1796–1799, 61 percent of commerce in the port was conducted with non-Spanish colonies. Many traders hailed from Curaçao, Saint Thomas, and Saint Croix. Another 30 percent of trade relied on smuggling networks that linked Spanish ports, including Santo Domingo, San Juan, Havana, and New Granada's ports of Cartagena and Santa Marta.[22] These commercial activities, both licit and illicit, transformed Maracaibo into a major Atlantic trading hub—more open, varied, and dynamic than inland cities because of the ever-fluctuating character of its population.[23] In late colonial Maracaibo, both foreigners and hinterland immigrants were familiar to the city's inhabitants, who regularly received foreigners of all colors and political inclinations. In fact, the arrival of two ships manned by black French corsairs raised few eyebrows—that is, until rumors of conspiracy began to circulate.

Suddenly, royal authorities called upon local men to defend the city against a possible invasion.

The two ships, named *El Bruto* and *La Patrulla*, arrived at night, towing an English ship, the *Harlequin*, in its wake. The captains of the French ships, the mulatto brothers Augustin Gaspar Bocé and Jean-Baptiste Gaspar Bocé, told port authorities that they had departed from Port-au-Prince in Saint-Domingue with the intention of exchanging coffee and other goods in Saint Thomas.[24] However, their trip had proved difficult: they had to make several stops on the mainland and at other islands in order to avoid enemies, and also to procure supplies and fresh water. Later, they had to stop once again in order to repair the mast of one of the ships. Contrary winds and bad weather accidentally brought them to the territory of the Guajiro Indians (on the Guajira Peninsula, bordering Maracaibo and New Granada), where they had observed three suspicious vessels hugging the coast. The corsairs decided to follow them, only to realize that the ships had raised their sails in an attempt to escape. The Saint-Domingue-based captains resolved to chase them, and finally they captured the *Harlequin*, a small ship flying the Union Jack. Having interrogated the crew and having appointed a Frenchman, Joseph Roman (also called "Romano" in the documentation), as the captain of the *presa* (prey), they decided to present the English ship to Spanish authorities in Tierra Firme, in this case at the port of Maracaibo. The corsairs asked permission to spend a few days in the port in exchange. Maracaibo's port authorities consented, since the captains had brought in an enemy ship and properly displayed their carte blanche, or letter of marque and reprisal. It had been issued in Léogâne, Saint-Domingue, at the beginning of 1799.[25]

Colonial authorities allowed the French corsairs to anchor within sight of Maracaibo, but they tried to limit their contact with locals by asking them to spend the night on their ships and to make only brief visits ashore. They also appointed Juan Sualbach, a soldier in a local militia company who spoke French, to accompany them in their business about town and to observe them closely for security reasons.[26] By May 11, all the legal paperwork was in order, and permissions were granted for the black French corsairs to remain stationed in the port of Maracaibo.[27] At this point, colonial authorities did not seem concerned about the presence of these so-called *negros franceses*, who were behaving in accordance with the law and the established regulations for corsairs. Officials even allowed the visitors to disembark, buy groceries, and take walks around the port.[28]

On the night of May 19, 1799, the governor of Maracaibo, don Juan Ignacio de la Armada, Marqués de Santa Cruz, opened the door of his house to find Tomás Ochoa, a corporal first class of the city's veteran battalion. Clearly worried, Ochoa carried an urgent message: a group of insurgents were plotting a rebellion that very evening. Ochoa told the governor that the thirty-five-year-old pardo tailor and sublieutenant Francisco Xavier Pirela had come to his house to report that a group of French black corsairs had revealed their conspiracy plans to him. Apparently, one of the ships' captains, Joseph Roman, had asked him to gather two hundred men, offering to pay him and anyone who was willing to participate in the movement. Pirela even showed Ochoa a piece of paper that contained the word that would be used as a *santo y seña* ("sign and signal"; i.e., a password) to announce the beginning of the uprising: *Antillen*—a word indicating someone from the Antilles.[29]

Maracaibo's governor immediately searched for Pirela, who was probably waiting to be arrested, since he immediately confessed the whole plan to the authorities. Pirela confided that he had had frequent contact with the French black corsairs because they had hired him as a tailor, and he regularly visited them on their ships. During his time onboard the vessels, Pirela and the "French blacks" shared meals and engaged in conversations about political events and ideas, and about recent developments in the French colonies. On one of these occasions, Captain Roman, who, unlike the other crew members, spoke Spanish, proposed that Pirela join a movement to take over the city of Maracaibo. The plan allegedly included "killing the governor, the white elite (*personas principales*), and the priests of the convent of San Francisco, with the exception of two who should be spared to ensure that locals would continue receiving the Holy Sacraments."[30]

Captain Roman told him that they would need two hundred local pardos or blacks to join the movement, and he offered to pay all participants. As for Pirela, the captain offered to appoint him, a pardo, as the governor of the city, "just as the blacks in Saint-Domingue have a black governor."[31] Pirela declared that, on that very morning, Roman had confirmed to him that everything "was prepared for the attack" and that all the crew members, including the crew of the British ship who were only pretending to be their prisoners, were ready to fight. Finally, he gave Pirela a small piece of paper with the code word that would signal the beginning of the uprising.

When asked which other locals were involved in the conspiracy, Pirela answered that he knew only two: Juan Sualbach, a soldier of the Fourth Company who had been assigned to guard and accompany the captains while they were in town, and José Francisco Suárez, a black slave and shoemaker. According to Pirela, Sualbach, who was originally from Europe and spoke French and Dutch, was lured by the French ideas of liberty and free commerce; he was seen secretly speaking with the captains and was almost certainly collaborating with them. The slave Suárez, according to the accuser, was further driven to collaborate with the French corsairs because he was from Santo Domingo and had witnessed firsthand the insurrection at Bayajá (Fort Dauphin). He was, in other words, well aware of French ideology and its reception by oppressed blacks.[32]

It was clear that neither Pirela nor the French captains had succeeded in recruiting the desired two hundred men for their movement. After hearing Pirela's confession, the governor recognized that the most important task was capturing the crew of the three ships. Six (some sources say ten) of these men were easily apprehended that very night in the houses of two local ladies who were offering dances. The rest of the crew was aboard the three ships; they were captured by dawn on May 20.[33] The soldiers and colonial officials who boarded the ships discovered that, in fact, these men were getting ready for a fight: "Their cannons were greased, and most of the crew had their rifles loaded."[34] The fight never occurred, and by 6:00 a.m. on May 20, sixty-eight men were imprisoned.

The French corsairs and crew members initially denied any involvement, claiming that they had simply been obeying their captains' instructions. They claimed that one of the captains had asked them to move their cargo of coffee to the smaller ship, to load the cannons, and to prepare their arms, but they declared that they were not even sure who their enemies were—they simply followed their superiors' orders.[35]

The governor also questioned the two other locals mentioned by Pirela. Juan Sualbach, the soldier in Maracaibo's Fourth Company, steadfastly denied any involvement. He admitted that he had shared meals with the French corsairs, with whom he spoke in French and Dutch, but he maintained a relationship with these men "only because he was appointed by the governor to observe them closely."[36] He did remark that the visitors had made connections with some local residents, including Suárez and Pirela, but he did not suspect them of organizing a plot. The black slave, Suárez, likewise denied participation. He acknowledged having witnessed the massacre of Bayajá and later describing the scene to the French blacks, but he insisted that he barely understood what they said because of the language barrier. Suárez mentioned that on a particular occasion one of the French captains mimed a beheading and hanging with his hands, but he insisted that he did not understand the meaning of these signs at the time, only later when he learned about the conspiracy. Suárez also mentioned that he overheard one of the captains asking Pirela in Spanish "how many troops guarded the port, who were the rich of the city, and where the gunpowder was kept, among other things."[37] Pirela apparently provided detailed answers to these inquiries.

Unlike the authorities at Coro, Maracaibo's colonial administrators respected the law and followed the appropriate criminal procedure. It took them more than three months to complete their investigation. The process was supervised first by Governor Armada and later by Fernando Mijares, who took over as governor of Maracaibo when Armada resigned for health reasons. Mijares provided Captain General Guevara y Vasconcelos with a detailed report on the criminal procedures and legal actions taken. For these colonial authorities, it was clear that the threat posed by the Maracaibo movement of 1799 had not warranted suspending the appropriate implementation of the law.[38]

The sworn declarations of the corsairs and crew suggest that Joseph Roman was one of the main leaders of the movement, and the only one who maintained a close relationship with the three locals involved. In his declaration, Roman revealed that he was born in Saint Thomas, where he used to work as a scribe.[39] Governor Mijares, then, wrote another letter warning that Roman was a particularly dangerous character: he was an educated man of color who had studied in Europe and spoke at least three languages (Spanish, English, and French, and apparently also Dutch). His rather exceptional education, the governor concluded, might allow him to attract "people of his same class to follow his model."[40]

There was, however, an important contradiction between Roman's and Pirela's declarations. While Pirela accused Roman of having planned the movement, Roman contended that Pirela was the one behind the plan and that he had contacted him for support. Roman reported that, a few weeks before the planned insurrection, Pirela asked him to meet onboard his ship. During this visit, they apparently discussed the French constitution and the rights of freedom and equality. Pirela confessed that, even though he was a pardo official, a person of rank, "people in the province treated pardos and blacks with contempt," and for this reason "they should plan a revolution against the city."[41] Roman offered to help Pirela by providing men, clarifying that in order to succeed they needed to know where the gunpowder was kept in the city, because this determination was the first serious step of any insurrection.

Other members of the crew confirmed Roman's declaration. According to Francisco Mequiet, for example, Pirela had mentioned that he already had found more than two hundred local men who were ready to fight. Arguing that they hardly understood Spanish, the other two captains, the Bocé brothers, denied any participation in the planning of the movement. Ultimately, the authorities found that Pirela and Roman had organized the movement, and the involvement of the other black Frenchmen remained dubious.[42]

The conspiracy evidently languished because its leaders had failed to secure sufficient popular support. On the one hand, Maracaibo, like Cartagena and other coastal cities on the mainland, was divided along stark socioracial lines that hindered any effort at collaboration between pardos and blacks. Many pardos in Maracaibo were slave owners and probably would not have been interested in joining a revolutionary movement organized by blacks, or one that advocated the abolition of slavery.[43] On the other hand, it is clear that the leaders of the movement lacked the time and strategic methods to promulgate their ideas, contextualize the goals of the movement, or coordinate common actions among different social groups. Local participation was minimal; the locals who did hear of the movement may well have perceived it as a foreign plan with little connection to the daily social reality of the city. They therefore chose to keep their distance, or, as Ochoa did, to report the plot to the colonial authorities.

For years, the colonial government fostered a general sense of animosity toward French people in Venezuela. By the end of the eighteenth century, this feeling had devolved into outright collective Francophobia. Spurred on by state officials, the local population treated French visitors with mistrust and, at times, downright contempt, especially if the visitors happened also to be blacks who may well have been inspired by the turbulent events in the French Caribbean. As we have seen, these revolutionary revolts—especially in Saint-Domingue—were often seen not only as threats to the social order but also as expressions of sacrilege and anarchism.

Unlike La Guaira's conspirators, the French black corsairs who visited Maracaibo in 1799 did little to organize local residents or to spread the political ideals that might sustain a revolutionary movement, but that does not mean that the movement did not have ideological roots or intentions. The lack of organization probably led Governor Mijares to conclude that the black corsairs' original plan was not to revolutionize the city of Maracaibo but to take advantage of a few incautious or credulous individuals, such as Pirela, to steal from the government and the wealthy families of the city. Ignoring and undermining the declarations of Pirela and Roman, who made very clear that the movement had political and ideological motivations, the authorities thus recast the movement as a mere act of piracy: "These men," the governor wrote, "are liars who lack any sort of authority for a cause, because their intentions were only to steal everything they could."[44] Pirela could have mentioned that he was indeed a victim of foreign villains who just wanted to sack the city, but he instead chose to speak about the turbulence of the French colonies, his interesting political conversations with the foreign visitors, the example of Saint-Domingue, and how French revolutionary ideas resonated with some locals' aspirations for racial equality and freedom. Roman, on the other hand, spoke about local frustrations with an unfair hierarchical system that mostly affected pardos and people of color, who felt diminished and discriminated against. Their testimonies put French revolutionary ideas and Saint-Domingue's recent changes at the center of the conspiracy, but colonial authorities preferred again to ignore this possibility, presenting the French blacks merely as villainous, amoral, and deceitful people with no education or political awareness, and locals as ignorant, thoughtless, and blind dupes. Despite these officials' representations of the movement as a simple act of pillage, the conspiracy left elites and colonial authorities with a nagging sense of vulnerability, and they responded by increasing their vigilance against any possible source of foreign contagion.

Beginning in 1799, rumors of Toussaint Louverture's alleged ambition to expand race war and emancipation to other colonies circulated throughout the Spanish Caribbean. For colonial authorities, French revolutionaries were determined to spread their destructive system to all other American territories, including Venezuela.[45] Moreover, Spanish colonial authorities believed that Toussaint also had intentions of taking over Mexico, Puerto Rico, and Cuba.[46] Their fears were partially confirmed two years later, in January 1801, when Toussaint invaded eastern Hispaniola, or Spanish Santo Domingo. Oral and written testimonies of Toussaint's invasion quickly reached Venezuelan shores, amplifying fear and alarm among the white elite but also awakening a sense of urgency to alleviate local blacks' discontent and secure their loyalty to their masters and the colonial government.

Toussaint Louverture Occupies Santo Domingo: Spanish Dominicans in Venezuela and Their Stories of Invasion

On January 20, 1801, the captain of the ship *Nuestra Señora del Carmen*, Josef Blade, arrived in Puerto Cabello on the central coast of Venezuela. Blade had left Puerto Cabello in December of the previous year with a load of foodstuffs and cacao, which he transported to Spanish Santo Domingo. On January 6, 1801, while Blade was still in Santo Domingo, the population received news that "the Black Toussaint and his people were heading to the city of Santo Domingo in order to take it." The governor of the Spanish half of the island, don Joaquín García, immediately ordered all men between the ages of sixteen and sixty to prepare to defend the city against the "atrocious actions that the black troops of Toussaint could commit."[47]

Blade left Santo Domingo on January 14 with twelve passengers—mostly white women fleeing the invasion of Toussaint. To the commander of Puerto Cabello, Miguel Marmión, Blade described a scene of mass exodus in Santo Domingo: people were boarding ships bound for destinations throughout the Caribbean, including Puerto Rico, Cuba, and the Venezuelan coast. He was sure that in the coming months many more ships would arrive in Venezuela, bringing refugees.[48] Indeed, between January and May 1801, more than one thousand immigrants from Spanish Santo Domingo arrived in Venezuela.[49]

The Haitian Revolution provoked an incredible migration of people throughout the Atlantic world. Plantations went up in flames; hundreds of people were killed; Spanish, British, and French armies invaded; and thousands of residents fled the island of Hispaniola for good. Throughout the last decade of the eighteenth century and during the early years of the nineteenth century, ships carried thousands of white refugees, their slaves, and free people of color from Saint-Domingue and Spanish Santo Domingo to ports throughout the Caribbean, Europe, Spanish America, and North America. The historiography of this migration is vast and rich. It has raised important questions about the discourses of race, freedom, and republicanism that these refugees took with them.[50] The stories told and retold by these refugees speak to the complex connections between the French and Haitian Revolutions, and the impact of both of these events on the rest of the Atlantic world.[51]

When Toussaint Louverture invaded the Spanish section of Hispaniola, a wave of Spanish Dominican refugees spread terrifying stories of the Haitian

Revolution and its black leaders. The refugees' accounts were almost inevitably framed in a narrative of victimhood: the violent revolution had spilled across territorial borders, invaded their hometowns, and forced them to abandon their land, their possessions, and their slaves. These refugees became masters of this narrative. They recounted in detail the fury of the sea, the threat of piracy, and the pain of separation from their families and possessions.[52] In Venezuela, the hardships endured by these unwilling migrants aroused the sympathy not only of colonial officials, who offered them monetary support, but also of the common people, who saw in these strangers a vivid and frightening version of the Haitian Revolution, featuring a black leader who was willing to expand his power, disregarding the most basic diplomatic and political rules.

The first Spanish Dominican families began to arrive in Venezuela at the end of 1795, when the Spanish section of Hispaniola was ceded to France, but the most significant wave of refugees arrived during the first months of 1801, in the wake of Toussaint Louverture's occupation of Spanish Santo Domingo. Most of these families did not settle in Venezuela; rather, they visited several ports in the greater Caribbean before settling on a final destination. The island of Cuba was particularly popular, as it allowed refugee families to re-create the same political, economic, and social conditions they had enjoyed in Santo Domingo.[53] Although their stay in Venezuela was usually temporary, Dominican refugees managed to spread a radical narrative of the Haitian Revolution: it was a political apocalypse that sowed disorder and destruction in its wake. They disseminated striking images of Hispaniola under the rule of blacks, who were depicted as savage, violent, insolent, and naturally prone to authoritarianism and, rather paradoxically, anarchism. These narratives represented a Manichean view of blacks and their communities, reinforcing elites' growing suspicions regarding their own slaves and free colored workers. The plight of the Spanish Dominicans also served as living evidence of the expansionist intentions of Toussaint and his revolution—a movement that, in the opinion of most refugees, did not follow any political plan and did not respect territorial boundaries or national sovereignty. As Ada Ferrer shows, many predicted that Toussaint would soon invade other Spanish territories, sowing anxiety among colonial authorities throughout the Spanish Caribbean.[54]

In 1798, tensions between the legitimate French authorities—assisted by the captain general of Santo Domingo, Joaquín García—and Toussaint Louverture reached a fever pitch. Toussaint had by then made up his mind to invade Santo Domingo. His reasons were several. In the first place, he wanted to abolish slavery and the slave trade on the entire island because he was sure that men, women, and children who were "French citizens" were kidnapped, taken to Santo Domingo, and sold as slaves. Second, Toussaint feared that the eastern part of the island might be used as a base for French military operations against his forces. Toussaint forced General Philippe Rose Roume de Saint-Laurent, the French agent in Santo Domingo, to issue a decree authorizing the occupation of Spanish Santo Domingo and to sign the capitulation. On April 27, 1800, Toussaint ordered the occupation of the Spanish section of Hispaniola, more than half of the island.[55]

Eight months later, having defeated André Rigaud in the south, Toussaint led his troops to San Juan de la Maguana and divided his army of twenty thousand men into two groups. One group entered the southern area of Santo Domingo, and the other, led by Toussaint's nephew, Moyse, entered the northern region. On January 10, rumors circulated among the population of Santo Domingo that Toussaint and his troops were close to the city. To prevent Toussaint from capturing the French generals Antoine Chanlatte and François-Marie Kerversau, Joaquín García gave them passports, and on January 13 they fled the city.[56]

The French generals arrived in Puerto Cabello, Venezuela, on January 18, 1801. Upon their arrival, the commander of Puerto Cabello, Miguel Marmión, ordered them to stay on board their ships, in accordance with the law that prohibited French people from entering the province. The French generals sent a letter to the captain general, Manuel de Guevara y Vasconcelos, pleading for permission to enter Venezuela: "Instead of rigorously applying the laws, the commander of Puerto Cabello should listen to the voice of humanity, politics, and the common cause that today unites Spain and France,"[57] they complained. In addition, they described Toussaint Louverture's invasion of Santo Domingo and explained the need to receive support from the Venezuelan government in order for them to continue their trip to France. The generals promised to communicate to the French government "the deplorable state to which the horrible ambition of Toussaint had reduced the entire Island of Santo Domingo." They were sure that Toussaint intended to extend his dominion beyond the limits of Hispaniola. In such a situation, the generals argued, "France would not have any direct information apart from those that Toussaint—the enemy—communicates."[58]

Captain General Guevara y Vasconcelos agreed to allow the French generals to enter the province. In his response, Guevara y Vasconcelos acknowledged the importance of the alliance between Spain and France in the face of the terrible menace of Toussaint. Furthermore, he offered to safeguard the archives that the generals had brought with them, which included documents relating to the military, administrative, and political affairs of both parts of Hispaniola.[59] Among these documents was a long report by General Chanlatte on the deterioration of relations between Toussaint and the French generals between 1799 and 1800. In the report, Toussaint Louverture—commonly referred to as just "Toussaint"—was described as a traitor, the "usurper of the Antilles," and a "tyrannical ruler who had submerged the island in the worst state of anarchy."[60]

While in Caracas, General Kerversau wrote another report on Toussaint's political program and its effects on Hispaniola. Kerversau again contended that Toussaint was a traitor who assumed whatever position and allied with whatever party the moment demanded, with the sole intention of pursuing his personal ambitions:

> I have witnessed Tusain [sic] oppressing whites while persuading them to join him; exterminating people of color while listening to their sacred songs and clamors for piety; and ruling blacks after having killed some of the chiefs that had influence over the population.[61]

In Kerversau's opinion, Toussaint used the "republic" as an instrument of tyranny and did not hesitate to oppress the general population, including people of his own race. He concluded:

> For those of you who do not know Toussaint, forget your illusions: as long as the colony continues, he alone will rule. There will be laws, but these simply reflect his will; there will be authority, but only his . . . because this is what happens in a colony ruled by an unruly and traitorous black.[62]

This last paragraph lays bare Kerversau's racial prejudice against the black leader. Kerversau argues that "republicanism" in the hands of blacks like Toussaint becomes a "tyrannical system," not because people of African descent do not understand republicanism but because "blacks have a haughty and arrogant character" and are prone to authoritarianism.[63]

In the following months, several sworn testimonies by Dominican refugees in Venezuela reinforced this negative image of Toussaint and his army.

These accounts could only have aggravated racial and social tensions in Venezuela. In January 1801, three ships carrying 271 Dominican refugees arrived in Maracaibo. Although Fernando Mijares, the governor of Maracaibo, was surprised by the unexpected arrival of these refugees, he soon made arrangements to receive them and ordered the residents of Maracaibo to welcome them into their homes and provide them with food and shelter. He also sent two of these ships back to Santo Domingo loaded with food from Venezuela, with orders to pick up more whites seeking to escape Toussaint.[64] As the governor soon noticed, the great majority of the refugees were women, children, and domestic servants. Of approximately twenty-five families, there were only four male heads of household. Joaquín García had ordered the men to stay on the island in order to confront Toussaint's troops. After García's capitulation on January 27, however, both white men and women in Santo Domingo tried to flee from the city with their families.

Interestingly, the first three ships that arrived in Maracaibo brought a total of 152 slaves (75 plantation slaves and 77 domestics), who represented 56 percent of the refugees aboard. This preponderance of slaves was exceptional; on subsequent ships, the proportion of slaves decreased drastically. Historian Carlos Deive provides an explanation for this situation: after entering the city of Santo Domingo, Louverture strictly prohibited Dominican masters from exporting their slaves. Toussaint argued that he could not allow the exit of the people upon whom the agriculture of the island depended. García tried to dissuade Toussaint, and he ultimately decided to allow departing Dominicans to take only their domestic slaves (who were included in the category "criados," or servants) with them. As a result, the number of slaves decreased, but the number of criados increased; there was probably a high percentage of domestic slaves among those criados.[65]

White refugees portrayed themselves as victims of Toussaint, whose invasion had forced them to leave their homes and haciendas, to abandon their slaves and possessions, and to bid farewell to their families and communities. Their narratives also emphasized the dangers they had faced at sea: a tempestuous climate with strong winds, plus the constant threat of piracy. This was, in fact, the situation confronted by the refugees onboard the *Ventura*. English pirates boarded their ship, took everything they could from the families (including twenty-four slaves), and destroyed everything else. When the pirates "tried to fondle the women," however, "the Priest Valverde bravely

Table 3. Arrival of Dominicans in Maracaibo, January–March 1801*

SHIP	WHITES	"CRIADOS"	SLAVES	TOTAL
Ventura (01/20/1801)	53	43	0	96
Santa Cecilia (01/22/1801)	11	6	11	28
Soledad (01/23/1801)	55	28	64	147
Nuestra Señora del Carmen (01/29/1801)	33	54	0	87
Ventura (02/04/1801)	101	68	0	169
Dinamarquesa† (02/14/1801)	85	12	0	97
San Cristobal (02/23/1801)	295	4	1	300
La Elisa‡ (02/22/1801)	4	6	0	10
Soledad (02/27/1801)	90	0	0	90
Nuestra Señora del Carmen (02/27/1801)	32	0	0	32
Americana (02/27/1801)	14	2	0	16
San Quins and Santa Julita (08/02/1801)	289	14	7	310
Nuestra Señora del Rosario (03/28/1801)	21	0	0	21
Total	1,083	237	83	1,403

* This table compiles thirteen reports in "Relaciones del número de personas emigradas de la Isla Española de Santo Domingo y llegadas al Puerto de Maracaibo (enero–marzo, 1801)," AGI, Estado, 60, no. 3.

† On this ship arrived don Leonardo Del Monte y Medrano with his family and five "criados." Del Monte was a magistrate of the Real Audiencia of Santo Domingo. Apparently, he stayed in Maracaibo until 1809, when he and his family moved to Cuba. His son, Domingo Del Monte, was born in Maracaibo on August 4, 1804. Domingo was a recognized man of letters and a critic; he was accused of participating in the La Escalera conspiracy in 1844.

‡ On this ship arrived the governor and captain general of Santo Domingo, don Joaquín García, and his family. García stayed in Maracaibo for three and a half months. He then went to Havana, arriving there on July 20, 1801.

opposed them, claiming that they would have to kill him before committing these atrocious actions against the women."[66] Such were the testimonies, loaded with high-seas drama. Another ship carrying families from Santo Domingo suffered the impact of strong winds and a heavy sea, and its captain was forced to change course. The ship reached land in the middle of the night. The passengers had to walk along the beach in the dark, suffering from hunger and fatigue, until they finally found help.[67]

Governor Joaquín García chose Maracaibo as a destination not only for himself and his family but also for other high-ranking Spanish refugees. These included the Cantabria Regiment, the commanders of Santo Domingo, some ministers of the royal treasury, magistrates of the royal court, secretaries, and important militiamen. According to Deive, García believed that the maritime route from Santo Domingo to Maracaibo was more secure than others, and he wanted to ensure the safety of the papers, money, and books that belonged to the Crown.[68] García landed in Maracaibo with his family, six domestic slaves, and Secretary Nicolás Toledo on February 22, 1801. Immediately after his arrival, he contacted the governor of Maracaibo and relayed his impressions of Toussaint Louverture's invasion. In a letter addressed to Venezuela's captain general, García contended that the black leader had taken the island by violence, brazenly breaking the terms of the Treaty of Basel. He had forced García to leave and had taken "everything that belonged to the king, establishing authoritarian rule, and setting a terrible example for the people of color and the slaves."[69] For García, it was clear that Toussaint represented a clear menace to the Spanish territories, and also a terrible example for people of African descent in the region.

On March 11, 1801, eighteen Dominicans who had settled in Maracaibo signed a letter to the governor of Caracas narrating the events of Toussaint's invasion of Santo Domingo:

> The consternation that from that awful moment invaded our hearts was such that there was no longer order nor agreement in Santo Domingo. Everyone tried immediately to abandon the unhappy fatherland with all their goods and possessions: each person boarded a ship wherever and however he could. Therefore our exit resembled more a precipitous escape than a planned emigration, and those who have managed it are fortunate, because the unfortunate who were not able to leave now find the port closed and are suffering the humiliations and shame that are the consequence of the Government of a despotic black, full of ambition and desire.[70]

The refugees depicted the actions of the blacks and mulattoes in Saint-Domingue as chaotic and destructive, devoid of any political plan or ideological purpose. For the Dominican refugees, it was not possible to imagine blacks and mulattoes fighting for the political ideals of liberty and equality, or for republicanism. None of these accounts mentioned Louverture's ideological grounds or political goals. For the white Dominicans, the blacks and mulattoes of Haiti were merely "ambitious" people whose only purpose was to kill whites, destroy their possessions, and take control of the Spanish capital city.

Although records show that 320 slaves (both domestic and agricultural) arrived with their masters in Maracaibo, there are no testimonies from the slaves that would allow us to assess their opinions of Toussaint, the revolution in Saint-Domingue, or the invasion of Santo Domingo. In Santo Domingo, according to Deive, free people of color favored Louverture and celebrated his arrival, and the remaining slaves on the island acclaimed him when he abolished slavery in August 1801.[71] In Venezuela, it was reported that black communities in Coro celebrated the invasion of the Spanish part of the island by Toussaint, while others in the rich agricultural valleys near Caracas "displayed great rejoicing and merriment at the news, using the chorus 'Look out for Tisón [Toussaint]' as others responded 'They'd better watch out.'"[72]

From January to April, more ships carrying refugees reached ports throughout Venezuela, such as Barcelona in the province of Cumaná, where Governor Vicente Emparan received thirty-one refugees, and Paraguaná de Coro, which became home to a smaller group of refugees. On January 27, 1801, Andrés Boggiero, commander and magistrate of Coro, received news that a ship from Santo Domingo had run aground at the port of La Vela de Coro. On board were approximately 120 refugees who had "fled from the revolution of blacks in Santo Domingo" and who had walked for more than twenty-four hours, from the beach to the city of Coro. Boggiero was uncertain whether to welcome these refugees, as he worried they might bring destabilizing rumors and information. He soon received an official order to admit them while keeping an eye out for any "French individuals" entering the province and preventing their communication with locals.[73]

The refugees who landed at La Vela de Coro brought updated but familiar stories about Toussaint's invasion, which they shared with Boggiero. Their accounts followed the same pattern as those told by other Dominican refugees: Toussaint was a traitor who did not respect the terms of the Treaty of Basel or the Capitulations; he took everything he could from the royal treasury; and he unilaterally freed all the slaves on the island.[74]

In March, Boggiero sent four accounts written by these refugees, who had temporarily settled in Coro, to Venezuela's captain general. The accounts described the events of the invasion: the number of Toussaint's troops, García's capitulation, and general reports regarding the black troops in the city. All four accounts argued that Toussaint had breached the Treaty of Basel and that his troops had allowed anarchy to reign in Santo Domingo. Don Bartolomé Segura, for example, asserted that Toussaint had come into the capital with "2,200 hungry and naked blacks" and had established "barbarism, disorder, despotism, sensuality, and other vices." Don Domingo Díaz Páez added: "The situation of our island is monstrous. The city, which before was a center of harmony and good order, has been reduced today to the most astonishing anarchy."[75] Another witness, don Andrés Angulo, observed:

> Toussaint's purpose is to make them [the blacks] masters of the entire island ... to destroying and annihilating it, and even to spreading its fire to neighboring possessions. This, I think, may be expected in view of his ambition and his daring nature.[76]

Another witness, don Francisco Mosquera y Cabrera, echoed these views:

> The purpose of the blacks is doubtless to extend their evil all over the island, destroying everything—like they did in the French part. Then they would happily extend this evil to other islands.[77]

The Maracaibo episode of 1799 and these accounts of victimhood at the hands of Toussaint Louverture and his followers soon afterward certainly increased the local elite's fear of invasion led by foreign blacks; it was clear now that *negros franceses* were willing to extend their revolution into neighboring Spanish-speaking regions. Enforcing military control over the coast and avoiding any communication between foreigners and locals were some of the measures authorities took to reduce the risk.

The events of 1799–1801, however, also led local whites to exhibit greater mistrust and apprehension of Venezuela's substantial African-descended population. Accounts from this period continually represented blacks not only as naturally prone to violence and revenge but also as incompetent and evil-minded political leaders, not necessarily because of their ignorance but because of their allegedly natural propensity for violence and authoritarian rule. French agents took pains to separate "French republicanism" from "black republicanism," depicting the latter as a system corrupted by the vices of blacks, yet conservative Spaniards and creoles argued that republicanism was itself the seed from which all chaos and disorder grew, promoting ambition and insolence among blacks. Local Spanish authorities knew all too well that revolutionary ideas were already circulating widely in Venezuela; at this point, it was crucial for them to continue spreading an image of republicanism as a destructive and chaotic system, convincing the local population (including the large free black population) that those events that we now call the Haitian Revolution only brought about misfortune, misery, and despair to all of Hispaniola's inhabitants, regardless of race and status. This official campaign needed to be accompanied, of course, by concrete actions that could distract the rebellious souls of the province. With the excuse of "calming the spirits," the colonial state, for example, allowed slaves and free blacks to present demands to local governments and to negotiate certain conditions with masters and local whites. Saint-Domingue not only increased white Venezuelans' fears and consternation regarding those who served them; it also opened new and significant spaces of interaction between whites, pardos, and blacks.

CONCLUSION

Venezuela and the Revolutionary Atlantic

IN AUGUST 1797, A DEEPLY CONCERNED PRIEST, JOSÉ IGNACIO Moreno, wrote a long essay describing the terrible circumstances that put the once calm and harmonious Captaincy General of Venezuela in imminent danger. For him, it was clear that the "fires of sedition and insubordination" that were spreading rapidly throughout Europe and the Americas had reached Venezuelan shores. Revolutionary France, he believed, was the original source of all evil and misfortune, and the tight bonds that linked Europe and the Americas allowed the effective expansion of a revolutionary disease that was "firing the most innocent and incautious hearts of the Province."[1] Moreno went on to offer a detailed analysis of the many factors that contributed to what he perceived as a pernicious contagion. He believed that the force of revolutionary ideas ("the disease"), coupled with the efficient and uncontrollable paths that connected nations, plus the weakness of local authorities who failed to jealously guard their territory, were responsible for the expansion of the "revolutionary fire" on the mainland.

This book has sought to illuminate the rich and complex realities that Father Moreno found so terrible and threatening. A key player in the densely interconnected Atlantic basin of Moreno's day, late colonial Venezuela was one of the many places visited by revolutionaries and their ideas. As Janet Polasky argues, the eighteenth-century revolutionaries' world was a world in motion, with no national borders.[2] In this world without boundaries, the exposed and unprotected coast of Venezuela offered a special opportunity to spread the seeds of change and insubordination in Spanish America. By the end of the eighteenth century, Venezuelans found themselves fully exposed to the revolutionary ideas and movements that had transformed the Atlantic world. This exposure had grown rapidly for many reasons. First, more people were engaging with written materials, expanding their sources of information and the kind of knowledge they consumed. This book has shown that the number of people who owned books had risen, and the size and diversity of private libraries had grown significantly, spurring an evolving process of secularization of reading practices. At the same time, an incipient but stable book market began to operate at the end of the eighteenth century. This led to the creation of new networks for the circulation of books and printed materials, while practices of lending books and manuscripts, transcribing texts, and reading excerpts aloud crossed social and racial boundaries, revealing the sociopolitical dimensions of print culture in late colonial Venezuela. A slow but steady transformation of everyday practices of reading and writing, and changes in readers' relationships with the written word, led to the emergence of new public spaces for the discussion of revolutionary ideas, different political projects, and novel social codes.

By the end of the eighteenth century, these emerging public spaces were also filled with a torrent of foreign pamphlets, broadsides, newspapers, and letters that trespassed the permeable frontiers of the Captaincy General of Venezuela and reached diverse social groups. In a society with no printing presses, these ephemeral materials facilitated the exchange of ideas and information among underprivileged groups. Thanks to their accessibility and also to their fugacious character, many of these texts eluded capture and censorship by the colonial state, the church, and the white elites; they offered different views of the French and Haitian Revolutions to readers and listeners. Written and spread by Caribbean and local actors, these ephemeral texts provided readers and listeners in Venezuela with concrete ideas about republicanism, emancipation, abolition, and equality and brought Venezuelans closer to the Caribbean's revolutionary struggles.

This book has also shown that by the time of the Atlantic revolutions, written knowledge expanded to social groups such as pardos, free blacks, and slaves formerly at the margins of literacy. These popular groups had found ways to learn the basic skills of reading, writing, and counting, taking part in a semiliterate culture where brief written texts intermingled with images, dialogues, songs, and performances. The social expansion of literacy and the existence of semiliterate media were coincidently reinforced by printed materials arriving from the revolutionary Caribbean near the end of the eighteenth century. Reading and writing, but also reciting, singing, and pamphleteering, became, then, deeply meaningful practices for socialization that contributed to the formation of an incipient public sphere and the configuration of local political communities.

Books, pamphlets, and newspapers were certainly not the only sources of information available to Venezuelans. Hundreds of visitors from France and the French Caribbean entered Venezuela, sharing with local inhabitants oral news of recent events in France and its colonies as well as their own political ideas and motivations. Together, visitors and local inhabitants of Venezuela contributed to the creation of images of the French and Haitian Revolutions—images that embodied and responded to local anxieties, fears, and hopes.

In his 1797 essay, Padre Moreno argued that the presence of revolutionary travelers and their papers was particularly damaging, because even the most loyalist Frenchmen offered venues for local inhabitants to question local authority, social hierarchies, and even the monarchical order. Moreno maintained that regardless of their political inclination, all the Frenchmen had been exposed to "ferocious Jacobins, and bastard and fanatical patriots";[3] and their words and written texts could not hide their republican tendencies, leaving ruinous impressions on the local population. Moreno's view was a clear reflection of the great fear that most members of Venezuela's white elite shared. This book has shown, however, that white paranoia was at times grounded in concrete facts, in the reality of a colonial state trying (and clearly failing) to "catch up" with the "revolutionary fire."

At the beginning of the 1790s, colonial authorities seemed concerned with the presence of a few unwelcome French subjects. These were quickly expelled from the province, but soon afterward local authorities faced a new source of "contagion": locals who frequently engaged in public discussions about political matters, displayed seditious posters in public spaces, and openly aired opinions against the colonial government or the socioracial order. By 1797, authorities struggled to placate a republican movement that stood for "liberty and equality" and whose leaders attracted remarkable support from a group of mixed-race pardos, whites, and free blacks as well as small merchants, artisans, and barbers. Their meeting place was La Guaira, the principal port city of the captaincy general and gateway to Caracas. As this book has shown, La Guaira's republican movement was entrenched within complex social networks and webs for the circulation of oral and written information. Proclamations, poems, short stories, songs, and copies of the "Declaration of the Rights of Man and of the Citizen" and other revolutionary documents from France and Spain offered diverse individuals opportunities for discussion and debate, all of which enabled the emergence of a genuine political community. This was, in effect, the most worrisome danger of the "revolutionary disease": it allowed individuals of any status or condition to think and act politically, making used of the language of republican rights that had been consecrated by the Atlantic revolutions.

Of course, most colonial authorities and elites failed to recognize the possibility of political action by subordinate groups of color. In their view, someone like José Leonardo Chirino, perceived as an ignorant zambo, could not comprehend the revolutions, much less follow any coherent plan. For political and social elites, the great Coro rebellion of 1795 never constituted a true political movement. Instead, it was depicted as an atrocious and chaotic revolt that sought to exterminate the white population and to establish a regime based on racial hatred.[4] For slaves and free blacks, on the other hand, the Coro rebellion allowed them, at least temporarily, to voice their demands for better material conditions and to become political actors who made use of new words, images, and symbols of revolution to open spaces for contestation and demand change. Saint-Domingue certainly remained a powerful image for the people of Coro, but it was an image that had contrasting meanings. For colonial officials, it referred to republicanism. For the white elite, it represented the extermination of white planters, the destruction of their means of production, and the establishment of a new sociopolitical order. For local free blacks and slaves, however, Saint-Domingue exemplified the chance to initiate dialogue with those in power, to reimagine their relationship with the colonial state and with white elites, and to negotiate their demands with colonial authorities.

During the last years of the eighteenth century, Venezuela's colonial officials became convinced that the tide of French Caribbean uprisings and associated ideological turbulence had reached the long coast of the captaincy general. This vast and thinly patrolled region was now frequently visited by black corsairs who not only attacked towns but also threatened to spread seditious ideas among locals to incite them to lead their own rebellions. The fear of possible invasion by black Frenchmen and the fear of revolutionary contagion reached a fever pitch that kept governors, port officials, and white elites in a constant state of alert. The general worry over a potential foreign invasion led officials to increase vigilance over coastal regions, and it also spurred white elites to strengthen their surveillance over the local African-descended population.

It is clear that the effective diffusion of information about the Atlantic revolutions, especially that of Haiti, plus the eruption of local rebellions and conspiracies and the growing fear of foreign invasion, altered socioracial relations in late colonial Venezuela. Colonial authorities and white elites began to pay more attention to pardos, free blacks, and slaves and to reconsider their relations with these subordinated groups of color, heightening their suspicions and undermining their confidence in them. At the end of his 1797 essay, Padre Moreno concluded that Venezuela was indeed sickened by the revolutionary disease. However, for him it was still possible to propose remedies: "The same way the human body recovers from an affliction, political societies should be able to restore themselves."[5] Moreno proposed strengthening the four pillars of colonial rule: the moral, the political, the military, and the economic. For him, such reinforcement could only be accomplished if the authorities increased control and repression.[6] But, were control and repression really the only possible remedies?

During the last decade of the eighteenth century, colonial officials and white elites responded to the perceived threat of black insurgency in the region in multiple ways. Between 1790 and 1808, both of Venezuela's captains general, first Pedro Carbonell and then Manuel de Guevara y Vasconcelos, issued orders limiting the importation of slaves and requiring greater surveillance of the black population by white masters and local authorities. Venezuelan masters and landowners also decided to curtail slave importation. By 1795, the number of enslaved Africans arriving in the captaincy general decreased dramatically; landowners preferred to hire free blacks and mixed-race laborers to work their haciendas.[7]

Officials in charge of Venezuela's ports and coastal areas clamped down on the entrance of maritime maroons from the Caribbean into the mainland. They did what they could to prevent their contact with local blacks. In 1790, Captain General Carbonell suspended application of the royal decree that conferred freedom on foreign slaves and also discouraged local masters from accepting any fugitives on their haciendas. They also began a campaign to repatriate those slaves who had recently arrived from the Caribbean. In regions where the presence of maritime maroon communities was evident, for example near the settlements of the luangos of the Serranía de Coro and Barlovento, colonial authorities made efforts to control the maroons and isolate them from local black communities. In Coro, they offered the luangos incentives, such as the right to use royal lands, in order to keep them contented and loyal to the Spanish Crown.

Officials implemented new surveillance strategies to optimize vigilance over the captaincy general's population of color. In different coastal regions and in the central valleys of the Province of Caracas, governors ordered white militia companies to be alert and to squelch potential uprisings. In port towns, they designated neighborhood magistrates with the responsibility of monitoring rumors and keeping track of suspicious gatherings. Special attention was given to local maroon communities, not just to monitor them but to break them up. From 1794 to 1797, the captain general relied on the formation and use of squadrons made up of soldiers and civilian residents throughout Venezuela to monitor slaves, dismantle maroon communities, and bring the population of color in rural regions into order.[8] Venezuela's merchant guild also paid for some of these semiprofessional squads, while others were financed by hacendados. From 1794 to 1797, for example, fifteen patrol squadrons of approximately twenty-four soldiers each were monitoring slaves and maroons in the Province of Caracas.

Colonial authorities in Venezuela, however, also acknowledged the need to keep blacks generally contented while quashing what they regarded as subversive movements. Authorities not only demanded greater vigilance on the part of local officials but also encouraged local authorities and masters to moderate their punishments and to use rational methods to discipline their slaves, even asking them to submit to some demands of their slaves and free people of color. As we have seen above, in some cases, governors even asked local authorities to set aside tribute collection orders among indigenous groups and to suspend some of the new and unpopular commercial taxes that had been implemented in the early 1790s. A royal decree of 1798, for example, ordered tax collectors in Coro to collect only the commercial taxes, tributes, and duties approved by the king, and charged the new commander of Coro, Andrés Boggiero, to watch for possible abuses on the part of tax collectors.

Slaves and free blacks perceived this shift in the disposition of local authorities and took advantage of these new spaces for negotiation to demand more attention, request concessions, and even file accusations of abuse against local authorities. Different colonial officials alerted local commanders and white masters to the importance of keeping their haciendas in order and to making certain their slaves were well treated. In contrast to the naked coercion employed in Coro in 1795 and in other regions of the Spanish

Caribbean such as Cuba,[9] colonial authorities in Venezuela used more subtle methods of control, often making concessions to improve the material conditions of slaves and mixed-race and free black workers, and curtailing the abuses of masters, tax collectors, shopkeepers, and local authorities.

The quick and thorough expansion of revolutionary ideas, the example of Saint-Domingue, the development of local rebellions and conspiracies, and the fear of foreign invasion and republican contagion all left strong impressions on the Venezuelan population. By the end of the eighteenth century, colonial officials and white elites began to reconsider their relationship with their slaves and with free blacks. Rumors of revolution made them suspicious of blacks and pardos, undermining a fragile sense of unity and loyalty that they imagined had existed before 1791. For them, the natural response to rebellion and conspiracy was fear, control, and repression, but the very sense of mistrust and consternation, surprisingly, encouraged colonial officials and white elites to also enter into new agreements with local free blacks and slaves. Daunted by the power of the Caribbean revolutions, authorities soon realized that it was essential to prevent discontent among the population of color. They thus gradually began to make concessions in an effort to defuse the political agitation that might otherwise have led to rebellion and unrest. This strategy, in turn, opened spaces for negotiation and contestation that allowed pardos and blacks to seek new social and political roles. Revolutionary images, impressions, and language had revealed new possibilities among contrasting socioracial groups in Venezuela, but the international tensions that continued through the first decade of the nineteenth century with the ascension to power of Napoleon in Europe and the definitive independence of Haiti in 1804 kept Venezuelans attentive.

As the process of Venezuelan independence unfolded in the second decade of the nineteenth century, creole patriotic leaders such as Simón Bolívar confronted the challenges of the "chaotic, unformed, and mixed-race reality"[10] of Venezuela, a reality that just a few years earlier had been "infected" by the revolutionary Caribbean "contagion," shaken by local republican conspiracies and slave rebellions, and fundamentally altered from within by the formation of an incipient yet vibrant public sphere. For these creole leaders and for the people of color who followed them, the close, familiar, and recognizable history and experience of Haiti might as well have served as an enduring political model, one that sought equality and liberty for all.

Appendix

List and Description of the Prohibited Books Seized in the Libraries of La Guaira's Conspirators during the Investigation and Sent by the Audiencia of Venezuela to Spain in 1802[1]

1. "One volume of the *Bibiothéque amusante et instructive, contenant des anecdotes interessantes et des histoires curieuses tirées des meilleurs auteurs*, a book written by Jean-Pierre Nicéron and François-Joachim Duport du Tertre."

Jean-Pierre Nicéron and François-Joachim Duport du Tertre, *Bibliothèque amusante et instructive, contenant des anecdotes interessantes et des Histoires curieuses tirées des meilleurs auteurs* (Paris: Chez Duchesne, 1755).

This book, found inside a drawer of José María España's desk, contains several essays about the diversity of human nature. From a comparative perspective, the authors explore differences and commonalities among a number of cultures. Topics such as beauty, memory, chastity, women, vengeance, marriage and infidelity, festivities, justice, health and medicines, death, and divination are studied comparatively, with the intention of enlightening the reader about people of different nations and regions. Indigenous communities of the Americas are mentioned several times to show how they differ from Europeans in their nature and the way they live.

2. "Two volumes of the *Dictionnaire de la marine françoise avec figures, par Charles Romme*."

Charles Romme, *Dictionnaire de la marine françoise avec figures* (Paris: Chez P. L. Chauvet, 1792).

This dictionary emphasizes the importance of the maritime sciences for the development of nations and commercial networks. The book was conceived as a guide introducing the general reader to the basic concepts of maritime science.

3. "Two volumes of the book *Histoire général de l'Amérique*."

R. P. Touron, *Histoire général de l'Amérique depuis sa découverte, qui comprend l'histoire naturelle, ecclesiéstique, militaire, morale e civile des contrées de cette grande partie du monde*, 14 vols. (Paris: Chez Jean-Thomas Hérissant, 1768–1770).

Although the title is incomplete, this is likely the multivolume work by R. P. Touron, *Histoire général de l'Amérique depuis sa découverte*, published in Paris in 1768.

4. "Ten volumes of the book *Histoire de l'Eglise*, written by the Abbot de Choisy between the years 1700 and 1723."

Abbé de Choisy, *Histoire de l'Eglise*, 10 vols. (Paris: Chez Christophe Davi, 1701–1723).

These ten volumes trace the history of the church from 100 BC to AD 1715. The Holy Office banned these volumes on the grounds that the author had committed many historical mistakes and imprecisions regarding the history of the church.

5. "Seven volumes of the book *Histoire philosophique et politique des établissements et du commerce des européens dans les deux Indes*, written by Abbé Guillaume Raynal."

Abbé Guillaume Raynal, *Histoire philosophique et politique des établissements et du commerce des européens dans les deux Indes* (Amsterdam: n.p., 1770).

Raynal was a French writer and philosopher who wrote several volumes on philosophy, politics, and commerce, as well as an encyclopedia on the Americas. The latter combined information on the New World with philosophical reflections on slavery and colonialism. In this work, Raynal praises commercial activities and trade but denounces slavery and calls into question the principles of colonialism. The volumes are considered Raynal's most significant work and his main contribution to liberal thought. After three successful editions, some including virulent attacks against despotic powers, the book was included in the French and Spanish index of prohibited books in 1774. According to documentation provided by the commissioners, these volumes belonged to José María España.

6. "One volume entitled *Histoire de Bayard*."

Guillaume-François Guyard de Berville, *Histoire de Pierre du Terrail, dit Chevalier Bayard, san peur et san reproche* (Lyon: Chez Barnuset, 1786).

This book is a biography of a French knight, the Chevalier de Bayard, who fought in the war between France and Italy in 1504. The book was considered a chivalric tale that praises French blood and braveness.

7. "Two volumes of an unidentified book entitled *Examen des finans*."

8. "One volume of an unidentified book entitled *Catechism de Bayonne*."

9. "One volume entitled *Lettres juives, ou correspondance philosophique, historique, et critique*."

Jean-Baptiste de Boyer, Marquis d'Argens, *Lettres juives, ou correspondance philosophique, historique, et critique entre un juif voyageur à Paris et ses correspondans en divers endroits* (La Haye en Touraine, France: Pierre Paupie, 1764).

This book offers a general description of life in Paris, with interesting comments on changing political and social relations. The book belonged to Captain José María Salas, who was interrogated for sharing some of his books with the La Guaira conspirators; he declared that, during his stay in the port, he attended several meetings with the insurgents, "but not those in which the virtue of the Republics of France or North America were a topic of conversation."

10. "The first volume of a book entitled *Oeuvres de J. J. Rousseau*."

Jean-Jacques Rousseau, *Oeuvres complets* (Paris: Chez de Maisonneuve, 1793–1800).

This book seems to be the first of the approximately eighteen volumes of the complete works of the French philosopher and political thinker Jean-Jacques Rousseau. Rousseau's writings, such as *Discourse on Inequality* and *The Social Contract*, are cornerstones of modern political and social thought and made a strong contribution to theories of democratic government. His books were prohibited in Spain because they were considered antimonarchical and a threat to social harmony. This book also belonged to Captain José María Salas, who had lent it to the conspirators.

11. "Two volumes, first and second, of an unidentified book *Histoire de Tamerlan*."

Jean-Baptiste Margat de Tilly, *Histoire de Tamerlan, empereur des Mongols et conquerant de l'Asie* (Paris: Chez Hippolyte-Louis Guérin, 1739).

12. "One volume of the book *Bibliothéque phissico economique instructive et amusante.*"

Jean-Baptiste Bory de Saint-Vincent, *Bibliothéque phissico economique instructive et amusante* (Paris: Chez Buisson, 1782–1793).

This book offers a general appraisal of the latest improvements and inventions in agricultural production, labor and new occupations, domestic economy and administration, healing, and diseases. The work comprised nineteen volumes, but the audiencia found only one.

13. "Two volumes, the third and fourth, of the book *Recueil de pieces galantes en prose et en vers*, written by Madame Henriette de Coligny, Comtesse de la Suze, and Monsieur Paul Pelisson."

Henriette de Coligny de la Suze and Paul Pelisson, *Recueil de pieces galantes en prose et en vers* (Lyon: Chez Antoine Bondet, 1695).

This is a book of belles lettres, which includes stories and poetry on human emotions such as love, joy, and jealousy.

14. "One volume of the book *Oeuvres choisies de J.-B. Rousseau, odes, cantantes, epitres, ét poesies diverses.*"

Jean-Baptiste Rousseau, *Oeuvres choisies de J.-B. Rousseau: odes, cantantes, epitres, ét poesies diverses.* Paris: Janet et Cotelle, 1823.

This book, first published in 1723, is divided into five parts: odes, odes in music, allegories, poetry, and epistles. It was written by Jean-Baptiste Rousseau, a French poet and writer who acquired a great reputation during the eighteenth century for his poetry and comedies, although he was also accused of writing obscene and libelous verses. In this work, he wrote several odes dedicated to social values such as justice, law, and the obligations of men.

15. "The seventh volume of the book *Nouveau voyage aux isles de L'Amerique contenant l'histoire naturelle de ces pays, l'origine, les moeurs, la religion et le gouvernment des habitants anciens et moderne.*"

Jean-Baptiste Labat, *Nouveau voyage aux isles de L'Amerique contenant l'histoire naturelle de ces pays, l'origine, les moeurs, la religion et le gouvernment des habitants anciens et moderne; les guerre ser les evenemens singulaires qui y son arrivez pendant le long séjour que l'auteur y a fait: le commerce et les manufactures qui y son établies, et les moyens de les augmenter* (La Haye en Touraine, France: Chez Pierre Husson, 1722–1724).

Labat was a French Dominican who was appointed procurator general of Dominican convents in the Antilles in 1696; this treatise is a compilation of his observations on the West Indies. It treats diverse subjects including the geography, flora, and fauna of Martinique, Guadeloupe, Grenada, and Saint-Domingue. Pere Labat's book paid special attention to the history and everyday life of black people, with a special chapter on "black wizards" and the system of slavery. The book also provides a complete description of the crops produced on each of the islands and devotes particular attention to the production of sugarcane, with several illustrations made by the author.

16. "One book entitled *La police de Paris dévoilée*."
Pierre Manuel, *La police de Paris dévoilée* (Paris: Chez J. B. Garnery, 1791).
Pierre Manuel was the procurator of the insurrectionary Paris commune in 1792 and a member of the National Assembly of Paris during the first years after the revolution. He wrote several additional revolutionary pamphlets such as *La bastille dévoilée* (1789) and *Lettres sur la révolution* (1792).

17. "One volume of an unidentified book entitled *Les contemporaines ou aventures des musjotier temmes de l'age present*."

Notes

Introduction

1. Humboldt, "Viaje a las regiones equinocciales," 124. In 1799 and 1800, Alexander von Humboldt traveled to the Captaincy General of Venezuela, where he visited many cities, including Cumaná, La Guaira and Caracas, Valencia, and Puerto Cabello, as well as rural regions.
2. Ibid., 125.
3. Ibid., 136.
4. "Observaciones de un Ciudadano sobre la conspiración descubierta en Caracas el día 13 de Julio del presente año y de los medios a qué podrá ocurrir el Gobierno para asegurar en lo sucesivo a sus habitantes de iguales insultos," by José Ignacio Moreno. Archivo General de Indias, Seville (hereafter AGI), Caracas, 434, 798.
5. "Observaciones de un Ciudadano . . .," by José Ignacio Moreno. AGI, Caracas, 434, 799.
6. Several "Sociedades de Amigos del País" were established in Spanish America after 1780 in towns such as Santiago de Cuba (1783), Mompox in New Granada (1784), Lima (1787), Quito and Havana (1791), and Guatemala (1794); these societies were related to local publication of newspapers, *gacetas*, and *mercurios*. See Rodríguez, *The Independence of Spanish America*.
7. In New Spain, for example, the printing press arrived as early as 1539, and in the Viceroyalty of Peru it arrived in 1581. By the end of the eighteenth century, the cities of Havana, Bogotá, Quito, Buenos Aires, and Santiago all had printing presses. The reasons why it came late to Venezuela are still the subject of debate: some historians argue that by the time Venezuela garnered administrative, political, and commercial interest on the peninsula, the menace of the circulation of revolutionary ideas in the Atlantic world eradicated any motivation for establishing printing presses in centers where they could become machines for disseminating dangerous revolutionary propaganda. See Grases, *La imprenta en Venezuela*.

8. Local periodical publications and the expansion of the print market were not necessary for the emergence of a public sphere in Venezuela, where an extensive public voiced, read, transcribed, and exchanged ideas about the Atlantic revolutions. Since the publication of Benedict Anderson's *Imagined Communities* in 1991, historians of late colonial Spanish America and of the newly independent Latin American states have focused on the role of print capitalism in the constitution of new identities and political communities but have provided little analysis to understand regions without printing presses. In the edited volume *Beyond Imagined Communities*, however, François-Xavier Guerra and John Charles Chasteen question both Anderson's premise that national consciousness preceded the wars of independence and the straightforward relation he drew between printing and the emergence of national identities. Guerra, "Forms of Communication, Political Spaces, and Cultural Identities," 3–32; and Chasteen, "Introduction: Beyond Imagined Communities," ix–xv.
9. The first Venezuelan press was established in Caracas by the printers Gallagher and Lamb in October 1808, when Spanish authorities decided to print texts supporting the rights of Ferdinand VII and legitimizing the *juntas* (*Gaceta de Caracas*, the first Venezuelan newspaper, was founded to promulgate these views). In the following years, the press in Caracas became a battleground in the conflict between royalists and patriots, and by 1810 both groups had established a number of newspapers and *semanarios*. See Millares Carlo, *Introducción a la historia del libro*; Martínez, *El libro en Hispanoamérica*; Grases, *Historia de la imprenta en Venezuela*; and Ramírez-Ovalles, *La opinión sea consagrada*.
10. For works that analyze the open dynamics and interimperial character of the Caribbean region, see Gaspar and Geggus, *A Turbulent Time*; Piqueras, *Las Antillas en la era de las luces*; Rupert, *Creolization and Contraband*; Gómez, "El síndrome de Saint-Domingue"; and Bassi, *An Aqueous Territory*.
11. Bassi, *An Aqueous Territory*. As Franklin W. Knight and Peggy Liss argue, port towns and cities were the most important nodes of European expansion in the Americas during conquest and colonial settlement. Later, port cities gained significance as the Atlantic world developed a complex trading system with its various geographic sectors built around maritime commerce. See Liss, *Atlantic Empires*; and Knight and Liss, *Atlantic Port Cities*. See also recent works, such as Fuente, *Havana and the Atlantic in the Sixteenth Century*; Rupert, "Marronage, Manumission and Maritime Trade"; and Helg, *Liberty and Equality in Caribbean Colombia*.
12. In his pioneering work on regional communication networks and the dissemination of revolutionary ideas in the Caribbean, Julius Scott argued that studies of commerce and trade in eighteenth-century America overlooked the most valuable commodity of exchange: information. Scott shows that communities of slaves, maroons, and free blacks not only followed and circulated news of political developments in the metropole but used this information to advance their

own political agendas. Scott, "The Common Wind." Scott's work was aligned with the emerging historiography of the Atlantic world. See, for example, the early work of Price, "Economic Function and the Growth of American Port Towns," 123–86; and Pocock, "Virtue and Commerce in the Eighteenth Century," 119–34. For Latin America, see Halperín Donghi, *Politics, Economics and Society*.

13. For an interesting analysis of the multiple media through which revolutionary ideas circulated in the Atlantic world, 1776–1804, see the recent study by Janet Polasky, *Revolutions without Borders*.

14. Trouillot, *Silencing the Past*; Geggus, *Haitian Revolutionary Studies*; Geggus, *The Impact of the Haitian Revolution*; Geggus and Fiering, *The World of the Haitian Revolution*; Ferrer, "Noticias de Haití en Cuba," 675–94; Ferrer, "Cuba en la sombra de Haití," 179–231; Ferrer, "Temor, poder y esclavitud en Cuba," 67–83; Ferrer, "Haiti, Free Soil, and Antislavery in the Revolutionary Atlantic," 40–66; Ferrer, *Freedom's Mirror*; Nesbitt, *Universal Emancipation*; Fischer, *Modernity Disavowed*; Fischer, "Unthinkable History?"; Calargé et al., *Haiti and the Americas*; and Gaffield, *Haitian Connections in the Atlantic World*.

15. Verna, *Pétion y Bolívar*; Thibaud, "Coupé têtes, brûlé cazes," 305–31; Helg, "Simón Bolívar and the Spectre of *Pardocracia*," 447–71; Dalleo, introduction to Calargé et al., *Haiti and the Americas*, 3–22; and Fischer, "Bolívar in Haiti," 25–53.

16. For popular royalism in Spanish America, see Sartorius, *Ever Faithful*; and Echeverri, *Indian and Slave Royalists*. Marcela Echeverri, in particular, dismantles previous historiographic assumptions that royalists were struggling to restore a traditional, static, and conservative order, and convincingly shows how royalist Indians and slaves in the northern Andes engaged with ideas of freedom and citizenship, using their political identities to advance profound changes in the system.

17. The lack of printing presses and the absence of a dynamic print market (like the one that existed in North American societies) did not prevent the emergence of a public sphere in Spanish America before the independence process. Historians William B. Taylor, Víctor Uribe-Urán, and Pablo Picatto argue that in Spanish America the public sphere began to take form during the Age of Revolutions and was even structured by colonial institutions and interests. See Taylor, "Between Global Process and Local Knowledge," 115–90; Uribe-Urán, "The Birth of a Public Sphere in Latin America," 425–57; Palti, "Recent Studies on the Emergence of a Public Sphere in Latin America," 255–66; and Piccato, "Public Sphere in Latin America," 165–92.

18. For an illuminating discussion on fragmentation and the public sphere, see Piccato, "Public Sphere in Latin America," 184–92. I adapted William Roseberry's definition of "language of contention" to the agitated reality of late colonial Venezuela. Roseberry defined "language of contention" as "a common material and meaningful framework . . . in part, discursive; a common language or way of talking about social relationships that sets out the central terms around which

and in terms of which contestation and struggle can occur." Although the turbulence of the times of late colonial Venezuela don't allow us to strictly use hegemony as a concept of analysis, we could still think of the Haitian Revolution and its republican values as a discursive framework used by different social groups to legitimize their positions and demands and to, ultimately, shape their struggle. See Roseberry, "Hegemony and the Language of Contention," 361.
19. There has been an increasing interest in exploring the connections between literacy, revolution, and the public sphere in Latin America in the eighteenth and nineteenth centuries. See, for example, Castro-Klarén and Chasteen, *Beyond Imagined Communities*; Guerra, *Modernidad e independencias*; Uribe-Urán, "The Birth of a Public Sphere in Latin America"; Rosas Lauro, "La imagen de la Revolución Francesa"; Peralta Ruiz, "Prensa y redes de comunicación"; Ferrer, "Noticias de Haití en Cuba"; and Acree, *Everyday Reading*.
20. See Chartier, *The Cultural Uses of Print*; Chartier, *The Cultural Origins of the French Revolution*; Darnton, "An Early Information Society"; Pettegree, *The Invention of News*; and Van Young, *The Other Rebellion*.
21. Latin American historians have greatly contributed to the public sphere debate in their studies of state formation and the transition to modern republicanism in the region. Pablo Piccato, in particular, has offered a rich analysis of what he has defined as the "historiographical map of the public sphere in Latin America." For Piccato, the concept of "public sphere" remains useful to our understanding of the relationship between meaning, communication, and politics and their interaction with cultural change and identity formation in Latin America. Picatto reminds us, above all, that the public sphere is an unfinished historical process rather than a stable structure. See Piccato, "Public Sphere in Latin America." See also Guerra, "Forms of Communication, Political Spaces, and Cultural Identities"; Guerra, *Modernidad e independencias*, 275–318; Uribe-Urán, "The Birth of a Public Sphere in Latin America"; and Tavárez, "Zapotec Time."
22. Janet Polasky notes this overlapping of political projects and proposals throughout the eighteenth-century Atlantic world. She argues: "No single all-encompassing vision united all of the eighteenth-century revolutionaries from four continents into a common party. . . . In a time of upheaval so turbulent that anything seemed possible, no simple dichotomies divided revolutionaries from counterrevolutionaries, or even radicals from conservatives." Polasky, *Revolutions without Borders*, 3.
23. Fischer, "Bolívar in Haiti."

Chapter 1

1. The foreign visitor Robert Semple commented about *pulperías*: "Pulpería is the name given in this country to establishments which are at the same time shops,

farms, and inns. These [small shops] are generally kept by natives of Biscay or Catalonia." Semple, *Sketch of the Present State of Caracas*, 67.
2. Ruiz, *Simón Rodríguez*; and Navarro, "Un episodio divertido."
3. Ruiz, *Simón Rodríguez*, 142–44.
4. Briggs, *Tropes of Enlightenment*. Since the parents of expósitos were unknown, it was difficult to determine the *calidad* or *naturaleza* of the child; in the case of Rodríguez it seems that his adoption by the priest could have allowed him to keep a calidad of white. Regarding the complex distinction between color and naturaleza, see Twinam, *Purchasing Whiteness*.
5. Leal, *Libros y bibliotecas en Venezuela colonial*; Soriano, "El correr de los libros"; and Soriano, "Bibliotecas, lectores y saber."
6. In regard to the French Revolution, for example, Roger Chartier argues that the new ideas of eighteenth-century French philosophy "did not become imprinted on the reader's minds, [and] it is perhaps risky to credit incontestable success to philosophical works with the increase in distance between French Society and the monarchy." Chartier, *The Cultural Origins of the French Revolution*, 85. See also Chartier, *The Cultural Uses of Print*; Chartier, *The Culture of Print*; Pettegree, *The Invention of News*; and Van Young, *The Other Rebellion*.
7. "Observaciones de un Ciudadano ... by José Ignacio Moreno," AGI, Caracas, 434; "Representaciones que remite el Gobernador de Caracas sobre noticias sediciosas, y sublevaciones, 22 de junio de 1799," AGI, Estado, 67, no. 67; and "Respuesta de los miembros de la Universidad de Caracas con respecto a los efectos de las Gracias al Sacar," in Rodulfo Cortés, *El régimen de las gracias al sacar*, 2:190–92.
8. See the twenty-six-book prohibition edicts published during 1762–1809, "Edictos de prohibición de libros," Archivo Arquidiocesano de Caracas (hereafter AAC), Santo Oficio, Carpetas I, II.
9. See, for example "Carta pastoral del Arzobispo de Caracas, Narciso Collt y Pratt, 1 de junio 1812," in Suria, *Iglesia y estado*, 118–25.
10. For a discussion on censors' bureaucratic operations in the ancien régime, see Darnton, *Censors at Work*; Álvarez Gómez and Tovar de Teresa, *Censura y revolución*; Nesvig, *Ideology and Inquisition*; and Guibovich, *Lecturas prohibidas*.
11. During most of the colonial period, the Province of Venezuela, often called Province of Caracas, was established as a *gobernación*, with the governor as the most important representative of the Spanish monarchy in the region. In 1777, when the Captaincy General was established, the governor of Caracas also became the captain general of Venezuela. Among foreigners, this change created some confusion about the political jurisdiction of the Captaincy General of Venezuela; however, Venezuelan officials had a very clear idea of the limits of their jurisdiction. The traveler Jean-François Dauxion-Lavaysse commented: "Almost all European geographers confound the General Government of Caracas or Venezuela, with the province, of which the town of Saint Leon de Caracas is the capital. This town was residence of the President, Captain general, Intendant, and

Audiencia [a supreme administrative and judicial court], on which depended the respective governors of the provinces of Cumana and New Andalusian, Maracaybo, Varinas, Guiana, and the Island of Trinidad." He added: "Venezuela is the national name adopted at present by the confederated provinces, and Caracas is their metropolis: the province of Venezuela has taken the name of Province of Caracas." See Dauxion-Lavaysse, *A Statistical, Commercial and Political Description*, 55.

12. Aizpurua, *Relaciones de trabajo*, 14–15.
13. The company's creation was, in fact, closely related to the Dutch presence on the nearby island of Curaçao and the significant illegal trade of cacao between Curaçao and Venezuela. Although commercial relations between the province and the Dutch were illegal, they had a profound impact on the local economy and were only partially interrupted by the activities of the Caracas Company. See Klooster, *Illicit Riches*; Hussey, *The Caracas Company*; Piñero, "The Cacao Economy"; and Rupert, *Creolization and Contraband*.
14. For an interesting analysis of Juan Francisco de León's rebellion, see Cromwell, "Covert Commerce."
15. Piñero, "The Cacao Economy"; and Eduardo Arcila Farías, "Economía, siglos XVI–XVIII," in *Diccionario de historia de Venezuela*, 2:155–58.
16. Arellano Moreno, *Orígenes de la economía venezolana*; Arcila Farías, "Comercio de cacao"; and Piñero, "The Cacao Economy."
17. Aizpurua, *Relaciones de trabajo*, 18–19.
18. Ibid, 181–82.
19. Lombardi, *People and Places in Colonial Venezuela*; and McKinley, *Caracas antes de la independencia*.
20. Slaves in Spanish America had the right—often called *coartación* or *manumisión*—to buy their freedom from their masters through a system of periodic deposits. This situation gave rise to a significant population of free blacks. For a detailed account, see Gilij, *Ensayo de historia americana*. For a historical discussion on this topic, see Lucena Salmoral, "El derecho de coartación del esclavo"; and Aizpurua, *Relaciones de trabajo*, chap. 3.
21. He also commented: "The slave treated with injustice or cruelty by his master, has a right to carry his complaint to the judge, who may order that he or she be sold to some other master of known humanity." Dauxion-Lavaysse, *A Statistical, Commercial and Political Description*, 178.
22. In most cases, slaves were given only a plot of land, where they had to build their own huts. Laws in Spanish America allowed slaves to exchange water, wood, land, and their own crops for money. In Venezuela, this situation developed into a "hacienda pattern": masters often did not supervise the process of production and established sharecropping arrangements with their slaves, some of whom eventually earned enough money to buy their freedom. See Acosta Saignes, *Vida de los esclavos negro*; Aizpurua, *Relaciones de trabajo*; and Blackburn, *The*

Making of New World Slavery, 497. French visitor François-Joseph de Pons remarked on this phenomenon: "The Spanish negroes receive from their master only a supply of prayers, since they are very scantily provided with food and clothes; and the law is silent on this project." Pons, *Travels in Parts of South America*, 45.

23. Although traditionally historians of Spanish America—and especially of colonial Mexico—have accepted the "caste system" for social demarcation, recent literature has put into question this understanding of "castes" as transparent and stable markers of identity in the colonial world. See Soriano de García-Pelayo, *Venezuela 1810–1830*; Pellicer, *La vivencia del honor*; Alonso, *Thread of Blood*; and Rappaport, *The Disappearing Mestizo*.
24. Salcedo Bastardo, *Historia fundamental de Venezuela*; Soriano de García-Pelayo, *Venezuela 1810–1830*; Pellicer, *La vivencia del honor*; Gómez, "The 'Pardo Question'"; and Rappaport, *The Disappearing Mestizo*.
25. On how colonial documents reproduce and legitimize social categories, see Dirks, "Annals of the Archive"; and Stoler, "Developing Historical Negatives." In her book *Along the Archival Grain: Epistemic Anxieties and Colonial Common Sense*, Stoler also discusses how colonial administrators were prolific producers of social categories.
26. Purity of blood (*limpieza de sangre*) refers to a concept used to differentiate truly Christian communities from outsiders. This idea crystallized in late fifteenth-century Spain when a series of edicts were used by Spaniards to discriminate against those who were believed not to have a clean blood, such as Jews, Moors, heretics, and people of African ancestry. On purity of blood, see Twinam, *Purchasing Whiteness*, 49–51.
27. See Gutiérrez, "Sex and Family"; McCaa, "Calidad, Clase, and Marriage"; Pellicer, *La vivencia del honor*; Alonso, *Thread of Blood*; and Rappaport, *The Disappearing Mestizo*.
28. The encomienda was a system of forced labor implemented by the Spaniards to control and regulate American Indian labor and behavior. The Spanish colonizer (encomendero) received grants of numbers of Indians, from whom they could exact labor or tribute, and in exchange the Indians (encomendados) were supposed to receive protection and religious education.
29. Because many indigenous communities in the province resisted Spanish rule and were never pacified, the demographic data about indigenous communities is incomplete. Most of the information was collected from indigenous groups that were under Spanish control, such as those located in Andean region, the region of Cumaná in the east, and the central valleys near the city of Caracas.
30. McKinley, *Caracas antes de la independencia*, 38–39; and Aizpurua, *Relaciones de trabajo*, chap. 2.
31. See for example, the case of Juan Bautista Olivares, who considered himself a pardo but who was described by colonial authorities as a mulatto. "Declaración

de Juan Bautista Olivares, acusado de promover la intraquilidad pública, haciendo circular ideas sediciosas de libertad e igualdad, trasladado a Cádiz, donde se le siguió declaración indagatoria," AGI, Caracas, 346.

32. In 1807, the French visitor Dauxion-Lavaysse commented: "In this metropolis, the word zambo is synonymous with worthless, idler, liar, impious, thief, villain, assassin, and etc." Dauxion-Lavaysse, *A Statistical, Commercial and Political Description*, 72–73. Another visitor, the British agent George Dawson Flinter, observed in 1816: "Sambos, a name which, to the people of this country—Venezuela—, comprehends every vice that is degrading to human nature; indeed, they are stigmatized for the commission of the blackest crimes." Flinter, *A History of the Revolution of Caracas*.

33. Rodríguez, "Los pardos libres en la colonia." As Joanne Rappaport argues, these cases show that the social criterion of calidad was relational in nature and highly dependent on the context. Rappaport, *The Disappearing Mestizo*, 5.

34. See Langue, "La pardocratie ou l'itineraire"; and Gómez, "The 'Pardo Question.'" See also Ann Twinam's excellent analysis of pardos in Venezuela and their quest to upgrade their calidad and social conditions in *Purchasing Whiteness*, chaps. 4–7.

35. The word *mantuano*, meaning "one with a shawl (*manta*)," identified white people who wore mantas during religious festivities. People of color and of lower status were not allowed to wear these shawls. The term *grandes cacaos* referred also to wealthy cacao planters. Rosenblat, "El mantuano y el mantuanismo"; Pellicer, *La vivencia del honor*; and Quintero, "Los nobles de Caracas." Venezuelan historian Inés Quintero has written fascinating biographies of different members of the creole elite and offers a revealing picture of their struggle to keep their social status during moments of social unrest and war. See for example, Quintero, *El último marqués*; and Quintero, *La criolla principal*.

36. Twinam, *Purchasing Whiteness*, 212.

37. Soriano de García-Pelayo, *Venezuela 1810–1830*, 56–57; and McKinley, *Caracas antes de la independencia*.

38. See Sosa Cárdenas, *Los Pardos*; Rodulfo Cortés, *El régimen de las gracias al sacar*; Leal Curiel, *Discurso de la fidelidad*; and Leal Curiel, "La querella por una alfombra."

39. "Informe que el Ayuntamiento de Caracas hace al Rey de España referente a la Real Cédula de 10 de febrero de 1795; Caracas, 28 de noviembre de 1796," in Rodulfo Cortés, *El régimen de las gracias al sacar*, 2:93–94.

40. For a complete discussion of the many challenges pardos confrontaron in colonial Venezuela, see Pellicer, *La vivencia del honor*; Leal Curiel, "La querella por una alfombra"; Rodulfo Cortés, *El régimen de las gracias al sacar*; and Twinam, *Purchasing Whiteness*, chap. 7.

41. For a comprehensive study and a documentary compilation of this royal decree, see Rodulfo Cortés, *El régimen de las gracias al sacar*; and Twinam, *Purchasing Whiteness*, chap. 7.

42. See "Informe que el Ayuntamiento de Caracas hace al Rey de España referente a la Real Cédula de 10 de febrero de 1795; Caracas, 28 de noviembre de 1796," in Rodulfo Cortés, *El régimen de las gracias al sacar*, 2:93–94.
43. Authors like Federico Brito Figueroa and Laureano Vallenilla Lanz argue that the frequency of social movements and rebellions made late colonial Venezuela a place of permanent tension between imperial reforms and local control, internal social divisions and rivalries. See Brito Figueroa, *Las insurrecciones de los esclavos negros*; Brito Figueroa, *El problema de la tierra y esclavos*; and Vallenilla Lanz, *Cesarimso democrático*.
44. Peter M. McKinley, for example, describes Venezuelan society of this period as "harmonious and stable." McKinley, *Caracas antes de la independencia*, 12–16.
45. Twinam, *Purchasing Whiteness*, 206.
46. People of color, for example, used religious brotherhoods as a strategy for social mobility. See Soto, "Purchasing the Status." For a rich discussion on ways people of African descent in late-eighteenth-century Venezuela used the colonial legal system to defend their honor, see Laurent-Perrault, "Black Honor."
47. Humboldt, *Viaje a las regiones equinocciales*, 140.
48. Pons, *Travels in Parts of South America*, 32–33.
49. Leal, *La cultura venezolana en el siglo XVIII*; Leal, *Libros y bibliotecas en Venezuela colonial*; Amézaga, "Los libros de la Caracas colonial"; Pérez Vila, *Los libros en la colonia*; Panera Rico, "Los libros de la ilustración"; Soriano, "Bibliotecas, lectores y saber"; and Soriano, "El correr de los libros."
50. I have studied 727 testaments in the Province of Caracas from 1770 to 1810. Archivo General de la Nación, Caracas (hereafter AGN), Testamentarías (1770–1810). Only ninety-two postmortem inventories contained lists of books. See Soriano, "Bibliotecas, lectores y saber."
51. On the methodological problems of analyzing literacy rates in past societies, see classic works such as Cipolla, *Literacy and Development in the West*; Cressy, *Literacy and the Social Order*; and Furet and Ozouf, *Reading and Writing*.
52. Based on my analysis of ninety-two inventories. AGN, Testamentarías (1770–1810).
53. Information based on an analysis of ninety-two library inventories. AGN, Testamentarías (1770–1810).
54. Ships' inventories show the frequency and quantity of books that were imported to Venezuela during the second half of the eighteenth century. See the book lists in "Registros de Navíos," AGI, Contratación 1693 (years 1770–1773), 1694 (years 1774–1776), and 1695 (years 1777–1778); and AGI, Indiferente General 2173, 2177, and 2178.
55. In the years 1773–1778, La Viuda Irisarri e Hijo sent an average of twenty *cajones* (boxes) of books once or twice a year. Compañía Guipuzcoana also sent a significant number of boxes of books every four or five months. AGI, Contratación, 1694 (1774–1776) and 1695 (1777–1778). These ship inventories are still waiting for

a detailed quantitative analysis, which would enrich our understanding of the book market in Venezuela at the end of the eighteenth century.
56. Data from an analysis of the ninety-two library inventories found during 1770–1810. AGN, Testamentarías. See the tables in Soriano, "Bibliotecas, lectores y saber," 244–45.
57. Book lists in "Registros de Navíos," AGI, Contratación 1693 (years 1770–1773), 1694 (years 1774–1776), and 1695 (years 1777–1778); and AGI, Indiferente General 2173, 2177, and 2178.
58. Study based on the quantitative analysis of forty-two library inventories (1770–1779 and 1800–1809) containing a total of 1,515 titles. AGN, Testamentarías (1770–1809). In a previous work, I offered similar numbers, but the continuing process of analysis and identification of the books' titles has refined the results. See Soriano, "Bibliotecas, lectores y saber," 248–52.
59. Soriano, "Bibliotecas, lectores y saber"; see also Duarte, *Mobiliario y decoración interior*, 32–35.
60. See, for example, the numerous individual shipments of books that were sent to La Guaira between 1765 and 1790. AGI, Contratación 1690–1693.
61. AGN, Testamentarías, 1787A and 1798N; and Pérez Vila, "Bibliotecas coloniales en Venezuela."
62. Most bodegas and pulperías offered several hundred cartillas, religious librillos, and books of saints. AGN, Testamentarías, 1774E, 1776P, 1778G, and 1784F; and AGN, Diversos, vol. 46, 46, 50–55.
63. This was the case of doña María Muñoz, who, in 1783, complained that she needed to urgently sell her husband's library in order to maintain her household. AGN, Testamentarías, 1783E. See also the list of readers attending the public auction and buying books from the priest don Simón Marciano Malpica in 1778. AGN, Testamentarías, 1778M; and Amézaga, "Los libros de la Caracas colonial," 11.
64. New titles were often publicized in several Spanish newspapers. The *Gaceta de Madrid*, for example, contained large lists of the new titles (and prices) offered in peninsular bookshops.
65. See "Representación que remite al exmo: Señor Don Diego de Gadorqui, el intendente de Caracas Don Antonio Lopez Quintana sobre medidas necesarias para que no se propague las doctrinas francesas," AGI, Caracas, 514. Likewise, the Real Audiencia wrote a lengthy report in 1793 in which it referred to diverse situations in which "seditious ideas" of liberty and equality were being discussed in public settings. See "Reporte de la Real Audiencia sobre peligros que representa para las Provincias de tierra firme, la presencia de prisioneros franceses de Santo Domingo en los Puertos de la Guaira y Cavello," AGI, Estado, 58.
66. "Cuadernillo de denuncias al Secretario del Santo Oficio," AAC, Santo Oficio, Carpeta II.
67. AGN, Testamentarías, 1771C, 1780M, 1781M, 1788M, 1789M, 1797V, and 1808M; and Pérez Vila, *Los libros en la colonia*, 3–29.

68. Pérez Vila, *Los libros en la colonia*, 3–29; see also Parra, *Filosofía universitaria venezolana*, 45; and Leal, *Libros y bibliotecas en Venezuela colonial*, 2:58–60.
69. Grases, *Historia de la imprenta en Venezuela*; Soriano, "El correr de los libros"; and Leal, *La cultura venezolana en el siglo XVIII*.
70. The *libro de pinturas* owned by Cuban artisan José Antonio Aponte represents a clear example of the intertextuality of the act of narrative creation through the production of handwritten texts, copied phrases, and illustrations. See Palmié, *Wizards and Scientists*, chap. 1. The copying, transcription, and translation of books is an interesting topic that requires further attention by Latin American historians. Fernando Bouza offers a comprehensive study of the circulation of manuscripts in seventeenth-century Spain in his book *Corre manuscrito: una historia cultural del siglo de oro*. On the process of translation and the appropriation of texts and songs in Latin America during the Age of Revolutions, see Bastin, Echeverri, and Campo, "La traducción en América Latina."
71. Parra, *Filosofía universitaria venezolana*, 45–50; and Leal, *Documentos para la historia*. I have also documented the case of the pardo Juan Bautista Olivares (see chap. 2 of this volume), who studied Latin, theology, and philosophy with books borrowed from San Felipe de Neri's priests.
72. "Cuadernillo de denuncias al Secretario del Santo Oficio," AAC, Santo Oficio, Carpeta II.
73. "Representación sobre la lectura de libros prohibidos en Caracas, 1782," AAC, Santo Oficio, Carpeta I. See also Watters, *A History of the Church in Venezuela*, 37.
74. Callahan, "La propaganda, la sedición y la Revolución Francesa."
75. "Real Cédula declarando que el Inquisidor General no publique Edicto alguno, Bula o Breve Apostólico sin que primero obtenga su Real Permiso (18 de enero de 1772)," AAC, Santo Oficio, Carpeta I. This decree is particularly interesting because the king clearly distinguished between "spiritual" responsibilities and civil matters corresponding to his "Royal Will and Authority." In this sense, Charles III seemed to be willing to put some limits on an institution that was depicted in other European nations as barbarous and obsolete.
76. Defourneaux, *Inquisición y censura de libros*, 206.
77. Reyes Gómez, *El libro en España y América*, 1:620–24.
78. "Real Cédula de S. M. y Señores del Consejo, por la cual se manda observar la ley veinte y tres, titulo primero de la Recopilación en quanto a que no se vendan libros que vengan de fuera del Reyno en qualquier idioma, y de qualquier material que sean, sin que primero se presente un exemplar en el consejo y se conceda licencia para su introducción o venta, con lo demás que se expresa (1 de Julio de 1784)," in Reyes Gómez, *El libro en España y América*, 1:11.
79. Río Barredo, "Censura inquisitorial y teatro."
80. "Real Cédula para que en los Reinos de Indias e Islas Filipinas se publique y observe el Edicto del Gobernador de Roma en que se manda a recoger el libro

Segunda Memoria Católica, 1789," AGN, Reales Cédulas, IV, 174–83; "Real Orden del 24 de septiembre de 1789," AGN, Reales Ordenes, X, 140; and "Real Orden para mandar a recoger papeles esparcidos por individuos de la Asamblea Nacional de Francia," AGN, Reales Ordenes, X, 198–99.

81. *Novísima recopilación de las leyes de España*, note 15, book 8, title XVIII, law XIII.
82. The Council of Castile also prohibited French catechisms such as "Catecismos Francés para la Gente del Campo," French letters like "The Manfiesto Reservado para el Rey Don Carlos IV, que Dios guarde y sus sublimes ministros," and several books, such as *La France libre* and *Des droits et devoirs de l'homme*. For the most complete history of censorship and prohibition of printed materials in Spain from the fifteenth through the eighteenth centuries, see Reyes Gómez, *El libro en España y América*.
83. "Representación del Presidente de la Real Audiencia de Caracas, sobre papeles sediciosos, Diciembre 1790," AGN, Gobernación y Capitanía General, XLIII, 96–97.
84. *Real Cédula de S. M. y Señores del Consejo*.
85. "Edictos de Prohibición de Libros," AAC, Santo Oficio, Carpetas I and II.
86. Watters, *A History of the Church in Venezuela*, 37.
87. "Cuadernillo de denuncias del Santo Oficio, 1806," AAC, Santo Oficio, Carpeta II.
88. Watters, *A History of the Church in Venezuela*, 37.
89. Defourneaux, *Inquisición y censura de libros*, 129–30; Scott, "The Common Wind"; and Pino Iturrieta, *La mentalidad venezolana*.
90. I found a total of thirteen prohibited titles in ninety-two postmortem library inventories (1770–1810). These titles surfaced in various libraries three or four times. Only 1 percent of the total identified titles in these libraries were prohibited. However, it is possible that these inventories failed to mention the forbidden titles that cautious heirs had removed from the libraries, either because they wanted to protect the memory of the deceased or because they wanted to take advantage of the money they could make by selling prohibited books clandestinely. See Leal, *La cultura venezolana en el siglo XVIII*. Prohibited titles found in these inventories included: Jean le Rond d'Alembert, *Mélanges de littérature, d'histoire, et de philosophie*; Abbé de Condillac, *Cours d'étude pour l'instruction du Prince de Parme*; Marquis de Condorcet, *Esquisse d'un tableau des progrès de l'esprit humain*; J.-F. Dauray de Brie, *Théorie des Lois Sociales*; Jacques Delille, *L'Énéide* and *La pitié, poeme*; Gaetano Filangieri, *La scienza della legislazione*; Pedro Montegnón y Paret, *Eusebio, parte primera sacada de las memorias que dejó el mismo*; Jean-Jacques Rousseau, *Du contrat social; ou principes du droit politique*; Voltaire, *Dictionnaire philosophique*; and Guillaume Thomas François Raynal, *Historia política de los establecimientos ultramarinos de las naciones europeas*. See postmortem library inventories, AGN, Testamentarías, 1770–1810.

91. On Inquisition edicts and special licenses to read forbidden books in Spanish America, see Guibovich, *Censura, libros e inquisición*; Guibovich, *Lecturas prohibidas*; and Nesvig, *Ideology and Inquisition*.
92. "Cuadernillo de denuncias del Santo Oficio, 1806," AAC, Santo Oficio, Carpeta II.
93. "Respuesta de los miembros de la Universidad de Caracas con respecto a los efectos de las Gracias al Sacar," in Rodulfo Cortés, *El régimen de las gracias al sacar*, 2:190–95.
94. The topic of "fear" of the French Revolution in Spanish America has received considerable attention. See, for example, Izard, *El miedo a la revolución*; Borrego Plá, *América Latina ante la Revolución Francesa*; Rosas Lauro, "El miedo a la revolución," 139–83; Ferrer, "Temor, poder y esclavitud en Cuba"; and Klooster, *Revolution in the Atlantic World*.
95. Fernández Heres, *La educación venezolana*; and Pellicer, *La vivencia del honor*.
96. See the book lists in "Registros de Navíos," AGI, Contratación 1693 (years 1770–1773), 1694 (years 1774–1776), and 1695 (years 1777–1778); AGI, Indiferente General 2173, 2177, and 2178; and AGN, Testamentarías, 1771C, 1780M, 1783T, 1785F, 1788M, 1794G, 1795P, 1796B, 1797M, 1797V, 1798N, 1800O, 1802M, 1804D, 1808M, 1809C, 1809O, and 1810C.
97. See Rodríguez de Campomanes, *Discurso sobre el fomento de la industria*; Rodríguez de Campomanes, *Discurso sobre la educación popular*; Jovellanos, *Memorias de la real sociedad económica*; Jerónimo Feijóo y Montenegro, *Theatro crítico universal*; Jerónimo Feijóo y Montenegro, *Cartas eruditas*; Uztáriz, *Theorica y practica del comercio*; and Ward, *Proyecto económico*. All of these titles are frequently found both in Caracas's postmortem inventories and in ship inventories between 1760 and 1780.
98. Aguilar Piñal, "La ilustración española."
99. AGN, Testamentarías, 1771C, 1780M, 1785F, 1788M, 1796B, 1797M, 1797V, 1800O, 1804D, 1808M, 1809C, and 1809O.
100. Jerónimo Feijóo y Montenegro, *Theatro critico universal*. See in particular the first discourse in volume 1, "De la voz del pueblo" (1:1–18), and the first discourse of the fourth volume, "Valor de la nobleza e influxo de la sangre" (4:1–20).
101. Rodríguez de Campomanes, *Discurso sobre la educación popular*, 5–6, 85, 111–17.
102. Jovellanos, *Memorias de la real sociedad económica*, 190–94.
103. See Leal, *Documentos para la historia*, lii. Later, in 1805, a group of elite pardos presented a second project for the creation of an elementary school for pardo children in Caracas, but these efforts were also ignored. Chachinca, *Antología documental*.
104. See "Petición de Diego Mexías Bejarano al Rey; Suplica se expida a su favor la Real Cédula sobre dispensa de calidad, 22 de junio 1797," in Rodulfo Cortés, *El régimen de las gracias al sacar*, 2:51–53; see also Pellicer, *La vivencia del honor*, 58–69.

105. Sosa Cárdenas, *Los Pardos*, 45–48.
106. Duarte, *Los Olivares en la cultura de Venezuela*.
107. Quoted by Leal, *Documentos para la historia*, lii.
108. According to the *Diccionario de Autoridades*, a cartilla is "a printed notebook with the letters of the alphabet and with the basic notions for learning to read." The cartilla was an essential tool for teaching literacy; it was very popular in Spain and Spanish America from the sixteenth to the eighteenth century. Cartillas were inexpensive and imported in great quantities to the Spanish American territories. Caracas's pulperías and small shops offered a large variety of them. See Torre Revello, "Las cartillas para enseñar a leer a los niños"; and Rueda Ramírez, "Las cartillas para aprender a leer."
109. Rodríguez, "Reflexiones sobre los defectos," 5–27.
110. Ibid., 6.
111. Ibid., 8, 10–11.
112. Religious catechisms were particularly popular in colonial Latin America; political catechisms were used later to educate popular groups during the independence period and the formation of the early republics in Latin America. See Ruiz, *Gobernantes y gobernados*.
113. Many pardos learned to read and write, but, as Rodríguez said, in "improper settings and in inadmissible ways"; Rodríguez found that as many as fifty children were being taught at different times in a single barbershop. See Rodríguez, "Reflexiones sobre los defectos," 11.
114. Soriano, "Libros y lectores en Caracas."
115. Regarding artisans who read papers and translated them for others, see the case of André Renoir, a hairdresser, who was asked to help with the translation of some paragraphs from French books. Aizpurua, "La conspiración por dentro."
116. In Spain and Spanish America, *tertulias* referred to formal or informal social gatherings where people discussed literary or artistic works, politics, and current affairs. Tertulias could develop in public settings like bars and coffeehouses, or in private homes.

Chapter 2

1. Real Cédula, "Educación, trato y ocupaciones de los esclavos en todos los dominios e Islas de Filipinas" (May 1789), AGI, Indiferente General, 802. For an understanding of the repercusiones of the edict in colonial Spanish America, see Torre Revello, "Origen y aplicación del código negrero." For a comprehension of its effects in colonial Venezuela, see Leal, "La aristocracia criolla."
2. During the 1780s, a number of small uprisings of free blacks and slaves took place in diverse regions of Venezuela, especially in the coastal region, where many

haciendas were established; these uprisings worried elites and officials, who debated the possible reasons that drove blacks to rebel. See Castillo Lara, *Apuntes para la historia colonial;* and Castillo Lara, *Curiepe: orígenes históricos.*
3. "Representación de la Real Audiencia al Rey sobre la Real Cédula de trato de esclavos de 1789, Julio 1790," AGI, Caracas, 167, no. 44.
4. Leal, "La aristocracia criolla," 68.
5. "Representación de la Real Audiencia al Rey sobre la Real Cédula de trato de esclavos de 1789, Diciembre 1789," AGI, Caracas, 167, no. 44.
6. "Representación de la Real Audiencia al Rey sobre la Real Cédula de trato de esclavos de 1789, Julio 1790," AGI, Caracas, 167, no. 44.
7. Ibid.
8. In his book *Silencing the Past: Power and the Production of History,* Michel-Rolph Trouillot argues that in spite of eighteenth-century philosophical debates and the rise of abolitionism, the Haitian Revolution represented an unthinkable event in the Western world because it challenged slavery and racism in unexpected ways. Sibylle Fischer, however, argues that in Europe a slave revolution was not as unthinkable. In her opinion, utopian novels such as *L'an 2440* (Louis-Sébastien Mercier, 1771) show that the idea of a slave revolution "was perfectly available but expressed itself . . . largely in utopias, fears, and fantasies." Fischer, *Modernity Disavowed*, 291–92. Following Fischer, I argue that this characterization of an "unthinkable event" becomes even more implausible in colonial America, where slavery was a tangible reality and masters' and slaves' everyday lives and relations shaped the slavery system itself. There are documents, such as the one I mention here, that show that white masters feared a possible slave revolution. We should also inquire if a slave revolution was also "thinkable" for the slaves. Most slaves could not write at all and therefore could not leave any records, but this does not mean that they could not have imagined a revolution on their own. See Fischer, "Unthinkable History?"
9. Earle, "Information and Disinformation in Late Colonial New Granada"; and Laviña, "Venezuela: entre la ilustración y la revolución."
10. There have been a growing number of historical studies focusing on the impact of manuscripts and ephemeral texts in early modern Europe and in the Americas. For manuscripts' circulation, see Love, *Scribal Publication in Seventeenth-Century England*; Woudhuysen, *Sir Philip Sidney*; Atherton, "The Itch Grown a Disease"; and Dierks, *In My Power.* For early modern Spain, see the comprehensive work of Fernando Bouza, *Corre manuscrito.*
11. The historiography on pamphleteering and revolutionary movements is vast; it covers different regions and historical junctures. See, for example, Earle, "Information and Disinformation in Late Colonial New Granada"; Davidson, *Propaganda and the American Revolution*; Sawyer, *Printed Poison*; Raymond, *Pamphlets and Pamphleteering*; Castillo Gómez, "There Are Lots of Papers Going Around"; and Reinders, *Printed Pandemonium*, 227–48.

12. The circulation of manuscripts, libels, and broadsides among diverse groups in societies with no printing presses has certainly extended the geographic and chronological boundaries of the concept of the public sphere. See, for example, Rospocher, *Beyond the Public Sphere*; Raymond, *Pamphlets and Pamphleteering*; Davies and Fletcher, *News in Early Modern Europe*; Dooley and Baron, *The Politics of Information*; and Fernando Bouza, *Papeles y opinión*. For Latin America, see Uribe-Urán, "The Birth of a Public Sphere in Latin America"; and Tavárez, "Zapotec Time."
13. "Expediente formado con las disposiciones referentes a evitar la introduccion en esta Provincia de papeles procedentes de la Francia, que contengan señales alucivas a la libertad," AGN, Diversos, LXVI, 290–93.
14. Juan Josef Mendiri, forty-two years old, was the guard and royal accountant of the port of La Guaira. See chapter 5.
15. Pettegree, *The Invention of News*, 326. See also Barker, *Newspapers, Politics and Public Opinion*; and Dooley, *The Dissemination of News*.
16. The number of newspapers published in the United States doubled between 1763 and 1775, and again in 1790. Newspaper publication became one of the most important props of the American publishing industry. See Pettegree, *The Invention of News*, chap. 16; Bailyn and Hench, *The Press and the American Revolution*; and Brown, *Knowledge Is Power*.
17. See Pettegree, *The Invention of News*, 340. See also Darnton and Roche, *Revolution in Print*; and Popkin, *Revolutionary News*.
18. Langlet, *El hablador juicioso y crítico imparcial*, 52.
19. Velasco, *Efemérides de la Ilustración de España*, 2.
20. See Defourneaux, *Inquisición y censura de libros*; and Reyes Gómez, *El libro en España y América*, 1:1. A recent study by Antonio Calvo Maturana offers a thoughtful analysis of the debates that Spanish enlightened absolutism confronted regarding information and public opinion at the end of the ancien régime. Convincingly, Calvo Maturana argues that the Bourbon dynasty intensified a two-pronged process: consolidation and protection of royal power, and ornamental adaptation to the liberal Enlightenment creed. The state's communicational strategies with the public responded to both concerns. Calvo Maturana, "Is It Useful to Deceive the People?"
21. For a comprehensive study of eighteenth-century Spanish newspapers and periodical publications, see Aguilar Piñal, *La prensa española en el siglo XVIII*. For an interesting view on the cultural impact of the press during the Spanish Enlightenment, see Urzainqui, "Un nuevo instrumento cultural."
22. See Torre Revello, *El libro: la imprenta y el periodismo en América*. Andrew Pettegree also argues that toward the end of the eighteenth century, newspapers in colonial and provincial settings reduced the amount of information taken from metropolitan newspapers and began to generate their own local information. At the end of the eighteenth century, local political controversies changed both the

role of the press and the circulation of papers in colonial towns. Pettegree, *The Invention of News*, chap. 16.
23. AGN, Testamentarías, 1797V, 1797M, 1802M, and 1809C; Leal, "Bibliotecas de los conspiradores"; and Callahan, "La propaganda, la sedición y la Revolución Francesa."
24. "Registro del Navío San Gabriel de la Real Compañía Guipuzcoana de Caracas, 2 de enero de 1770," AGI, Contratación, 1693. The list included the Recopilación de Leyes de Indias, which he bought in Cádiz days before his departure.
25. "Registro del Navío San Carlos de la Real Compañía Guipuzcoana de Caracas que salió para La Guaira el 10 de mayo de 1775," AGI, Contratación, 1694.
26. "Informe de la Real Audiencia sobre lectura de libros y papeles sediciosos relacionados con la sublevacion de la Guaira, 1797," AGI, Caracas, 432, 434, 436; AGN, Testamentarías (1770–1810); Callahan, "La propaganda, la sedición y la Revolución Francesa"; and Leal, *La cultura venezolana en el siglo XVIII*.
27. Discourse 5, "Fábulas Gazetales," in Jerónimo Feijóo y Montenegro, *Theatro critico universal*, 8:61–84.
28. *Gaceta de Madrid*, no. 13, February 15, 1790, 103; and *Gaceta de Madrid*, no. 61, August 2, 1791, 533. On news about the American Revolution in Spain, see García Melero, *La independencia de los Estados Unidos de Norteamérica*.
29. *Gaceta de Madrid*, no. 91, November 15, 1791, 832.
30. "Observaciones de un Ciudadano . . ." by José Ignacio Moreno, AGI, Caracas, 434; and "Representaciones que remite el Gobernador de Caracas sobre noticias sediciosas, y sublevaciones, 22 de junio de 1799," AGI, Estado, 67, no. 67. See also García Melero, *La independencia de los Estados Unidos de Norteamérica*; and Rosas Lauro, *El miedo en el Perú*.
31. "Real Orden del 24 de septiembre de 1789," AGN, Reales Ordenes, X, 140; and *Novísima recopilación de las leyes de España*, note 15, book 8, title XVIII, law XIII.
32. "Orden del Consejo prohibiendo la introducción y curso del 'Correo de París o Publicista Francés,' no. 54, 5 de enero de 1790," quoted in Reyes Gómez, *El libro en España y América*, 1:627.
33. "Real Cédula de su Majestad sobre introducción en el Reyno de papeles sediciosos y contrarios a la fidelidad, 10 de septiembre de 1791," published in the *Gaceta de Madrid*, no. 74, September 16, 1791, 665–72.
34. Frequently, eighteenth-century Spanish newspapers included texts taken from prohibited French and English books that passed unnoticed. Prohibited texts by Rousseau and Montesquieu were extracted, translated, and transformed into short essays in Spanish magazines and gazettes. See Deacon, "La libertad de expresión en España"; and Aragón, "Traducciones de obras francesas." On the erasure of France from Spanish publications, see Reyes Gómez, *El libro en España y América*, 1:632.
35. "Expediente de la Intendencia relativo a asuntos de Francia," AGN, Diversos, LXVI, 290–95.

36. "Sobre destierro del redactor de la Gaceta o papel publico de ocurrencias semanales de la Ysla de Trinidad," AGI, Caracas, 153, no. 10; and "Noticias sobre Introducción de papeles extranjeros," AGI, Caracas, 115.
37. The Province of Trinidad had been recently added to the Captaincy General of Venezuela; unlike Caracas and many other important cities that lacked printing presses, Trinidad possessed a small printing press that printed brief papers about news and current events. The relative insignificance of Trinidad allowed the entry and functioning of a printing press on that island during the eighteenth century to pass unnoticed by the authorities, contrary to the case of Caracas, where permission for a printing press was emphatically denied on different occasions. Millares Carlo, *La imprenta y el periodismo en Venezuela*.
38. "Sobre destierro del redactor de la Gaceta o papel publico de ocurrencias semanales de la Ysla de Trinidad," AGI, Caracas, 153, no. 10.
39. Aragón, "Traducciones de obras francesas"; and Gómez, "Le syndrome de Saint-Domingue."
40. Claudia Rosas Lauro shows that newspapers printed in Lima in 1793–1794 offered ample information about the French Revolution. The viceroy of Peru, Francisco Gil de Taboada, promoted special editions, arguing that it was important to "offer an official version of the Revolutionary events." Rosas Lauro, "El miedo a la revolución," 139–83.
41. Ada Ferrer notes that the captain general of Cuba, the Marquis of Someruelos, expressed his concerns in regard to the public circulation and spread of the *Gaceta* in different corners of the island of Cuba: "Everyone buys them, and they circulated widely among the blacks," he expressed. Ferrer, "Noticias de Haití en Cuba," 687–89.
42. *Gaceta de Madrid*, no. 11, February 17, 1793, 86–87; and *Gaceta de Madrid*, no. 53, June 28, 1793, 619.
43. *Gaceta de Madrid*, no. 53, June 28, 1793, 620; *Gaceta de Madrid*, no. 55, July 9, 1793, 649–50; and *Gaceta de Madrid*, no. 58, July 19, 1793, 693–94.
44. *Gaceta de Madrid*, no. 67, August 20, 1793, 827–28.
45. *Gaceta de Madrid*, no. 94, November 25, 1791, 856–57.
46. *Gaceta de Madrid*, no. 100, December 16, 1791, 915.
47. Some issues offered very detailed information about the destruction of the French colony. One issue in particular specified the number of white people who had died at the hands of the rebels (150 white men, 48 women, and 18 children) and further mentioned that 353 sugar and coffee plantations had been burned, 94 others destroyed, and 2 villages completely razed to the ground. *Gaceta de Madrid*, no. 104, December 30, 1791, 949.
48. *Gaceta de Madrid*, several issues published between March and May 1802. See also Ferrer, *Freedom's Mirror*, 154–55.
49. *Gaceta de Madrid*, no. 56, October 7, 1804, 604.

50. Pettegree, *The Invention of News*; Bouza, *Corre manuscrito*; and Earle, "Information and Disinformation in Late Colonial New Granada."
51. Sellers-García, *Distance and Documents*.
52. Earle, "Information and Disinformation in Late Colonial New Granada," 174.
53. The epistolary relation between the captain general in Venezuela and other Spanish Caribbean authorities intensified during the last decade of the eighteenth century. Multiple bounds at the AGI, in the Caracas and Estado sections, hold the hundreds of official letters that Spanish authorities in the Caribbean exchanged among themselves. See AGI, Caracas 99, 102, 105, 115, 131, 310, 521; and AGI, Estado, vols. 58–70. The governor of Trinidad, in particular, maintained a frequent correspondence with the captain general before the British invaded the island. He provided him with information about the arrival of French families from Saint-Domingue, the presence of foreign ships, the situation of Martinique and Cuba, and, of course, what was happening in Saint-Domingue. See diverse communications from the governor of Trinidad, José María Chacón, to the captain general of Venezuela, in AGN, Gobernación y Capitanía General, XLIII, 48; XLVII, 14; XLVIII, 218, 297, 307, 348; and XLVII, 14. See also Ferrer, *Freedom's Mirror*; Sevilla Soler, "Las repercusiones de la Revolución Francesa"; Córdova Bello, *La independencia de Haití*; and Deive, *Las emigraciones dominicanas a Cuba*.
54. Ferrer, "Cuba en la sombra de Haití"; and Ferrer, *Freedom's Mirror*, chap. 2.
55. Trouillot, *Silencing the Past*; and Fischer, *Modernity Disavowed*, introduction.
56. "Carta del Gobernador de Caracas al Comandante Interior de La Guaira," AGN, Gobernación y Capitanía General, LIX, 256. The same happened in other regions such as Spanish Santo Domingo and Cuba. In the case of Cuba, Ada Ferrer notes that, although colonial authorities did not hesitate to implement measures of control to limit contagion, they did not seek to control slavery's expansion; Cuban authorities never considered ending or curtailing the slave trade in order to avoid the fate of Haiti. Ferrer, *Freedom's Mirror*, 80–82.
57. "Sobre la introducción de libros y papeles franceses en estas provincias," AGN, Reales Ordenes, XII, 85–86.
58. "Expediente creado con motivo de haberse descubierto la introduccion de un papel de la Asamblea de Paris, titulado *Extracto del manifiesto que la Convencion Nacional hace de todas las naciones*," AGI, Estado, 65, no. 20. It is also mentioned in García Chuecos, *Estudios de historia colonial venezolana*; and Callahan, "La propaganda, la sedición y la Revolución Francesa."
59. Thibaud, *Un nouveau monde républicain*, chap. 2. I thank Clément Thibaud for sharing this information and his manuscript with me.
60. "Expediente creado con motivo de haberse descubierto la introduccion de un papel de la Asamblea de Paris, titulado *Extracto del manifiesto que la Convencion Nacional hace de todas las naciones*," AGI, Estado, 65, no. 20.
61. Ibid.

62. Juan Xavier Arrambide, born in Villa del Puerto Real (Cádiz, Spain), was a thirty-five-year-old merchant in the port of La Guaira, while Juan Josef Mendiri, forty-two years old, was the *guardamayor* of the port and royal accountant. See chapter 5 of this volume.
63. Carrera Montero, *Las complejas relaciones de España con la Española*.
64. "Sobre introducción y circulación de Papel 'Instrucción que debe servir de regla al Agente Interino Francés destinado á la Parte Española de Santo Domingo,'" AGI, Estado, 58, no. 8; and AGI, Caracas, 169, no. 86.
65. "Instrucción que debe servir de regla al agente interino Francés, destinado a la parte Española de la Ysla de Santo Domingo," AGN, Gobernación y Capitanía General, LIX, 237–39.
66. "La dificultad es pues, . . . , probar al mundo entero por medio de una unión íntima con los Jefes españoles quan facil es, establecer una perfecta armonía entre ambas naciones, aprovechándose de la diferencia que existe entre los principios políticos." Ibid.
67. "Persuadir para desimpresionar a aquellos ciudadanos de las falsas ideas que hayan podido imprimirseles de la revolución Francesa, y disipar en su espíritu cuantos recelos se les haya inspirado del libre ejercicio de su religión." Ibid., 238.
68. "Si el acto constitucional aniquila el dro. Horrible de esclavitud de un hombre sobre otro hombre dotado igualmente de un alma racional, es claro que este articulo no puede mirarse como una infraccion del dro. de propiedad colonial, sino por gentes llenas de preocupación o cargadas de un vil interes. Y esta objeción debe tener aun menos fuerza entre los españoles, los quales sobre tener menos esclavos que las demas naciones europeas, los han tratado siempre con una humanidad capaz de grangearlos por amigos. Deben pues, los nuevos colonos humanos y generosos esperar que sus esclavos libres ya, no abusaran de su libertad, sino que seran al contrario siempre adictos, y que no se separaran jamas de sus lados como hijos reconocidos." Ibid., 239.
69. Ibid., 237–39.
70. "Contestación del Gobernador de Barinas sobre circulación de papel 'Instrucción que debe servir de regla,'" AGN, Gobernación y Capitanía General, LIX, 19; "Contestación del Gobernador de Trinidad sobre circulación de papel 'Instrucción que debe servir de regla,'" AGN, Gobernación y Capitanía General, LIX, 258; and "Contestación del Gobernador de Coro sobre circulación de papel 'Instrucción que debe servir de regla,'" AGN, Gobernación y Capitanía General, LIX, 45.
71. "El Gobernador de Barinas, Don Fernando Mijares, remite al Capitán General dos copias que encontró del papel prohibido: 'Instrucción que debe seguir de regla,'" AGN, Gobernación y Capitanía General, LIX, 296.
72. "Carta del Gobernador de Trinidad al Gobernador de Caracas, comunicándole que pondrá en ejercicio su orden de recoger y remitir papeles que se introduzcan por la via de Santo Domingo," AGN, Gobernación y Capitanía General, LIX, 258.
73. "Observaciones de un Ciudadano . . ." by José Ignacio Moreno, AGI, Caracas, 434.

74. "Para que recojan todos los papeles abiertos que vinieren de Santo Domingo ó de otra parte, y puedan conceptuarse nocivos á la tranquilidad publica y subordinación de vida á su Majestad y a sus Ministros," AGN, Gobernación y Capitanía General, LIX, 219–23.
75. The first letter started: "Después de las muchas noticias recividas yo me lisonjeo" and ended: "Olvidad pues el agravio que os ha hecho vuestro antiguo Gobierno, y asociaos á nosotros para el bien de la Francia, y de la Espana Europea y Americana"; the second one started: "Carta Enciclica de muchos y otros Obispos de Francia a sus hermanos los demas Obispos y a las sedes vacantes" and ended: "Siguen las firmas de cinco Obispos"; and the third one: "Paris, 19 de Octubre del año del Señor de mil setecientos noventa y cinco, o cuarto de la República" and ended: Gregorio Obispo de la Diócesis de Laya y miembro de la convencion de Francia." AGN, Gobernación y Capitanía General, LIX, 219–23.
76. "Acuerdo de la Real Audiencia sobre los papeles provenientes de Santo Domingo," AGN, Gobernación y Capitanía General, LIX, 219–23.
77. "Del Capitán General de Venezuela a los Comandantes y Goberadores de su jurisdicción, sobre introducción de papeles provenientes de Santo Domingo," AGN, Gobernación y Capitanía General, LIX, 224; and AGN, Gobernación y Capitanía General, LIX, 270.
78. "Gobernador de Caracas al Príncipe de la Paz," AGN, Gobernación y Capitanía General, LIX, 235–36; also AGI, Estado, 65, no. 54.
79. "Despues de las noticias recividas, yo me lisonjeo," AGN, Gobernación y Capitanía General, LIX, 240–44.
80. Jenson, "Toussaint Louverture, Spin Doctor?"
81. He dedicated several paragraphs of the piece to explaining the political context in which the treaty had been negotiated, and depicted the Spanish as deceitful and dangerous partners. "Despues de las noticias recividas, yo me lisonjeo," AGN, Gobernación y Capitanía General, LIX, 240–44.
82. "Pero el Ministerio Español al volber de su terror, y panico, olvidó toda la sangre que vosotros haveis derramado tantas veces en los Valles, en las Sabanas, y en las Montanas de Hayti, despues de mas de trescientos anos que convatio por la gloria y utilidad de la Monarquia; ya fuese contra los antiguos Yndios, duenos legitimos de la Ysla, ya contra los Yngleses mandados por Drak Pen, y Venables [¿] o ya haya sido finalmente contra los fieros Filibustieres. No se acordó ya mas de vros. Gastos, de vras. Fatigas, y de vros. trabajos, de vro. intrepido valor por el descubrimiento y conquistas de las Yslas, y continente de la America." "Despues de las noticias recividas, yo me lisonjeo," AGN, Gobernación y Capitanía General, LIX, 242.
83. "Va a dedicarse enteramente a haceros todo el bien de que sois merecedores, y conzolaros de la ingratitude y insulto que se os ha hecho." "Despues de las noticias recividas, yo me lisonjeo," AGN, Gobernación y Capitanía General, LIX, 242.
84. "Despues de las noticias recividas, yo me lisonjeo," AGN, Gobernación y Capitanía General, LIX.

85. "Vosotros vivis juntos con ellos (los esclavos), los manejais, los alimentais, los vestis, los cuidais; y vosotros no los haveis tratado jamas a ellos con tanta inconsequencia, ni barbarie, como os ha tratado a vosotros el Gobierno espano." "Despues de las noticias recividas, yo me lisonjeo," AGN, Gobernación y Capitanía General, LIX.
86. "Cuadernillo de denuncias al Secretario del Santo Oficio," AAC, Santo Oficio, Carpeta II.
87. "El Gobernador a Vicente Emparan," AGN, Gobernación y Capitanía General, XLIX, 213; also quoted in Callahan, "La propaganda, la sedición y la Revolución Francesa," 184.
88. Pérez Aparicio, *Perdida de la isla de Trinidad*.
89. "Informe de Don Vicente Emparan al Gobernador Carbonell acerca del estado de la Provincia de Cumaná y también sobre la isla de Trinidad," AGN, Gobernación y Capitanía General, LXVII, 109.
90. Ibid.
91. Dauxion-Lavaysse, *A Statistical, Commercial and Political Description*, 30.
92. "Acuerdo de la Junta de Caracas, 19 de mayo de 1796," AGI, Estado, 58.
93. "Informe que da cuenta de lo ocurrido con aquella Audiencia sobre darle el voto consultivo en un expediente grave relativo á la Introducción de un papel sedicioso de la Asamblea de Paris que se aprehendio," AGI, Estado, 58, no. 5.
94. As Ranajit Guha argues in the case of colonial India: "Writing was socially privileged. The production of verbal messages in graphic form for purposes of insurgency was feasible only when individuals of elite origin were induced by circumstance or conscience or a combination of both to make common cause with the peasantry, or when a few among the latter had managed, against all odds, to acquire the rudiments of literacy and put these at the service of an uprising." Guha, *Elementary Aspects of Peasant Insurgency*, 247.
95. "Del Gobernador al Duque de Alcudia, 16 de febrero de 1795," AGN, Gobernación y Capitanía General, LIV, 126–127; see also AGI, Caracas, 346.
96. Ibid.
97. "Manuscrito de Juan Bautista Olivares, Cárcel de Cádiz, 16 de Julio de 1796," AGI, Caracas, 346; Manuel Pérez Vila, "Juan Bautista Olivares," in *Diccionario de historia de Venezuela*, 3:399–400; and Duarte, *Los Olivares en la cultura de Venezuela*.
98. These serious accusations against Olivares complicated an already confrontational relationship between Olivares and the church. In 1791, Olivares had introduced a petition to the diocesan authorities to enter in ecclesiastical order, but the church's official attorney ignored his petition. Later, in 1794, the general attorney of the diocese opposed Olivares's petition, alleging that the pardo was a descendent of "blacks and mulattos" and that someone with impure blood could not enter in "positions exclusive to people who are clean of all bad race." See "Documento relativo a la petición que hace Juan Bautista Olivares ante el

Provisor y Vicario General para que le conceda licencia para vestir los hábitos clericales, Caracas, febrero 1795," AGN, Gobernación y Capitanía General, LIV, 127.
99. "Declaración de Juan Bautista Olivares, acusado de promover la intraquilidad pública, haciendo circular ideas sediciosas de libertad e igualdad, trasladado a Cádiz, donde se le siguió declaración indagatoria," AGI, Caracas, 346.
100. Nieremberg, *Diferencia entre lo temporal y lo eterno*; more than 40 percent of private libraries in Caracas had a copy of Nieremberg's book.
101. "Declaración de Juan Bautista Olivares, acusado de promover la intraquilidad pública, haciendo circular ideas sediciosas de libertad e igualdad, trasladado a Cádiz, donde se le siguió declaración indagatoria," AGI, Caracas, 346.
102. Ibid.
103. "Declaración de Juan Bautista Olivares." As mentioned earlier in this chapter, the *Gaceta de Madrid* contained information regarding the revolutionary movements in France and Saint-Domingue. Ada Ferrer asserts that this information "may have not caused reactions in Madrid, but in places like Havana could have moved the readers." Ferrer, "Noticias de Haití en Cuba," 197.
104. "Manuscrito de Juan Bautista Olivares, escrito en la cárcel de Cádiz," AGI, Caracas, 346.
105. This decision could show the Crown's tendency to take advantage of the discriminatory situations that the majority of pardos and mixed-race people experienced in colonial Spanish America. In 1795, Madrid offered a way out of the "stain of slavery" to individuals of mixed African ancestry by extending the sale of *gracias al sacar* (legitimation of status change) to pardos and quinterones. Regarding the theme of honorability, race, and status in Colonial Spanish America, see Twinam, *Public Lives, Private Secrets*.
106. "El Gobernador al Príncipe de la Paz, Agosto, 1796," AGN, Gobernación y Capitanía General, LIX, 234.
107. "Edicto del Santo Oficio de Caracas, 1809," AAC, Santo Oficio, Carpeta II.

Chapter 3

1. "Sobre extrañar de estas Provinicias a los negros extranjeros que no sean de Guinea, y providencia observada contra de Don Francisco Diego Hernández por su inobservancia," AGN, Gobernación y Capitanía General, LXXI, 1-4.
2. This is a transcription of a song sang in French by a small boy from Curaçao to Spanish-speaking authorities. There are illegible and incomplete verses, probably because the boy did not pronounced them clearly, or because the authorities could not understand or transcribe them.
3. The literal transcription of some of the verses: "Sansculote republicain amie de la Liberté / Vive la République Français, la liberté et Egalité Française"; "Aller

sitoyen français formé vos bataillon / A vos cannon marché . . . marché"; and "Comba mourir pour sa Patri France." "Sobre extrañar de estas Provincias a los negros extranjeros que no sean de Guinea, y providencia observada contra de Don Francisco Diego Hernández por su inobservancia," AGN, Gobernación y Capitanía General, LXXI, 1–4.

4. "Acuerdo del Gobernador de Caracas sobre esclavos de Curazao en el Puerto de La Guaira, 27 de julio de 1797," AGN, Gobernación y Capitanía General, LXXI, 6.
5. Ibid.
6. For songs, political propaganda, and popular politics see Mason, *Singing the French Revolution*; Mason, "Song: Mixing Media"; and Oettinger, *Music as Propaganda in the German Reformation*, esp. the chapter "Popular Song as Resistance."
7. Goody, *The Interface between the Written and the Oral*, chap. 8; Mason, *Singing the French Revolution*; and Mason, "Song: Mixing Media."
8. Scott, "The Common Wind."
9. There is abundant historiography regarding the impact of the mobilization of people during the Haitian Revolution. See Gaspar and Geggus, *A Turbulent Time*; Geggus, *The Impact of the Haitian Revolution*; González-Ripoll et al., *El rumor de Haití en Cuba*; Gómez, *Fidelidad bajo el viento*; Gómez, "Le syndrome de Saint-Domingue"; Piqueras, *Las Antillas en la era de las luces*; Garraway, *Tree of Liberty*; Nesbitt, *Universal Emancipation*; Geggus and Fiering, *The World of the Haitian Revolution*; Helg, *Liberty and Equality in Caribbean Colombia*; Klooster, *Revolution in the Atlantic World*; and Landers, *Atlantic Creoles in the Age of Revolutions*.
10. For an interesting and complete analysis of the emotional effects of the Haitian Revolution on the Atlantic world, see Gómez, "Le syndrome de Saint-Domingue."
11. As Ranajit Guha asserts, rumor is often the catalyst for insurgent movements: "Rumour is both a *universal* and *necessary* carrier of insurgency in any pre-industrial, pre-literate society." Guha, *Elementary Aspects of Peasant Insurgency*, 251. On rumor as a form of transgression and a trigger of insurgency and popular movements, see also Lefevbre, *The Great Fear of 1789*; Mayer, *The Furies*; Geggus, "Slavery, War, and Revolution"; Dubois, *A Colony of Citizens*, chap. 3; and Van Young, *The Other Rebellion*, chap. 14.
12. Since the mid-twentieth century, social psychologists, sociologists, and historians have tended to perceive rumor not as an expression of a reality but as a socially constructed mode of communication. In 1947, Gordon Allport and Leo Postman published one of the first and most complete studies of rumor. In a social-psychological analysis, Allport and Postman argue that rumor circulates when important events happen in the lives of individuals; news conveyed through rumor, however, is necessarily incomplete, ambiguous, or uncertain. Allport and Postman conceive of rumors as social spaces that provide a broader interpretation of various puzzling features of one's environment, "playing a

prominent part in the intellectual drive to render the surrounding world intelligible." Allport and Postman, *The Psychology of Rumor*, 2. Tamotsu Shibutani added several sociological observations to Allport and Postman's study, characterizing rumors not as false or unverified representations but as "improvised news" that are in constant construction as they respond not to a specific reality but to a process of social consensus. Shibutani, *Improvised News*. See also Hunt, "Rumour, Newsletters, and the Pope's Death"; Kapferer, *Rumors: Uses, Interpretation, and Images*; Ewing, "Invasion of Lorient"; Stewart and Strathern, *Witchcraft, Sorcery, Rumors, and Gossip*, chap. 2; Aldrin, "Penser la rumeur"; and Rosnow and Fine, *Rumor and Gossip*.
13. For similar examples of how rumors and verbal enunciations permeated official reports and written evidence, see Dubois, *A Colony of Citizens*; and Van Young, *The Other Rebellion*. For a rich discussion on confronting colonial state archives and the multiple ways to navigate the official circuits of communication and state secrets, see Stoler, *Along the Archival Grain*, chaps. 2, 3.
14. Stoler, *Along the Archival Grain*, 21.
15. "Real Cédula de su Majestad sobre introduccion en el Reyno de papeles sediciosos y contrarios a la fidelidad, 10 de septiembre de 1791," *Gaceta de Madrid*, no. 74, September 16, 1791, 665–72.
16. "Real Orden del Conde de Floridablanca, 24 de septiembre de 1789," AGN, Reales Ordenes, X, 140.
17. Ibid., 198–99.
18. Dubois, *A Colony of Citizens*, 23–124; and Paquette and Engerman, *The Lesser Antilles in the Age of European Expansion*.
19. "Orden del Presidente de la Real Audiencia de Caracas," AGN, Gobernación y Capitanía General, XLIII, 96–97. On many occasions when neighboring islands like Trinidad and Margarita asked for military reinforcements from the mainland, colonial authorities fabricated the same kind of excuses based on the lack of military troops. In one letter, the governor of Cumaná wrote: "How are we going to send reinforcements if we do not have enough soldiers to guard our own coasts from pirate attacks or possible invasions?" See "Carta de Vicente Emparan al Capitán General Carbonell, 1793," AGI, Caracas, 94, no. 221; see also Aizpurua, *Curazao y la costa de Caracas*; and Rupert, *Creolization and Contraband*, chap. 5.
20. "Orden del Presidente de la Real Audiencia de Caracas," AGN, Gobernación y Capitanía General, XLIII, 99.
21. "Carta del Gobernador de Trinidad al Primer Ministro, Conde de Floridablanca, 28 de Junio de 1791," AGI, Estado, Leg. 66, no. 5.
22. Ibid.; and "Reservada entre el Comandante Interior de La Guaira y el Gobernador de Caracas," AGN, Gobernación y Capitanía General, LIX, 268.
23. Shibutani, *Improvised News*.
24. Stoler, *Along the Archival Grain*, 26.

25. Lefevbre, *The Great Fear of 1789*; Mayer, *The Furies*; Newman, *A History of Terror*; and Edelstein, *The Terror of Natural Right*, 127–69.
26. "Orden a los Tenientes Justicias Mayores de Coro," AGN, Gobernación y Capitanía General, XLVII, 68.
27. Ibid., 69.
28. "Orden del Teniente Justicia Mayor de El Tocuyo," AGN, Gobernación y Capitanía General, XLVII, 50. Also cited in Callahan, "La propaganda, la sedición y la Revolución Francesa"; Laviña, "Revolución Francesa y control social"; and Pino Iturrieta, *La mentalidad venezolana*, 36.
29. "Expediente del caso del Doctor Francés Víctor Droin," AGI, Caracas, 15, nos. 8, 13.
30. In the eyes of the Spanish Crown, the French Revolution was sacrilegious and impious; anyone who supported it was depicted as violent, godless, or even anarchist. The Crown and the church developed a royalist discourse based on a loyalty that was at once sociopolitical and religious. See Rosas Lauro, "El miedo a la revolución." For Venezuela, see Straka, *La voz de los vencidos*; and Plaza, "El miedo a la ilustración en la provincia de Caracas."
31. "Expediente del caso del Doctor Francés Víctor Droin," AGI, Caracas, 15, nos. 8, 13.
32. Ibid. Among the French witnesses, there was a French doctor named Pedro Canibens, who was married to Josefa Joaquina España, sister of the "conspirator" of La Guaira, don José María España. In 1797, Canibens worked as a doctor at the La Guaira hospital and was accused of participating in the republican conspiracy of Gual and España. See López, *Juan Bautista Picornell*; and Aizpurua, "La conspiración por dentro."
33. "Por Ley está prohibido pasar a las Indias, y permanecer en ellas qualesquiera extranjeros que no estén habilitados con carta de naturaleza y Licencia Real, . . . Así mismo se ordena limpiar los Reinos de Indias de estos extranjeros." "Expediente del caso del Doctor Francés Víctor Droin," AGI, Caracas, 15, nos. 8, 13.
34. In 1794, for example, Francisco Combret, a Frenchman who worked as a tobacconist in the city of Maracay, was accused by his workmates of expressing subversive ideas in the workplace and in public. Combret was arrested "along with all his books and papers" and sent to Cádiz in 1795. Accompanying Combret in the same ship was a Basque merchant, Santiago Albi, who was accused by his neighbors of celebrating the fall of the port of San Sebastián to the French with fireworks and joyful cries. In an official report, Albi was described as "an insolent, vain, and atheistic young man, capable of inspiring and moving others with the project that the National Assembly of Paris has spread." "El Gobernador a Juan N. Pedroza, noviembre de 1794," AGN, Gobernación y Capitanía General, LIII, 30; also quoted in Callahan, "La propaganda, la sedición y la Revolución Francesa," 183.

35. "Real Cédula sobre presencia de extranjeros en la Provincia, especialmente de franceses que pudiesen alterar el orden y la tranquilidad pública," AGI, Caracas, 169, no. 85.
36. French families in Trinidad received diverse benefits: the governor assigned them land for agricultural development, while they provided their own slaves. Also, the Real Hacienda offered monetary aid for each of the refugees, including elderly people and children. See "Sobre Ayuda monetaria a emigrados franceses en Trinidad," AGI, Caracas, 153, no. 60.
37. In 1788, Trinidad had 9,816 inhabitants; 3,807 were free and 6,009 slaves. By 1797, when the British invaded the island, there were a total of 17,700 inhabitants, many of whom had come from Saint-Domingue. See Sevilla Soler, "Las repercusiones de la Revolución Francesa"; and Brereton, *A History of Modern Trinidad*.
38. "Carta del Gobernador de Trinidad al Capitán General, julio de 1793," AGI, Caracas, 153, no. 37.
39. Sevilla Soler, "Las repercusiones de la Revolución Francesa," 120–25.
40. The governor of Trinidad, in particular, was in regular correspondence with the captain general of Caracas. He provided him with information about the arrival of French families from Saint-Domingue, the presence of foreign ships, the situation in Martinique and Cuba, and, of course, what was happening in Saint-Domingue. By the beginning of the 1800s, after the British had assumed control of the island, French families controlled the slave labor force and, by extension, much of the economy of the island. See diverse communications from Governor Chacón to the captain general of Venezuela, in AGN, Gobernación y Capitanía General, XLIII, 48; XLVII, 14; XLVIII, 218, 297, 307, 348; and XLVII, 14; also, AGI, Caracas, 115; and AGI, Estado, 66. See also Brereton, *A History of Modern Trinidad*, chap. 2; Noel, *Trinidad, provincia de Venezuela*; and Newson, "Inmigrantes extranjeros en América española."
41. "Oficio reservado del Gobernador de Cumaná sobre haberse introducido persona sospechosa en los pueblos de Indios," AGI, Caracas, 514, no. 8.
42. "Reservada del Gobernador de Cumaná al Capitán General sobre persona sospechosa y de sus peligrosas máximas que se han introducido en el pueblo de San Bernardino y otros lugares de la Provincia," AGN, Gobernación y Capitanía General, LIV, 205.
43. "Real Orden a los Gobernadores de La Guaira, Puerto Cabello, Coro y Cumaná, con copia a la Real Hacienda," AGI, Caracas, 514, no. 8.
44. "Reservada del Gobernador de Cumaná al Capitán General sobre persona sospechosa y de las peligrosas máximas que se han introducido en el pueblo de San Bernardino y otros lugares de la Provincia," AGN, Gobernación y Capitanía General, LIV, 206.
45. "Representación de Fray Vicente Blasco al Gobernador de Cumaná," AGN, Gobernación y Capitanía General, LIV, 207.

46. "Orden de la Real Audiencia sobre apresar a sospechoso que incita a los Indios a la desobediencia," AGI, Caracas, 514, no. 9.
47. "Reservada no. 21 al Intendente de los Reales Exercitos de Caracas," AGI, Caracas, 514.
48. Roger Chartier shows how even French Enlightenment political thinkers and writers such as the Marquis de Condorcet, Jean-François Marmontel, and Jean le Rond d'Alembert maintained a clear distinction between the educated public and the "people" who were perceived as ignorant and easy to persuade. Chartier comments that "subject to extremes, inconstant, contradictory, blind, the *people* of eighteenth-century dictionaries remained true to its portrayal in classical tragedy: always quick to change course, from one minute to the next docile or furious, but always manipulable." Chartier, *The Cultural Origins of the French Revolution*, 28.
49. Roger Chartier also comments on deep-rooted prerevolutionary representations of popular groups as incapable of acting politically, or of participating in government, because of their loyalty to the sovereign. Chartier, *The Cultural Origins of the French Revolution*. In colonial India, Ranajit Guha observes the same situation, explaining how authorities insinuated that outsiders had robbed peasants of their innocence. Guha, *Elementary Aspects of Peasant Insurgency*, 220. For similar cases in the rebellious Andes, see Walker, *Smoldering Ashes*; and Thomson, *We Alone Will Rule*.
50. In the Catholic tradition, a scandal is a situation in which "one person, through words or actions, persuades others to sin," along with conducting impiety and blasphemy. This "sin" was considered a terrible indiscretion, often thought to be committed by "false" revolutionary philosophers and other persons spreading revolutionary ideas among the "incautious" population. See Plaza, "Vicisitudes de un escaparate de cedro."
51. See O'Phelan, *La gran rebelión en los Andes*; and Fisher, Kuethe, and McFarlane, *Reform and Insurrection*. For Venezuela, see Castillo Lara, *Apuntes para la historia colonial*; Brito Figueroa, *Las insurrecciones de los esclavos negros*; and Magallanes, *Luchas e Insurrecciones en la Venezuela Colonial*. See also chapters 4, 5, and 6 of this volume.
52. Scott, "The Common Wind."
53. "Circular reservada del Capitán General de Venezuela a los Gobernadores sobre introducción de embarcaciones francesas," AGN, Gobernación y Capitanía General, VI, 29.
54. See, for example, the cases of Cuba and Trinidad, where white planters were not convinced of the need to disrupt the slave trade and proposed new ways of controlling the black population. See Naranjo, "La amenaza haitiana, un miedo interesado"; Ferrer, "Cuba en la sombra de Haití"; and Sevilla Soler, "Las repercusiones de la Revolución Francesa."

55. Although *bozales* made up the bulk of rebel forces in slave insurrections, at this point the colonial authorities were more interested in the "ideas" that could stir mobilization. They tried to limit the entry of slaves from the French Antilles, clearly preferring slaves imported directly from Africa. Izard, *El miedo a la revolución*.
56. "Sobre temporada extendida de comerciante francés de negros," AGN, Gobernación y Capitanía General, XLVII, 53.
57. "Comunicación del Comandante Sucre al Capitán General de Venezuela sobre llegada de navíos franceses," AGN, Gobernación y Capitanía General, XLVIII, 68.
58. AGN, Reales Ordenes, XI, 306.
59. Brito Figueroa argues that in Venezuela the slave trade ended well before the 1810, in response to sudden economic stagnation. According to him, miscegenation and manumission led to a new social group of free, mixed-race small farmers who were hired by masters and landowners to replace African slaves. Brito Figueroa, *Estructura económica de Venezuela colonial*; and Brito Figueroa, *El problema de la tierra y esclavos*. See also McKinley, *Caracas antes de la independencia*, 38.
60. Borucki, "Trans-Imperial History in the Making of the Slave Trade," 43. José María Aizpurua agrees with this interpretation, arguing that "warfare among the different European powers and the social upheaval in the Caribbean region completely disrupted the importation of slaves to the region." Aizpurua, *Relaciones de trabajo*, 78.
61. Borucki, "Trans-Imperial History in the Making of the Slave Trade"; Lombardi, *People and Places in Colonial Venezuela*; Lombardi, *The Decline and Abolition of Negro Slavery*; and McKinley, *Caracas antes de la independencia*.
62. Castillo Lara, *Apuntes para la historia colonial*; Aizpurua, "Coro y Curazao en el siglo XVIII"; and Aizpurua, "En busca de la libertad." See also "Real Cédula de Su Majestad sobre declarar por libres a los negros que viniesen de los ingleses u holandeses a los reinos de España buscando el agua del bautismo, Buen Retiro, 24 de septiembre de 1750," AGN, Caracas, Reales Cédulas, X, 332.
63. "Real Orden reservada del 21 de mayo de 1790," AGI, Caracas, 115.
64. "Real Orden sobre Introducción de negros extranjeros, julio 1790," AGI, Caracas, 115. This order reverted the previous royal decree of 1750. See "Real Cédula de Su Majestad sobre declarar por libres a los negros que viniesen de los ingleses u holandeses a los reinos de España buscando el agua del bautismo, Buen Retiro, 24 de septiembre de 1750," AGN, Caracas, Reales Cédulas, X, 332.
65. The governor contends: "Por ahora cese el uso de la libertad de los esclavos que se refugían en nuestras colonias, ... y que se suspenda entre tanto el cumplimiento de las Cédulas declaratorias de la libertad, que conforme al Derecho de Gentes se han expedido en diferentes ocasiones a casos particulares a favor de los

esclavos que se han refugiado en nuestro Dominio de América." Quoted in Castillo Lara, *Apuntes para la historia colonial*, 600; see also AGI, Caracas, 115.

66. In a report written to the Spanish king in 1794, the captain general of Venezuela alerted about the danger that the proximity between Curaçao and Coro represented for the province: "The closeness of that Province [Coro] to the Island of Curaçao is such that one might estimate that it is almost a Dutch possession in the Coast." "Comunicado del Capitán General de Venezuela al Rey, 13 de marzo de 1794," AGI, Caracas, 95. See also Aizpurua, "Esclavitud, navegación y fugas de esclavos"; Aizpurua, "En busca de la libertad"; and Rupert, *Creolization and Contraband*, esp. the chapter "Curaçao and Tierra Firme."

67. "El Gobernador de Caracas informa sobre la situación con esclavos luangos viviendo en la Provincia de Coro," AGI, Estado 58, 2-1.

68. "Borrador a los Gobernadores sobre las circunstancias de las Islas Francesas y la llegada de familias a la Isla de Curazao, 20 de diciembre de 1791," AGN, Gobernación y Capitanía General, XLVI, 308, 311.

69. "Comunicación del Gobernador de Curazao suplicando apoyo y asistencia para retornar a Curazao unos negros esclavos de Casper Luis Van Nytrech," AGN, Real Intendencia y Ejército, LVIII, 43.

70. Castillo Lara, *Apuntes para la historia colonial*; and Rupert, *Creolization and Contraband*, chap. 5. See also chapter 4 of this volume.

71. Like the black rebellion of Coro, other social movements involving slaves, maroons, and free people of African descent erupted in Barlovento and the Valleys of Curiepe, Capaya, Caucagua, and El Guapo. "Reservada no. 25, sobre expedición para contener a los negros cimarrones de Caucagua, Curiepe y El Guapo, Mayo de 1793," AGI, Caracas, 95. See Castillo Lara, *Apuntes para la historia colonial*; and chapter 4 of this volume.

72. "Representación de la Real Audiencia al Rey Sobre la Real Cédula de trato de esclavos de 1789, Diciembre 1789," AGI, Caracas, 167, no. 44.

73. I borrow the term "imaginary decree of emancipation" from Wim Klooster's article "Le décret d'émancipation imaginaire: monarchisme et esclavage en Amérique du Nord et dans la Caraïbe au temps des révolutions."

74. Chapter 4 in this book shows how, during the Coro rebellion, the white elite argued that false rumors of emancipation were a crucial factor in igniting the rebellion of blacks. See Scott, "The Common Wind"; and Klooster, "Le décret d'émancipation imaginaire."

75. Dubois, *A Colony of Citizens*, chap. 3; and Geggus, "Slavery, War, and Revolution."

76. "Reporte del Gobernador de Trinidad, José María Chacón, al Secretario de Estado sobre la situación en las Islas Francesas, 1 febrero 1791," AGI, Estado 66, no. 2.

77. Ibid.; and "Reporte del Gobernador de Trinidad, José María Chacón, al Secretario de Estado sobre el cumplimiento de la Real Orden del 28 de mayo sobre

doblar vigilancia de papeles y noticias de Francia y sus Islas, Diciembre 1791," AGI, Estado 66, no. 6.
78. "Reporte de Josef Damián Cuenca, Auditor de Guerra de la Isla de Trinidad al Capitán General, Diciembre 1794," AGI, Estado 66, no. 26; and several official reports by the governor of Trinidad to the captain general, AGI, Estado 66, nos. 29, 35, 37, 42.
79. "Reporte de Josef Damián Cuenca, Auditor de Guerra de la Isla de Trinidad al Capitán General, Diciembre 1794," AGI, Estado 66, no. 26.
80. "Informe de Don Vicente Emparan al Gobernador Carbonell acerca del estado de la Provincia de Cumaná y también sobre la isla de Trinidad," AGN, Gobernación y Capitanía General, LXVII, 109.
81. See Acosta Saignes, *Vida de los esclavos negros*, 158–59; Aizpurua, "La insurrección de los negros"; and Gil Rivas, Dovale, and Bello, *La insurrección de los negros*.
82. *Cumbes* and *palenques* were relatively autonomous maroon communities made up of fugitive slaves that were established near haciendas or urban centers.
83. As Jane Landers contends: "Located on the peripheries of European cities, and also on the fringes of indigenous worlds, maroon communities borrowed elements they found useful from both the dominant and native cultures." Landers, "*Cimarrón* and Citizen," 123.
84. "Sobre establecimiento de patrullas de vigilancia en Caracas, Agosto 1794," AGN, Real Consulado, Actas, 2526, 37–38; "Del Capitán General de Venezuela al Justicia Mayor de Carora, sobre establecimiento de milicias urbanas para controlar alzamientos de esclavos y de gente de color, junio 1795," AGN, Gobernación y Capitanía General, LV, 353; and "Lista de los esclavos cimarrones aprehendidos por las Patrullas, de las que se han presentado a sus dueños después de su establecimiento, Mayo 1795," AGN, Diversos, LXIX, 113.
85. These squadrons operated in the following departments of Caracas: Caracas, Petare, Sabana de Ocumare, Guarenas, Caucagua, Capaya, Guapo, Turmero, Cupira, Río Chico, San Felipe, Puerto Cabello, Maracay, and La Guaira. See "Lista de los esclavos cimarrones aprehendidos por las Patrullas, de las que se han presentado a sus dueños después de su establecimiento, Mayo 1795," AGN, Diversos, LXIX, 113.
86. Captains of the squadrons were asked to compile lists with the names of the *cimarrones* (maroons), the number of years they had been living in these conditions, where they had been captured, and the products and/or animals they possessed or ostensibly had stolen. "Lista de los esclavos cimarrones aprehendidos por las Patrullas, de las que se han presentado a sus dueños después de su establecimiento, Mayo 1795," AGN, Diversos, LXIX.
87. I studied approximately thirty declarations by these supposedly runaway men and women living in the Province of Caracas. Twenty-four were runaways, and about half of these runaways declared that they had escaped because of the

humiliations and severe punishments they suffered at the hands of their masters and *mayordomos*. Four declared that they had escaped because working conditions were unbearable: they had to work when they were sick. Four others said that they fled because they did not receive enough food or clothing, and one said that he was unhappy because his master did not give him enough tobacco. There were six free blacks who had been captured by mistake; one said that he was lost because he was a "Dutch" slave and could not speak Spanish. More than half of the twenty-four runaways I investigated were working as free laborers (jornaleros) on haciendas in the area, but ten of them declared that they lived in a small maroon community. They lived in small houses they built themselves, surrounded by fields cultivated by them for their own consumption. They organized their work in the fields and followed a leader (captain). "Procedimientos contra esclavos fugitivos en los montes de Capaya, y sus declaraciones," AGN, Diversos, LXVI, 469–500.
88. Ibid., 479.
89. Ibid., 544.
90. Ibid., 545.
91. "Cartas de Vicente Emparan al Capitán General, sobre a la conspiración de los negros de Cariaco, cree que la tentativa es obra del Gobernador Picton, Cumaná, 16 de enero de 1798," AGN, Gobernación y Capitanía General, LXVIII, 224–26. See also Magallanes, *Luchas e insurrecciones*, 203–4; and *Documentos para el estudio de los esclavos negros*, vol. 103, doc. no. 95, 329.
92. "Vicente Emparan al Gob. y Cap. Gral. Anuncia regreso de los hombres que fueron a Cariaco a dominar una sublevación de negros, Cumaná, 2 de marzo de 1798," AGN, Gobernación y Capitanía General, LXVIII, 351–52.
93. "Para el Gobernador de Curaçao sobre 18 negros fugados de Cumaná por seducción de dos holandeses, febrero 1800," AGN, Gobernación y Capitanía General, LXXXIII, 106.
94. For a complete description of the cession of Santo Domingo to France, see Schaeffer, "The Delayed Cession of Spanish Santo Domingo to France," 46–48; and Deive, *Las emigraciones dominicanas a Cuba*.
95. "Testimonio del Expediente de Don José Peralta y varios vecinos del comercio, solicitando se les declare libres de impuestos los efectos que traen por su emigración a la Provincia de Venezuela, 5/1796," AGI, Caracas, 507, no. 991.
96. "Comunicación de Esteban Fernández de León a Don Diego de Gardoqui, 6/1796," AGI, Caracas, 507, no. 991.
97. "Carta del Gobernador de Caracas al Comandante Interior de La Guaira, 1796," AGN, Gobernación y Capitanía General, LIX, 256.
98. "Reservada entre el Comandante Interior de La Guaira y el Gobernador de Caracas, 1796," AGN, Gobernación y Capitanía General, LIX, 268.
99. On the extraordinary mobility, adaptability, and political skills of African and African-descended actors who traveled throughout the Atlantic world in their

quest for freedom during the Atlantic revolutions, see Landers, *Atlantic Creoles in the Age of Revolutions*; Ferrer, *Freedom's Mirror*; and Polasky, *Revolutions without Borders*.

100. "Reservada del Presidente y Gobernador cumpliendo orden de vigilar introduccion de papeles y libros, y extranjeros que pudiesen esparcir ideas sediciosas. junio de 1797," AGI, Caracas, 434.

101. See also the case of a mulatto immigrant from Spanish Santo Domingo, Josef María González, who was mistakenly identified by another Dominican immigrant in Venezuela named José Sotolongo as a mulatto leader who had ordered the killing of more than two thousand souls and was known by his cruelty during Toussaint's invasion. Authorities detained González until his innocence was proved. AGN, Archivo de Aragua, LVI, 1805, 173–90.

102. Rivière was originally a member of a royalist squadron that had been sent from France to Martinique in 1790. When the Colonial Assembly repudiated its loyalty to the metropole, royalists like Rivière lost all support from the colonists of Martinique. As the situation deteriorated, he and his men believed that a good way to oppose the revolutionaries and remain loyal to the Bourbon family was by moving to the Spanish territories and offering their services to the Spanish king. See Sanz Tapia, "Refugiados de la Revolución Francesa en Venezuela"; and Gómez, *Fidelidad bajo el viento*.

103. "Correspondencia entre el Gobernador de Trinidad y el Capitán General de Venezuela, sobre lo ocurrido con los buques del Mando de M. Rivière, acompaña copia traducida de carta de Rivere," AGI, Caracas, 153, no. 37.

104. "Capitán General de Venezuela acusa recibo de la Real Orden que aprueba la Buena acogida que dió el Gobernador de Trinidad al Brigadier de Francia M. de Rivière, julio de 1793," AGI, Caracas, 94, no. 174.

105. "Comunicación de Don Vicente Emparan al Capitán General Carbonell en la cual da parte de los realistas que se han refugiado en Trinidad, 1793," AGN, Gobernación y Capitanía General, XLVI, 308. See also Sanz Tapia, "Refugiados de la Revolución Francesa en Venezuela," 839.

106. Puerto Cabello was a relatively small port town on the central coast of the captaincy general. "Carta del Gobernador de Pedro Carbonell a M. Rivière, julio 1793," AGN, Gobernación y Capitanía General, XLV, 307, 348.

107. "Representación de Joaquín de Fressineaux, teniente coronel del regimiento del mariscal de Turena al Gobernador, septiembre de 1793," AGN, Gobernación y Capitanía General, X, 45. Quoted in Gómez, *Fidelidad bajo el viento*, 116, 119.

108. Sanz Tapia, "Refugiados de la Revolución Francesa en Venezuela," 841.

109. "Oficio de Joaquín de Fressineaux para el Capitán General, octubre 1793," AGN, Gobernación y Capitanía General, X, 114. Quoted in Gómez, *Fidelidad bajo el viento*, 122.

110. "Oficio del Capitán General para el Exmo. Sr. Conde del Campo de Alange, diciembre 1793," AGN, Gobernación y Capitanía General, X, 328–30. Quoted in Gómez,

Fidelidad bajo el viento, 123. Gómez remarks that one French official committed suicide in Puerto Cabello; this event had a great impact on the residents of the town, reinforcing their perceptions of the French as irreligious people.

111. "Reservada de la Junta de Guerra convocada por el Gobernador para tratar los recelos que a la tranquilidad de aquellas Provincias ocasionan los oficiales emigrados de la Ysla de Martinica, diciembre 1793," AGI, Caracas, 505, no. 13.
112. Sanz Tapia, "Refugiados de la Revolución Francesa en Venezuela," 845.
113. "Informe de la Junta extraordinaria convocada por el Gobernador de la Provincia para tratar problema de los prisioneros de Santo Domingo, 30 de noviembre de 1793," AGI, Estado, 58, no. 3.
114. Although he proposed Santo Domingo as a final destination for Commander Fressinaux, the captain general told him that "if some of your militiamen want to go back to Trinidad or to another island, I could consider their case and give them a passport." Quoted in Gómez, *Fidelidad bajo el viento*, 130.
115. "Informe de la Junta extraordinaria convocada por el Gobernador de la Provincia para tratar problema de los prisioneros de Santo Domingo, 30 de noviembre de 1793," AGI, Estado, 58, no. 3.
116. Ibid., no. 4.
117. "Que dos negros esclavos en la Guayra ocupados de amasar pan, se animaban al trabajo, diciendose en confianza de no ser oydos: que dentro de un ano serian tan libres como los del Guarico." Ibid.
118. "Esta es buena ocacion para sacudir la esclavitud y yugo de los españoles, como han sacudido el de los Franceses los Negros del Guarico." Ibid.
119. Ibid.
120. "Que un esclavo no debia serlo ni hombre alguno de otro." Ibid.
121. "Respondió descaradamente que no habia entre las dos desigualdad que la del color pues en lo demas eran iguales." Ibid.
122. Ibid.
123. In the report, the authorities mentioned that "even young women" in La Guaira talked freely about freedom and equality. The city of Valencia is located sixty miles away from Caracas and La Guaira, and only ten miles from Puerto Cabello. It was surrounded by haciendas in the Valleys of Aragua. Ibid.
124. Ibid.
125. Ibid.
126. Ibid.
127. Ibid.
128. These slaves were brought to La Guaira on the condition that they could be sold to local planters and that the money from their sale would go directly to the Real Hacienda of the province.
129. "Informe de la Junta extraordinaria convocada por el Gobernador de la Provincia para tratar problema de los prisioneros de Santo Domingo, 30 de noviembre de 1793," AGI, Estado, 58, no. 4.

130. Ibid.; see also "Reservada del Intendente del Ejército Don Esteban Fernández de León, donde da cuenta de haber concurrido la Junta Extraordinaria convocada por el Gobierno para tratar sobre los recelos que a la tranquilidad pública de aquellas provincias ocasionan los oficiales franceses," AGI, Caracas, 505.
131. "Reservada del Intendente de la Isla de Puerto Rico al Intendente de Reales Ejércitos de Caracas, mayo de 1794," AGI, Caracas, 506, no. 1; and "Real Orden sobre traslado de esclavos franceses, diciembre de 1794," AGI, Caracas, 514, nos. 1, 2.
132. "Real Orden sobre traslado de esclavos franceses, diciembre de 1794," AGI, Caracas, 596, no. 1.
133. "Representación del Intendente de Caracas, Don Antonio López de Quintana al Exmo; Señor Don Diego de Gardorqui, sobre medidas necesarias para que no se propaguen las doctrinas francesas por parte de los prisioneros y esclavos franceses que se hallan en La Guaira, febrero de 1795," AGI, Caracas, 472, 514.
134. Ibid.
135. "Lista de los esclavos franceses prisioneros que se embarcan para Puerto Cabello con destino final Cuba," AGI, Caracas, 506, no. 16.
136. "Expediente a Luis Alejandro Espinosa por mostrar públicamente expresiones subversivas relativas a la igualdad," AGI, Caracas, 430.
137. "Expediente a Luis Alejandro Espinosa por mostrar públicamente expresiones subversivas relativas a la igualdad," AGI, Caracas, 430. See also Hernández, "Doctrina y gobierno en la conspiración de Gual y España."
138. "Informe de la Junta extraordinaria convocada por el Gobernador de la Provincia para tratar problema de los prisioneros de Santo Domingo, 30 de noviembre de 1793," AGI, Estado, 58, no. 3.
139. "Informe de De La Torre al Gobernador interino Joaquin Zubillaga, sobre sospecha de sedición en los Valles, 25 Septiembre 1796," AGN, Diversos, LXVI, 566–69.
140. Ibid, 567.
141. Ibid.
142. "Comunicación del Gobernador y Capitán General al Justicia Mayor de Curiepe, 11/1/1798," AGN, Gobernación y Capitanía General, LXVII, 240.
143. "Comunicación de Don José Anís al Gobernador y Capitán General, acusa recibo de su carta, 22/1/98," AGN, Gobernación y Capitanía General LXVIII, 261–63.

Chapter 4

1. Doña Felipa Caro was either the legitimate daughter or the sister of don Ignacio Caro, brigadier in Santo Domingo and an officer in the Spanish army in Santo Domingo who in 1793 had helped persuade Hyacinthe, one of black leaders of Saint-Domingue, to join the Spanish forces against France. Later, don Ignacio Caro moved to Havana and collaborated with the Spanish authorities in process of negotiation with Saint-Domingue. "Reservada de Doña Felipa Caro, viuda

emigrada de Santo Domingo, solicitando pension, no. 3," AGI, Caracas, 95. See also Ferrer, *Freedom's Mirror*, 100, 160.

2. "Reservada de Doña Felipa Caro, viuda emigrada de Santo Domingo, solicitando pension, no. 3," AGI, Caracas, 95; and "Reservada de Doña Felipa Caro al Gobernador y Capitán General, Abril de 1796," in *Documentos de la insurrección de José Leonardo Chirinos*, 1:167, 226.

3. It is possible that the same ideological and political forces that silenced and camouflaged the Haitian Revolution in the Western Hemisphere, depicting it as "not a commendable model of emancipation," were also responsible for hindering historical critique and dialogue about the Coro rebellion in Venezuela's history. Fischer, *Modernity Disavowed*, 4; see also Trouillot, *Silencing the Past*. For a critical view of Trouillot's argument about the silence around the Haitian Revolution, see Ada Ferrer, "Talk about Haiti"; and Fischer, *Modernity Disavowed*, 1–38.

4. Arcaya, "Insurrección de los negros" (1960); and Arcaya, *Insurrección de los negros* (1949).

5. The Asociación Cultural José Leonardo Chirino and the Asociación Rescate de Tradiciones José Leonardo Chirino, for example, located in the Valley of Curimagua, have both engaged in the production of historical texts, songs, plays, performances, festivals, and historical routes collectively commemorating the black insurrection. For the political uses of the memories of the Coro rebellion in contemporary Venezuela, see Ruette-Orihuela and Soriano, "Remembering the Slave Rebellion of Coro."

6. Arcaya claims that "rumors about the upheaval of the blacks of Haiti were circulating, and José Leonardo, who had met [the blacks of Saint-Domingue] years before and knew that they were no better than he was, convinced himself that he could lead a revolution." Describing the first events of the rebellion, Brito Figueroa writes: "José Leonardo remained in the 'sierra' applying the 'Law of the French'—or better said, the law of Toussaint Louverture's and Dessalines' black Jacobins." In this sentence, Brito Figueroa evidences the influence of C. L. R. James's *The Black Jacobins: Toussaint l'Ouverture and the San Domingo Revolution*. See Arcaya, *La insurrección de los negros* (1949); and Brito Figueroa, *Las insurrecciones de los esclavos negros*, 69–71.

7. Aizpurua, "La insurrección de los negros."

8. Laviña, "Indios y negros sublevados de Coro"; and Gil Rivas, Dovale, and Bello, *La insurrección de los negros*.

9. Official histories tend to reproduce the colonial elite's perceptions of rebellions as movements that were incited from the outside, depicting leaders and local participants of these movements as people politically unprepared. Characterizing rebellions as responses to local junctures would imply the recognition that the colonial system itself had serious problems. It was more appropriate for colonial authorities and elites to depict social uprisings as spontaneous and unplanned reactions to outside forces. See Guha, *Elementary Aspects of Peasant*

Insurgency; Childs, "A Black French General Arrived to Conquer the Island"; and Fick, *The Making of Haiti*.

10. Curaçao's slave rebellion in 1795, Maracaibo's and Cartagena's conspiracies in 1799, Charles Deslondes's slave rebellion in Louisiana in 1811, José Antonio Aponte's conspiracy in Cuba in 1812, the Barbados slave revolt in 1816, and Denmark Vesey's slave conspiracy in Charleston, South Carolina, in 1822 are some of the most studied examples. See Geggus, *The Impact of the Haitian Revolution*.

11. Davis, "Impact of the French and Haitian Revolutions," 3–9.

12. Eugene Genovese argues that the Haitian revolution exercised a decisive influence on the political agendas of subsequent slave revolts, which evolved from "restorationist movements"—based on traditional African forms of social organization—to rebellions inspired by modern political discourses. David Geggus, on the other hand, has insisted that abolitionism, not the republican ideologies of the French and Caribbean revolutions, underlay most of these rebellions. Genovese, *From Rebellion to Revolution*; Geggus, "The French and Haitian Revolutions"; and Geggus, *Haitian Revolutionary Studies*.

13. Sibylle Fischer comments that "a very narrow notion of influence may unwittingly prevent us from recognizing the ideological and symbolic impact of the Haitian Revolution and thus make it impossible to recognize the cultural formation . . . in which knowledge of Haiti was taken for granted and which we *know* existed." Fischer, *Modernity Disavowed*, 2. On the distinction between "influence" and "repercussions," see Ferrer, "Talk about Haiti"; Ferrer, "Cuba en la sombra de Haití"; and Sklodowska, *Espectros y espejismos*.

14. See, for example, Jordan, *Tumult and Silence at Second Creek*; Johnson, "Denmark Vesey and His Co-Conspirators"; Paquette and Egerton, "Of Facts and Fables"; Childs, *The 1812 Aponte Rebellion*; and Finch, *Rethinking Slave Rebellion in Cuba*.

15. See also Jordan, *Tumult and Silence at Second Creek*; and Martínez, "The Black Blood of New Spain."

16. Sharples, "Discovering Slave Conspiracies."

17. The Intendencia de Ejército y Real Audiencia was a crucial institution of the Spanish colonial administration. In Venezuela, it was created in 1776 as a way of restructuring the economic organization of the province. The royal intendant was responsible for administering and controlling the Real Hacienda, including the establishment of new taxes and public spending. In 1791, Esteban Fernández de León was commissioned as the royal intendant in Venezuela, and as early as 1793 conflicts between Carbonell and Fernández de León emerged. Both sent several letters to the king accusing each other of abuse of power or excesses regarding their roles and responsibilities. See "Intendencia de Real Ejército y Hacienda," *Diccionario de historia de Venezuela*, 2:812–13; and García Chuecos, *Siglo dieciocho venezolano*, 300–305.

18. Fernández de León ignored the fact that free blacks and slaves in Coro did, in fact, pay commercial taxes to transport and sell products in the urban centers. Cited in García Chuecos, *Siglo dieciocho venezolano*, 302.
19. Roseberry, "Hegemony and the Language of Contention," 361.
20. "Testimonio del Expediente formado sobre la sublevación de los negros sambos, mulatos esclavos y libres de la jurisdicción de Coro," AGI, Caracas, 426. The expediente was published in 1994 as *Documentos de la insurrección de José Leonardo Chirinos*, in two volumes.
21. As Stephan Palmié argues, historians of slave rebellions in the Americas struggle to "reconstruct a history that never was and whose creator was killed in the act of its enunciation." Palmié, *Wizards and Scientists*, 93; and Trouillot, *Silencing the Past*, 25–30.
22. Jordán, "Acercamiento a la rebelión," 1:16–17; and Gil Rivas, Dovale, and Bello, *La insurrección de los negros*.
23. The city of Coro is located in the present-day Venezuelan state of Falcón, in the northwest of the country. In the eighteenth century, the region was known as the Provincia de Coro, with the city of Coro as its capital. During colonial times, the Province of Coro fell under the jurisdiction of the Government of Caracas, and later, in 1777, of the Captaincy General of Venezuela.
24. Altolaguirre y Duvale, *Relaciones geográficas de la gobernación de Venezuela*, 191. Altolaguirre compiled a description made by Pedro Felipe de Llamas in 1768 when he was *teniente de justicia mayor* of Coro.
25. Arcaya, *La insurrección de los negros* (1949), 20.
26. Rupert, *Creolization and Contraband*, chap. 5.
27. Lovena Reyes, "Coro y su espacio geohistórico."
28. According to Linda Rupert, by the 1650s Coro was already a center of intercolonial trade, primarily conducted by small-scale merchants and seafarers. Smuggling between Coro and Curaçao underwent several cycles throughout the seventeenth and eighteenth centuries, and it became crucial for the economic growth of both regions. Rupert, *Creolization and Contraband*, chap. 5. Ramón Aizpurua also provides convincing evidence of the economic and social significance that Coro had for the island of Curaçao throughout the eighteenth century. Aizpurua, *Curazao y la costa de Caracas*; Aizpurua, "Coro y Curazao en el siglo XVIII"; Aizpurua, "En busca de la libertad," 69–102; and Aizpurua, "El comercio curazoleño-holandés."
29. "Informe detallado de Don Manuel Carrera al Capitán General de Caracas, 26 de septiembre de 1796," in *Documentos de la insurrección de José Leonardo Chirinos*, 1:160.
30. This census only takes into consideration the population living in the twenty-three small towns that presumably composed the region; however, there were some isolated "haciendas" and *conucos* (small plots of land where people cultivated for domestic consumption) not necessarily attached to those small towns.

31. Of the 30 percent of Indians, 28 percent did not pay tribute and 2 percent did. "Testimonio del expediente formado sobre la sublevación de los negros, sambos, mulatos esclavos y libres de la jurisdicción de Coro, 1796," *Documentos de la insurrección de José Leonardo Chirinos*, 1:158–59. During the early colonization of Coro, the Spanish established encomiendas of indigenous groups, such as the Jirajaras and the Ajaguas. Originally, these encomiendas belonged to important Spanish families who commanded tribute and labor from the indigenous groups; however, by the eighteenth century most of these had disappeared, and the Indian population worked as free jornaleros and lived in Indian communities.
32. Free blacks included mulattos and zambos who worked as artisans in the urban areas or as peasants in the local haciendas. "Testimonio del expediente formado sobre la sublevación de los negros, sambos, mulatos esclavos y libres de la jurisdicción de Coro, 1796," AGI, Caracas, 426. Also in *Documentos de la insurrección de José Leonardo Chirinos*, 1:158–59.
33. In their study, Gil Rivas, Dovale, and Bello present slightly different numbers on the Coro social composition. They contend that approximately 64 percent of the population was black (44 percent free blacks and 20 percent enslaved), 24 percent were Indians, and 12 percent were whites. Their numbers shows that the majority of the population was of African descent, and that the number of free blacks was double that of slaves. Gil Rivas, Dovale, and Bello, *La insurrección de los negros*, 100–120.
34. Javier Laviña comments: "The composition and social structure of Coro notably differed from that of the rest of Venezuela. There was a big mass of free blacks that contrasted with the higher proportion of slaves in other areas of the captaincy general; this phenomenon was, in part, due to the economic marginality of Coro regarding official circuits, and the closeness to Curaçao, whose maroons became part of the free blacks who worked, along with the slaves, in the Haciendas." Laviña, "Indios y negros sublevadoss de Coro," 99.
35. Rupert, *Creolization and Contraband*, chap. 5; Aizpurua, "Coro y Curazao en el siglo XVIII"; and Aizpurua, "En busca de la libertad."
36. The term "maritime marronage" is borrowed from N. A. T. Hall in his chapter "Maritime Maroons: Grand Marronage from the Danish West Indies."
37. Rupert contends: "Once in Tierra Firme, many fugitive Afro-Curaçaoans also participated actively in the contraband trade. Afro-Curaçaoan runaways often established close links with communities of Afro-Venezuelans who were already involved in smuggling, including maroons, urban free men and women, and enslaved laborers who worked on the cacao plantations." Rupert, *Creolization and Contraband*, 197.
38. A Spanish royal decree of 1750 freed all slaves from foreign colonies (the Dutch, French, and British islands). See "Real Cédula de Su Majestad sobre declarar por libres a los negros que viniesen de los ingleses u holandeses a los reinos de España

buscando el agua del bautismo. Buen Retiro, 24 de septiembre de 1750," AGN, Reales Cédulas, X, 332.
39. Aizpurua, "Coro y Curazao en el siglo XVIII," 232.
40. Arcaya explains: "Since the master really produced just a small plot of land, above which he believed he had entire dominion, he allowed his slaves to develop their crops in small *conucos*. There was the land of the Lord surrounded by smaller ones, belonging to the 'serfs.' So it was considered normal that slaves only worked the time necessary to finish the job that was assigned to them." Arcaya, *Insurrección de los negros* (1949), 17; see also Acosta Saignes, *Vida de los esclavos negros*; and Blackburn, *The Making of New World Slavery*, 497.
41. Generally speaking, Venezuelan masters did not support, and frequently impeded, marriages between free blacks and slaves, because they believed that it had negative effects on the "natural submission" of slaves, and also because they believed that the need to get money to support the family frequently drove slaves to steal. Legally, masters had the right to control their slaves' marriages, but despite this, slaves and free blacks found ways to bind and have families. "Procedimientos contra esclavos fugitivos en los montes de Capaya y sus declaraciones," AGN, Diversos, LXVI, 469–569; and Acosta Saignes, *Vida de los esclavos negros*, chaps. 11–14.
42. David Geggus observes that free colored leadership in a slave movement was rather frequent in the Atlantic World. Almost a dozen of the slave revolts and conspiracies that occurred during the period 1791–1815 were led by free blacks who seemed to know well about the libertarian ideology of the French Revolution. Geggus, "Slavery, War, and Revolution."
43. Aizpurua, "Coro y Curazao en el siglo XVIII."
44. Laviña, "Indios y negros sublevados de Coro," 95–100.
45. This is demonstrated by the creation of diverse black cofradias in various cities of the Province of Venezuela and by the formation of separated "militias" such as the pardo company and the luango company in Coro. In Coro, conflicts among hacendados, local free blacks, and luangos started long before 1795. See "Autos sobre disensiones y bullicios de los Negros Esclavos fugitivos de la Isla de Curazao a la Jurisdicción de Coro, 1770," AGN, Diversos, XL.
46. Manuel Carrera, a hacendado who collaborated in capturing black rebels, commented that "it was rather bizarre and negligent that blacks from Curaçao were allowed to form in the mountains a confusing *incorporación* [company], with a Captain." See "Informe detallado de Don Manuel Carrera al Capitán General de Caracas, 2 de junio de 1795," in *Documentos de la insurrección de José Leonardo Chirinos*, 1:45.
47. Pedro Arcaya, *Insurrección de los negros* (1949), 20–25.
48. Gil Rivas, Dovale, and Bello, *La insurrección de los negros*, 50–65.
49. José Caridad González was an African-born black who lived first in Curaçao and later fled to Coro, where he settled. He spoke different languages and helped

other Curaçao slaves move to Coro. He became the militia leader of the luango community in Macuquita after he traveled to Spain and returned with a royal decree that authorized luangos to continue using the land. "Reservada no. 26, del Capitán General de Caracas al Real y Supremo Consejo noticias relativas a los sucesos de la Sublevación de Coro, 15 de junio de 1795," AGI, Caracas, 95; and Laviña, "Indios y negros sublevados de Coro," 108.

50. "Juan Guillelmi acusa recibo de la Real Orden sobre José Caridad González, Mayo 1792," AGI, Caracas, 93, no. 351; also cited in Gil Rivas, Dovale, and Bello, *La insurrección de los negros*.

51. This was not the first land dispute that occurred between local people and luangos in Coro. In 1770, for instance, a luango uprising revealed a struggle for land and access to water among these groups, with the consequent elimination of the company of luangos and their relocation from Santa María de la Chapa a Macuquita. See "Autos sobre disensiones y bullicios de los Negros Esclavos fugitivos de la Isla de Curazao a la Jurisdicción de Coro, 1770," AGN, Diversos, XL. See also Rivera, "Social Control on the Eve of a Slave Rebellion."

52. The people who descended from the serranía to the city and to the small towns to sell agricultural products commonly passed through Caujarao (the southern entry to Coro). Aizpurua, "La insurrección de los negros," 712; and Gil Rivas, Dovale, and Bello, *La insurrección de los negros*, 108–10.

53. "Informe de Josef Tellería al Real Consulado de Comercio, no. 15," cited in Rivera, "Social Control on the Eve of a Slave Rebellion."

54. "Informe detallado de Don Manuel Carrera al Capitán General de Caracas," in *Documentos de la insurrección de José Leonardo Chirinos*, 1:45. Manuel Carrera contends that this false rumor spread in Coro thanks to a royal decree given to the luango captain, José Caridad González, which stated that the royal lands of Macuquita were to be occupied and used by luango communities.

55. Ibid.

56. "Informe del Justicia Mayor de Coro, Ramírez Valderrain sobre la insurrección de Coro, 28 de enero de 1796," AGI, Caracas, 95.

57. "Oficio de Ramírez Valderrain, 11 de mayo de 1795," in *Documentos de la insurrección de José Leonardo Chirinos*, 1:33–34.

58. "Ellos me batieron su bandera y hicieron una embajada expresiva de decir se les concediese la libertad a los esclavos y la excepción de derechos de alcabala demas impuestos a los libres, y que nada se ofreceria, entregandoles así la ciudad." "Oficio de Ramírez Valderrain, 15 de mayo de 1795," in *Documentos de la insurrección de José Leonardo Chirinos*, 1:34–35. There is no description of the colors of the flag in the documents, but contemporary oral accounts mention that it was a purple flag. Ruette-Orihuela and Soriano, "Remembering the Slave Rebellion of Coro."

59. "Oficio de Ramírez Valderrain, 15 de mayo de 1795," in *Documentos de la insurrección de José Leonardo Chirinos*, 1:34–35.

60. Ibid.

61. "Oficio de Ramírez Valderrain, 15 de mayo de 1795," in *Documentos de la insurrección de José Leonardo Chirinos*, 1:35.
62. Carbonell wrote: "I consider it important for this case that Your Mercy send a report on the dead and sentenced, and information about the declarations that *in voce* were taken from some with other news and facts that Your Mercy may consider necessary for clarity's sake in the case." "Oficio del Capitán General Don Pedro Carbonell, 26 de mayo de 1795," in *Documentos de la insurrección de José Leonardo Chirinos*, 1:37.
63. "Authorities should allow those sentenced to give evidence and have legitimate self defense, consulting final sentences with the criminal chamber of the respective districts or with the Council. . . . On the contrary Your Majesty will feel unserved and will proceed against those who become transgressors of his sovereign intentions." "Disposición general de las Leyes y demas reales resoluciones sobre los artículos diecisiete y diecinueve de la Real Pragmática de diez y siete de Abril de 1774," AGI, Estado 58, no. 22.
64. "Oficio de Ramírez Valderrain, 17 y 18 de mayo de 1795," in *Documentos de la insurrección de José Leonardo Chirinos*, 1:57–58.
65. "Oficio de Ramírez Valderrain, 23 de mayo de 1795," in *Documentos de la insurrección de José Leonardo Chirinos*, 1:30.
66. "Venían los sublevados a coger la Ciudad, y poner en execucion sus designios de matar a todos los blancos, quitar la contribución de Reales derechos, apoderarse del todo de la ciudad, y seguir de resto la Ley de los Franceses." Ibid.
67. According to Manuel Carrera's brief, only one luango, Nicolás Flores, was officially recognized to have actively participated in the rebellion. Aizpurua, "La insurrección de los negros."
68. If it were true that José Caridad González was a ringleader of the rebellion, it seems strange that he would put himself at risk of being captured by the authorities. His capture and that of the rest of luangos accompanying him were, in fact, the only arrests that occurred in the city of Coro.
69. "Los de Curazao, sin ser delicuentes averiguados, no los tengo por santos." Gil Rivas, Dovale, and Bello, *La insurrección de los negros*, 86.
70. "Informe del Gobernador y Capitán General de la Provincia de Venezuela, del 12 de junio de 1795," in *Documentos de la insurrección de José Leonardo Chirinos*, 1:71–73.
71. The demands described by Carbonell seem contradictory. How could rebels demand the formation of a republic and, at the same time, exoneration from taxes? It seems obvious that political control of the city and the subsequent creation of a republic would reduce or even eliminate those taxes. Several possibilities allow us to explain this ambiguity: first, the contradictory demands were simply invented or imagined by the official discourse; second, the demands were made by rebels at different moments; or third, the two sets of demands were made by different groups of rebels. Unfortunately, the lack of testimony from the rebels prevents us from resolving this question.

72. "Oficio de Ramírez Valderrain, 23 de mayo de 1795," in *Documentos de la insurrección de José Leonardo Chirinos*, 1:33–34.
73. "Se le presentaron en número de más 350 y batiendo la bandera le hicieron embajada, en que pedía libertad de esclavos y exención de alcabalas y demás contribuciones para los libres, entregándoles la ciudad con el fin de establecer la república que torpe y delincuentemente envolvieron en su idea y procuraban con la atrocidad de sus manos, manchadas con las sangre de sus amos y otros blancos destrozados ya la feroz de su ignominia." "Informe de Pedro Carbonell en que alaba al Teniente Justicia Mayor con motivo de la rebelión de los negros esclavos de Coro, 12 de junio de 1795," in *Documentos de la insurrección de José Leonardo Chirinos*, 1:72.
74. "Informe de Pedro Carbonell en que alaba al Teniente Justicia Mayor con motivo de la rebelión de los negros esclavos de Coro, 12 de junio de 1795," in *Documentos de la insurrección de José Leonardo Chirinos*, 1:73.
75. "Proclamando la libertad de esclavos, el exterminio de los blancos, la servidumbre de las blancas, la extinción de los derechos Reales, el pillaje universal, la insolencia, el atrocimiento y la invasion de la Ciudad de Coro." "Informe de Don Hilario Bustos," in *Documentos de la insurrección de José Leonardo Chirinos*, 1:41.
76. "Informe de Don Andrés Manuel de Goribar del 22 de mayo de 1795," in *Documentos de la insurrección de José Leonardo Chirinos*, 1:39.
77. "Presentados en son de Batalla a la entrada de la Ciudad, a tiempo que por parte de ella se le esperava mandaron un emisario a decir que no se ofrecia novedad siempre que se quitasen las alcabalas, y se diese livertad a los esclavos; la respuesta fue dispararles una piesa de canon." "Informe de Juan Hilario de Armas al Gobernador de Caracas, Carora, 31 de mayo de 1795," in *Documentos de la insurrección de José Leonardo Chirinos*, 1:42–43.
78. "Informe de Juan Hilario de Armas al Gobernador de Caracas. Carora, 31 de mayo de 1795," in *Documentos de la insurrección de José Leonardo Chirinos*, 1:43.
79. "Informe de Don Manuel Carrera," in *Documentos de la insurrección de José Leonardo Chirinos*, 1:51.
80. As Jordan comments: "Even when slaves were able to seize temporary local control, as during several revolts in Jamaica and at Stono in South Carolina in 1739, there were no such actual instances during the myriad excitements over slave plots in the entire history of the Anglo-American colonies and nation." Jordan, *Tumult and Silence at Second Creek*, 150. See also Sharples, "Discovering Slave Conspiracies"; and Martínez, "The Black Blood of New Spain."
81. This discourse was often used by British and Spanish colonists to characterized the "cruelty" or lustful nature of Indians, free blacks, and "uncivilized" others. Ana María Alonso, for example, shows that in northern Mexican warfare, both the colonists and the Apaches captured and enslaved women and children. "The capture of 'barbaric' women by 'civilized' men was represented as the redemption of these beings from a life of savagery. By contrast, the taking of 'civilized' women by the 'barbarians' was viewed as an insult to the honor of the colonist."

Alonso, *Thread of Blood*, 96. White women had the advantage over women of color in every aspect of sexual coercion; for women of color, protective patriarchs were absent figures or, at worst, able to use their status to sexually oppress with impunity. See Block, *Rape and Sexual Power in Early America*; and Sanday, *A Woman Scorned*.

82. Laurent Dubois connects the perceived violence of the Haitian Revolution to the politics of representation and, in particular, to questions on how black leaders chose to represent this revolutionary violence. See Dubois, "Avenging America," 111–24; and Nesbitt, *Universal Emancipation*.

83. See Popkin, *Facing Racial Revolution*, chaps. 3, 5. Popkin analyzes an account of an anonymous author who survived the insurrection; this survivor wrote: "I showed them [two blacks guards] how astonished I was at everything they told me, but I didn't make any response to it. I simply asked them why they were sparing the priests, the surgeons, and the women. They replied that they were keeping the priests so that religious services could be held, the surgeons to heal their maladies, and the women to take for their own and get pregnant." Popkin, *Facing Racial Revolution*, 53.

84. Within the Iberian idea of honor, the attacks on the sexual purity of women (mothers, sisters, wives, and daughters) were considered serious insults that put courage, virility, and virtue into question and that had to be avenged if honor was to be restored. Therefore, women were a medium through which men could be dishonored; the chastity of women was what ensured the integrity of the patriarchal domain, the honor of the family, and ethnic purity. See Alonso, *Thread of Blood*; and Pellicer, *La vivencia del honor*.

85. "Mas vale negro con placa, que caveza de blanco: candela arriba, candela abajo, saca la machaca, corta la cabeza, come los zamuros, beva la aguardienta." In "Tercera pieza de Audiencia sobre Sublevación de los Negros Esclavos y libres de aquella ciudad. Contiene las declaraciones de su Teniente, Don Josef de Zabala, Don Francisco Jacot y algunos más," quoted in Castillo Lara, *Curiepe: orígenes históricos*, 41. See Josefina Jordán, "Acercamiento a la rebelión encabezada por José Leonardo Chirinos en 1795," in *Documentos de la insurrección de José Leonardo Chirinos*, 1:16–29.

86. "Candela abajo, candela arriba, muera lo blanco, lo negro viva: y Joséf Leonardo con su pandilla, junta a los negros en Macanilla, y con su volero de Palma Real, muera lo blanco, negro semillan: Blanco cava, negro queda para semillan, quien viviere lo verá." In "Tercera pieza de Audiencia sobre Sublevación de los Negros Esclavos y libres de aquella ciudad. Contiene las declaraciones de su Teniente, Don Joséf de Zabala, Don Francisco Jacot y algunos más," quoted in Castillo Lara, *Curiepe: orígenes históricos*, 42.

87. These parties were usually permitted during Catholic festivities such as Christmas, Easter Sunday, and Cruz de Mayo, among others. Arcaya, "Insurrección de los negros" (1960).

88. "Que con esta expresión querían decir los negros que trataban de extender su generación en las blancas." "Tercera pieza de Audiencia sobre Sublevación de los Negros Esclavos y libres de aquella ciudad. Contiene las declaraciones de su Teniente, Don Joséf de Zabala, Don Francisco Jacot y algunos más," quoted in Castillo Lara, *Curiepe: orígenes históricos*, 43.
89. Alonso, *Thread of Blood*, 90–96; and Martínez, "The Black Blood of New Spain."
90. "Que no había de quedar blanco barón, ni para semilla, que las hembras se havían de acomodar a sus nuevas leyes, que ya no havia esclavitud, ni Alcabalas." "Informe de Doña Nicolasa de Acosta, testigo de la insurrección de Coro," in *Documentos de la insurrección de José Leonardo Chirino*, 1:112.
91. "Informe de Doña Nicolasa de Acosta, testigo de la insurrección de Coro," in *Documentos de la insurrección de José Leonardo Chirino*, 1:113–14.
92. Ibid.
93. "Bamos no me vengas con bromas, esta no sabe lo que hay." "Declaración de Maria Dolores Chirino, 23 de septiembre de 1795," in *Documentos de la insurrección de José Leonardo Chirino*, 1:116–17.
94. Ibid.
95. "Declaración de Maria Dolores Chirino, 23 de septiembre de 1795," and "Declaración de Petrona Janeit, 23 de septiembre de 1795," in *Documentos de la insurrección de José Leonardo Chirino*, 1:117.
96. "Muy Señor, halládome en este empeño de ver su se acaban estos pechos que nos matan, propongo a ustedes la gente que me puedan dar para ir a hacer una demanda Buena a Coro, a ver si los cogemos para tener un buen alivio. Con eso no pagarán demore, y es cuanto se ofrece por ahora rogar a Dios me los guarde muchos años. De su afectísimo Servidor que besa sus manos. José Leonardo Chirino." Archivo Histórico de Coro, Fondo Arcaya, vol. 7, 72. Cited in Gil Rivas, Dovale, and Bello, *La insurrección de los negros*, 80.
97. "Declaración del miliciado blanco Manuel Jose Quero, quien escribió la misiva al cacique de Pecaya dictada por José Leonardo," in *Documentos de la insurrección de José Leonardo Chirino*, 2:84–87.
98. "Informe del Intendente del Real Ejército y Hacienda, Fernández de León, sobre eliminación de tributos a Indios de Pecaya, 8 de Septiembre de 1795," in *Documentos de la insurrección de José Leonardo Chirino*, 1:113–14. See also Gil Rivas, Dovale, and Bello, *La insurrección de los negros*, 80–82.
99. "Informe de Josef Tellería al Real Consulado de Comercio, no. 15," cited in Enrique Rivera, "Social Control on the Eve of a Slave Rebellion."
100. In his report, Tinoco affirms that in Coro "everyone of every class uniformly agrees that the main cause of the rebellion was the insulting and abusing ways with which tax agents proceeded while collecting taxes and tributes," and later he declares: "Most of the blacks have been decapitated without *sumaria*, accusation, confession, sentence or any other legal formality, not even notifying the slave's owners about their slaves' fate." "Informe de Gerónimo Tinoco sobre la

rebellion de Coro, 2 de septiembre de 1795," in *Documentos de la insurrección de José Leonardo Chirino*, 1:107–11.
101. "Informe de Gerónimo Tinoco sobre la rebellion de Coro, 2 de septiembre de 1795," in *Documentos de la insurrección de José Leonardo Chirino*, 1:110.
102. Ibid.
103. Pedro Arcaya, "Insurrección de los negros" (1960), 322.
104. "Informe de Josef Tellería al Real Consulado de Comercio, no. 15," cited by Rivera, "Social Control on the Eve of a Slave Rebellion."
105. Chirino apparently mentioned that he had heard Tellería say, after having a fight with a member of the Zárraga-Zabala family over the report about the abuses of the collectors, that "he won't defend the city when the French come to take it, Zárraga-Zabala and his family will have to do it." As mentioned earlier, throughout the eighteenth century the Tellerías and the Chirinos had engaged in several conflicts with the Zárraga-Zabala family. Arcaya, "Insurrección de los negros" (1960), 323–24.
106. Ibid., 326.
107. Ibid., 331.
108. Dubois, *Avengers of the New World*, 105.
109. Ibid., chaps. 4–7.
110. Ramón Aizpurua suggests that "to kill whites, blacks rebels [of Coro] did not need the example of the Haitians, because they had their own experience of suffering the exploitation, abuse, and insults for more than two hundred years." Aizpurua, "La insurrección de los negros," 717.
111. "Borrador para Don Miguel Aranza. Da Cuenta de haberse exceutado la sentencia de Muerte de José Leonardo Chirino, 6 de marzo de 1797," AGN, Gobernación y Capitanía General, LXII, 7; and "Expediente sobre la Insurrección de los negros proyectada en las inmediaciones de Coro, 1795," AGI, Caracas, 426.
112. Historians of the insurrections in the eighteenth-century Andes have offered similar interpretations of the corporeal dismemberment of Túpac Amaru's body by Spanish officials in Peru (1781). For an insightful analysis on the notion of *reconstitution* elaborated by indigenous Aymara activists in present-day Bolivia, see Thomson, "La descolonización de la memoria"; and Thomson, "Moments of Redemption."
113. "Real Cédula sobre el establecimiento en Coro de una Comandancia Militar, como consecuencia del Movimiento Revolucionario de José María Chirino, 27/10/1798," AGN, Diversos, LXXV, 139–53.
114. "Que el unico origen de aquella sublevacion . . . ha sido la negligencia de los dueños de las Haciendas del mismo Valle en la educación y cuidado christiano y politico de los esclavos y dependientes, que abandonados a sus pasiones, arrasaron violentamente todo lo que encontraban." "Informe de Carbonell a la Real Audiencia, 26 de diciembre de 1796," AGI, Estado 58, no. 7.
115. Manumission by testament refers to a case in which an individual decides to

grant freedom to his or her slaves in his testament, as an expression of gratitude or as an ultimate expression of Christian charity.
116. De Lima, "Libertades en la jurisdicción de Coro"; Blanca De Lima, personal communication with the author, July 2007.
117. "Real Cédula sobre el establecimiento en Coro de una Comandancia Militar, como consecuencia del Movimiento Revolucionario de José Leonardo Chirino, 27/10/1798," AGN, Diversos, LXXV, 139–53.
118. Ibid.
119. Ibid.
120. "Carta de Andrés Boggiero al Capitán General de Venezuela, 24/2/1801," AGN, Gobernación y Capitanía General, XCV, 217.
121. "Sobre recibimientos de las noticias de Santo Domingo por los negros de Coro," AGN, Gobernación y Capitanía General, XCVI, 115, 152, 225.
122. Racine, *Francisco de Miranda*, 159–64.

Chapter 5

1. Level de Goda, "La Revolución de Gual y España," 38–39; and López, *Juan Bautista Picornell*, 149.
2. "Soneto Americano," AGI, Caracas, 434, no. 2. According to López, this song was sung at the celebrations and meetings that the conspirators attended. López, *Juan Bautista Picornell*, 375.
3. In a report about the causes of the movement of La Guaira, the priest José Ignacio Moreno commented that people in La Guaira were influenced by the revolutionary ideas of liberty and equality, which easily entered the city by the coast. In Caracas, he reflected, "the seed of republicanism had not yet been planted," and Montesinos was wrong to think that he could win the "fidelity of the people of Caracas" for the revolutionary cause. See "Observaciones de un ciudadano . . . by José Ignacio Moreno, 22/03/1798," AGI, Estado, 58, no. 24.
4. López, *Juan Bautista Picornell*, 150.
5. "Informe de la Real Audiencia de Caracas sobre sublevación, 8/8/1797," AGI, Caracas, 434, no. 233; López, *Juan Bautista Picornell*, 149–50; Aizpurua, "La conspiración por dentro"; and Gaylord, "The Early Revolutionary Career of Juan Mariano Picornell."
6. "Informe de la Real Audiencia de Caracas sobre la sublevación que se ha descubierto en aquella Capital, 18/7/1797," AGI, Caracas, 434, no. 232; and "Observaciones de un ciudadano . . . by José Ignacio Moreno, 22/03/1798," AGI, Estado, 58, no. 24.
7. López Bohórquez, *Manuel Gual y José María España*; and Grases, *La conspiración de Gual y España*.
8. See Gil Fortoul, *Historia constitucional de Venezuela*; Grases, *Derechos del*

hombre y del ciudadano; Grases, *La conspiración de Gual y España*; López Bohórquez, *Manuel Gual y José María España*; Pérez, *Los movimientos precursores*; and Lynch, *The Spanish American Revolutions*.

9. A collection of essays by historians Juan Carlos Rey, Rogelio Pérez Perdomo, Ramón Aizpurua, and Adriana Hernández analyzes the political roots of the movement, its social complexity, and its ideological strength. Rey et al., *Gual y España*. Ramón Aizpurua offers an interesting picture of the social networks upon which the movement was structured. His work clarifies the motivations, aspirations, and frustrations of the groups of men and women who gathered to discuss political ideas and economic concerns, ultimately generating alliances based on what seemed to be a common cause. Adriana Hernández offers an equally fascinating analysis of how republicanism was adapted to the Venezuelan context. Her work focuses on "programmatic documents"—texts produced by the insurgents in order to explain the motivations, goals, and procedures of the movement.

10. Here, I use both primary and secondary sources. Most of the primary documentation has been drawn from the court records housed in the Archivo General de Indias, and particularly from the Expediente. For this chapter, I have particularly analyzed documentation that contains information regarding written materials and reading practices, especially bounds 430, 432, 433, 434, and 436. AGI, Caracas, 427–36.

11. These court records, known as "Expediente de la conspiración de Gual y España," are housed in the Archivo General de Indias, section Caracas, bounds 427–36. The Archivo General de la Nación in Caracas also has several copies and originals of these records. For an analysis of the diverse texts written by the participants of the movement, see Grases, *La conspiración de Gual y España*; Grases, *Derechos del hombre y del ciudadano*; and Hernández, "Doctrina y gobierno en la conspiración de Gual y España."

12. Guerra, *Modernidad e independencias*, chap. 8. In the case of Venezuela, both Christopher Conway's study of the *Gaceta de Caracas* and Rodolfo Ramírez-Ovalles's study of public opinion in Caracas emphasize the role of printing for the diffusion of political ideas and the proliferation of public spaces for reading and intellectual gatherings in nineteenth-century Venezuela. Conway, "Letras combatientes"; and Ramírez-Ovalles, *La opinión sea consagrada*.

13. Recently, Víctor Uribe-Urán provided comparative evidence that at least an incipient public sphere emerged within Spanish American society in the late colonial period, before independence. Uribe-Urán, "The Birth of a Public Sphere in Latin America."

14. Gil Fortoul, *Historia constitucional de Venezuela*; López Bohórquez, *Manuel Gual y José María España*; Grases, *La conspiración de Gual y España*; and Lynch, *The Spanish American Revolutions*.

15. López, *Juan Bautista Picornell*, 354.

16. At the beginning of the eighteenth century, the Crown received alarming reports about the success of smuggling activities among Venezuelan merchants and the Dutch. The establishment of Compañía Guipuzcoana was closely related to the Dutch presence in Curaçao and their illegal trade with the province. Rey et al., *Gual y España*. See also Hussey, *The Caracas Company*; Aizpurua, *Curazao y la costa de Caracas*; Rupert, *Creolization and Contraband*; and Piñero, "The Cacao Economy."
17. See McKinley, *Caracas antes de la independencia*, chap. 4; Arcila Farías, *Economía colonial de Venezuela*, 2:97; Hussey, *The Caracas Company*; and Piñero, "The Cacao Economy." Caracas received European goods through La Guaira that were either consumed in the city or distributed to others towns; Caracas also provided storage for local agricultural products that were transported to La Guaira to be exported to Europe. The port of La Guaira also received products directly from other areas such as the coast of Barlovento and the central coast. See Banko, *El capital comercial en La Guaira y Caracas*, 340–43.
18. González, *La Guayra: conquista y colonia*, 157; and Banko, *El capital comercial en La Guaira y Caracas*.
19. González, *La Guayra: conquista y colonia*, 157; and Miller, "Status and Royalty of Regular Army Officers."
20. Dauxion-Lavaysse, *A Statistical, Commercial and Political Description*, 55–56.
21. Semple, *Sketch of the Present State of Caracas*, 35.
22. Ibid.; also see González, *La Guayra: conquista y colonia*; and McKinley, *Caracas antes de la independencia*.
23. These were the cases of Martín Antonio de Goenaga, Francisco Sinza, Juan Xavier Arrambide, and José Montesinos y Rico, all very influential merchants at the port. White creoles José María España and Fermín Medina were hacendados in La Guaira, and Agustín García, commander of La Guaira. Juan Josef Mendiri was the royal accountant and guardamayor of the port, and Joaquín Sorondo, an employer of the Real Hacienda. See López, *Juan Bautista Picornell*; and Aizpurua, "La conspiración por dentro."
24. For example, Narciso del Valle (a barber in La Guaira), André Renoir (a hairdresser and jeweler in La Guaira), Josefina Acosta (a domestic servant in La Guaira), and Martín Amador and Juan de Andueza (both bodegueros). See "Reservada entre el Comandante Interior de La Guaira y el Gobernador de Caracas," AGN, Gobernación y Capitanía General, LIX, 268; see also López, *Juan Bautista Picornell*; and Aizpurua, "La conspiración por dentro."
25. "Informe de la Junta extraordinaria convocada por el Gobernador de la Provincia para tratar problema de los prisioneros de Santo Domingo, 30 de noviembre de 1793," AGI, Estado, 58, no. 4; see also "Reservada del Intendente del Ejército Don Esteban Fernández de León, donde da cuenta de haber concurrido la Junta Extraordinaria convocada por el Gobierno para tratar sobre los recelos que a la tranquilidad pública de aquellas provincias ocasionan los oficiales franceses,"

AGI, Caracas, 505; and "Representación del Intendente de Caracas, Don Antonio López de Quintana al Exmo. Señor Don Diego de Gardorqui, sobre medidas necesarias para que no se propaguen las doctrinas francesas por parte de los prisioneros y esclavos franceses que se hallan en La Guaira, febrero de 1795," AGI, Caracas, 472, 514.

26. "Real Audiencia informa a V. M. con mas extensión y documentos lo que va resultando del proceso concerniente a la conjuración que se empezó a descubrir en la noche del 13 de julio de 1797," AGI, Caracas, 434, no. 233.
27. "Informe de José María Reina, 15 de agosto de 1797," AGI, Caracas, 430, no. 44.
28. "Observaciones de un ciudadano... by José Ignacio Moreno, Agosto, 1797," AGI, Caracas, 434, 797–815.
29. "Declaración de Manuel del Pino, 14 de noviembre de 1797," AGI, Caracas, 431, no. 64; quoted in Aizpurua, "La conspiración por dentro," 253.
30. "Declaración de José María España del 2 de mayo de 1798," AGI, 433, no. 91.
31. "Declaración de José de Rusiñol, del 10 de noviembre de 1797," AGI, Caracas, 430, no. 51.
32. "Declaración de Narciso del Valle, 29 de julio de 1797," AGI, Caracas, 430, 50, 20–37.
33. See list of the accused, incriminated, and sentenced in "Razón de los Reos en la Causa de Intentada Sublevación, Descubierta en Esta Ciudad y Puerto de La Guaira el 13 de Julio de 1797, y de sus Respecitvas sentencias Confirmadas por S. M. por Real Cédula de 19 de Julio de 1801," in López Bohórquez, *Manuel Gual y José María España*, 63–72.
34. A similar case of a socially diverse conspiracy with a substantial presence of artisans has been studied by Lyman Johnson in his book *Workshop of Revolution: Plebeian Buenos Aires and the Atlantic World, 1776–1810*, chap. 5.
35. "Declaración de José Antonio Noguera, del 4 de agosto de 1797," AGI, Caracas, 428, 23, 80–87.
36. "Carta del Gobernador de Caracas al Comandante Interior de La Guaira," AGN, Gobernación y Capitanía General, LIX, 256; "Sobre introducción y circulación de Papel 'Instrucción que debe servir de regla al Agente Interino Francés destinado á la Parte Española de Santo Domingo,'" AGI, Estado, 58, no. 8; and AGI, Caracas, 169, no. 86.
37. "Declaración de José Rusiñol, 4 de Agosto de 1797," AGI, Caracas, 430, no. 51.
38. Landaeta Rosales, "Don Manuel Gual y José María España"; and Landaeta Rosales, "La familia españa en Venezuela."
39. Although García denied his attendance at these meetings or anything to do with the reading of seditious documents, José de Rusiñol asserted that in previous years he had seen a paper in the hands of García's secretary that contained "several articles referred to the planning of an Aristocratic republic, preserving the nobility, slavery, and class distinctions, but proposing various dispositions against religious institutions," in "Declaración de Rusiñol, 31 de octubre de 1797," AGI, 430, no. 51; quoted in Aizpurua, "La conspiración por dentro," 232.

40. See "Declaración de José Rusiñol, 6 de junio de 1797," AGI, Caracas, 430, no. 51; and "Declaración de Juan Francisco Arenaza, del 9 de agosto de 1797," AGI, Caracas 427, 17, 1-4. Arenaza declared that, while he was sick, Rusiñol had lent him a manuscript notebook that expressed ideas about how the Spanish monarchy oppressed its vassals with taxes. He later discovered that this notebook had circulated among different people he knew.
41. Grases, *La conspiración de Gual y España*; López, *Juan Bautista Picornell*; and Aizpurua, "La conspiración por dentro."
42. Manuel Gual was the son of Mateo Gual, who arrived in Venezuela in 1743 with the Victoria Regiment. In 1744, the elder Gual decided to remain in Venezuela, and the Crown rewarded him by granting him the title of lieutenant colonel. Gary Miller notes: "He repeatedly asked the crown for a promotion, each time noting that officers who entered the service when he did were by then generals in Spain, while he floundered in Venezuela as lieutenant colonel. Although he served interim appointments as commander in Puerto Cabello and as governor of Cumaná, he remained a lieutenant colonel for nearly 30 years until his death in 1777." Manuel Gual suffered the same fate as his father; he retired from the army with the rank of captain in 1796 in part because his repeated pleas for promotion went unanswered. Miller, "Status and Royalty of Regular Army Officers," 683.
43. Grases, *La conspiración de Gual y España*; López, *Juan Bautista Picornell*; and Edsel, "Gual o la pasión revolucionaria," 649-52.
44. "Declaración de José Francisco Montilla, 19 de Julio de 1797," AGI, Caracas 429, 38.
45. Grases, *La conspiración de Gual y España*; López, *Juan Bautista Picornell*; and Aizpurua, "La conspiración por dentro." Salas declared that "Don Agustín García, Don Patricio Ronán, Don Pedro Canibens, and Don Manuel Gual, when he was in town," also joined the group for these hikes."Declaración de José María Salas, 17 de agosto de 1797," AGI, Caracas, 431, no. 59; also quoted in Aizpurua, "La conspiración por dentro," 262.
46. "Declaración de Narciso del Valle, 13 de octubre de 1797," AGI, Caracas, 430, no. 50; and "Declaración de Manuel del Pino, 14 de noviembre de 1797," AGI, Caracas, 431, no. 64.
47. "Declaración de Lorenzo Acosta, 5 de agosto de 1797," AGI, Caracas, 429, no. 30; quoted in Aizpurua, "La conspiración por dentro," 307.
48. "In the history of this revolution, the name of José Rusiñol is barely mentioned, merely to say that he was condemned. . . . The names of Narciso del Valle, Agustín Serrano, José Manuel del Pino, and Juan Moreno are hardly mentioned either. They were humble soldiers who gave their heads in order to give us liberty." López, *Juan Bautista Picornell*, 90.
49. Gaylord, "The Early Revolutionary Career of Juan Mariano Picornell"; Grases, "Juan Bautista Picornell," 673-77; and Sanoja Hernández, "La obra revolucionaria de Juan Bautista Picornell," 693-94.

50. Gaylord, "The Early Revolutionary Career of Juan Mariano Picornell"; and López, *Juan Bautista Picornell*.
51. Gaylord, "The Early Revolutionary Career of Juan Mariano Picornell."
52. Historians assert that José de Rusiñol updated Picornell on all the political activities and meetings that had been taking place in La Guaira since 1794. He put Picornell in contact with España, Gual, and Valle, and provided him with the necessary materials to write and disseminate his texts. Salcedo Bastardo, "Picornell, Gual y España," 547–58.
53. López, *Juan Bautista Picornell*, 75.
54. Sanoja Hernández, "La obra revolucionaria de Juan Bautista Picornell," 673–77.
55. López, *Juan Bautista Picornell*; Gaylord, "The Early Revolutionary Career of Juan Mariano Picornell"; Aizpurua, "La conspiración por dentro"; and Salcedo Bastardo, "Picornell, Gual y España," 547–58.
56. One of the conspirators, the engineer Patricio Ronán, declared that Picornell was frequently visited by other insurgents of La Guaira and that he "constantly wrote inflammatory papers" that could endanger the tranquility of the province. "Declaración de Patricio Ronán, 18 de agosto de 1797," AGI, Caracas, 427, 7, 75–81.
57. AGI, Caracas, 427, 3, 16–26. I thank Ramón Aizpurua for sharing these documents with me.
58. Soriano, "Bibliotecas, lectores y saber."
59. This list contained books belonging to different libraries; some belonged to José María España, others to Manuel Gual, and others to José de Rusiñol, Manuel Montesinos y Rico, and José María Salas, a captain in La Guaira who did not participate in the plot but who attended some meetings and shared readings with some of the conspirators. "Libros que se recoxieron a los reos de la Sublevación descubierta en 1797," AGI, Caracas, 434, no. 352. The books apparently remained in the hands of the members of the Real Audiencia, who used them in their investigations until they sent them to Spain in 1802. See, for example, "Declaración de José María Salas del 23 de octubre de 1797," AGI, Caracas, 431, no. 59.
60. For a complete analysis of this translation of the "Déclaration des droits de l'homme et du citoyen," see Grases, *Derechos del hombre y del ciudadano*; and Graces, *Traducciones de interés politico-cultural*.
61. "Libros que se recoxieron a los reos de la Sublevación descubierta en 1797," AGI, Caracas, 434, no. 352.
62. "Real Audiencia de Caracas prohibe la lectura del librillo titulado Derechos del Hombre y del Ciudadano, y cualquier otro papel sedicioso, 18 de diciembre de 1797," AGI, Caracas, 432, no. 85.
63. "Auto de Antonio Fernández de León y Francisco Espejo, 23 de agosto de 1797," AGI, Caracas, 427, no. 3.
64. Chartier, *The Cultural Origins of the French Revolution*, 71.

65. According to Renoir, he only helped them translate French books on medicine and grammar, and some comedies. See "Declaración de André Renoir, 4 de agosto de 1797," AGI, Caracas, 428, no. 23.
66. Picornell was the author of *Examen publico, cathechistico, historico y geografico a que expone Don Juan Picornell y gomila social de la real sociedad económica de Madrid a su hijo Juan Antonio Picornell y Obispo*; *Discurso teórico-práctico sobre la educación de la infancia dirigido a los padres de familia*; *El maestro de primeras letras, instruido perfectamente en todas las obligaciones y prerrogativas*; and *Discursos sobre los mejores medios de escitar y fomentar el patriotismo en una monarquía*.
67. López, *Juan Bautista Picornell*, chap. 2.
68. This was, in fact, the argument that members of the Caracas elite used in their demand for royal permission to have a local printing press in 1800. They argued that printing was fundamental to the development of agriculture, commerce, education, and the arts in Venezuela: "With it, the experienced farmers will communicate with other fellow countrymen all the knowledge they have obtained in their fields in order to improve crops; artists will do the same for the benefit of their class, and other citizens will feel encouraged to share the product of their chores in the country." In "Carta del Real Consulado al Rey de España, Febrero 1800," AGI, Caracas, 914.
69. Unfortunately, substantial parts of these papers were burned or hidden from the authorities. Once colonial officials uncovered the conspiracy, many of the conspirators sought to destroy any written evidence. In order to learn about their content, we have had to rely on the numerous declarations that describe the texts.
70. José María España, for example, commented: "In order to prepare the minds, [Picornell] produced a text in jail entitled 'The Life of Vitatusa' which was basically directed against the King, the nobility, and the priests; another one entitled 'Revelation of Father Fr. Joseph de la Concepción,' in which the zambo martyr José Leonardo, principal accused for the rebellions in Coro, is canonized, and where the Americans are incited to declare their freedom; and another entitled 'Letter from a Grandfather to His Grandchild,' in which the grandfather exhorts the child to follow the cause of freedom in the event that an upheaval should take place in the Americas." "Declaración de José María España, 2 de mayo de 1799," AGI, Caracas, 433, no. 91, 49–49v.
71. Tropes of rage and abuse infused representations that people of African descent shared about Chirino and his frustrated insurrection. Picornell seemed to have perceived these feelings and articulated them in his writings. He must have heard about Chirino from José de Rusiñol, who escorted and accompanied Chirino after he was captured and submitted to the port. Aizpurua, "La conspiración por dentro," 239.
72. López, *Juan Bautista Picornell*, 80–81.
73. "Declaración de José Cordero, 27 de octubre de 1797," AGI, Caracas, 428, no. 25.

74. Hernández, "Doctrina y gobierno en la conspiración de Gual y España," 365.
75. "Declaración de Juan de la Tasa," AGI, Caracas, 428, no. 23.
76. "Declaración de José Cordero, del 16 de agosto de 1797," AGI, Caracas, 428, no. 25; "Declaración de José Manuel del Pino, 15 de noviembre de 1797," AGI, Caracas, 431, no. 64; and "Declaración de Miguel Granadino, del 2 de agosto de 1797," AGI, Caracas, 428, no. 23.
77. "Declaración de José Rusiñol, 4 de noviembre de 1797," AGI, Caracas, 430, no. 51.
78. For a fascinating narrative of the San Blas conspirators' escape from La Guaira prison, see López, *Juan Bautista Picornell*, 105–16.
79. "Auto de Antonio Fernández de León y Francisco Espejo, 23 de agosto de 1797," AGI, Caracas, 427, 3, 16–26.
80. Different versions of these texts are to be found in the archives. López, for example, referred to the copies that belonged to Montesinos y Rico (AGI, Caracas, 427, no. 1), which differed slightly from the copies to be found at the Archivo de la Academia Nacional de la Historia in Caracas. López, *Juan Bautista Picornell*, 347–56.
81. "Ordenanzas," AGI, Caracas, 427, no. 1; in López, *Juan Bautista Picornell*, 347–56. For an interesting and detailed analysis of the political and social implications of the "Ordenanzas," see Hernández, "Doctrina y gobierno en la conspiración de Gual y España."
82. In this sense, the La Guaira conspiracy responded to the motivations of many of the eighteenth-century popular movements in Latin America: the mounting economic grievances that followed increases in taxes and commercial monopolies. Examples include the Túpac Amaru rebellion, the insurrection of Aymara highland communities against La Paz, the Indian uprising of northern Potosí, the *comuneros* rebellion in New Granada, and even the black rebellion of Coro, all of which occurred during the last quarter of the eighteenth century. See Langley, *The Americas in the Age of Revolution*; Serulnikov, *Subverting the Colonial Authority*; and Thomson, *We Alone Will Rule*.
83. "Ordenanzas," in López, *Juan Bautista Picornell*, 354.
84. In fact, documents of the conspiracy show that on several occasions the authors adapted their texts to the audience. They alternated, for example, between "blacks" and "morenos" depending on circumstances, using "morenos" in documents addressed to literate white collaborators and "blacks" in the songs and dialogues addressed to people of color.
85. "Soneto Americano," AGI, Caracas, 434, no. 2. According to López, this song was sung at the celebrations and meetings that the conspirators attended. López, *Juan Bautista Picornell*, 375.
86. In revolutionary France, the sansculottes were the radical militants of the lower classes who made up the bulk of the revolutionary army during the first years of the revolution. Their demands included popular democracy and social and economic equality. See Soboul, *The Sans-Culottes*.

87. "Carmañola Americana," AGI, Caracas, 434, no. 85. For an interesting comparative analysis of the translation and adaption of the French "La Carmagnole" to the Spanish "Carmañola," see Bastin and Díaz, "Las tribulaciones de la Carmañola."
88. "Carmañola Americana," AGI, Caracas, 434, no. 85.
89. López, *Juan Bautista Picornell*, 354. As Adriana Hernández comments, it is clear that the conspirators had to consider seriously the issue of the abolition of slavery and its economic effects. They proposed an interesting solution, similar to expropriation: the *justa compensación*, which would apply only to those masters who voluntarily presented their slaves to the junta. Hernández, "Doctrina y gobierno en la conspiración de Gual y España," 375.
90. "Ordenanzas," in López, *Juan Bautista Picornell*, 354.
91. Ibid.
92. "Instrucciones para el Comandante en Xefe del Exercito Revolucionario del Pueblo Americano de Caracas," AGI, Caracas, 434, no. 16. López quoted another version found in AGI, Caracas, 429, no. 35.
93. "Instrucciones para el Comandante en Xefe del Exercito Revolucionario del Pueblo Americano de Caracas," AGI, Caracas, 434, no. 16.
94. There was another document entitled "Borrador de plan globo de revolución," also written by Picornell, that contained the same articles as the "Instrucciones" and sustained the idea that anyone could be part of the Junta Gubernativa. Hernández, "Doctrina y gobierno en la conspiración de Gual y España," 370.
95. "Instrucciones para el Comandante en Xefe del Exercito Revolucionario del Pueblo Americano de Caracas," AGI, Caracas, 434, no. 16. López quoted another version found in AGI, Caracas, 429, no. 35. López, *Juan Bautista Picornell*, 360–61.
96. "Instrucciones para el Comandante en Xefe del Exercito Revolucionario del Pueblo Americano de Caracas," AGI, Caracas, 434, no. 16.
97. "Declaración de Manuel Montesinos y Rico, 6 de septiembre de 1797," AGI, Caracas, 431, no. 62; "Declaración de Martín de Goenaga, 24 de julio de 1797," AGI, Caracas, 428, no. 21; and "Declación de Jean Lartigue, 4 de agosto de 1797," AGI, Caracas, 427, no. 16; all quoted in Aizpurua, "La conspiración por dentro," 264–65.
98. "Declaración del sargento Miguel Granadino, 31 de julio de 1797," AGI, Caracas 428, no. 23; and "Declaración de Narciso del Valle, del 29 de julio de 1797," AGI, Caracas, 427, no. 7.
99. Alejandro Gómez and Ramón Aizpurua argue that the revolution led by Victor Hugues in Guadeloupe, who agreed to grant freedom to the slaves but recommended that they remain in the haciendas while the General Board decided their final destination, could have been an appropriate model for the whites in the La Guaira conspiracy. As Laurent Dubois argues, Hugues's system condemned slaves to a permanent political incapacity, "as it prevented them for becoming

anything other than plantation laborers." Dubois, *A Colony of Citizens*. Gómez shows that Manuel Gual and Patricio Ronán in fact corresponded with Victor Hugues, who even agreed to support the revolution in Tierra Firme. Aizpurua, "La conspiración por dentro," 284–87; and Gómez, "La revolución de Caracas."

100. "Comunicado del Capitán General de Venezuela sobre las intenciones de los ministros ingleses de animar a los españoles a la independencia, 31 de Julio de 1800," AGI, Caracas 96.

101. Ibid.

Chapter 6

1. Scott, "The Common Wind"; Geggus, "Slavery, War, and Revolution"; Dubois, *A Colony of Citizens*; Gómez, "La ley de los franceses"; Gómez, "El síndrome de Saint-Domingue"; and Helg, *Liberty and Equality in Caribbean Colombia*.
2. "Real Orden e Instruccion del Rey a los Jefes de las Provincias en America, para prevenirles sobre el peligro de las Insurrecciones acontecidas en las Provincias, noviembre de 1791," AGN, Reales Ordenes, XI, 70.
3. Geggus, "Slavery, War, and Revolution," 23–24.
4. Dubois, *A Colony of Citizens*; and Gómez, "La Ley de los franceses."
5. Dubois comments that, by 1795, 25 ships operated in the waters around Guadeloupe, but by the end of Hugues's regime, in 1798, the corsairs had proliferated, reaching 121 ships. In four years, these corsairs destroyed or captured 1,800 merchant vessels. Dubois, *A Colony of Citizens*, 242.
6. Geggus, "Slavery, War, and Revolution," 23–24; and Pompeian, "Spirited Enterprises."
7. Ibid.
8. Gómez, "La Ley de los franceses,"18–19.
9. "Borrador al Capitán General," AGN, Gobernación y Capitanía General, LXVIII; also cited in Gómez, "La ley de los franceses."
10. "Testimonio del expediente formado sobre la sublevación de los negros, sambos, mulatos esclavos y libres de la jurisdicción de Coro, 1796," in *Documentos de la insurrección de José Leonardo Chirinos*, 1:158–59; and "Comunicación del Capitán General a todos los dueños de haciendas de los Valles de Río Chico, Panaquire y Tapipta, Caracas, 19 de marzo de 1801," AGN, Gobernación y Capitanía General, XCVI, 156.
11. The list of denunciations of the presence of French corsairs on the Venezuelan coast from 1798 to 1801 is long. See "Expediente sobre negros y mulatos franceses dejados en la Península Goajira, 1799," AGI, Estado, no. 60; "Comunicación del gobernador de Maracaibo sobre presencia de corsarios franceses en Río de Hacha, mayo 1799," AGN, Gobernación y Capitanía General, LXXVII, 76; "Comunicación de Fernando Mijares al Capitán General, sobre presencia de

Corsarios franceses, junio 1799," AGN, Gobernación y Capitanía General, LXXIX, 223-27; "Don Manuel Ayala Informa al Capitán General sobre ataque de 40 negros franceses en pueblo del Valle de Ocumare, julio 1799," AGN, Gobernación y Capitanía General, LXXIX, 212; "Comunicación del Capitán General de Venezuela al Virrey de Santa Fé sobre presencia de corsarios franceses en las costas, octubre 1799," AGN, Gobernación y Capitanía General, LXXXI, 287; "Comunicación del Gobernador de Maracaibo para el Capitán General sobre presencia de corsarios con 120 franceses de color, julio 1800," AGN, Gobernación y Capitanía General, LXXXVIII, 7; and "Informe del Comandante de Coro, Andrés Boggiero al Capitán General, enero 1801," AGI, Estado, no. 60.

12. "Copia de la carta del Gobernador Anastasio Zejudo para el Virrey de Santa Fé, sobre la sublevación de los negros esclavos, Cartagena, 9 de abril 1799," in Troconis de Veracochea, *Documentos para el estudio de los esclavos negros*, 325-28; and "Oficio de Pedro Mendinueta para el Virrey de Santa Fé, sobre la conjuración tramada por los negros esclavos de Cartagena de Indias, 19 de mayo de 1799," in Troconis de Veracochea, *Documentos para el estudio de los esclavos negros*, 323-24. See also Helg, "A Fragmented Majority"; and Helg, *Liberty and Equality in Caribbean Colombia*.

13. Helg, "A Fragmented Majority."

14. "Comunicación del Gobernador de Maracaibo, Don Juan Ignacio de la Armada, al Capitán General de Venezuela, Guevara Vasconcelos, May 1799," AGI, Estado 71, no. 3.

15. Helg maintains that the extreme fragmentation of the region, the weak presence of colonial authorities in the small towns dotting the coast, and the undefined nature of the unconquered land inhabited by indigenous communities precluded mass rebellion along New Granada's Caribbean shores. Helg, "A Fragmented Majority," 162.

16. "Comunicado del Capitan General de Venezuela, Carbonell, a los Gobernadores de la Provincia," AGN, Gobernación y Capitanía General, LV, 235.

17. The movement has been mentioned and analyzed in some Venezuelan historical works that either study series of colonial insurgent movements or compile the history of the region of Maracaibo. See Salcedo Bastardo, *Historia fundamental de Venezuela*; Brito Figueroa, *El problema de la tierra y esclavos*; Magallanes, *Luchas e insurrecciones*; Arocha, *Diccionario geográfico, estadístico e histórico*; and Besson, *Historia del Zulia*. Only three Venezuelan historians have written monographs focused exclusively on Pirela's movement; see Brice, *La sublevación de Maracaibo de 1799*; Leal, "Francisco Javier Pirela"; and Manzanilla Celis, *La sublevación de Francisco Javier Pirela*. Manzanilla offers the first detailed analysis of the complete file (*expediente*) of the conspiracy; he not only connects the events of Maracaibo with other, similar events developing in Cartagena and Curaçao but also offers a complete and detailed analysis of the failed plot and the different strategies that colonial officials developed in order to control it.

18. Manzanilla, for example, argues that evident connections of this movement to similar plots in Curaçao, Cartagena, and Santiago de Cuba lead him to think that this was part of a larger plan to export the revolution from Saint-Domingue to other regions. Alejandro Gómez, on the other hand, maintains that the fact that the corsairs ended up in Maracaibo by accident, together with the lack of evidence for any conjoined plan in Saint-Domingue, shows that the plot was more an "act of piracy" organized by the corsairs, who acted on their own, and on many occasions, without direction or approval from the government in Saint-Domingue. See Manzanilla Celis, *La sublevación de Francisco Javier Pirela*; Gómez, "La ley de los franceses"; and Gómez, "La caribeanidad revolucionaria de la 'Costa de Caracas.'"
19. Authorities in Maracaibo argued that that a Captaincy General of Maracaibo should be created, while authorities in New Granada demanded to maintain jurisdiction over the province, because three-fourths of the products commercialized in Maracaibo originated in New Granadan territory. See "Provincia de Maracaibo," *Diccionario de historia de Venezuela*, 3:39–42; and Cardozo, "Maracaibo: de la aldea colonial al puerto atlántico."
20. Cardozo, "Maracaibo: de la aldea colonial al puerto atlántico."
21. See "Provincia de Maracaibo," *Diccionario de historia de Venezuela*, 3:39–42; Vázquez de Ferrer, "El comercio marabino"; and Urdaneta, "San José de Cucúta."
22. Vázquez de Ferrer, "El comercio marabino."
23. Cardozo, "Maracaibo: de la aldea colonial al puerto atlántico."
24. Brice, *La sublevación de Maracaibo*; Leal, "Francisco Javier Pirela"; and Manzanilla Celis, *La sublevación de Francisco Javier Pirela*.
25. Gómez, "La ley de los franceses," 22.
26. "Informe no. 1 que hizo Fernando Miyares, sobre el proceso seguido por el gobierno de Maracaibo, contra los capitanes franceses Agustín Gaspar, Juan Bautista Gaspar Bocé y las tripulaciones de los dos corsarios titulados 'El Bruto' y 'La Patrulla,' por la insurrección intentada contra la ciudad, Maracaibo, 13 de Julio de 1799," in Manzanilla Celis, *La sublevación de Francisco Javier Pirela*, 363.
27. "Expediente de entrega del cargamento de la Goleta inglesa 'El Arlequín,' hecha presa pot los Capitanes de los corsarios franceses 'El Bruto' y 'La Patrulla,' Maracaibo, 11 de mayo de 1799," AGN, Diversos, LXXIV, 242–51.
28. The ship *El Bruto* had a crew of forty-three people, most of them black or mulatto, originally from Saint-Domingue (Port-au-Prince, Léogâne, Petit-Goâve, and Guarico); *La Patrulla* had a crew of twenty-five people, the majority also blacks from Saint-Domingue, but there were some from Guinea, Spanish Santo Domingo, and New York. The British ship had only seven people, five of whom were whites: the captain from Saint Thomas, a sailor from Wales, one from Sweden, one from England, and one from Urhan in Ireland. The two blacks on board were from Curaçao. See Manzanilla Celis, *La sublevación de Francisco Javier Pirela*, 166–71.

29. "Reporte del Gobernador de Maracaibo, Juan Ignacio de la Armada sobre la conspiración de los negros franceses en el Puerto de Maracaibo, 20 de Mayo de 1799," AGN, Primera Pieza del Expediente Conspiración de Pirela, 1–2; and "Declaración de Tomás Ochoa sobre conspiración de los negros franceses en el Puerto de Maracaibo, 20 de Mayo de 1799," AGN, Primera Pieza del Expediente Conspiración de Pirela, 3.
30. "Reporte del Gobernador de Maracaibo, Juan Ignacio de la Armada sobre la conspiración de los negros franceses en el Puerto de Maracaibo, 20 de Mayo de 1799," AGN, Primera Pieza del Expediente Conspiración de Pirela, 1–2; and "Declaración de Francisco Pirela, subteniente de la Compañía de Pardos, 20 de mayo 1799," AGN, Primera Pieza del Expediente Conspiración de Pirela, 4.
31. "Declaración de Francisco Pirela, subteniente de la Compañía de Pardos, 20 de mayo 1799," AGN, Primera Pieza del Expediente Conspiración de Pirela, 4.
32. "Declaración de Francisco Pirela, subteniente de la Compañía de Pardos, 20 de mayo 1799," AGN, Primera Pieza del Expediente Conspiración de Pirela, 4. He is presumably talking about the events of January 1, 1792, when black rebel forces took Fort Dauphin and announced that more French troops would come to support them. See Ferrer, *Freedom's Mirror*, 51; and Dubois, *Avengers of the New World*, 125–29.
33. "Reporte del Gobernador de Maracaibo, Juan Ignacio de la Armada sobre la conspiración de los negros franceses en el Puerto de Maracaibo, 20 de Mayo de 1799," AGN, Primera Pieza del Expediente Conspiración de Pirela, 1–2; and "Informe no. 1 que hizo Fernando Miyares, sobre el proceso seguido por el gobierno de Maracaibo, contra los capitanes franceses Agustín Gaspar, Juan Bautista Gaspar Bocé y las tripulaciones de los dos corsarios titulados 'El Bruto' y 'La Patrulla,' por la insurrección intentada contra la ciudad, Maracaibo, 13 de Julio de 1799," in Manzanilla Celis, *La sublevación de Francisco Javier Pirela*, 363.
34. "Declaración de Don Salvador Pérez, residente de Maracaibo, 20 de mayo 1799," AGN, Primera Pieza del Expediente Conspiración de Pirela, 9; and "Declaración de Don Fabián Salinas, 20 de mayo 1799," AGN, Primera Pieza del Expediente Conspiración de Pirela, 10.
35. "Declaración de Juan Arrizon, marinero del corsario 'La Patrulla,' 20 de mayo 1799," AGN, Primera Pieza del Expediente Conspiración de Pirela, 8; "Declaración de Juan José Prospero, mariner negro del corsario 'La Patrulla,'" AGN, Primera Pieza del Expediente Conspiración de Pirela, 8; and "Oficio del Gobernador de Maracaibo, Don Juan Ignacio de la Armada para el Capitán General de Venezuela, 21 de mayo 1799," in Manzanilla Celis, *La sublevación de Francisco Javier Pirela*.
36. "Declaración de Juan Sualbach, soldado de la 4ta compañía veterana de la plaza, 20 de mayo 1799," AGN, Primera Pieza del Expediente Conspiración de Pirela, 5–6.
37. "Declaración del esclavo José Francisco Suárez, 20 Mayo 1799," AGN, Primera Pieza del Expediente Conspiración de Pirela, 5.

38. "Reporte del Gobernador de Maracaibo, Fernando Mijares, sobre la causa de revolución intentada en Maracaibo, noviembre 1799," AGN, Gobernación y Capitanía General, LXXXII, 57–60.
39. "Declaración de Joseph Romano, Capitán de la presa 'El Arlequín,'" AGN, Segunda Pieza del Expediente Conspiración de Pirela, 280–84.
40. "Informe de Fernando Mijares al Capitán General, Agosto 1799," AGN, Gobernación y Capitanía General, LXXX, 76–77.
41. "Declaración de Joseph Romano, Capitán de la presa 'El Arlequín,'" AGN, Segunda Pieza del Expediente Conspiración de Pirela, 280–84.
42. "Informe de Fernando Mijares al Capitán General, Agosto 1799," AGN, Gobernación y Capitanía General, LXXX, 76–77; Brice, *La sublevación de Maracaibo*; and Leal, "Francisco Javier Pirela."
43. Gómez, "La ley de los franceses"; and Gómez, "La caribeanidad revolucionaria de la 'Costa de Caracas.'"
44. "Comunicación de Fernando Mijares al Capitán General, 19 junio 1799," AGN, Gobernación y Capitanía General, LXXVIII, 224.
45. "Reporte del Gobernador de Maracaibo, Juan Ignacio de la Armada para el Capitán General sobre la Junta de Guerra formada para proporcionar medios adecuados de seguridad y defensa, 27 mayo 1799," AGN, Gobernación y Capitanía General, LXXVIII, 6–13.
46. Ferrer, *Freedom's Mirror*, 152.
47. "Comunicación de Don Miguel Marmión, Teniente de Puerto Cabello, al Capitán General de Venezuela, 20/1/1801," AGN, Gobernación y Capitanía General, XCVI, 229–34.
48. Ibid.
49. See "Estado que manifiesta el número de personas emigradas en este Puerto, así particulares como de los Cuerpos Político y Militar, y de la Real Hacienda procedentes de la Ysla Española de Santo Domingo, Maracaibo, 21 de marzo de 1801," quoted in Carrera Montero, *Las complejas relaciones de España con la Española*, 505.
50. On Saint-Domingue refugees, their mobilizations, and their stories, see Brasseaux and Conrad, *The Road to Louisiana*; Geggus, "Slavery, War, and Revolution"; Meadows, "Engineering Exile"; Sevilla Soler, "Las repercusiones de la Revolución Francesa"; White, *Encountering Revolution*; Branson and Patrick, "Etrangers dans un Pays Etrange"; and Pierce, "Discourses of the Dispossessed".
51. As Ashli White contends, Saint-Dominguan exiles "raised as many questions about being a republic as they did about slaveholding," and, in the case of the United States, these questions forced Americans to confront the paradox of being a slaveholding republic. White, *Encountering Revolution*, 3.
52. Natalie Zemon Davis argues that when the condemned seek to portray themselves as victims, they become masters of the narrative. See Davis, *Fiction in the*

Archives. For interesting discussions of the politics of victimization, see Torpey, *Politics and the Past*; and Elias, *The Politics of Victimization*.
53. On Dominican refugees in Cuba, see Deive, *Las emigraciones dominicanas a Cuba*; Ferrer, "Cuba en la sombra de Haití"; and Ferrer, *Freedom's Mirror*.
54. Ferrer, *Freedom's Mirror*, chap. 4.
55. See Schaeffer, "The Delayed Cession of Spanish Santo Domingo to France," 46–48; Deive, *Las emigraciones dominicanas a Cuba*; Dubois, *Avengers of the New World*, chaps. 10, 11; and Ferrer, *Freedom's Mirror*, chaps. 4, 5.
56. "Pasaporte otorgado por Joaquín García a Antonio Chanlatte, General de Brigada francés en la parte española de Santo Domingo, 13/01/1801," AGI, Estado, 59, no. 14, 3.
57. "Carta de los Generales Chanlatte y Kerversau al Gobernador y Capitán General de Venezuela," AGI, Estado, 59, no. 14. Following the Treaty of Aranjuez, Spain became an active ally of France on June 27, 1796, and the following November a war started between Spain and England. See Schaeffer, "The Delayed Cession of Spanish Santo Domingo to France," 55.
58. "Comunicación de los Generales Franceses al Capitán General de Venezuela, 3/1801," AGN, Gobernación y Capitanía General, XCVI, 51–52, 85–87.
59. "Comunicación del Capitán General de Venezuela autorizando el desembarco de los Generales Franceses, 23/01/1801," AGI, Estado, 59, no. 14.
60. "Relación sobre el estado de la parte francesa y de la parte española de Santo Domingo, por Antonio Chanlatte, General de Brigada y Comisario del Gobierno Francés en la parte española, 8/5/1800," AGI, Estado, no. 14.
61. "Extracto de la principal relación sobre los acontecimientos de Santo Domingo por el General Kerversau," AGN, Gobernación y Capitanía General, LXXXV, 316–324v, 317.
62. Ibid., 322.
63. Ibid., 323–24.
64. "Comunicación del Gobernador Fernando Mijares al Capitan General de Venezuela, 23/01/1801," AGI, Estado 60, no. 3.
65. Deive, *Las emigraciones dominicanas a Cuba*, 95. In Latin America, the term *criado* usually referred to a person raised by the family, a poor relative, or someone from the hacienda who depended on the family. The term did not normally apply to slaves. However, because Toussaint prohibited the emigration of field slaves and allowed only that of domestic slaves, Dominicans masters seem to have included their domestic slaves under the category "criados" in order not to call the attention of the authorities. Table 3 shows how the number of criados significantly increased right after the prohibition on taking slaves went into effect; in the following months, however, the numbers decreased, probably because Toussaint restricted the exit of criados, or because masters had already taken all the slaves they could.

66. "Comunicación del Gobernador Mijares al Capitán General de Venezuela, 14/02/1801," AGI, Estado, 60, no. 13, 211.
67. Ibid.
68. Deive, *Las emigraciones dominicanas a Cuba*, 93–96; and "Comunicación del Gobernador Mijares al Capitán General de Venezuela, 24/2/1801 y 3/2/1801," AGI, Estado, 60, no. 13, 218, 219, 220.
69. "Comunicación de Joaquín García al Capitán General de Venezuela sobre situación de Santo Domingo, la toma de la plaza por las tropas de Toussaint, 24/02/1801," AGI, Estado 60, no. 3.
70. "La consternación que desde aquel fatal momento se apoderó de nuestros corazones; fue tal que no hubo mas orden no concierto en Sto. Domingo; todos trataron inmediatamente de abandonar una patria infeliz y con ella todos sus bienes, y posesiones: cada cual se embarcó donde pudo, y como pudo, suerte que nuestra salida mas ha parecido una fuga precipitada que una emigración arreglada, y . . . dichosos los que lo hemos verificado! Pues los desgraciados que no han podido efectuarla, ya tienen cerrado el Puerto, y están sufriendo las vejaciones y aprobios que son consecuentes al Gobierno de un negro déspota, lleno de ambición y de codicia." "Comunicado de los emigrados de Santo Domingo residentes en Maracaibo," AGN, Gobernación y Capitanía General, XCVI, 102–3. On February 8, 1801, Toussaint forbade any inhabitant of Spanish Santo Domingo from leaving the island, with the exception of the governor, the ministers, and the Cantabria Regiment. With this decision, Toussaint clearly violated the terms of both the Treaty of Basel and the Capitulations. See Carrera Montero, *Las complejas relaciones de España con la Española*, 473.
71. Black Dominican refugees would likely have felt similarly and would probably have spread favorable rumors about the black rebellion and about freedom and equality in Santo Domingo.
72. "Sobre recibimientos de las noticias de Santo Domingo por los negros de Coro," AGN, Gobernación y Capitanía General, XCVI, 115, 152, 225; and "Recibimiento de las Noticias de Toussaint en los Valles de Aragua, Febrero 1801," Archivo de la Academia de la Historia (AAH), civiles, A13-5159-2; quoted in Geggus, *The Haitian Revolution: A Documentary History*, 188.
73. "Comunicación de Andrés Boggiero al Capitán General de Venezuela, 24/01/1801," AGI, Estado 60, no. 3, 176.
74. The truth is that Toussaint did not abolish slavery in the Spanish part of Santo Domingo until August 1801. He did prohibit the sale of slaves as well as their emigration from the island. Slaves had to remain in the custody of the republic, as a way of preventing their dispersion and the loss of agricultural production. See Carrera Montero, *Las complejas relaciones de España con la Española*, 472.
75. "Información que remiten los emigrados de Sto. Domingo habitantes en Coro, 1801," AGN, Gobernación y Capitanía General, XCVI, 66–67.

76. "Las miras de Tousain es de creerse que podran senorearse en toda la Ysla como dueño absoluto de esta, destruirla y aniquilarla y aun extender el fuego por defuera de sus posesiones vecinas. Esto digo puede esperarse de su ambicion y genio." Ibid.
77. Ibid.

Conclusion

1. "Observaciones de un Ciudadano . . ." by José Ignacio Moreno, AGI, Caracas, 434, 798–99.
2. Polasky, *Revolutions without Borders*, 8–10.
3. "Observaciones de un Ciudadano . . ." by José Ignacio Moreno, AGI, Caracas, 434, 799–800.
4. This image probably prevailed throughout the nineteenth century; even the leaders of Venezuela's movement for independence, such as Simón Bolívar and Francisco de Miranda, avoided mentioning the Coro rebellion, as if the movement had never occurred.
5. "Observaciones de un Ciudadano . . ." by José Ignacio Moreno, AGI, Caracas, 434, 802.
6. He suggested not only establishing an Inquisition Court in the province in order to counter moral disorder but also closely supervising pardo militias.
7. Borucki, "Trans-Imperial History in the Making of the Slave Trade"; and Aizpurua, *Relaciones de trabajo*, 78.
8. "Sobre establecimiento de patrullas de vigilancia en Caracas, Agosto 1794," AGN, Real Consulado, Actas, 2526, 37–38; "Del Capitán General de Venezuela al Justicia Mayor de Carora, sobre establecimiento de milicias urbanas para controlar alzamientos de esclavos y de gente de color, junio 1795," AGN, Gobernación y Capitanía General, LV, 353; and "Lista de los esclavos cimarrones aprehendidos por las Patrullas, de las que se han presentado a sus dueños después de su establecimiento, Mayo 1795," AGN, Diversos, LXIX, 113.
9. Ferrer, *Freedom's Mirror*, chap. 7; and Childs, *The 1812 Aponte Rebellion*.
10. Fischer, "Bolívar in Haiti," 31.

Appendix

1. "Auto de Antonio Fernández y Francisco Espejo, del 23 de agosto de 1797," AGI, Caracas, 427.

Bibliography

Archival Sources

Venezuela

Archivo General de la Nación (AGN)
    Sección Archivo de Aragua
    Gobernación y Capitanía General
    Reales Cédulas
    Reales Ordenes
    Reales Provisiones
    Real Intendencia y Ejército
    Sección Diversos
    Sección Testamentarías (1770–1810)
Archivo de la Academia de la Historia (AAH)
    Sección Civiles
Archivo Arquidiocesano de Caracas (AAC)
    Sección Santo Oficio
Biblioteca Nacional (Caracas)
    Sala de Libros Raros

Spain

Archivo General de Indias, Seville (AGI)
    Sección Caracas
    Sección Contratación
    Sección Santo Domingo
    Sección Estado
    Sección Indiferente General
Biblioteca Nacional (Madrid)

United States

Center for Southwest Research and Special Collections, University of New Mexico.

John Carter Brown Library, Brown University.
Kislak Center for Special Collections, Rare Books, and Manuscripts, University of Pennsylvania.

Published Primary Sources

Alembert, Jean le Rond d'. *Mélanges de littérature, d'histoire, et de philosophie*. Amsterdam: Zacharie Chatelain and Fils, 1767.
Altolaguirre y Duvale, Ángel de. *Relaciones geográficas de la gobernación de Venezuela, 1767-1768*. Madrid: Real Sociedad Geográfica, 1908.
Bory de Saint-Vincent, Jean-Baptiste. *Bibliothéque phissico economique instructive et amusante*. Paris: Chez Buisson, 1782-1793.
Castillo Lara, Lucas G. *Apuntes para la historia colonial de Barlovento*. Caracas: Academia Nacional de la Historia, 1981.
Choisy, Abbé de. *Histoire de l'Eglise*. 10 vols. Paris: Chez Christophe Davi, 1701-1723.
Coligny de la Suze, Henriette de, and Paul Pelisson. *Recueil de pieces galantes en prose et en vers*. Lyon: Chez Antoine Bondet, 1695.
Condillac, Abbé de. *Cours d'étude pour l'instruction du Prince de Parme*. Geneva: Deifart, 1789.
Condorcet, Marquis de. *Esquisse d'un tableau des progrès de l'esprit humain*. Madrid: n.p., 1794.
Dauray de Brie, J.-F. *Théorie des Lois Sociales*. Paris: Demonville, 1804.
Dauxion-Lavaysse, Jean-François. *A Statistical, Commercial and Political Description of Venezuela, Trinidad, Margarita and Tobago*. London: G. and W. B. Whittaker, 1820.
Delille, Jacques. *L'Énéide*. Paris: Chez Guiguet et Michaud, 1804.
———. *La pitié, poeme*. Paris: Chez Guiguet et Michaud, 1803.
Diccionario de Autoridades (1726-1742). Madrid: Gredos, 1976.
Diderot, Denis, and Jean le Rond d'Alembert. *Encyclopédie ou dictionaire raisonné des sciences, des arts et des métiers*. Paris: Chez du Le Breton, 1751-1772.
Documentos de la insurrección de José Leonardo Chirinos. 2 vols. Caracas: Ediciones "Fundación Historia y Comunicación," 1994.
Documentos para el estudio de los esclavos negros. Colección "Fuentes para la Historia Colonial." Caracas: Academia Nacional de la Historia, 1969.
Filangieri, Gaetano. *La scienza della legislazione*. Genoa: Ivone Gracian, n.d.
Flinter, George Dawson. *A History of the Revolution of Caracas: Comprising an Impartial Narrative of the Atrocities Committed by the Contending Parties, Illustrating the Real State of the Contest, Both in a Commercial and Political Point of View, Together with a Description of the Llaneros, or People of the Plains of South America*. London: T. and J. Allman, 1819.

Gilij, Felipe Salvador. *Ensayo de historia americana: estado presente de la tierra firme.* Bogotá: Editorial Sucre, 1955. First published, 1784.

Guyard de Berville, Guillaume-François. *Histoire de Pierre du Terrail, dit Chevalier Bayard, san peur et san reproche.* Lyon: Chez Barnuset, 1786.

Humboldt, Alexander von. "Viaje a las regiones equinocciales del nuevo mundo." In *Alejandro de Humboldt por tierras de Venezuela.* Caracas: Fundación de Promoción Cultural de Venezuela, 1987.

Jerónimo Feijóo y Montenegro, Fray Benito. *Cartas eruditas, y curiosas, en que por la mayor parte, se continua el designio del theatro critico universal, impugnado, o reduciendo a dudosas, varias opinions communes.* Madrid: Francisco del Hierro, 1742.

———. *Theatro crítico universal, o discursos varios, en todo género de materias, para desengaño de errores communes, dedicado al General de la Congregación de San Benito de España.* 8 vols. Madrid: Lorenzo Francisco Mujados, 1726–1739.

Jovellanos, Gaspar Melchor de. *Memorias de la real sociedad económica de Madrid.* Madrid: Antonio Sancha, 1795.

Labat, Jean-Baptiste. *Nouveau voyage aux isles de L'Amerique contenant l'histoire naturelle de ces pays, l'origine, les moeurs, la religion et le gouvernment des habitants anciens et moderne; les guerre ser les evenemens singulaires qui y son arrivez pendant le long séjour que l'auteur y a fait: le commerce et les manufactures qui y son établies, et les moyens de les augmenter.* La Haye en Touraine, France: Chez Pierre Husson, 1722–1724.

Langlet, Abate. *El hablador juicioso y crítico imparcial: cartas y discursos eruditos sobre todo género de materias útiles y curiosas.* Madrid: Imprenta de Francisco Javier García, 1763.

Manuel, Pierre. *La police de Paris dévoilée.* Paris: Chez J. B. Garnery, 1791.

Montengón y Paret, Pedro. *Eusebio, parte primera sacada de las memorias que dejó el mismo.* Madrid: Antonio Sancha, 1786.

Nicéron, Jean-Pierre, and François-Joachim Duport du Tertre. *Bibliothèque amusante et instructive, contenant des anecdotes interessantes et des histoires curieuses tirées des meilleurs auteurs.* Paris: Chez Duchesne, 1755.

Nieremberg, Juan Eusebio. *Diferencia entre lo temporal y lo eterno: crisol de desengaños en la memoria de la eternidad, postrimerías humanas y misterios divinos.* Madrid: Manuel Martin, 1762.

Novísima recopilación de las leyes de España. Dividida en XII libros. En que se reforma la recopilación publicada por el Señor Don Felipe II en el año de 1567, reimpresa últimamente en el de 1775. Y se incorporan las pragmáticas, cédulas, decretos, órdenes y resoluciones reales, y otras providencias no recopiladas, y expedidas hasta el de 1804. Mandada formar por el señor don Carlos IV. Madrid: Antonio Sancha, 1805.

Picornell, Juan Bautista. *Discurso teórico-práctico sobre la educación de la infancia dirigido a los padres de familia.* Salamanca: Andrés García Rico, 1786.

———. *Discursos sobre los mejores medios de escitar y fomentar el patriotismo en una monarquía*. Madrid: n.p., 1790.

———. *Examen publico, cathechistico, historico y geografico a que expone Don Juan Picornell y gomila social de la real sociedad económica de Madrid a su hijo Juan Antonio Picornell y Obispo*. Salamanca: Andrés García Rico, 1785.

———. *El maestro de primeras letras, instruido perfectamente en todas las obligaciones y prerrogativas*. Madrid: n.p., 1786.

Pons, François-Joseph de. *Travels in Parts of South America, during the Years 1801, 1802, 1803 & 1804: Containing a Description of the Captain-Generalship of Caracas, with an Account of the Laws, Commerce, and Natural Productions of That Country; as Also a View of the Customs and Manners of the Spaniards and Native Indians*. London: Richard Phillips, 1806.

———. *Viaje a la parte oriental de tierra firme en la América meridional*. 2 vols. Caracas: Banco Central de Venezuela, 1960.

Raynal, Guillaume Thomas François. *Histoire philosophique et politique des établissement et du commerce des européens dans les deux Indes*. Amsterdam: n.p., 1770.

———. *Historia política de los establecimientos ultramarinos de las naciones europeas*. Madrid: Antonio de Sancha, 1784.

Real Cédula de S. M. y Señores del Consejo, en que se prohíbe la introducción y curso en estos Reynos de qualesquiera cartas o papeles sediciosos y contrarios a la fidelidad, y a la tranquilidad pública, y se manda a las Justicias procedan en este asunto sin disimulo y con la actividad y vigilancia que requiere; en la conformidad que se expresa. Madrid: Imprenta de la Viuda de Marín, 1791.

Rodríguez, Simón. "Reflexiones sobre los defectos que vician la escuela de primeras letras de Caracas y medio de lograr su reforma por un nuevo establecimiento, 19 de mayo de 1794." In *Simón Rodríguez, Escritos*, edited by Pedro Grases, 5–27. Caracas: Imprenta Nacional, 1954.

Rodríguez de Campomanes, Pedro. *Discurso sobre el fomento de la industria*. Madrid: Antonio Sancha, 1774.

———. *Discurso sobre la educación popular de los artesanos y su fomento*. Madrid: Antonio Sancha, 1775.

Romme, Charles. *Dictionnaire de la marine françoise avec figures*. Paris: Chez P. L. Chauvet, 1792.

Rousseau, Jean-Baptiste. *Oeuvres choisies de J.-B. Rousseau: odes, cantantes, epitres, ét poesies diverses*. Paris: Janet et Cotelle, 1823.

Rousseau, Jean-Jacques. *Du contrat social; ou principes du droit politique*. Amsterdam: Marc Michel Rey, 1762.

———. *Oeuvres complets*. Paris: Chez de Maisonneuve, 1793–1800.

Sempere y Guarinos, Juan. *Ensayo de una biblioteca española de los mejores escritores del reynado de Carlos III*. Madrid: Imprenta Real, 1785.

———. *Historia del luxo y de las leyes suntuarias de España*. Madrid: Imprenta Real, 1788.
Semple, Robert. *Sketch of the Present State of Caracas; Including a Journey from Caracas through La Victoria, and Valencia to Puerto Cabello*. London: Robert Baldwin, 1812.
Uztáriz, Gerónimo de. *Theorica y practica del comercio y la marina en diferentes discursos y calificados exemplares*. Madrid: Antonio Sanz, 1757.
Velasco, Julián de. *Efemérides de la ilustración de España*. Madrid: Imprenta de Manuel Caballero, no. 1, 1804.
Voltaire. *Dictionnaire philosophique*. Amsterdam: Varberg, 1766.
Ward, Bernardo. *Proyecto económico en que se proponen varias providencias dirigidas a promover los intereses de España*. Madrid: Joaquín Ibarra, 1779.

Secondary Sources

Acosta Saignes, Miguel. *Vida de los esclavos negros en Venezuela*. Caracas: Vadell Hermanos, 1984.
Acree, William Garrett, Jr. *Everyday Reading: Print Culture and Collective Identity in the Río de la Plata, 1780–1910*. Nashville: Vanderbilt University Press, 2011.
Adelman, Jeremy. *Sovereignty and Revolution in the Iberian Atlantic*. Princeton, NJ: Princeton University Press, 2006.
Aguilar Piñal, Francisco. "La ilustración española, entre el reformismo y el liberalismo." In *La literatura española de la ilustración: homenaje a Carlos III*, edited by Francisco Aguilar Piñal, 39–51. Madrid: Universidad Complutense de Madrid, 1989.
———. *La prensa española en el siglo XVIII: diarios, revistas y pronósticos*. Madrid: Consejo Superior de Investigaciones Científicas, 1978.
Aizpurua, José María. *Relaciones de trabajo en la sociedad colonial venezolana*. Caracas: Centro Nacional de la Historia, 2009.
Aizpurua, Ramón. "El comercio curazoleño-holandés, 1700–1756." *Anuario de Estudios Bolivarianos* 10, no. 11 (2004): 11–88.
———. "La conspiración por dentro: un análisis de las declaraciones de la conspiración de La Guaira de 1797." In Rey et al., *Gual y España*, 213–344.
———. "Coro y Curazao en el siglo XVIII." *Tierra Firme*, no. 14 (1986): 229–40.
———. *Curazao y la costa de Caracas: introducción al estudio del contrabando en la provincia de Venezuela en tiempos de la Compañía Guipuzcoana (1730–1780)*. Caracas: Academia Nacional de la Historia, 1993.
———. "En busca de la libertad: los esclavos fugados de Curazao a Coro en el siglo XVIII." In *II Encuentro para la promoción y difusión del patrimonio de los países andinos*, 69–102. Caracas: Fundación Bigott, 2002.

———. "Esclavitud, navegación y fugas de esclavos en el Curazao del siglo XVIII." Paper presented at the eleventh Encuentro-Debate América Latina Ayer y Hoy, Barcelona, November 2007.

———. "La insurrección de los negros de la serranía de Coro en 1795: una revisión necesaria." *Boletín de la Academia Nacional de la Historia*, no. 283 (1983): 705–23.

———. "Santa María de la Chapa y Macuquita: en torno a la aparición de un pueblo de esclavos fugados de Curazao en la Sierra de Coro en el siglo XVIII." *Boletín de la Academia Nacional de la Historia*, no. 345 (2004): 109–28.

Aldrin, Philippe. "Penser la rumeur: une question discutée des sciences sociales." *Genèses: Sciences Sociales et Histoire* 50 (2003): 126–41.

Allport, Gordon, and Leo Postman. *The Psychology of Rumor*. New York: Russell and Russell, 1947.

Alonso, Ana María. *Thread of Blood: Colonialism, Revolution, and Gender in Mexico's Northern Frontier*. Tucson: University of Arizona Press, 1995.

Álvarez de Castrillón, Gonzalo Añes. "España y la Revolución Francesa." In *Revolución, contrarrevolución e independencia: la Revolución Francesa, España y América*, 17–39. Madrid: Turner Publicaciones, 1989.

Álvarez Gómez, Cristina, and Guillermo Tovar de Teresa. *Censura y revolución: libros prohibidos por la Inquisición de México (1790–1819)*. Madrid: Trama Editorial; Mexico City: Consejo de la Crónica de la Ciudad de México, 2009.

Amézaga, Vicente. "Los libros de la Caracas colonial." *El Farol* 30, no. 28 (1969): 10–13.

Amodio, Emanuele. *La casa de Sucre: sociedad y cultura en Cumaná al final de la época colonial*. Caracas: Centro Nacional de la Historia, 2010.

Anderson, Benedict. *Imagined Communities: Reflections on the Origin and Spread of Nationalism*. New York: Verso, 1991.

Aragón, María Aurora. "Traducciones de obras francesas en la *Gaceta de Madrid* en la década revolucionaria (1790–1799)." PhD diss., Universidad de Oviedo, Spain, 1992.

Arcaya, Pedro Manuel. *La insurrección de los negros de la Serranía de Coro*. Caracas: Instituto Panamericano de Geografía e Historia, 1949.

———. "Insurrección de los negros de la Serranía de Coro." In *Discurso de Incorporación a la Academia Nacional de la Historia, 11 de diciembre de 1910*, 311–42. Caracas: Archivo Nacional de Historia, 1960.

Arcila Farías, Eduardo. "Comercio de cacao en el siglo XVII." *Revista Nacional de Cultura* 43 (1944).

———. *Economía colonial de Venezuela*. 2 vols. Caracas: Italgráfica, 1973.

———. *El régimen de la encomienda en Venezuela*. Caracas: Instituto de Investigaciones, Facultad de Economía, Universidad Central de Venezuela, 1996.

Arellano Moreno, Antonio. *Orígenes de la economía venezolana*. Mexico City: Ediciones Edime, 1947.

Arocha, José Ignacio. *Diccionario geográfico, estadístico e histórico del Estado Zulia*. Caracas, Editorial Avila, 1949.

Ashforth, Adam. *The Politics of Official Discourse in Twentieth-Century South Africa*. Oxford: Clarendon Press, 1990.
Atherton, Ian. "'The Itch Grown a Disease': Manuscript Transmission of News in the Seventeenth Century." In *News, Newspapers, and Society in Early Modern Britain*, edited by Joad Raymond, 39–65. London: Frank Cass, 1999.
Bailyn, Bernard, and John B. Hench, eds. *The Press and the American Revolution*. Worcester, MA: American Antiquarian Society, 1980.
Banko, Catalina. *El capital comercial en La Guaira y Caracas (1821–1848)*. Caracas: Academia Nacional de la Historia, 1990.
Barker, Hannah. *Newspapers, Politics and Public Opinion in Late Eighteenth-Century England*. Oxford: Clarendon Press, 1998.
Bassi, Ernesto. *An Aqueous Territory: Sailor Geographies and New Granada's Transimperial Greater Caribbean World*. Durham, NC: Duke University Press, 2016.
——. "Between Imperial Projects and National Dreams: Communication Networks, Geopolitical Imagination, and the Role of New Granada in the Configuration of a Greater Caribbean Space, 1780–1810." PhD diss., University of California, Irvine, 2012.
Bastin, Georges L., and Adriana L. Díaz. "Las tribulaciones de la Carmañola (y de la Marsellesa) en América Latina." *Trans* 8 (2008): 29–39.
Bastin, Georges L., Álvaro Echeverri, and Ángela Campo. "La traducción en América Latina: propia y apropiada." *Estudios, Revista de Investigaciones Literarias y Culturales* 24 (2004): 69–94.
Besson, Juan. *Historia del Zulia*. Maracaibo: Ediciones del Banco Hipotecario del Zulia, 1973.
Blackburn, Robin. *The Making of New World Slavery: From the Baroque to the Modern, 1492–1800*. London: Verso, 1998.
Block, Sharon. *Rape and Sexual Power in Early America*. Chapel Hill: University of North Carolina Press, 2006.
Borrego Plá, María del Carmen. *América Latina ante la Revolución Francesa*. Mexico City: Universidad Nacional Autónoma de México, 1993.
Borucki, Alex. "Trans-Imperial History in the Making of the Slave Trade to Venezuela, 1526–1811." *Itinerario* 36, no. 2 (2012): 29–54.
Bouza, Fernando. *Corre manuscrito: una historia cultural del siglo de oro*. Madrid: Marcial Pons, 2001.
——. *Papeles y opinión: políticas de publicación en el siglo de oro*. Madrid: Consejo Superior de Investigaciones Científicas, 2008.
Branson, Susan, and Leslie Patrick. "Etrangers dans un Pays Etrange: Saint-Dominguan Refugees of Color in Philadelphia." In Geggs, *The Impact of the Haitian Revolution*, 193–208.
Brasseaux, Carl A., and Glenn R. Conrad, eds. *The Road to Louisiana: The Saint-Domingue Refugees, 1792–1809*. Lafayette: Center for Louisiana Studies, University of Southwestern Louisiana, 1992.

Brereton, Bridget. *A History of Modern Trinidad, 1783–1962*. London: Heinemann, 1981.
Brice, Ángel Francisco. *La sublevación de Maracaibo de 1799: manifestación de su lucha por la independencia*. Caracas: Academia Nacional de la Historia, 1960.
Briggs, Ronald. *Tropes of Enlightenment in the Age of Bolívar: Simón Rodríguez and the American Essay at Revolution*. Nashville: Vanderbilt University Press, 2010.
Brito Figueroa, Federico. *Estructura económica de Venezuela colonial*. Caracas: Universidad Central de Venezuela, 1963.
———. *Historia económica y social de Venezuela*. 2nd ed. Caracas: Universidad Central de Venezuela, 1976.
———. *Las insurrecciones de los esclavos negros en la sociedad colonial venezolana*. Caracas: Cantaclaro, 1961.
———. *El problema de la tierra y esclavos en la historia de Venezuela*. Caracas: Teoría y Praxis, 1973.
Brown, Richard D. *Knowledge Is Power: The Diffusion of Information in Early America, 1700–1865*. New York: Oxford University Press, 1989.
Calargé, Carla, Raphael Dalleo, Luis Duno-Gottberg, and Clevis Headley, eds. *Haiti and the Americas*. Jackson: University Press of Mississippi, 2013.
Callahan, William J. "La propaganda, la sedición y la Revolución Francesa en la capitanía general de Venezuela, 1780–1796." *Boletín histórico* 14 (May 1967): 177–205.
Calvo Maturana, Antonio. "Is It Useful to Deceive the People? The Debate of Public Information in Spain at the End of the Ancien Régime (1780–1808)." *Journal of Modern History* 86, no. 1 (2014): 1–46.
Cardozo, Germán "Maracaibo: de la aldea colonial al puerto atlántico." *Tierra Firme*, no. 14 (1986): 149–64.
Carrera Montero, Fernando. *Las complejas relaciones de España con la Española: el Caribe hispano frente a Santo Domingo y Saint Domingue, 1789–1803*. Santo Domingo: Fundación García Arévalo, 2004.
Carrington, Selwyn H. H. *The British West Indies during the American Revolution*. Providence, RI: Foris Publications, 1988.
Caso González, José Miguel. *De ilustración y de ilustrados*. Oviedo, Spain: Instituto Feijoo de Estudios, 1988.
Castillo Gómez, Antonio. "'There Are Lots of Papers Going Around and It'd Be Better if There Weren't': Broadsides and Public Opinion in the Spanish Monarchy in the Seventeenth Century." In Rospocher, *Beyond the Public Sphere*, 227–48.
Castillo Lara, Lucas G. *Curiepe: orígenes históricos*. Caracas: Biblioteca de Autores y Temas Mirandinos, 1981.
Castro-Klarén, Sara, and John Charles Chasteen, eds. *Beyond Imagined Communities: Reading and Writing the Nation in Nineteenth-Century Latin America*. Baltimore, MD: Johns Hopkins University Press, 2003.

Cavallo, Guglielmo, and Roger Chartier, eds. *A History of Reading in the West.* Amherst: University of Massachusetts Press, 1999.
Chanchica, Aureliano, et al. *Antología documental: historia de las ideas pedagógicas en Venezuela.* Caracas: Universidad Central de Venezuela, 1997.
Chartier, Roger. *Cultural History: Between Practices and Representations.* Cambridge: Polity Press, 1988.
——. *The Cultural Origins of the French Revolution.* Translated by Lydia G. Cochrane. Durham, NC: Duke University Press, 1991.
——. *The Cultural Uses of Print in Early Modern France.* Princeton, NJ: Princeton University Press, 1987.
——, ed. *The Culture of Print: Power and the Uses of Print in Early Modern Europe.* Translated by Lydia G. Cochrane. Princeton, NJ: Princeton University Press, 1989.
——. *The Order of Books: Readers, Authors, and Libraries in Europe between the Fourteenth and Eighteenth Centuries.* Translated by Lydia G. Cochrane. Stanford, CA: Stanford University Press, 1994.
Chasteen, John Charles. "Introduction: Beyond Imagined Communities." In Castro-Klarén and Chasteen, *Beyond Imagined Communities*, ix–xv.
Childs, Matt D. *The 1812 Aponte Rebellion in Cuba and the Struggle against Atlantic Slavery.* Chapel Hill: University of North Carolina Press, 2006.
——. "'A Black French General Arrived to Conquer the Island': Images of the Haitian Revolution in Cuba's 1812 Aponte Rebellion." In Geggus, *The Impact of the Haitian Revolution*, 135–56.
Cipolla, Carlo. *Literacy and Development in the West.* London: Penguin, 1970.
Conway, Christopher. "Letras combatientes: relectura de la *Gaceta de Caracas*, 1808–1822." *Revista Iberoamericana* 214 (2006): 77–92.
Córdova Bello, Eleazar. *La independencia de Haití y su influencia en Hispanoamérica.* Caracas: Instituto Panamericano de Geografía e Historia, 1967.
Cressy, David. *Literacy and the Social Order: Reading and Writing in Tudor and Stuart England.* Cambridge: Cambridge University Press, 1981.
Cromwell, Jesse. "Covert Commerce: A Social History of Contraband Trade in Venezuela." PhD diss., University of Texas, 2012.
Crossley, Nick, and John Michael Roberts, eds. *After Habermas: New Perspectives on the Public Sphere.* Oxford: Blackwell, 2004.
Dalleo, Raphael. Introduction to Calargé et al., *Haiti and the Americas*, 3–22.
Darnton, Robert. *Censors at Work: How States Shaped Literature.* New York: W. W. Norton, 2014.
——. "An Early Information Society: News and the Media in Eighteenth-Century Paris." *American Historical Review* 105, no. 1 (2000): 1–35.
——. *The Forbidden Best-Sellers of Pre-Revolutionary France.* New York: W. W. Norton, 1995.

Darnton, Robert, and Daniel Roche, eds. *Revolution in Print: The Press in France, 1775–1800*. Berkeley: University of California Press, 1989.
Davidson, Philip. *Propaganda and the American Revolution, 1763–1783*. Chapel Hill: University of North Carolina Press, 1940.
Davies, Simon F., and Puck Fletcher, eds. *News in Early Modern Europe: Currents and Connections*. Leiden: Brill, 2014.
Davis, David Brion. "Impact of the French and the Haitian Revolutions." In Geggus, *The Impact of the Haitian Revolution*, 3–9.
Davis, Natalie Zemon. *Fiction in the Archives: Pardon Tales and Their Tellers in Sixteenth-Century France*. Stanford, CA: Stanford University Press, 1987.
Deacon, Philip. "La libertad de expresión en España en el período precedente a la Revolución Francesa." *Estudios de Historia Social* 1–2, nos. 36–37 (1986): 17–21.
Defourneaux, Marcelin. *Inquisición y censura de libros en la España del siglo XVIII*. Madrid: Taurus, 1973.
Deive, Carlos Esteban. *Las emigraciones dominicanas a Cuba (1795–1808)*. Santo Domingo: Fundación Cultural Dominicana, 1989.
De Lima, Blanca. "Libertades en la jurisdicción de Coro, 1750–1850." *Revista de Historia Mañongo* 12, no. 23 (July–December 2004): 79–96.
Diccionario de historia de Venezuela. 4 vols. Caracas: Fundación Polar, 2010.
Dierks, Konstantin. *In My Power: Letter Writing and Communications in Early America*. Philadelphia: University of Pennsylvania Press, 2009.
Dirks, Nicholas. "Annals of the Archive: Ethnographic Notes on the Sources of History." In *From the Margins: Historical Anthropology and Its Futures*, edited by Brian Keith Axel, 47–65. Durham, NC: Duke University Press, 2002.
Dooley, Brendan, ed. *The Dissemination of News and the Emergence of Contemporaneity on Early Modern Europe*. Farnham, Surrey, England: Ashgate, 2010.
Dooley, Brendan, and Sabrina Baron, eds. *The Politics of Information in Early Modern Europe*. London: Routledge, 2001.
Drescher, Seymour. "The Limits of Example." In Geggus, *The Impact of the Haitian Revolution*, 10–14.
Duarte, Carlos F. *Mobiliario y decoración interior durante el período hispánico venezolano*. Caracas: Ediciones Armitano, 1995.
———. *Los Olivares en la cultura de Venezuela*. Caracas: Fundación John Boulton, 1967.
Dubois, Laurent. *Avengers of the New World: The Story of the Haitian Revolution*. Cambridge, MA: Harvard University Press, 2004.
———. "Avenging America: The Politics of Violence in the Haitian Revolution." In Geggus and Fiering, *The World of the Haitian Revolution*, 111–24.
———. *A Colony of Citizens: Revolution and Slave Emancipation in the French Caribbean, 1787–1804*. Chapel Hill: University of North Carolina Press, 2004.
Earle, Rebecca. "Information and Disinformation in Late Colonial New Granada." *The Americas* 54, no. 2 (1997): 167–84.

Echeverri, Marcela. *Indian and Slave Royalists in the Age of Revolution: Reform, Revolution, and Royalism in the Northern Andes, 1780–1825*. Cambridge: Cambridge University Press, 2016.
Edelstein, Dan. *The Terror of Natural Right: Republicanism, the Cult of Nature, and the French Revolution*. Chicago: University of Chicago Press, 2009.
Edsel, Carlos. "Gual o la pasión revolucionaria." In López Bohórquez, *Manuel Gual y José María España*, 649–52.
Elias, Robert. *The Politics of Victimization: Victims, Victimology and Human Rights*. New York: Oxford University Press, 1986.
Elliott, John H. "Mundos parecidos, mundos distintos." In *Mezclado y sospechoso: movilidad e identidades, España y América (siglos XVI–XVIII)*, edited by Gregoire Salinero, xi–xxviii. Madrid: Casa de Velázquez, 2005.
Ewing, Tabetha. "Invasion of Lorient: Rumor, Public Opinion, and Foreign Politics in 1740s Paris." In *Into Print: Limits and Legacies of the Enlightenment; Essays in Honor of Robert Darnton*, edited by Charles Walton, 101–12. University Park: Pennsylvania State University Press, 2011.
Fernández Heres, Rafael. *La educación venezolana bajo el signo de la ilustración, 1770–1870*. Caracas: Academia Nacional de la Historia, 1995.
Ferrer, Ada. "Cuba en la sombra de Haití: noticias, sociedad y esclavitud." In González-Ripoll et al., *El rumor de Haití en Cuba*, 179–231.
―――. *Freedom's Mirror: Cuba and Haiti in the Age of Revolution*. Cambridge: Cambridge University Press, 2014.
―――. "Haiti, Free Soil, and Antislavery in the Revolutionary Atlantic." *American Historical Review* 117, no. 1 (2012): 40–66.
―――. *Insurgent Cuba: Race, Nation, and Revolution, 1868–1898*. Chapel Hill: University of North Carolina Press, 1999.
―――. "Noticias de Haití en Cuba." *Revista de Indias* 63, no. 229 (2003): 675–94.
―――. "Talk about Haiti: The Archive and the Atlantic's Haitian Revolution." In Garraway, *Tree of Liberty*, 21–40.
―――. "Temor, poder y esclavitud en Cuba en la época de la Revolución Haitiana." In Piqueras, *Las Antillas en la era de las luces*, 67–83.
Fick, Carolyn. *The Making of Haiti: The Saint Domingue Revolution from Below*. Knoxville: University of Tennessee Press, 1990.
Finch, Aisha. *Rethinking Slave Rebellion in Cuba: La Escalera and the Insurgencies of 1841–1844*. Chapel Hill: University of North Carolina Press, 2015.
Fischer, Sibylle. "Bolívar in Haiti: Republicanism in the Revolutionary Atlantic." In Calargé et al., *Haiti and the Americas*, 25–53.
―――. *Modernity Disavowed: Haiti and the Cultures of Slavery in the Age of Revolution*. Durham, NC: Duke University Press, 2004.
―――. "Unthinkable History? Some Reflections on the Haitian Revolution, Historiography, and Modernity on the Periphery." In *A Companion to African*

American Studies, vol. 2, edited by Lewis Gordon and Jane Gordon, 360–79. Malden, MA: Blackwell, 2006.
Fisher, John R. *Commercial Relations between Spain and Spanish America in the Era of Free Trade, 1778–1796*. Liverpool: Center for Latin American Studies, University of Liverpool, 1985.
Fisher, John R., Allan J. Kuethe, and Anthony McFarlane, eds. *Reform and Insurrection in Bourbon New Granada and Peru*. Baton Rouge: Louisiana State University Press, 1990.
Fuente, Alejandro de la. *Havana and the Atlantic in the Sixteenth Century*. Chapel Hill: University of North Carolina Press, 2008.
Furet, François, and Jacques Ozouf. *Reading and Writing: Literacy in France from Calvin to Jules Ferry*. Cambridge: Cambridge University Press, 1982.
Gaffield, Julia. *Haitian Connections in the Atlantic World: Recognition after Revolution*. Chapel Hill: University of North Carolina Press, 2015.
García Chuecos, Héctor. *Estudios de historia colonial venezolana*. 2 vols. Caracas: Tipografía Americana, 1938.
———. *Siglo dieciocho venezolano*. Caracas: Ediciones Edime, 1957.
García Melero, Luis Angel. *La independencia de los Estados Unidos de Norteamérica a través de la prensa española: Gaceta de Madrid y Mercurio Histórico Político, 1763–1776*. Vol. 1, *Trabajos monográficos sobre la independencia de América*. Madrid: Ministerio de Asuntos Exteriores, 1977.
Garraway, Doris L., ed. *Tree of Liberty: Cultural Legacies of the Haitian Revolution in the Atlantic World*. Charlottesville: University of Virginia Press, 2008.
Gaspar, David Barry, and David Patrick Geggus, eds. *A Turbulent Time: The French Revolution and the Greater Caribbean, 1789–1815*. Bloomington: Indiana University Press, 1997.
Gaylord, Harris. "The Early Revolutionary Career of Juan Mariano Picornell." *Hispanic American Historical Review* 22, no. 1 (1942): 57–81.
Geggus, David Patrick. "The French and Haitian Revolutions and Resistance to Slavery in the Americas: An Overview." *Revue Française d'Histoire d'Outre-Mer* 76 (1989): 107–24.
———. *The Haitian Revolution: A Documentary History*. Indianapolis: Hackett, 2014.
———. *Haitian Revolutionary Studies*. Bloomington: Indiana University Press, 2002.
———, ed. *The Impact of the Haitian Revolution in the Atlantic World*. Columbia: University of South Carolina Press, 2001.
———. "Slavery, War, and Revolution in the Greater Caribbean, 1789–1815." In Gaspar and Geggus, *A Turbulent Time*, 1–50.
Geggus, David Patrick, and Norman Fiering, eds. *The World of the Haitian Revolution*. Bloomington: Indiana University Press, 2009.
Genovese, Eugene D. *From Rebellion to Revolution: Afro-American Slave Revolts in the Making of the Modern World*. Baton Rouge: Louisiana State University Press, 1992.

Gestrich, Andreas. "The Early-Modern State and the Rise of the Public Sphere." In Rospocher, *Beyond the Public Sphere.*
———. "The Public Sphere and the Habermas Debate." *German History* 24, no. 3 (2006): 413–30.
Gil Fortoul, José. *Historia constitucional de Venezuela.* Caracas: Ministerio de Educación, 1954.
Gil Rivas, Pedro, Luis Dovale, and Luzmila Bello. *La insurrección de los negros de la sierra coriana, 10 de mayo de 1795.* Caracas: Universidad Central de Venezuela, 1996.
Gómez, Alejandro. "La caribeanidad revolucionaria de la 'Costa de Caracas': visión prospectiva (1793–1815)." In *Las independencias hispanoamericanas: un objeto de historia*, edited by Véronique Hébrard and Geneviève Verdo, 35–48. Madrid: Casa de Velázquez, 2013.
———. "¿Ciudadanos de color?" *Nuevo Mundo, Mundos Nuevos*, Bibliothèque des Auteurs du Centre (2007). At http://nuevomundo.revues.org/index9973.html.
———. *Fidelidad bajo el viento: revolución y contrarevolución en las Antillas francesas en la experiencia de algunos oficiales emigrados a tierra firme 1790–1795.* Mexico City: Siglo XXI, 2004.
———. "La ley de los franceses: una reinterpretación de las insurrecciones de inspiración jacobina en la costa de Caracas." *Akademos* 7, no. 1 (2006): 97–132.
———. "The 'Pardo Question': Political Struggles on Free Coloreds Right to Citizenship during the Revolution of Caracas, 1797–1813." *Nuevo Mundo, Mundos Nuevos*, Matériaux de Séminaires (2008). At http://nuevomundo.revues.org/index34503.html.
———. "La revolución de Caracas *desde abajo*." *Nuevo Mundo, Mundos Nuevos*, Débats (2008). At http://nuevomundo.revues.org/index32982.html.
———. "El síndrome de Saint-Domingue: percepciones y sensibilidades de la Revolución Haitiana en el Gran Caribe (1791–1814)." *Caravelle* 86 (2006): 125–56.
———. "Le syndrome de Saint-Domingue: perceptions et représentations de la révolution haïtienne dans le monde atlantique, 1790–1886." PhD diss., École de Hautes Études en Sciences Sociales, Paris, 2010.
González, Luis Enrique. *La Guayra: conquista y colonia.* Caracas: Grafarte, 1982.
González González, Alfonso F. *El oriente venezolano a mediados del siglo XVIII: a través de la visita del gobernador Diguja.* Caracas: Academia Nacional de la Historia, 1977.
González-Ripoll, María Dolores, Consuelo Naranjo, Ada Ferrer, Gloria García, and Josef Opatrný, eds. *El rumor de Haití en Cuba: temor, raza y rebeldía, 1789–1844.* Madrid: Consejo Superior de Investigaciones Científicas, 2004.
Goody, Jack. *The Interface between the Written and the Oral.* Cambridge: Cambridge University Press, 1993.

———. *The Logic of Writing and the Organization of Society*. Cambridge: Cambridge University Press, 1986.

Grases, Pedro. *La biblioteca de Francisco de Miranda*. Caracas: Cromotip, 1966.

———. *La conspiración de Gual y España y el ideario de la independencia*. Caracas: Academia Nacional de la Historia, 1997.

———. *Derechos del hombre y del ciudadano*. Caracas: Academia Nacional de la Historia, 1959.

———. *Historia de la imprenta en Venezuela hasta el fin de la primera república, 1812*. Caracas: Ediciones de la Presidencia de la República, 1967.

———. *La imprenta en Venezuela*. Caracas: Seix Barral, 1981.

———. "Juan Bautista Picornell." In López Bohórquez, *Manuel Gual y José María España*.

———. *Libros y libertad*. Caracas: Ediciones de la Presidencia de la República, 1974.

———. *Traducciones de interés politico-cultural en la epoca de la independencia de Venezuela*. Caracas: Ediciones Guadarrama, 1961.

Guerra, François-Xavier. "Forms of Communication, Political Spaces, and Cultural Identities in the Creation of Spanish American Nations." In Castro-Klarén and Chasteen, *Beyond Imagined Communities*, 3–32.

———. *Modernidad e independencias: ensayos sobre las revoluciones hispánicas*. Mexico City: Fondo de Cultura Económica, 2001.

Guha, Ranajit. *Elementary Aspects of Peasant Insurgency in Colonial India*. Durham, NC: Duke University Press, 1999.

Guibovich, Pedro. *Censura, libros e inquisición en el Perú colonial, 1570–1754*. Madrid: Consejo Superior de Investigaciones Científicas, 2003.

———. *Lecturas prohibidas: la Censura Inquisitorial en el Perú tardío colonial*. Lima: Fondo Editorial de la Pontificia Universidad Católica del Perú, 2013.

Gutiérrez, Ramón. "Sex and Family: Social Change in Colonial New Mexico, 1690–1846." PhD diss., University of Wisconsin, 1980.

Habermas, Jürgen. *The Structural Transformation of the Public Sphere: An Inquiry into a Category of Bourgeois Society*. Translated by Thomas Burger. Cambridge, MA: MIT Press, 2000.

Hall, N. A. T. "Maritime Maroons: Grand Marronage from the Danish West Indies." In *Caribbean Slave Society and Economy*, edited by Hilary Beckles and Verene Shepherd, 387–400. New York: New Press, 1993.

Halperín Donghi, Tulio. *Politics, Economics and Society in Argentina in the Revolutionary Period*. Cambridge: Cambridge University Press, 1975.

Helg, Aline. "Bolívar and the Spectre of *Pardocracia*: José Padilla in Post-Independence Cartagena." *Journal of Latin American Studies* 35, no. 3 (August 2003): 447–71.

———. "A Fragmented Majority: Free 'of All Colors,' Indians, and Slaves in Caribbean Colombia during the Haitian Revolution." In Geggus, *The Impact of the Haitian Revolution*, 157–75.

———. *Liberty and Equality in Caribbean Colombia, 1770–1835*. Chapel Hill: University of North Carolina Press, 2004.
Hernández, Adriana. "Doctrina y gobierno en la conspiración de Gual y España: una mirada desde el expediente judicial." In Rey et al., *Gual y España*, 345–428.
Herr, Richard. *España y la revolución del siglo XVIII*. Madrid: Aguilar, 1964.
Herzog, Don. *Poisoning the Minds of the Lower Orders*. Princeton, NJ: Princeton University Press, 1998.
Hunt, John M. "Rumour, Newsletters, and the Pope's Death in Early Modern Rome." In Davies and Fletcher, *News in Early Modern Europe*, 143–54.
Hussey, Roland Dennis. *The Caracas Company, 1728–1784: A Study in the History of Spanish Monopolistic Trade*. Cambridge, MA: Harvard University Press, 1934.
Irazábal, Carlos. *Venezuela esclava y feudal*. Caracas: Pensamiento Vivo Editores, 1964.
Izard, Miguel. *El miedo a la revolución: la lucha por la libertad en Venezuela (1777–1830)*. Madrid: Tecnos, 1979.
———. *Tierra firme: historia de Venezuela y Colombia*. Madrid: Alianza, 1986.
James, C. L. R. *The Black Jacobins: Toussaint l'Ouverture and the San Domingo Revolution*. New York: Vintage Books, 1989.
Jenson, Deborah. "Toussaint Louverture, Spin Doctor? Launching the Haitian Revolution in the French Media." In Garraway, *Tree of Liberty*, 41–62.
Johnson, Lyman L. *Workshop of Revolution: Plebeian Buenos Aires and the Atlantic World, 1776–1810*. Durham, NC: Duke University Press, 2012.
Johnson, Michael P. "Denmark Vesey and His Co-Conspirators." *William and Mary Quarterly*, 3rd ser., 58, no. 4 (2001): 915–76.
Jordán, Josefina. "Acercamiento a la rebelión encabezada por José Leonardo Chirinos en 1795." In *Documentos de la insurrección de José Leonardo Chirinos*, 1:16–29.
Jordan, Winthrop D. *Tumult and Silence at Second Creek: An Inquiry into a Civil War Slave Conspiracy*. Baton Rouge: Louisiana State University Press, 1996.
Jouve Martín, José Ramón. *Esclavos de la ciudad letrada: esclavitud, escritura y colonialismo en Lima (1650–1700)*. Lima: Instituto de Estudios Peruanos, 2005.
Kantorowicz, Ernest. *The King's Two Bodies: A Study in Mediaeval Political Theology*. Princeton, NJ: Princeton University Press, 1957.
Kapferer, Jean-Noël. *Rumors: Uses, Interpretation, and Images*. New Brunswick, NJ: Transaction Publishers, 2013.
Klooster, Wim. "Le décret d'émancipation imaginaire: monarchisme et esclavage en Amérique du Nord et dans la Caraïbe au temps des révolutions." *Annales Historiques de la Révolution Française* 363 (January–March 2011): 109–29.
———. *Illicit Riches: Dutch Trade in the Caribbean, 1648–1795*. Leiden: Koninklijk Instituut voor Taal-, Land- en Volkenkunde, 1998.
———. *Revolution in the Atlantic World: A Comparative History*. New York: New York University Press, 2009.

Knight, Franklin W., and Peggy Liss. *Atlantic Port Cities: Economy, Culture, and Society in the Atlantic World, 1650–1850*. Knoxville: University of Tennessee Press, 1991.
Landaeta Rosales, Manuel. "Don Manuel Gual y José María España." In López Bohórquez, *Manuel Gual y José María España*, 168–72.
———. "La familia españa en Venezuela." In López Bohórquez, *Manuel Gual y José María España*, 173–82.
Landers, Jane G. *Atlantic Creoles in the Age of Revolutions*. Cambridge, MA: Harvard University Press, 2010.
———. "*Cimarrón* and Citizen: African Ethnicity, Corporate Identity, and the Evolution of Free Black Towns in the Spanish Circum-Caribbean." In Landers and Robinson, *Slaves, Subjects, and Subversives*, 111–46.
Landers, Jane G., and Barry M. Robinson, eds. *Slaves, Subjects, and Subversives: Blacks in Colonial Latin America*. Albuquerque: University of New Mexico Press, 2006.
Langley, Lester D. *The Americas in the Age of Revolution, 1750–1850*. New Haven, CT: Yale University Press, 1998.
Langue, Frédérique. "La pardocratie ou l'itineraire d'une 'classe dangereuse' dans le Vénezuela des XVIIIe et XIXe siècles." *Caravelle* 67 (1997): 57–72.
Laurent-Perrault, Evelyne. "Black Honor: Intellectual Marronage in Venezuela, 1760–1809." PhD diss., New York University, 2015.
Laviña, Javier. "Indios y negros sublevados de Coro." In *Poder local, poder global en América Latina*, edited by Gabriela Dalla Corte, Pilar García Jordán, Javier Laviña, Lola G. Luna, Ricardo Piqueras, José Luis Ruiz-Peinado Alonso, and Meritxell Tous, 97–112. Barcelona: Universitat de Barcelona, 2008.
———. "Revolución Francesa y control social." *Tierra Firme* 7, no. 27 (1989): 272–85.
———. "Venezuela: entre la ilustración y la revolución." *El Taller de la Historia* 6, no. 6 (2014): 311–42.
Leal, Ildefonso. "La aristocracia criolla y el código negrero de 1789." *Revista de Historia* 26, no. 1 (1961): 61–81.
———. "Bibliotecas de los conspiradores." In López Bohórquez, *Manuel Gual y José María España*, 30–50.
———. *La cultura venezolana en el siglo XVIII*. Caracas: Academia Nacional de la Historia, 1971.
———. *Documentos para la historia de la educación en Venezuela*. Caracas: Academia Nacional de la Historia, 1968.
———. "Francisco Javier Pirela y su intento de sublevar a Maracaibo en 1799." *Revista de Historia* 4, no. 21 (1964): 41–69.
———. *Libros y bibliotecas en Venezuela colonial (1633–1767)*. 2 vols. Caracas: Academia Nacional de la Historia, 1978.
Leal Curiel, Carole. *Discurso de la fidelidad: construcción social del espacio como símbolo del poder regio*. Caracas: Academia Nacional de la Historia, 1990.

———. "La querella por una alfombra, o la cuestión del buen orden de la república: Valencia, Venezuela, finales del siglo XVIII." *Revista Historia y Memoria*, no. 9 (July–December, 2014): 163–87.

Lefevbre, George. *The Great Fear of 1789: Rural Panic in Revolutionary France*. New York: Schocken Books, 1989.

Level de Goda, Andrés. "La revolución de Gual y España en La Guaira." In López Bohórquez, *Manuel Gual y José María España*.

Liss, Peggy. *Atlantic Empires: The Network of Trade and Revolution, 1713–1826*. Baltimore, MD: Johns Hopkins University Press, 1983.

Lombardi, John. *Decadencia y abolición de la esclavitud en Venezuela (1820–1854)*. Caracas: Universidad Central de Venezuela, 2004.

———. *The Decline and Abolition of Negro Slavery in Venezuela, 1820–1854*. Westport, CT: Greenwood Press, 1971.

———. *People and Places in Colonial Venezuela*. Bloomington: Indiana University Press, 1976.

López, Casto Fulgencio. *Juan Bautista Picornell y la conspiración de Gual y España*. Madrid: Ediciones Nueva Cádiz, 1955.

López Bohórquez, Alí Enrique, ed. *Manuel Gual y José María España: valoración múltiple de la conspiración de La Guaira de 1797*. Caracas: Comisión Presidencial del Bicentenario de Gual y España, 1997.

Love, Harold. *Scribal Publication in Seventeenth-Century England*. Oxford: Clarendon Press, 1993.

Lovena Reyes, Elina. "Coro y su espacio geohistórico en la época colonial." *Tierra Firme*, no. 14 (1986): 221–27.

Lucena Salmoral, Manuel. "El derecho de coartación del esclavo en la América española." *Revista de Indias* 59, no. 216 (1999): 357–74.

———. "La sociedad de la provincia de Caracas a comienzos del siglo XIX." *Anuario de Estudios Americanos* 37 (1980): 157–89.

Lynch, John. *The Spanish American Revolutions, 1808–1826*. New York: W. W. Norton, 1973.

Magallanes, Manuel. *Luchas e insurrecciones en la Venezuela colonial*. Caracas: Academia Nacional de la Historia, 1982.

Manzanilla Celis, Ángel Francisco. *La sublevación de Francisco Javier Pirela: Maracaibo, 1799–1800; una nueva perspectiva histórica e historiográfica*. Caracas: Academia Nacional de la Historia, 2011.

Martínez, José Luis. *El libro en Hispanoamérica: origen y desarrollo*. Madrid: Fundación Germán Díaz Sánchez Ruipérez, 1987.

Martínez, María Elena. "The Black Blood of New Spain: Limpieza de Sangre, Racial Violence, and Gendered Power in Early Colonial Mexico." *William and Mary Quarterly*, 3rd ser., 61, no. 3 (2004): 479–520.

Martínez Shaw, Carlos. "El despotismo ilustrado en España y en las Indias." In *El imperio sublevado: monarquía y naciones en España e Hispanoamérica*, edited by

Víctor Mínguez and Manuel Chust, 123–78. Madrid: Consejo Superior de Investigaciones Científicas, 2004.

Mason, Laura. *Singing the French Revolution: Popular Culture and Politics, 1787–1799.* Ithaca, NY: Cornell University Press, 1996.

———. "Song: Mixing Media." In Darnton and Roche, *Revolution in Print.*

Mayer, Arno J. *The Furies: Violence and Terror in the French and Russian Revolutions.* Princeton, NJ: Princeton University Press, 2000.

McCaa, Robert. "Calidad, Clase, and Marriage in Colonial Mexico: The Case of Parral, 1788–1790." *Hispanic American Historical Review* 64, no. 3 (1984): 477–501.

McKenzie, Donald F. *Bibliography and the Sociology of Texts.* Cambridge: Cambridge University Press, 1999.

McKinley, Peter M. *Caracas antes de la independencia.* Caracas: Monteávila, 1993.

McKitterick, Rosamond. *The Uses of Literacy in Early Mediaeval Europe.* Cambridge: Cambridge University Press, 1995.

Meadows, R. Darrell. "Engineering Exile: Social Networks and the French Atlantic Community, 1789–1809." *French Historical Studies* 23, no. 1 (2000): 67–102.

Millares Carlo, Agustín. *La imprenta y el periodismo en Venezuela (desde sus orígenes hasta mediados del siglo XIX).* Caracas: Monteávila, 1969.

———. *Introducción a la historia del libro y de las bibliotecas.* Mexico City: Fondo de Cultura Económica, 1986.

Miller, Gary. "Status and Royalty of Regular Army Officers in Late Colonial Venezuela." *Hispanic American Historical Review* 66, no. 4 (1986): 667–96.

Molas Ribalta, Pere. "Política, economía y derecho." In *Historia literaria de España en el siglo XVIII*, edited by Francisco Aguilar Piñal, 915–63. Madrid: Consejo Superior de Investigaciones Científicas, 1996.

Nalle, Sara T. "Literacy and Culture in Early Modern Castile." *Past and Present* 125 (1989): 65–96.

Naranjo, Consuelo. "La amenaza haitiana, un miedo interesado: poder y fomento de la población blanca en Cuba." In González-Ripoll et al., *El rumor de Haití en Cuba*, 83–178.

Navarro, Nicolás Eugenio. "Un episodio divertido de la primera educación de Bolívar." *Boletín de la Academia Nacional de la Historia*, no. 49 (1955): 3–15.

Nesbitt, Nick. *Universal Emancipation: The Haitian Revolution and the Radical Enlightenment.* Charlottesville: University of Virginia Press, 2008.

Nesvig, Martin A. *Ideology and Inquisition: The World of the Censors in Early Mexico.* New Haven, CT: Yale University Press, 2009.

Newman, Paul. *A History of Terror: Fear and Dread through the Ages.* Stroud, Gloucestershire, England: Sutton Publishing, 2000.

Newson, Linda. "Inmigrantes extranjeros en América española: el experimento colonizador de la isla de Trinidad." *Revista de Historia de América* 87 (1979): 79–103.

Noel, Jesse A. *Trinidad, provincia de Venezuela: historia de la administración española de Trinidad.* Caracas: Academia Nacional de la Historia, 1972.
Oettinger, Rebecca Wagner. *Music as Propaganda in the German Reformation.* Farnham, Surrey, England: Ashgate, 2001.
O'Phelan, Scarlett. "La construcción del miedo a la plebe en el siglo XVIII a través de las rebeliones sociales." In Rosas Lauro, *El miedo en el Perú*, 123–38.
———. *La gran rebelión en los Andes: de Túpac Amaru a Túpac Catari.* Cuzco: Centro de Estudios Rurales Andinos "Bartolomé de las Casas," 1995.
———. *Un siglo de rebeliones anticoloniales: Perú y Bolivia, 1700–1783.* Cuzco: Centro de Estudios Rurales Andinos "Bartolomé de Las Casas," 1988.
Osterhammel, Jürgen. *The Transformation of the World: A Global History of the Nineteenth Century.* Princeton, NJ: Princeton University Press, 2014.
Pagden, Anthony. *Spanish Imperialism and the Political Imagination: Studies in European and Spanish-American Social and Political Theory, 1513–1830.* New Haven, CT: Yale University Press, 1990.
Palmié, Stephan. *Wizards and Scientists: Explorations in Afro-Cuban Modernity and Tradition.* Durham, NC: Duke University Press, 2002.
Palti, Elías José. "Recent Studies on the Emergence of a Public Sphere in Latin America." *Latin America Research Review* 36, no. 2 (2001): 255–66.
Panera Rico, Carmen. "Los libros de la ilustración: iglesia, ideología, y mentalidad en Venezuela (1759–1789)." PhD diss., Universidad de Sevilla, 1998.
Paquette, Robert L., and Douglas R. Egerton. "Of Facts and Fables: New Light on the Denmark Vesey Affair." *South Carolina Historical Magazine* 105, no. 1 (2004): 8–48.
Paquette, Robert L., and Stanley L. Engerman, eds. *The Lesser Antilles in the Age of European Expansion.* Gainesville: University Press of Florida, 1996.
Parra, Caracciolo. *Filosofía universitaria venezolana (1780–1821).* Caracas: Parra Hermanos, 1934.
Pellicer, Luis F. *La vivencia del honor en la provincia de Venezuela, 1774–1809: estudios de casos.* Caracas: Fundación Polar, 1996.
Peralta Ruiz, Víctor. "Prensa y redes de comunicación en el virreinato del Perú, 1790–1821." *Tiempos de América* 12 (2005): 1–20.
Pérez, Joseph. *Los movimientos precursores de la emancipación en Hispanoamérica.* Madrid: Alhambra, 1977.
Pérez Aparicio, Josefina. *Perdida de la isla de Trinidad.* Seville: Escuela de Estudios Hispano-Americanos, 1966.
Pérez Díaz, Víctor. "State and Public Sphere in Spain during the Ancient Regime." *Daedalus* (1998): 251–79.
Pérez Vila, Manuel. "Bibliotecas coloniales en Venezuela." *Revista de Historia* 3, no. 12 (1962): 15–25.
———. *La formación intelectual del Libertador.* Caracas: Ediciones de la Presidencia de la República, 1979.

———. "El gobierno deliberativo: hacendados, comerciantes y artesanos frente a la crisis, 1830–1848." In *Política y economía en Venezuela, 1810–1976*, edited by Alfredo Boulton. Caracas: Fundación John Boulton, 1976.

———. *Los libros en la colonia y en la independencia*. Caracas: Oficina Central de Información, 1970.

Pettegree, Andrew. *The Invention of News: How the World Came to Know about Itself*. New Haven, CT: Yale University Press, 2014.

Piccato, Pablo. "Public Sphere in Latin America: A Map of the Historiography." *Social History* 32, no. 2 (2010): 165–92.

Pierce, Jennifer. "Discourses of the Dispossessed: Saint-Domingue Colonists on Race, Revolution, and Empire, 1789–1825." PhD diss., State University of New York at Binghamton, 2005.

Piñero, Eugenio. "The Cacao Economy of the Eighteenth-Century Province of Caracas and the Spanish Cacao Market." *Hispanic American Historical Review* 68, no. 1 (1988): 75–100.

Pino Iturrieta, Elías. *La mentalidad venezolana de la emancipación (1810–1812)*. Caracas: Instituto de Estudios Hispanoamericanos, Facultad de Humanidades, Universidad Central de Venezuela, 1971.

Piqueras, José, ed. *Las Antillas en la era de las luces y la revolución*. Madrid: Siglo XXI, 2005.

Plaza, Elena. "El miedo a la ilustración en la provincia de Caracas, 1790–1810." *Politeia* 14 (1990): 311–48.

———. "Vicisitudes de un escaparate de cedro con libros prohibidos." *Politeia* 13 (1989): 331–60.

Pocock, J. G. A. "Virtue and Commerce in the Eighteenth Century." *Journal of Interdisciplinary History* 3 (1972): 119–34.

Polasky, Janet. *Revolutions without Borders: The Call to Liberty in the Atlantic World*. New Haven, CT: Yale University Press, 2015.

Pompeian, Edward P. "Spirited Enterprises: Venezuela, the United States, and the Independence of Spanish America, 1789–1823." PhD diss., College of William and Mary, 2014.

Popkin, Jeremy. *Facing Racial Revolution: Eyewitness Accounts of the Haitian Insurrection*. Chicago: University of Chicago Press, 2007.

———. *Revolutionary News: The Press in France, 1789–1799*. Durham, NC: Duke University Press, 1990.

Price, Jacob. "Economic Function and the Growth of American Port Towns in the Eighteenth Century." *Perspectives in American History* 8 (1974): 123–86.

Quintero, Inés. *La criolla principal: María Antonia Bolívar, la hermana del libertador*. Caracas: Santillana, 2008.

———. "Los nobles de Caracas y la independencia de Venezuela." *Anuario de Estudios Americanos* 64, no. 7 (2007): 209–32.

———. *El último márques: Francisco Rodríguez del Toro, 1761-1851*. Caracas: Fundación Bigott, 2005.
Racine, Karen. *Francisco de Miranda: A Transatlantic Life in the Age of Revolution*. Wilmington, DE: Scholarly Resources, 2003.
Ramírez-Ovalles, Rodolfo. *La opinión sea consagrada: articulación e instauración del aparato de opinión pública republicana, 1810-1821*. Caracas: Fundación Bancaribe y Academia Nacional de la Historia, 2009.
Rappaport, Joanne. *The Disappearing Mestizo: Configuring Difference in the Colonial New Kingdom of Granada*. Durham, NC: Duke University Press, 2014.
Raymond, Joad. *Pamphlets and Pamphleteering in Early Modern Britain*. Cambridge: Cambridge University Press, 2003.
Reinders, Michel. *Printed Pandemonium: Popular Print and Politics in the Netherlands, 1650-72*. Leiden: Brill, 2013.
Reis, João José, and Flávio dos Santos Gomes. "Repercussions of the Haitian Revolution in Brazil, 1791-1850," In Geggus and Fiering, *The World of the Haitian Revolution*, 284-313.
Rey, Juan Carlos, Rogelio Pérez Perdomo, Ramón Aizpurua Aguirre, and Adriana Hernández, eds. *Gual y España: la independencia frustrada*. Caracas: Fundación Polar, 2007.
Reyes Gómez, Fermín de los. *El libro en España y América: legislación y censura (siglos XV-XVIII)*. 2 vols. Madrid: Arco Libros, 2000.
Río Barredo, María José del. "Censura inquisitorial y teatro de 1707 a 1819." *Hispania Sacra* 37 (1986): 279-330.
Rivera, Enrique. "Social Control on the Eve of a Slave Rebellion: The Case of Coro, 1795." Master's thesis, University of Maryland, 2013.
Rodríguez, Jaime. *The Independence of Spanish America*. Cambridge: Cambridge University Press, 1998.
Rodríguez, Manuel Alfredo. "Los pardos libres en la colonia y la independencia." In *Discursos de incorporación 1992-1998*, vol. 8. Caracas: Academia Nacional de la Historia, 2002.
Rodulfo Cortés, Santos. *El régimen de las gracias al sacar en Venezuela durante el período Hispánico*. 2 vols. Caracas: Academia Nacional de la Historia, 1978.
Rosas Lauro, Claudia. "La imagen de la Revolución Francesa en el virreinato peruano a fines del siglo XVIII." Undergraduate diss., Pontificia Universidad Católica del Perú, Lima, 1997.
———. "El miedo a la revolución: rumores y temores desatados por la Revolución Francesa en el Perú, 1790-1800." In Rosas Lauro, *El miedo en el Perú*, 139-83.
———, ed. *El miedo en el Perú, siglo XVI al XX*. Lima: Fondo Editorial de la Pontificia Universidad Católica del Perú, 2005.
Roseberry, William. "Hegemony and the Language of Contention." In *Everyday Forms of State Formation: Revolution and the Negotiation of Rule in Modern Mexico*,

edited by Gilbert M. Joseph and Daniel Nugent, 355–66. Durham, NC: Duke University Press, 1994.

Rosenblat, Ángel. "El mantuano y el mantuanismo en la historia social de Venezuela." *Nueva Revista de Filología Hispánica* 24, no. 1 (1975): 64–88.

Rosnow, Ralph L., and Gary Alan Fine. *Rumor and Gossip: The Social Psychology of Hearsay.* New York: Elsevier, 1976.

Rospocher, Massimo, ed. *Beyond the Public Sphere: Opinions, Publics, Spaces in Early Modern Europe.* Bologna: Società Editrice il Mulino; Berlin: Duncker und Humblot, 2012.

Rueda Ramírez, Pedro. "Las cartillas para aprender a leer: la circulación de un texto escolar en Latinoamérica." *Cultura Escrita y Sociedad* 11 (December 2010): 15–42.

Ruette-Orihuela, Krisna, and Cristina Soriano. "Remembering the Slave Rebellion of Coro: Historical Memory and Politics in Venezuela." *Ethnohistory* 63, no. 2 (April 2016): 327–50.

Ruiz, Gustavo A. *Simón Rodríguez: maestro de escuela de primeras letras.* Caracas: Academia Nacional de la Historia, 1990.

Ruiz, Nydia. *Gobernantes y gobernados: los catecismos políticos en España e Hispanoamérica (siglos XVIII-XIX).* Caracas: Universidad Central de Venezuela, 1997.

Rupert, Linda M. *Creolization and Contraband: Curaçao in the Early Modern Atlantic World.* Athens: University of Georgia Press, 2012.

———. "Marronage, Manumission and Maritime Trade in the Early Modern Caribbean." *Slavery and Abolition* 30, no. 3 (2009): 361–82.

Rydjord, John. "The French Revolution in Mexico." *Hispanic American Historical Review* 9, no. 1 (1929): 60–98.

Salcedo Bastardo, José Luis. *Historia fundamental de Venezuela.* Caracas: Fundación Gran Mariscal de Ayacucho, 1977.

———. "Picornell, Gual y España." In López Bohórquez, *Manuel Gual y José María España.*

Sanday, Peggy. *A Woman Scorned: Acquaintance Rape on Trial.* New York: Doubleday, 1996.

Sanoja Hernández, Jesús. "La obra revolucionaria de Juan Bautista Picornell y su influencia sobre los rebeldes venezolanos." In López Bohórquez, *Manuel Gual y José María España.*

Sanz Tapia, Ángel. *Los militares emigrados y los prisioneros franceses en Venezuela durante la guerra contra la revolución: un aspecto fundamental de la época de la pre-emancipación.* Caracas: Instituto Panamericano de Geografía e Historia, 1977.

———. "Refugiados de la Revolución Francesa en Venezuela (1793–1795)." *Revista de Indias* 47, no. 181 (1987): 833–67.

Sartorius, David. *Ever Faithful: Race, Loyalty, and the Ends of Empire in Spanish Cuba.* Durham, NC: Duke University Press, 2013.

Sawyer, Jeffrey K. *Printed Poison: Pamphlet Propaganda, Faction Politics, and the Public Sphere in Early Seventeenth-Century France*. Berkeley: University of California Press, 1990.
Schaeffer, Wendell G. "The Delayed Cession of Spanish Santo Domingo to France, 1795–1801." *Hispanic American Historical Review* 29, no. 1 (1949): 46–48.
Scott, James C. *Domination and the Arts of Resistance: Hidden Transcripts*. New Haven, CT: Yale University Press, 1990.
Scott, Julius, III. "The Common Wind: Currents of Afro-American Communication in the Era of the Haitian Revolution." PhD diss., Duke University, 1986.
Sellers-García, Sylvia. *Distance and Documents at the Spanish Empire's Periphery*. Stanford, CA: Stanford University Press, 2013.
Serulnikov, Sergio. *Subverting the Colonial Authority: Challenges to Spanish Rule in Eighteenth-Century Southern Andes*. Durham, NC: Duke University Press, 2003.
Sevilla Soler, Rosario. "Las repercusiones de la Revolución Francesa en el Caribe español: los casos de Santo Domingo y Trinidad." *Cuadernos Americanos Nueva Época* 5, no. 17 (1989): 117–33.
Sharples, Jason T. "Discovering Slave Conspiracies: New Fears of Rebellion and Old Paradigms of Plotting in Seventeenth-Century Barbados." *American Historical Review* 120, no. 3 (2015): 811–43.
Shibutani, Tomutso. *Improvised News: A Sociological Study of Rumors*. Indianapolis: Bobbs-Merrill, 1966.
Sklodowska, Elzbieta. *Espectros y espejismos: Haití en el imaginario cubano*. Madrid: Iberoamericana; Frankfurt: Vervuert, 2009.
Soboul, Albert. *The Sans-Culottes: The Popular Movement and Revolutionary Government, 1793–1794*. Translated by Rémy Inglis Hall. Princeton, NJ: Princeton University Press, 1980.
Soriano, Cristina. "Bibliotecas, lectores y saber en Caracas durante la segunda mitad del siglo XVIII." In *El libro en circulación en la América Colonial: producción, circuitos de distribución y conformación de bibliotecas en los siglos XVI-XVIII*, edited by Idalia García and Pedro Rueda Ramírez, 239–58. Mexico City: Ediciones Quivira, 2014.
———. "Buscar libros en una ciudad sin imprentas: la circulación de los libros en la Caracas de finales del siglo XVIII." In *El libro en circulación en el mundo moderno en España y Latinoamérica*, edited by Pedro Rueda Ramírez, 108–27. Madrid: Calambur, 2012.
———. "El correr de los libros en la cotidianidad caraqueña: Mercado y redes de circulación de libros en Caracas durante el siglo XVIII." In *Mezclado y sospechoso: movilidad e identidades, España y América (siglos XVI-XVIII)*, edited by Gregoire Salinero, 229–49. Madrid: Casa de Velázquez, 2005.
———. "Libros y lectores en Caracas durante el siglo XVIII." Undergraduate diss., Universidad Central de Venezuela, Caracas, 1999.

Soriano de García-Pelayo, Graciela. *Venezuela 1810–1830: aspectos desatendidos de dos décadas*. Caracas: Lagoven, 1988.
Sosa Cárdenas, Diana. *Los pardos: Caracas en las postrimerías de la colonia*. Caracas: Universidad Católica Andrés Bello, 2010.
Soto, Andreína. "Purchasing the Status: Religious Confraternities in Late-Colonial Venezuela." *Concept* 39 (April 2016): 72–97.
Stefano, Luciana de. *La sociedad estamental de la baja Edad Media española a la luz de la literatura de la época*. Caracas: Universidad Central de Venezuela, 1966.
Stewart, Pamela J., and Andrew Strathern. *Witchcraft, Sorcery, Rumors, and Gossip*. Cambridge: Cambridge University Press, 2004.
Stoler, Ann Laura. *Along the Archival Grain: Epistemic Anxieties and Colonial Common Sense*. Princeton, NJ: Princeton University Press, 2009.
———. "Developing Historical Negatives: Race and the (Modernist) Visions of a Colonial State." In *From the Margins: Historical Anthropology and Its Futures*, edited by Brian Keith Axel, 156–88. Durham, NC: Duke University Press, 2002.
Straka, Tomás. *La voz de los vencidos: ideas del partido realista de Caracas, 1810–1821*. Caracas: Universidad Católica Andrés Bello, 2007.
Suria, Jaime. *Iglesia y estado*. Caracas: Ediciones del Cuatricentenario de Caracas, Editorial Sucre, 1967.
Tavárez, David. "Zapotec Time, Alphabetic Writing, and the Public Sphere." *Ethnohistory* 57, no. 1 (2010): 73–85.
Taylor, William B. "Between Global Process and Local Knowledge: An Inquiry into Early Latin American Social History, 1500–1900." In *Reliving the Past: The Worlds of Social History*, edited by Oliver Zunz, 115–90. Chapel Hill: University of North Carolina Press, 1985.
Thibaud, Clément. "'Coupé têtes, brûlé cazes': peurs et désirs d'Haïti dans l'Amérique de Bolivar." *Annales: Histoire, Sciences Sociales* 58, no. 2 (March–April 2003): 305–31.
———. *Un nouveau monde républicain: les premiers états sans roi dans l'atlantique hispanique*. Mordelles, France: Les Perséides, forthcoming.
Thomson, Sinclair. "La descolonización de la memoria: el cuerpo reconstituido del Tupaj Katari." In *Corporalidades*, edited by Maya Aguiluz Ibargüen and Pablo Lazo Briones. Mexico City: Universidad Nacional Autónoma de México, 2010.
———. "Moments of Redemption: Decolonization as Reconstitution of the Body of Katari." *Caribbean Rasanblaj* 12, no. 1 (2015). At http://hemisphericinstitute.org/hemi/en/emisferica-121-caribbean-rasanblaj/thomson.
———. *We Alone Will Rule: Native Andean Politics in the Age of Insurgency*. Madison: University of Wisconsin Press, 2002.
Torpey, John C., ed. *Politics and the Past: On Repairing Historical Injustices*. Lanham, MD: Rowman and Littlefield, 2003.

Torre Revello, José. "Las cartillas para enseñar a leer a los niños en América Española." *Thesaurus* 15, no. 1 (1960): 214-34.

———. *El libro: la imprenta y el periodismo en América durante la dominación española.* Buenos Aires: Facultad de Filosofía y Letras, 1940.

———. "Origen y aplicación del código negrero en América Española (1788-1794)." *Boletín del Instituto de Investigaciones históricas* 15, no. 53 (1932): 42-50.

Troconis de Veracochea, Ermila. *Documentos para el estudio de los esclavos negros de Venezuela.* Caracas: Academia Nacional de la Historia, 1969.

Trouillot, Michel-Rolph. *Silencing the Past: Power and the Production of History.* Boston: Beacon Press, 1997.

Twinam, Ann. *Public Lives, Private Secrets: Gender, Honor, Sexuality, and Illegitimacy in Colonial Spanish America.* Stanford, CA: Stanford University Press, 1999.

———. *Purchasing Whiteness: Pardos, Mulattos, and the Quest for Social Mobility in the Spanish Indies.* Stanford, CA: Stanford University Press, 2015.

Urdaneta, Arlene. "San José de Cucúta en el comercio marabino del siglo XIX." *Tierra Firme*, no. 14 (1986): 177-92.

Uribe-Urán, Víctor. "The Birth of a Public Sphere in Latin America during the Age of Revolution." *Comparative Studies in Society and History* 42, no. 2 (2002): 425-57.

Urzainqui, Inmaculada. "Un nuevo instrumento cultural: la prensa periódica." In *La república de las letras en la España del siglo XVIII*, edited by Joaquín Álvarez Barrientos, François López, and Inmaculada Urzainqui, 125-214. Madrid: Consejo Superior de Investigaciones Científicas, 1995.

Vallenilla Lanz, Laureano. *Cesarismo democrático: estudios sobre las bases sociológicas de la constitutición efectiva de Venezuela.* Caracas: Tipografía Garrido, 1961.

Van Young, Eric. *The Other Rebellion: Popular Violence, Ideology, and the Mexican Struggle for Independence, 1810-1821.* Stanford, CA: Stanford University Press, 2001.

Vázquez de Ferrer, Belín. "El comercio marabino en las postrimerías del gobierno hispánico." *Tierra Firme*, no. 14 (1986): 165-76.

Verna, Paul. *Pétion y Bolívar: una etapa decisiva en la emancipación de Hispanoamérica, 1790-1830.* Caracas: Ediciones de la Presidencia de la República, 1980.

Viotti da Costa, Emilia. *Crowns of Glory, Tears of Blood: The Demerara Slave Rebellion of 1823.* New York: Oxford University Press, 1994.

Walker, Charles. *Smoldering Ashes: Cuzco and the Creation of Republican Peru, 1780-1840.* Durham, NC: Duke University Press, 1999.

Watters, Mary. *A History of the Church in Venezuela, 1810-1930.* Chapel Hill: University of North Carolina Press, 1933.

White, Ashli. *Encountering Revolution: Haiti and the Making of the Early Republic.* Baltimore, MD: Johns Hopkins University Press, 2010.

Woudhuysen, H. R. *Sir Philip Sidney and the Circulation of Manuscripts, 1558-1640.* Oxford: Oxford University Press, 1996.

Index

Page numbers in italic text indicate illustrations.

abolition: conspiracy of La Guaira, 151, 179, 275n89; in France, 64, 96; papers about, 63–68; rebellion of Coro and, 134–38, 141–44; whites opposing, 22, 47–49
Acosta, José, 163
Acosta, Nicolasa de, 138
Acosta Saignes, Miguel, 226n22
African-descended cultural organizations, 118, 256n5
Age of Revolutions, 3, 4, 6, 11; newspapers, 51–58; oral communication, 79–81; racial war, 135, 136
Aizpurua, José María, 21
Aizpurua, Ramón, 94, 119, 123, 132, 151, 160, 162, 275n99
alcabala, derechos de (commercial taxes), 118, 126, 127, 140, 141
alcaldes de barrio, 110, 112
American Revolution, 4; conspiracy of La Guaira, 121, 160, 174; Miranda and, 147, papers from, 161, 162, 174; Spanish newspapers, 55
Arrambide, Juan Xavier, 162, 166
Arcaya, Pedro Manuel, 118, 119
Ariztizabal, Admiral Gabriel, 103
Armada, Juan Ignacio de la (governor of Maracaibo), 191, 193

Audiencia of Caracas (colonial high court), 27, 34, 47; conspiracy of La Guaira, 150, 157; Coro rebellion, 122, 138; French visitors, militiamen, prisoners, and slaves, 87, 90, 95, 105, 109; invasion of Santo Domingo, 120; Juan Bautista Olivares, 74; prohibited papers, 62, 64, 65

barbershops, 44–46, 172; Valle's, 159, 171–73
Bassi, Ernesto, 4
black code, 47, 48, 95; elite's reactions to, 47; pasquinades about, 48–49, *48*. *See also código negrero* of 1789
blacks, 24, 26, 27; *bozales* and *criollos*, 24; enslaved population, 24, 27; free, 24, 27; free in Coro, 124; free in La Guaira, 156; fugitives from the French Caribbean, 82–84
blancos. See whites
Boggiero, Andrés (commander of Coro), 146, 203
Bogotá, Santa Fé de, 189
Bolívar, Simón, 5, 6, 16, 213
books: circulation of, 35–37; importation of, 32–34; market of, 34–35, 37
Borucki, Alex, 93

311

Bourbon reforms, 21, 27, 29, 127, 189; Maracaibo, 189; newspapers, 55, 236n20; postal system, 59; tax agents and collectors, 127, 140, 146
Brito Figueroa, Federico, 119
broadsides, 49, 50, 235n11; from France, 38, 62, 64, 65, 72; from Saint-Domingue, 62–67; smuggling practices, 68–70; from Trinidad, 65, 69. *See also* pasquinades

cacao economy, 19–22; haciendas, 156
calidad, 23–25
Caracas, Province of, 19, 225n11; economic activities of, 21, 22; map of, xvi; and Maracaibo, 189; population of, 25, 26, *26*
Caracas City Council (*cabildo*), 15, 28, 44, 47
Caracas Company, 20, 31, 33, 126, 154, 156, 226n13. *See also* Compañía Guipuzcoana
Carbonell, Pedro (captain general), 51, 61, 66, 69, 74, 78, 82, 120, 130
Cariaco, rebellion of, 99
Carmañola Americana, 177, 275n87
Cartagena de Indias, 186, 189
cartillas, 234n108
Catholic Church, 18; censorship, 25, 50, 66, 86; conspiracy of La Guaira and, 173, 174; Coro and, 145, 146; education and social control, 37, 39, 74, 85; republicanism, 63, 91
cattle economy, 19, 20, 123
Chacón, José María (governor of Trinidad), 56, 57, 64, 95, 96, 103
Chanlatte, General Antoine, 198, 199
Charles III, King of Spain, 37, 53, 231n75
Chartier, Roger, 168, 224n20, 225n6, 248n48, 248n49
Chirino, José Leonardo, 117, 122, 125, 129, 139–42; death of, 144, 145; testimony of, 142–43; writings about, 170, 171
Chirino, María Dolores, 125, 139, 144
Chirino, Pedro, 141
coartación, 22, 226n20
Cocofío (black healer in Coro), 127, 128
código negrero of 1789, 47, 48, 95; elite's reactions to, 47; pasquinades about, 48–49, *48*
Compañía Guipuzcoana, 20, 31, 33, 126, 154, 156, 226n13. *See also* Caracas Company
Comunero rebellion, 91
conspiracy of La Guaira, 51, 62, 71, 151–54; abolition of slavery, 178, 179; black population, 162, 163, 169, 170, 174; elimination of Indian tributes, 178; government board, 175, 178; political plan, 175–79; private libraries, 166–69; social equality, 160, 163, 175–79; social networks, 160–65; tributary plan, 175
conspiracy of Maracaibo, 187–95; Francophobia, 194; pardos and free blacks, 193–95; piracy, 188, 195; Saint-Domingue, 195
conspiracy of San Blas, 163, 164, 169
contraband, 20, 51, 69, 97, 98, 125, 127, 154, 189, 269n16
Cordero, José, 158
Coro, province of, 122–28, 258n23; black rebellion of, 117–22; City Council, 139–41; connections with Curaçao, 123; connections with Saint-Domingue, 121, 122; economy, 123, 124; free blacks of, 124; labor, 124; population, 124; royalism, 147; smuggling activities, 123; sugar production, 123; white families of, 126, 127; tax collectors, 141, 146
corsairs, black, 183–88, 191, 194, 195, 210
Cortés de Campomanes, Manuel, 164, 174, 176, 177

INDEX 313

criados, 281n65
Cuba, 11, 20, 59, 108–10, 188, 195–97, *201*, 212
Cumaná, 4; connections with Trinidad, 69, 70
Curaçao: connections with Coro, 123, 124, 250n66; connections with Maracaibo, 189; slaves from, 77, 78
Curiepe (black town), 113, 173

Dauxion-Lavaysse, Jean-François, 22, 156, 225n11
Declaration of the Rights of Man, 51, 57, 70, 152, 154, 167, 170, 209
Deive, Carlos, 200, 202, 203
De Pons, François-Joseph, 30, 227n22
Desfourneaux, General Étienne, 185
dispensa de calidad, 28, 43, 233n104, 243n105. *See also* Gracias al Sacar
Dubois, Laurent, 95, 143, 264n82, 275n99

El Bruto (ship), 190, 278n28
Emparan, Vicente, Governor of Cumaná, 69, 89, 203
España, José María, 150, 158, 160

Feijóo y Montenegro, Benito Jerónimo, 41, 42, 55, 166
Ferrer, Ada, 60, 119, 197, 238n41, 239n56
Fischer, Sibylle, 12, 119, 257n13
Francophobia, 87, 103, 167, 194, 233n94
free trade, 11, 21, 151, 156, 168
French Laws, 103. *See also* Law of the French
French Revolution: in Coro, 142–44; fear of, 38, 82, 185, 186, 208, 233n94; impressions about, 4, 66, 85, 225n6, 246n30; in La Guaira, 151, 153, 163, 160, 166, 175–77; in Maracaibo, 195; news about, 29, 38, 57; objects from, 38; papers from, 38, 52, 65, 66, 74, 166; rumors about, 80, 83; songs, 77, 78, 177, 244n6
French visitors and militiamen, 84–88, 102–13, 246n34; in La Guaira, 104–8, 157; in Puerto Cabello, 103, 104, in Trinidad, 84, 88, 89, 103; blacks in Venezuela, 101–2, 185
Fressinaux, Commander Joaquin, 103, 104

García, Commander Agustín, 160
García, Joaquín (governor of Santo Domingo), 106, 196–98, 200, *201*, 202, 203
Gaspar Bocé, Augustin, 190, 194, 278n26
Gaspar Bocé, Jean-Baptiste, 190, 194, 278n26
Geggus, David, 95, 184
Gómez, Alejandro, 25, 103, 275n99
González, José Caridad, 126, 129, 130, 132, 260n49
Gracias al Sacar, 28, 43, 233n104, 243n105. *See also dispensa de calidad*
Guadeloupe, 82, 102, 106, 184, 185
Gual, Manuel, 150, 160, 161, 174, 271n42
Guarico (Cap-Français, Saint-Domingue), 102, 106, 179, 180
Guerra, François-Xavier, 153, 224n21
Guevara Vasconcelos, Manuel (captain general), 146, 181, 198, 199
Guillelmi, Juan (captain general), 86, 94

Haitian Revolution, 4–6; bicentennial celebration, 5; conspiracy of La Guaira, 177; migratory movements, 196, 244n9, 280n50; in newspapers, 56–60; papers about, 40–42; oral news and rumors about, 60, 80; rebellion of Coro, 118–22; slave revolts in the Atlantic world, 5, 119–20
Harlequín, the (ship), 190

Havana: Caracas and, 2; Maracaibo and, 189; sending prisoners to, 108
Helg, Aline, 186, 277n15
Hispanic patriotism, 169
Hugues, Commander Victor, 184
Humboldt, von Alexander, 1, 30

Inquisition, 19, 34, 35, 37, 75; officers of, 19, 35, 37–40; and the Spanish Crown, 37, 38
Independence of Venezuela, 118, 151, 152, 203; wars of, 147
Indian tributes, 89, 120, 127; elimination of, 151, 178
indios (indigenous peoples), 24; *Ajaguas*, 259n31; in Coro, 124, 129; in Cumaná, 89; *encomiendas de*, 24, 227n28; *Goajiro*, 190; from Guaybacoa; 129; *Jirajaras*, 259n31; of Pecaya, 140; *pueblos de*, 24, 89, 120; tributary and free, 24
Intendencia de Ejército y Real Audiencia, 257n17
Iturbe, Manuel, 127

Jacot, Captain Francisco, 136, 137
Jordan, Josefina, 136
Jordan, Winthrop, 135

Kervesau, General François-Marie, 101, 198, 199

La Gaceta de Madrid, 55–58, 74; the American Revolution, 55; the French Revolution, 57; the Haitian Revolution, 57–59
La Guaira: 4, 111, 154; commerce 32, 34, 154; French visitors, militiamen, and prisoners in, 80, 102–13; military protection, 155; population, 156; port agents, 51, 61; slaves in, 77, 78
La Macanilla (sugar plantation) 137, 140, 142

La Patrulla (ship), 190, 278n15
Lavaux, General Étienne, 101
Laviña, Javier, 119, 125, 259n34
Law of the French, 118, 119, 131, 133–37. See also French Laws
Letters, official, 59–60, 81, 239n53
López, Casto Fulgencio, 160, 164
Louverture, Toussaint: abolition of slavery, 198; celebrating, 203; in Coro, 143; invasion of Santo Domingo, 66, 147, 187, 198, 200, 204; in Maracaibo, 187; news and rumors about, 58, 143, 187, 202–4; troops, 200, 203
luangos (or *loangos*): communities, 95, 125, 211; in Coro, 125, 130, 132

mantuanos: 25, 228n35. See also *personas principales*
manumission, 22, 64; in Coro, 145
manuscripts, 35, 36, 231n70, 235n10
Maracaibo, Province of, 188–90; commercial activities, 189; conspiracy in, 186–95; society, 186
Marmión, Miguel (commander of Puerto Cabello), 196, 198
maroons: local communities, 98–100, 251n82, 251n87; maritime, 93, 97; squadrons to control, 98, 99, 112, 212, 251n85
Mendiri, Juan Josef, 51, 52, 161, 166
Mijares, Fernando (governor of Maracaibo), 193, 194, 200
Miranda, Francisco de, 5, 147
Montesinos y Rico, Manuel, 149, 179
Moreno, José Ignacio, 2, 35, 65, 158
mulattos, 24, 28, 77

New Granada, Viceroyalty of, 185, 189
newspapers, 51–60; British, 51, 55; censorship, 53, 56; French, 55, 56, 71; Spanish, 54, 55; Spanish-American,

53; Spanish reformism and, 52, 53; revolutionary movements and, 52, 55, 57

Olivares, Juan Bautista, 43, 72–74
oral information, Atlantic Revolutions, 84; politics, 79–82

Paine, Thomas, 40, 66, 161
pardos, 24, 25, 27, 28; education, 29, 30, 43; elite, 27, 28; literacy, 41, 44, 45; prohibited papers and, 71–73; schools for, 43, 44
pasquinades, 49, 50; from France, 38, 62, 64, 65, 72; from Saint-Domingue, 62–67; smuggling practices of, 68–70; from Trinidad, 65, 69. *See also* broadsides
Pecaya, cacique de, 139, 140, 142
personas principales, 25; *personas de condición*, 26; *personas de baja condición*, 26
Piccato, Pablo, 223n17, 224n21
Picornell, Juan Bautista, 72, 150, 163–65; manuscript writings, 169–73; political plan, 173–79
Picton, Thomas, 99
piracy, 184, 185, 197, 200
Pirela, Lieutenant Francisco Xavier, 188, 191–95, 277n17
Polasky, Janet, 207, 224n22
Port-au-Prince, Saint-Domingue, 188, 190
private libraries, 18, 31–35; Caracas, 31–33, 36; clergy, 31, 35; La Guaira, 34, 36; inventories, 31–33, 33, 35; manuscripts in, 35, 36; newspapers in, 54; public auctions, 34; shipping lists, 3–34; white elite, 31
prohibited books: conspiracy of La Guaira, 165–69; denunciations of, 35, 38, 232n90; edicts, 19, 38, 39; from France, 40; royal decrees, 38, 39; smuggling, 39, 70
public education, 41–44
public sphere, 3, 6–8, 46, 153, 181, 208, 209, 236n12; in Latin America, 153, 268n13
Puerto Cabello, 103, 104
purity of blood, 227n26

racial war, 118, 134, 147
Ramírez Valderrain, Lieutenant Mariano, 128–34
Raynal, Abbé Guillaume Thomas François, 40, 166, 169
Real Consulado, 27
rebellion: slave, 20, 234n2, 250n71; Cariaco, 99; Comunero, 91; Coro, 117–22; memories of the Coro's, 118–20; Túpac Amaru, 91
republicanism, 12, 50, 51, 60–63, 103, 111, 119–21, 131, 170, 196, 204, 205, 208
revolutionary songs, 78, 176–78
Rivière, Monsieur (French squadron commander), 103, 253n102
Rochambeau, General Jean-Baptiste, 101
Rodríguez, Pedro (Conde de Campomanes), 42
Rodríguez, Simón, 15, 16, 43–45
Roman, Captain Joseph, 190–95
Roseberry, William, 223n18, 258n19
Roume de Saint-Laurent, Phillipe Rose, 62, 65, 101, 198
Rousseau, Jean-Jacques, 5, 37, 39, 167, 168, 169
rumors, 85, 244n11, 244n12; conspiracy and insurrection, 112, 149; emancipatory decree, 95–98, 121, 128; French militiamen and officers, 104, 105; French slaves in Venezuela, 110–12
runaways. *See* maroons
Rupert, Linda, 123, 259n37

Rusiñol, Sergeant José de, 159, 161, 164

Saint-Domingue, 4–7; black corsairs, 183; conspiracy of La Guaira, 179; conspiracy in Maracaibo, 185–88; Coro rebellion, 121, 122, 134, 137, 142, 143; news about, 59, 60, 91; prisoners and slaves from, 106–8; rebellions in, 49, 91
Santo Domingo, 63; families, 100, 101, 197–202; French occupation, 101; Maracaibo, 189; papers, 66–68; prisoners and slaves in La Guaira, 106–8, 157; Toussaint Louverture's invasion, 147, 197–99
Scott, Julius, 79, 91
sedition, 80, 90, 91, 158, 185, 207, 248n50
Semple, Robert, 156
Serranía de Coro. *See* Coro, province of
Sharpless, Jason T., 120
slavery: abolition of, 22; population, 26, 27; Venezuelan, 21, 22
slaves: African, 21; decreased importation, 93; Cumaná, 94; Curaçao, 77, 94, 95; Dutch Esequibo, 94; marriages, 260n41; population, 24, 27; Santo Domingo, 101–2; slaves' escapes, 99, 100; songs 77, 78, 137; trade, 92–94; Trinidad, 94
social estates, 23–25
social mobility, 16, 27–29, 229n46
"Soneto Americano," 149, 176, 177, 267n2
Spanish reformism, 18; authors, 41, 42; education, 17, 18, 29, 41–44; newspapers and, 52, 53
Stoler, Ann Laura, 81, 85
Sualbach, Juan, 190–92
Suárez, José Francisco (slave), 192, 193
sugar: plantations, 118, 123, 124, 126; production, 19, 20, 168, 189, 219

Tellería, Josef, 127, 139–41
tertulias, 234n116
Thibaud, Clément, 61, 239n59
Tinoco, Gerardo, 141
Torre, Agustín de la, 112, 113
Treaty of Basel, 63, 66, 67, 100, 101, 117, 202–4, 282n72
Trinidad: British invasion of, 69, 97; connections with Cumaná, 69, 70, 89, 90, 96, 97, 99; French visitors and militiamen, 84, 88, 89, 103, 247n36; papers from, 69, 70, 162, 167; printing press, 56, 57, 238n37; smuggling activities, 69
Trouillot, Michel-Rolph, 223n14, 235n8, 256n3, 256n3
Túpac Amaru rebellion, 91
Twinam, Ann, 27, 29

Valle, Narciso del, 72, 158, 159, 162, 164; barbershop, 172
Venezuela, Captaincy General, 4, 19, 225n11; economy, 19–21, 33; labor, 21, 22; map of, *xvi*; Maracaibo, 189; population, 25; social structure, 22–27; topography, 83
Ventura (ship), 200

Wars of Independence. *See* Independence of Venezuela
whites, 23, 24; *criollos,* 24; 179; *de orilla,* 24; *peninsulares,* 24

Yturén, Manuel, 185

zambas (African dances), 136
zambos, 24, 28, 228n32
Zejudo, Anastasio (governor of Cartagena), 185

www.ingramcontent.com/pod-product-compliance
Lightning Source LLC
Chambersburg PA
CBHW030521230426
43665CB00010B/717